KEY CONCEPTS IN CINEMA STUDIES

Key Concepts in Cinema Studies is a comprehensive glossary of the main terms and concepts in film theory and film production. The book includes definitions of:

- key film genres, from Westerns to Musicals
- major movements of world cinema, from New German Cinema to Third Cinema
- theories used in the study of cinema, from auteur theory to psychoanalysis and to feminist film theory
- key film production terms, from film editing to zoom lens

Major entries are accompanied by suggestions for further reading, and there is also a bibliography of essential writings in cinema studies.

Susan Hayward is a Senior Lecturer in French Studies at the University of Birmingham. She is the author of *French National Cinema* (Routledge, 1993) and co-editor, with Ginette Vincendeau, of *French Film: Texts and Contexts* (Routledge, 1989).

To my students

KEY CONCEPTS IN CINEMA STUDIES

Susan Hayward

London and New York

First published 1996
by Routledge
11 New Fetter Lane, London EC4P 4EE

Simultaneously published in the USA and Canada
by Routledge
29 West 35th Street, New York, NY 10001

Routledge is an International Thomson Publishing company

© 1996 SUSAN HAYWARD

Typeset in Bembo by Florencetype Limited
Printed and bound in Great Britain by
Clays Ltd, St. Ives PLC

British Library Cataloguing in Publication Data
A catalogue record for this book is available from the British Library

Library of Congress Cataloging in Publication Data
A catalogue record for this book has been requested.

ISBN 0–415–10718–0 (hbk)
      0–415–10719–9 (pbk)

CONTENTS

PREFACE

Key Concepts in Cinema Studies has been two years in the writing. It is intentionally an in-depth glossary which, it is hoped, will provide students and teachers of film studies and other persons interested in cinema with a useful reference book on key theoretical terms and, where appropriate, the various debates surrounding them. The glossary also gives historical overviews of key genres, film theory and film movements. Naturally, not 'everything' is covered by these entries. In a later edition further entries may be included, and I would welcome suggestions of further entries from readers. The present book is based on my perception of students' needs when embarking on film studies; its intention is also to give teachers synopses for rapid reference purposes. Entries have been written as lucidly and as succinctly as possible, but doubtless there will be some 'dense' areas; again I welcome feedback. My own students have been very helpful in this area.

All cross-references are in bold. Sometimes the actual concept cross-referred may not be the precise form in the entry (for example, **ideological** in bold actually refers to an entry on ideology). Bibliographical citations at the end of certain entries refer to the bibliography at the end of the book. Wherever it is useful to explain the particular relevance or direction of a suggested text, this has been done. Cross-references and bibliographies are given in order of importance wherever this seemed significant, otherwise in alphabetical order.

Finally, instead of a table of contents in traditional style I have supplied a list of all concepts dealt with in this book. Where a concept is part of a larger issue, the entry is a cross-reference to the main entry where it is discussed (thus, 'jouissance' is entered under the 'J' entries but as a cross-reference to 'psychoanalysis' where it is explained. At the beginning of most entries there is a parenthesis suggesting that you consult other entries – I believe you will find this dipping across useful and that it will help widen the issue at hand.

ACKNOWLEDGEMENTS

I would like to thank various people who have helped this project along. First, Rebecca Barden, my editor, whose unfailing enthusiasm for the project has made it such an enjoyable book to write. Second, Valerie Swales whose wide-ranging knowledge on theory has helped me considerably on some of the more difficult entries. Third, colleagues, students and Routledge readers who put a lot of effort into giving me feedback on the different entries. In that regard, I would particularly like to thank Alex Hughes, Catherine Hadoke, Sarah Clarke, Anne Hamilton and Barbara Rasmussen for their thoughtful and helpful responses. Fourth, I must express my thanks to the British Film Institute for its existence and the extremely helpful librarians who made my task that much easier. Finally, my thanks go to my Head of Department, Jennifer Birkett, who – because of her progressive policies on research – supported this project and made its reasonably swift completion possible.

KEY CONCEPTS

A

absence/presence
agency
ambiguity
anamorphic lens
animation
apparatus
art cinema
aspect ratio
asynchronization/asynchronous sound
audience
auteur/auteur theory/politique des auteurs/Cahiers du cinéma
avant-garde

B

backstage musical *see* musical
Black cinema/Blaxploitation movies
B-movies
body horror films *see* horror films
British New Wave
buddy films

C

D

G

gangster/criminal/detective thriller/private-eye films
gaze/look
gender
genre/sub-genre
German expressionism
Germany/New German cinema
gesturality
gothic horror *see* horror

H

Hammer horror *see* horror
Hays code
hegemony
historical films/reconstructions
Hollywood
Hollywood blacklist
Hollywood majors *see* classic Hollywood – cinema studio system
horror/gothic horror/Hammer horror/horror
   thriller/body horror/vampire movies

I

iconography
identification *see* distanciation spectator-identification
identity *see* psychoanalysis, spectator-identification, subjectivity
ideology
image
Imaginary/Symbolic
independent cinema
intertextuality
Italian neo-realism

J

jouissance see psychoanalysis
jump cut

L

lap-dissolve *see* dissolve
lighting
look *see* gaze/look, Imaginary/Symbolic, scopophilia, suture

M

mainstream cinema *see* dominant/mainstream cinema
match cutting
mediation
melodrama and women's films
metalanguage
metaphor *see* metonymy/metaphor
method acting
metonymy/metaphor
mise-en-abîme
mise-en-scène
misrecognition *see* psychoanalysis, suture
modernism
montage *see* editing, Soviet cinema
motivation
musical
myth

N

narrative/narration
naturalizing
naturalism
neo-realism *see* Italian neo-realism
New German cinema *see* Germany/New German Cinema
New Wave/*Nouvelle Vague see* French New Wave

O

Oedipal trajectory
180-degree rule

opposition *see* narrative, sequencing
oppositional cinema *see* counter-cinema

P

paradigmatic/syntagmatic *see* structuralism/post-structuralism
parallel reversal
parallel sequencing *see* editing
patriarchy *see* Imaginary/Symbolic, Oedipal trajectory, psycho-
    analysis
performance *see* gesturality, star system
plot/story *see* classical Hollywood cinema, discourse, narrative
point of view/subjectivity *see* subjective camera, subjectivity
politique des auteurs *see* auteur, French New Wave, mise-en-
    scène
postmodernism
post-structuralism *see* structuralism/post-structuralism
preferred reading
presence *see* absence/presence
private-eye films *see* gangster films
projection *see* apparatus, psychoanalysis
projector *see* apparatus
psychoanalysis
psychological thriller *see* thriller

Q

queer cinema

R

realism
reconstructions *see* historical films
repetition/variation/opposition *see* narration, sequencing
representation *see* feminist film theory, gender, sexuality,
    stereotypes, subjectivity
resistances *see* avant-garde, counter-cinema
reverse-angle shot *see* shot/reverse-angle shot

road movie
rules and rule-breaking *see* counter-cinema, jump cut

S

science fiction films
scopophilia/scopic drive/visual pleasure
seamlessness
semiology/semiotics/sign and signification
sequencing/sequence
setting
sexuality
shots
shot/reverse-angle shot
sign/signification *see* semiology/semiotics
social realism
sound/soundtrack
Soviet cinema/school
Soviet montage *see* editing, Soviet cinema
space and time/spatial and temporal contiguity
spectator/spectator-identification/female spectator
stars/star system/star as capital value/star as
   construct/star as deviant/star as cultural value: sign
   and fetish/star-gazing and performance
stereotype
structuralism/post-structuralism
studio system
subject/object
subject/subjectivity
subjective camera
surrealism
suture
syntagmatic *see* paradigmatic

T

theory
Third Cinema/Third World Cinema

30-degree rule
thriller/psychological thriller
time and space *see* spatial/temporal contiguity
tracking shot/travelling shot/dollying shot
transitions *see* cut, dissolves, fade, jump cut, unmatched shots,
   wipe
transparency/transparence
travelling shot *see* tracking shot

U

underground cinema
unmatched shots

V

vampire movies *see* horror movies
variation *see* repetition
violence *see* censorship, voyeurism/fetishism
visual pleasure *see* scopophilia
voyeurism/fetishism

W

war films
westerns
wipe
women's films *see* melodrama and women's films

Z

zoom

absence/presence (*see also* **apparatus**) *A first definition:* cinema makes absence presence; what is absent is made present. Thus, cinema is about illusion. It is also about temporal illusion in that the film's **narrative** unfolds in the present even though the entire filmic text is prefabricated (the past is made present). Cinema constructs a 'reality' out of selected images and sounds.

This notion of absence/presence applies to character and **gender** representation within the filmic text and confers a reading on the narrative. For example, an ongoing **discourse** in a film on a central character who is actually off-screen implies either a reification (making her or him into an object) or a heroization of that character. Thus, discourses around absent characters played by the young Marlon Brando, in his 1950s films, position him as object of desire, those around John Wayne as the all-time great American hero. On the question of gender-presence, certain **genres** appear to be gender-identified. In the **western**, women are, to all intents and purposes, absent. We 'naturally' accept this narrative convention of an exclusively male point of view. But what happens when a western is centred on a woman, for example Mae West in *Klondike Annie* (Raoul Walsh, 1936) and Joan Crawford in *Johnny Guitar* (Nicholas Ray, 1954)? Masquerade, mimicry, cross-dressing and gender-bending maybe, but also a transgressive (because it is a female) point of view – absence made presence.

1

Absence/presence also feeds into nostalgia for former times. This is most clearly exemplified in the viewing of films where the **stars** are now dead. Obviously, the nostalgia evoked is for different types of 'realities' depending on the star yearned after. For example, Marilyn Monroe and James Dean elicit different nostalgia responses from those of Cary Grant and Deborah Kerr.

A second definition (*see also* **apparatus**, **Imaginary/Symbolic**, **psychoanalysis**, **suture**): film theorists (Baudry, Bellour, Metz, Mulvey (all 1975) making psychoanalytic readings of the dynamic between screen and **spectator** have drawn on Sigmund Freud's discussions of the libido drives and Jacques Lacan's of mirror stage to explain how film works at the unconscious level. The mirror stage is the moment when the mother holds the child up to the mirror and the child imagines an illusory unity with the mother. This is a first moment of identification, with the mother as object. This moment is short-lived, for the child subsequently perceives either his difference from or her similarity with the mother. At this point the child imagines an illusory identification with the self in the mirror but then senses the loss of the mother. In Lacanian psychoanalytic terms this part of the mirror stage is termed the Imaginary. The next phase of the mirror stage is termed the Symbolic and can be explained as follows. The child, having sensed the loss of the mother, now desires reunification with her. But this desire is sexualized and so the father intervenes. He enters as the third term into the mirror/reflection, forming a triangle of relationships. He prohibits access to the mother by saying 'No'. In this way language functions as the Symbolic order. For the child to become a fully socialized being/**subject**, she or he must obey the father's 'No': that is, the 'Law of the Father'. In so doing, the child enters the realm of language (enters the Symbolic Order): she or he conforms to the Law of the Father which is based in language (the uttered 'No'). The process of socialization for the male child is complete, supposedly, when he finds eventual fulfilment in a female other; the female child, for her part, turns first to her father as object of desire and later transfers that desire onto a male other. (For further clarification see **Imaginary/Symbolic** and **Oedipal trajectory**; and for a full discussion see Lapsley and Westlake, 1988, 80–90.)

By analogy with this psychoanalytic description of the mirror stage, the screen is defined as the site of the Imaginary: making absence presence (bringing into the spectator's field of vision images of people or stars who are not in real life present). The screen also functions to make presence absence: the spectator is absent from the screen upon which she or he gazes. However, the interplay between absence and presence does not end here; if it did it would end in spectator alienation. Although the spectator is absent from the screen, she or he becomes presence as the hearing, seeing subject: without that presence the film would have no meaning. In this respect the screen is seen as having analogies with the mirror stage. The screen becomes the mirror into which the spectator peers. At first the spectator has a momentary identification with that image and sees herself or himself as a unified being. She or he then perceives her or his difference and becomes aware of the lack, the absence or loss of the mother. Finally, she or he recognizes herself or himself as perceiving subject. According to this line of analysis, at each film viewing there occurs a re-enactment of the unconscious processes involved in the acquisition of sexual difference (the mirror stage), of language (entry *of* the Symbolic) and of autonomous selfhood or subjectivity (entry *into* the Symbolic order and rupture with the mother as object of identification). It is through this interplay of absence/presence that cinema constructs the spectator as subject of the look and establishes the desire to look with all that it connotes in terms of visual pleasure for the spectator (see **gaze**). But this visual pleasure is also associated with its opposite: the shame of looking. Absence/presence now functions so as to position the spectator as 'she or he who is seeing without being seen'. In this regard, cinema makes possible the re-enactment of the primal scene – that is, according to Freud, the moment in a child's psychological development when it, unseen, watches its mother and father copulating (see **scopophilia**, **voyeurism/fetishism**).

3

A third definition: woman as absence (as object of male desire), man as presence (as perceiving subject). The woman is eternally fixed as feminine, but not as subject of her own desire. She is eternally fixed and, therefore, mute. (For further discussion, see **feminist film theory**, **gaze**, **scopophilia**, **spectator-identification**.)

agency (*see also* **subjectivity**) Refers essentially to issues of control and operates both within and outside the film. Within the film, agency is often applied to a character in relation to desire. If that character has agency over desire it means that she or he (though predominantly in **classic narrative cinema** it is 'he') is able to act upon that desire and fulfil it (a classic example is: boy meets girl, boy wants girl, boy gets girl). Agency also functions at the level of the **narrative** inside and outside the film. Whose narration is it? A character in the film? A character outside the film? The director's? **Hollywood**'s? And finally, agency also applies to the **spectator**. In viewing the film, the spectator has agency over the text in that she or he produces a meaning and a reading of the filmic text.

ambiguity (*see also* **film noir** and **naturalizing**) 'Double meaning', a term that has been incorporated into film analysis. Ambiguity can occur at all levels of a film: characterization, **narrative**, type of **shot, space and time**. Often the **mise-en-scène** and **lighting** function to signal ambiguity. For example, mirrors offering reflections of a character point not just to the **myth** of Narcissus but also to the idea of duplicity. The use of highlighting through side-lighting of a character's face when all else is in shadow and the use of contrasting light and dark within one **shot**, are two lighting effects that signal character ambiguity. These particular **codes** are common to **film noir** and are employed to point to the moral ambiguity of the central protagonist. But ambiguity is not exclusive to this **genre** and can be found in both mainstream and **art cinema**. In the former case, Clint Eastwood's later **westerns** are exemplary because he uses character ambiguity to question the **genre** itself (as in *Pale Rider*, 1985, and *Unforgiven*, 1992, both directed by and starring Eastwood). The hero's own self-doubt or questioning leads to the genre itself being ambiguously positioned. The genre itself now questions what its codes and conventions serve to normalize (the opposition of 'good' and 'bad', the 'civilized' White man and the 'natural' Indian, and so on). In art cinema where film-makers are seeking to question film-making practices and the standardization of genres, ambiguity is one of the means used to achieve that effect. For example, lack of **diegetic/narrative** continuity creates a sense of ambiguity and has a destabilizing effect on both the film itself and the **spectator**. Codes of time and space are deconstructed through the use of **jump cuts** and **asynchronism** between image and sound, causing the spectator to feel disorientated. Often the central characters will appear to reflect a similar disorientation or confusion, revelatory of states of mind that cannot easily be read by the spectator.

Ambiguity, then, can come about as a result of more than one focused reading: that is, there is not a single **preferred reading**. The above are some examples of how this is achieved, but mention should also be made of the effect of the **depth of field** shot and multi-track **sound**. In both cases it is the closeness of these effects to 'reality' that paradoxically signifies their ambiguity. Bazin (1967, 23ff.) qualifies depth of field filming as objective **realism**. He makes the point that it is an open **shot** that allows the spectator greater reading potential because its meaning is not as strongly encoded as is the case with **montage**. Although it constitutes a unity of image in time and space and as such is a realistic structure, none the less because it is open to wider interpretation it does not lose its potential for ambiguity. Similarly, the greater fidelity and range of multi-track **sound**, if there is no foregrounding of one sound over another, can lead to a greater realism and a less encoded meaning. One sound is not artificially privileged over another; rather, the

5

spectator hears the sounds in their 'true' relation and can evaluate the significance of that relation.

anamorphic lens (*see also* **aspect ratio**) A French invention devised by Henri Chrétien for military use during the First World War, this is a wide-angle lens that permits 180-degree vision (see **180-degree rule**). It was not introduced into cinema until 1928 when it was used experimentally by the French film-maker Claude Autant-Lara. Characteristically, the French film industry did not invest in this new technology which could have done much to aid its ailing fortunes, and it was the United States who bought the rights to the system in 1952. The following year Fox **studios** was the first to release what was termed a **cinemascope** film, *The Robe* (Henry Koster). The wide-screen effect of cinemascope is achieved by a twofold process using the anamorphic lens. First, the lens on the camera squeezes the width of the image down to half its size so that it will fit on to the existing width of the film (traditionally 35 mm). Then the film is projected through a projector supplied with an anamorphic lens which produces the wide-screen effect with an **aspect ratio** of 2.35:1. Without the anamorphic lens on the projector the image would be virtually square and its contents hugely distorted – horizontally squashed and vertically stretched as if caught in a concave mirror. The wide-angle effect is now more usually accomplished without the anamorphic lens, through the use of the wide-gauge 70 mm film or by printing 35 mm onto 70 mm film for special releases.

animation Traditionally, animation has been achieved by shooting inanimate objects, such as drawings, frame by frame in stop-motion photography. In succeeding frames the object has very slightly shifted positions so that when the stop-motion photos are run at standard speed (twenty-four frames per second) the object seems to move. Animation dates back to the early days of cinema. It first appeared in the form of an insert in a live-action film with Georges Méliès's animation of the moon in *Voyage à la lune*, 1902. Later, in 1914, Winsor McCay produced the first animated short, *Gertie the Dinosaur*. Full-length cartoons did not come into their own until Walt Disney's *Snow White and the Seven Dwarfs* (1937). In terms of animated dolls, arguably the most famous is the gorilla doll who is the eponymous hero of *King Kong* (Ernest B. Schoedask, 1933). Recent technological advances have seen the introduction of computer-aided graphics, producing a greater **realism** in terms of movement. This new technology should reduce production costs. One minute of traditional animation requires on average fifteen hundred drawings and the medium is therefore very costly and labour-intensive. However, it is sobering to recall that Steven Spielberg's dinosaurs in *Jurassic Park* (1992) cost $25 m alone (representing over a third of the total costs of $66 m). (For further reading see Hoffer, 1981; Grant, 1987; Culham, 1988).

apparatus (*see also* **agency**, **spectator-identification** and **suture**) Baudry (1970) was among the first film theorists to suggest that the cinematic apparatus or technology has an **ideological** effect upon the **spectator**. In the simplest instance the cinematic apparatus purports to set before the eye and ear realistic images and sounds. However, the technology disguises how that reality is put together frame by frame. It also provides the illusion of perspectival space. This double illusion conceals the work that goes into the production of meaning and in so doing presents as natural what in fact is an **ideological** construction, that is, an idealistic reality. In this respect, Baudry argues, the spectator is positioned as an all-knowing **subject** because he (*sic*) is all-seeing even though he is unaware of the processes whereby he becomes fixed as such. Thus the omniscient spectator-subject is produced by, is the *effect* of the filmic text. A contiguous, simultaneous ideological effect occurs as a result of the way in which the spectator is positioned within a theatre (in a darkened room, the eyes projecting towards the screen with the projection of

7

the film coming from behind the head). Because of this positioning, an identification occurs with the camera (that which has looked, before the spectator, at what the spectator is now looking at). The spectator is thereby interpellated by the filmic text, that is the film constructs the subject, the subject is an effect of the film text (see **ideology**). That is, the spectator as subject is constructed by the meanings of the filmic text.

Later, after 1975, discussion of the apparatus moved on from this anti-humanist reading of the spectator as subject-effect, and the presupposition that the spectator is male. Now, the spectator is also seen as an active producer of meaning who is still positioned as subject, but this time as agent of the filmic text. That is, she or he becomes the one viewing, the one deriving pleasure (or fear, which is another form of pleasure) from what she or he is looking at. She or he also interprets and judges the text. On the 'negative' side of this positioning it could be said that, in becoming the camera, the apparatus places the spectator voyeuristically, as a colluder in the circulation of pleasure which is essential to the financial well-being of the film industry (Metz, 1975). The economic viability of the latter depends on the desire of the former to be pleasured. Cinema in this respect becomes an exchange commodity based on pleasure and capital gain – pleasure in exchange for money. On the 'positive' side it could be said that as agent the spectator can resist being fixed as **voyeur**, or indeed as effect, and judge the film critically. (For further discussion see Lapsley and Westlake, 1988, 79–86; Mayne, 1993, 13–76; De Lauretis and Heath, 1980.)

art cinema (*see* **avant-garde**, **counter-cinema**)   This term refers predominantly to a certain type of European cinema that is experimental in technique and **narrative**. This cinema, which typically produces low- to mid-budget films, attempts to address the aesthetics of cinema and cinematic practices and is primarily, but not exclusively, produced outside **dominant cinema** systems. For example, the **French New Wave** and the new **German cinema**, which come under this label, received substantial financing from the state. Other art cinemas, such as the American **underground cinema** were funded by the film-makers themselves. Art cinema is also produced by individuals – often women film-makers – who do not come under any particular movement (for example Agnès Varda, Liliani Cavani, Nelly Kaplan and Chantal Akerman).

Art cinema has been rightly associated with eroticism since the 1920s when sexual desire and nudity were explicitly put up on screen. However, for American audiences during the censorship period under the **Hays code** (1934–68), 'art cinema' came to mean sex films. With an eye to the export market, film producers were quick to exploit art cinema's sexual cachet. Perhaps one of the most famous instances of this is the case of Jean-Luc Godard's *Le Mépris* (1963), starring Brigitte Bardot. Upon its completion, two of its producers (Levine and Ponti) insisted that Godard should insert some nude scenes of Bardot. He did this, but not with the anticipated results – far from titillating or sexual, these scenes are moving, tragic.

The term *cinéma d'art*, was first coined by the French in 1908 to give cinema – which until then had been a popular medium – a legitimacy that would attract the middle classes to the cinema. This earliest form of art cinema was filmed theatre (mostly actors of the Comédie Française) accompanied by musical scores of renowned composers – making it a quite conservative artefact. During the 1920s, however, owing to the impact of **German expressionism** and the French avant-garde, art cinema became more closely associated with the **avant-garde**. From the 1930s onwards, partly owing to the French and Italian realist movements, its connotations widened to include social and psychological **realism**. And the final legitimation came in the 1950s when the *politique des auteurs* made the term **auteur** sacrosanct. This *politique* or polemic argued that certain film-makers could be identified as auteurs – as generators or creators rather than producers of films. This further widening of its frame of reference has meant that, although art cinema is considered primarily a

9

European cinema, certain Japanese, Indian, Australian, Canadian and Latin-American film-makers are also included in the canon – as well as certain films made by representatives of some minority groups: women, Blacks and self-called queers (see **Black cinema, queer cinema**; for women's cinema see Kuhn, 1990).

Historically, art cinema was not intentionally devised as a counter-**Hollywood** cinema, even though its production is clearly not associated with Hollywood. It is interesting to note, however, that the 1920s art cinema was a period of great cross-fertilization between Hollywood and European cinema. Generally speaking, in art cinema narrative **codes and conventions** are disturbed, the **narrative** line is fragmented so that there is no **seamless** cause-and-effect storyline. Similarly, characters' behaviour appears contingent, hesitant rather than assured and 'in the know' or motivated towards certain ambitions, desires or goals. Although these films are character- rather than plot-led, there are no heroes – in fact this absence of heroes is an important feature of art cinema. Psychological realism takes the form of a character's subjective view of events; **social realism** is represented by the character in relation to those events. The point of view can take the form of an interior monologue, or even several interior monologues (Alain Resnais's and Ingmar Bergman's films are exemplars of this). **Subjectivity** is often made uncertain (whose 'story' is it?) and so too the safe construction of time and space. This cinema, in its rupture with **classic narrative cinema**, intentionally distances **spectators** to create a reflective space for them to assume their own critical space or subjectivity in relation to the screen or film.

aspect ratio   This refers to the size of the image on the screen and to the ratio between the width and height. It dates back to the days of silent cinema, when the ratio was fixed at 1.33:1 (width to height) thanks to a standardization of technology brought about by hard-nosed business strategies on the part of the Edison company. Edison contracted its rivals into a cartel which had to use Edison equipment and pay royalties to the company. The cartel dominated the market from 1909 to 1917 when an anti-trust law broke it up. Edison went out of business, but the aspect ratio for a standard screen remained the norm internationally, until the early 1950s, when the threat posed to film **audiences** by television obliged the film industry to find visual ways to attract or retain audiences. Ironically, this ratio was the one adopted by television for its own screens. Although there had been experimentation with other screen sizes, it was not until economic necessity forced the film industry to invest heavily in technology that screens took on different dimensions. The first innovation in size was **cinemascope** with a standard aspect ratio of 2.35:1. Nowadays, films are more commonly projected either from the wide-gauge 70 mm film frame with an aspect ratio of 2.2:1 or from 35 mm film with its top and bottom pre-cropped with an aspect ratio of 1.85:1 in the United States and 1.66:1 in European cinemas.

asynchronization/asynchronous sound (*see also* **sound, seamlessness, space and time**) Asynchronization occurs when the sound is either intentionally or unintentionally out of sync with the image. In the latter case this is the result of faulty editing (for example a spoken voice out of sync with the moving lips). In the former, it has an aesthetic and/or **narrative** function. First, asynchronization calls attention to itself: thus the **spectator** is made aware that she or he is watching a film (so the illusion of identification is temporarily removed or deconstructed). Second, it serves to disrupt time and space and thereby narrative continuity, and as such points to the illusion of reality created by **classic narrative cinema** through its seamless **continuity editing**. Finally, it can be used for humorous effect, as occasionally in the earliest talkies when the advent of sound was met by film-makers with mixed reactions. There were two camps of thought: those who embraced the new technology and those who feared it would transform cinema into filmed theatre. As an example of this latter camp, the French film-maker René Clair was concerned that sound would limit visual experimentation and remove the poetic dimension inherent in silent film. His early sound films (mostly comic operettas) play with sound. By confounding the actual source of sound (for example, we see a woman singing framed in a window, then there is a cut and we go into her room and we realize that in fact she is miming to a record player), he draws attention to its pretensions at the 'reality effect' (see his *A nous la liberté*, 1931).

audience *(for a fuller discussion see* **spectator***)* Always recognized as important by film distributors and exhibitors, the audience has now become an important area of research for film theorists and sociologists (for references see **spectatorship**). Considerable work has been done on reception theory (how the audience receives and/or is positioned by the film). More recently, the debate has focused on how the **spectator** both identifies with the film and becomes an active producer of meaning as **subject** of the film (see **agency**). The film industry has since its beginnings targeted films to attract large audiences; this has meant that the product is predominantly audience-led. As the audience changes (for example, from working-class men and women before the Second World War to women after the War, to youth from the late 1950s), so too does the type of product.

auteur/auteur theory/politique des auteurs/Cahiers du cinéma *Auteur* is a term that dates back to the 1920s, in the theoretical writings of French film critics and directors of the silent era. At that time, the debate centred on the auteur (author of script and film-maker as one and the same) versus the scenario-led film (scripts commissioned from authors or scriptwriters) – a distinction that fed into the original high-art/low-art debate. After 1950 this debate was 'picked up' again and popularized – with the effect, as we shall see, of dissolving the high-art/low-art issue – by the newly launched film review *Cahiers du cinéma* (1951). This review, still in existence, was at that time headed by André Bazin, a film critic, and was written by a regular group of film critics, known as the *Cahiers* group. This group did not pursue the 1920s theorists' thinking (see **avant-garde**); in fact, they either ignored or totally dismissed it. This later debate is the one that has been carried forward into film theory. Through the *Cahiers* discussions on the *politique des auteurs* (that is, the polemical debate surrounding the concept of auteurism), the group developed the notion of the auteur by binding it closely up with the concept of **mise-en-scène**. This shift in the meaning of the auteur was largely due to the avid attention the *Cahiers* group paid to American/ **Hollywood** cinema. During the German occupation of France in the Second World War, American films had been proscribed. Suddenly, after the war, hundreds of such films, heretofore unseen, flooded the French cinema screens. This cinema, directed by the likes of Alfred Hitchcock, Howard Hawkes, John Ford and Samuel Fuller, seemed refreshingly new and led the *Cahiers* group to a reconsideration of Hollywood's production. They argued that just because American directors had little or no say over any of the production process bar the staging of the **shots**, this did not mean that they could not attain auteur status. Style, as in mise-en-scène, could also demarcate an auteur. Thanks to the *Cahiers* group, the term auteur could now refer either to a director's discernible style through mise-en-scène or to film-making practices where the director's signature was as much in evidence on the script/scenario as it was on the film product itself. Exemplars of auteurism in this second form (total author) are Jean Vigo, Jean Renoir, Jean-Luc Godard, Agnès Varda in France, Rainer Werner Fassbinder, Wim Wenders, Margarethe von Trotta in Germany, Orson Welles and David Lynch in the United States. Certain film-makers (mostly of the mise-en-scène form of auteur) have had this label ascribed to them by the *Cahiers* group even though their work may pre-date this use of the term (for example Hawkes, Ford, Fuller and Hitchcock on the American scene).

13

The *politique des auteurs* was a polemic initiated by the *Cahiers* group not just to bring favourite American film-makers into the canon but also to attack the French cinema of the time which they considered sclerotic, ossified. Dubbing it *le cinéma de papa*, they accused it of being script-led, redolent with safe psychology, lacking in social realism and of being produced by the same old scriptwriters and film-makers whose time was up (François Truffaut was by far the most virulent in his attacks). This quasi-Oedipal polemic established the primacy of the author/auteur and as such proposed a rather romantic and, therefore, conservative aesthetic. And, given the hot political climate in France during the 1950s, it is striking how apolitical and unpoliticized the group's writings were – pointing again to a conservative positioning. A further problem with this polemic is that by privileging the auteur it erases context (that is, history) and therefore side-steps **ideology**. Equally, because film is being looked at for its formalistic, stylistic and thematic structures, unconscious structure (such as the unspoken dynamics between film-maker and actor, the economic pressures connected with the industry) is precluded. Interestingly, of two of the writers in the *Cahiers* group who went on to make films, Godard and Truffaut, it is Truffaut's work that is locked in the conservative romantic ideology of the *politique des auteurs* and Godard's which has constantly questioned auteurism (among other things).

This *politique* generated a debate that lasted well into the 1980s, and auteur is a term which still prevails today. Given its innate conservatism one might well ask why. The first answer is that it helped to shift the notion of film theory, which until the 1950s had been based primarily in sociological analysis. The second answer is that the debate made clear that attempts to provide a single film theory just would not work and that, in fact, film is about multiple theories.

What follows is a brief outline of the development of auteur theory through three phases (for more detail see Andrew, 1984; Caughie, 1981; Cook, 1985; Lapsley and Westlake, 1988). The figure outlined gives a graphic representation of auteurism:

14

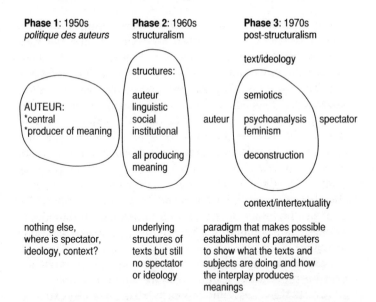

Phase 1: 1950s
politique des auteurs

Phase 2: 1960s
structuralism

Phase 3: 1970s
post-structuralism

text/ideology

structures:

AUTEUR:
*central
*producer of meaning

auteur
linguistic
social
institutional

all producing
meaning

semiotics

auteur   psychoanalysis   spectator
          feminism

deconstruction

context/intertextuality

nothing else,
where is spectator,
ideology, context?

underlying
structures of
texts but still
no spectator
or ideology

paradigm that makes possible
establishment of parameters
to show what the texts and
subjects are doing and how
the interplay produces
meanings

The term 'auteur theory' came about in the 1960s as a mistranslation by the American film critic Andrew Sarris. What had been a 'mere' polemic now became a full-blown theory. Sarris used auteurism to nationalistic and chauvinistic ends to elevate American/Hollywood cinema to the status of the 'only good cinema', with but one or two European art films worthy of mention. As a result of this misuse of the term, cinema became divided into a canon of the 'good' or 'great' directors and the rest. The initial impact of this on film courses and film studies in general was considerable, the tendency being to study only the good or great canon. Thankfully the impact of cultural studies on film studies in the late 1970s has served to redress this imbalance as well as developments in film theory.

The debate did not end there. It was picked up in the late 1960s in the light of the impact of **structuralism**. In France, the *Cahiers du cinéma* was obliged to rethink and readjust its thinking around auteurism, and in Britain the film journal *Movie* significantly developed the debate. As a concept, structuralism dates back to the beginning of the twentieth century

15

primarily in the form of Ferdinand de Saussure's linguistic theories. However, it remained little known until the theories were brought into the limelight by the French philosopher-semiotician Roland Barthes in the 1950s – especially in his popularizing essays *Mythologies* (1957). Saussure, in his *Cours de linguistique générale*, sets out the base paradigm by which all language can be ordered and understood. The base paradigm *langue/parole* was intended as a function that could simultaneously address and speak for the profound universal structures of language or language system (*langue*) and their manifestations in different cultures (*parole*). Claude Lévi-Strauss's anthropological structuralism of the 1960s (which looked at American Indian myths) continued in a similar vein, although this time it was applied to **narrative** structures. Lévi-Strauss's thesis was that since all cultures are the products of the human brain there must be, somewhere, beneath the surface, features that are common to all.

Structuralism was an approach that became extremely popular in France during the 1960s. Following the trend set by Barthes and Lévi-Strauss, the Marxist philosopher Louis Althusser adapted it into his discussions on ideology and Jacques Lacan into his writings on **psychoanalysis**. The fundamental point to be made about this popularization of structuralism in France is socio-political and refers to structuralism's strategy of total theory. This popularization of structuralism coincided with Charles de Gaulle's return to presidential power in 1958. His calls for national unity (in the face of the Algerian crisis), the era of economic triumphalism and the consequent nationalism that prevailed were in themselves symptomatic of a desire for structures to be mobilized to give France a sense of national identity. Thus, the desire for total structure, as exemplified by structuralism, can be read as an endeavour to counter the real political instability of the 1960s.

It is also worth labouring the point that this 'rethinking' of film theory in the 1960s did not come via film criticism (as it did in the 1950s) but through other disciplines, namely structural linguistics and semiotics. This pattern would repeat itself in the 1970s with psychoanalysis and philosophy pushing the debate along, and then history in the 1980s. The significance of this new trend of essayists and philosophers turning to cinema to apply their theories cannot be underestimated. Not to put too simplistic a reading on their importance, it is unquestionably their work which has legitimated film studies as a discipline and brought cinema firmly into the academic arena.

Structuralism was eagerly seized upon by proponents of auteurism because it was believed that, with its scientific approach, it would facilitate the establishing of an objective basis for the concept and counter the romantic subjectivity of auteur theory. Furthermore, apart from its potential to give a scientific legitimacy to auteurism, the attraction of structuralism for film theory in general lay in the theory's underlying strategy to establish a total structure.

Symptomatic of this desire for order in film theory were Christian Metz's endeavours (in the mid-1960s) to situate cinema within a Saussurian semiology. Metz, a semiotician, was the first to set out, in his *Essais sur la signification au cinéma*, a total theory approach in the form of his *grande syntagmatique*. He believed that cinema possessed a total structure. To adopt Saussurian terms, he perceived cinema as *langue* and each film as being *parole*. His endeavour – to uncover the rules that governed film language and to establish a framework for a semiotics of the cinema – pointed to a fundamental limitation with such an all-embracing, total approach: that of the theory overtaking the text and occluding other aspects of the text. What gets omitted is the notion of pleasure and **audience** reception, and what occurs instead is a crushing of the aesthetic experience through the weight of the theoretical framework.

This is not to say that structuralism did not advance the debate on film theory and auteurism. It did. Auteur-structuralism brought about a major positive change to auteur theory (*à la* Sarris). The British film journal *Movie* pointed out the problems of a resolutely romantic aesthetic in relation to cinema, but saw ways to deal with them. By situating

17

the auteur as one level among others – such as the notion of **genre** and the film industry – producing meaning, the theory would yield to a greater flexibility. *Cahiers du cinéma* was also critical of the romantic notion of auteurship because the auteur is not a unified and free creative spirit and film as a text is a 'play of tensions, silences and repressions' (Caughie, 1981, 128). Thus the auteur was displaced from the centre of the work and was now one structure among several others making up the film text. This displacement allowed other structures to emerge, namely, the linguistic, social and institutional structures and the auteur's relationship to them. And even though in the late 1960s the tendency was still to perceive the auteur structure as the major one, it was also recognized that the **studio** and **stars** – amongst others – were equally important contributors to the production of meaning in film. Still absent from the debate, however, was the **spectator** – the question of pleasure and ideology.

After 1968 *Cahiers* made a first attempt to introduce ideology into the debate in its exploration of Hollywood films that either 'resisted' or reflected dominant ideology. (In what is referred to as 'the *Young Mr Lincoln* debate', the *Cahiers* group claimed that this film mediated Republican values to counter Roosevelt's Democratic New Deal measures of 1933–41 and to promote a Republican victory in the 1940 Presidential elections.) Althusser's discussions on ideology, particularly his concept of interpellation, made it possible for both *Cahiers* and the British journal *Screen* to start to address the screen–spectator relationship. At this juncture, both journals accepted what, with hindsight, turned out to be a profoundly anti-humanist analysis of spectator positioning. According to Althusser, ideological state apparatuses (ISAs) interpellate individuals as **subjects**: that is, as pre-existing structures, ISAs function to constitute the individual as a subject to the ideology. ISAs manifest themselves as institutions of the state: the police, government, monarchies are ISAs. Just to illustrate: the British are subjects *to* the monarchy. The individual is, therefore, an effect of ISAs and not an agent. As subject–effects, individuals give meaning to ideology by colluding with and acting according to it. A mirroring process occurs which provides the subject with a reassuring sense of national identity (of belonging). Applied to film this means that cinema, in terms of meaning production, positions the spectator as a subject-effect who takes as real the images emanating from the screen. Thus, meaning is received, but not constructed, by the subject.

It would take the impact of post-structuralism (see **structuralism**), psychoanalysis, feminism and **deconstruction** to make clear finally that a single theory was inadequate and that what was required was a pluralism of theories that cross-fertilized each other. Post-structuralism, which does not find an easy definition, could be said to regroup and, to some extent, cross-fertilize the three other theoretical approaches (psychoanalysis, feminism and deconstruction). As its name implies, it was born out of a profound mistrust for total theory, and started from the position that all texts are a double articulation of **discourses** and non-discourses (that is, the said and the non-said, *le dit et le non-dit*). In terms of auteur theory the effect was multiple: 'the intervention of **semiotics** and psychoanalysis' 'shattering' once and for all 'the unity of the auteur' (Caughie, 1981, 200). Because post-structuralism looks at all relevant discourses (said or unsaid) revolving around and within the text, many more areas of meaning-production can be identified. Thus, semiotics introduced the theory of the textual subject: that is, subject positions within the textual process, including that of the spectator and the auteur, all producing meanings. Furthermore, semiotics also made clear that the text is a series of **signs** producing meanings.

Having defined the auteur's place within the textual process, auteur theory could now be placed within a theory of textuality. Since there is no such thing as a 'pure' text, the **intertextuality** (effects of different texts upon another text) of any film text must be a major consideration, including auteurial intertextuality. That is, the auteur is a figure constructed out of her or his film: because of x hallmarks the film is ostensibly a certain film-maker's and also influenced by that of others, etc. Psychoanalysis introduced the theory of the sexual, specular, divided subject (divided by the fact of difference, loss of and separation from the mother (see **psychoanalysis**)). Questions of the subject come into play: who is the subject (the text, auteur, spectator)? What are the effects of the **enunciating** text (i.e. the film as performance) on the spectator and those on the filmic text of the spectator? What are the two-way ideological effects (film on spectator and vice versa) and the pleasures derived by the spectator as she or he moves in and out of the text (see **spectator-identification**)? To speak of text means too that the context must also come into play in terms of meaning production: modes of production, the social, political and historical context. Finally and simultaneously, one cannot speak of a text as transparent, natural or innocent: therefore it is to be unpicked, deconstructed so that its modes of representation are fully understood.

avant-garde   It is perhaps curious that a military term should come to define what is now usually an anti-establishment positioning. The term *avant-garde* was first used in the modern sense to typify various aesthetic groupings immediately before and after the First World War, from about the dates given: cubism and **futurism** (both 1909), dadaism (1916), Constructivism (1920) and **surrealism** (1924). It is also curious to note that, in part, it was in reaction to the horrors of that war that the later avant-garde movements came about. The avant-garde seeks to break with tradition and is intentionally politicized in its attempts to do so. In cinema the avant-garde cachet was first used in the 1920s when a group of French film theorists (most famously Louis Delluc, Germaine Dulac and Jean Epstein) turned their hand to film-making and sought to create a cinema of the avant-garde. The first point to be made about this loosely banded collective is the pluralism of its members' theoretical approaches to cinema, which clearly inflected their film-making practices. Between them, they addressed issues of high and popular art, realist versus naturalist film, the **spectator**–screen relationship, **editing**

styles (particularly that of the **Soviet school** and **montage**), simultaneity, **subjectivity**, the unconscious, and the psycho-analytical potential of film, **auteur** cinema, cinema as rhythm and as a sign (see **semiology**). Once they turned their hands to making film, experimentation was central to their practice. This experimentation functioned on three overlapping levels: reworking genres, exploring the possibilities of film language and redefining the representation of subjectivity. **Genres** were mixed, intercalated and juxtaposed. Similarly the popular was fused with the experimental (mainstream cinema with **counter-cinema**), socio-realism with the subjective (**documentary** with **melodrama**). Working within these popular genres allowed them to extend, distort, even subvert dominant **discourses**. In so doing, these avant-garde film-makers attacked the precept of filmic **narrative** and spectator omniscience. Their films raised questions about subjectivity and its representation by disrupting **diegetic** time and space. This was achieved in a number of ways: shifts from diegetic continuity to discontinuity, fast editing, disruption of conventional transitional **shots**, disorientating shots through **unmatched shots** or a simultaneous representation of a multiplicity of perspectives. Thus, the fetishizing **gaze** of the male was also examined, showing an awareness of the under-privileging of female subjectivity. Subjectivity not only became a question of point of view but also included the implicit notion of **voyeurism** and speculation (of the female other – see **gaze**) as well as the issue of desire, and the functioning of the conscious and the unconscious mind (see Abel, 1984, 241–95; Flitterman-Lewis, 1990; Hayward, 1993, 76–80 and 106–11).

Soviet cinema and **German expressionism** with, respectively, their characteristic editing and **lighting** practices greatly influenced this first avant-garde, as did the surrealist movement and **psychoanalysis**. This avant-garde went through three different stages: subjective cinema (showing the interior life of a character, as in *La Souriante Mme Beudet*, Dulac, 1923), pure cinema (film signifying in and of itself through its plasticity and rhythms, as in *Entr'acte*, René Clair, 1924) and surrealist cinema (a collision of the first two stages

with the intention of giving filmic representation to the ratio-
nality and irrationality of the unconscious and dream state,
as in *La Coquille et le clergyman*, Dulac, 1927 and *Un Chien
andalou*, Luis Buñuel, 1929).

Since that period, other influences have also come into
play. And, interestingly, once again there are three dominant
types: first, what Wollen (1982, 92) calls the self-reflexive
avant-garde (predominantly American), or what Andrew
(1984, 124) terms the American romantic; second, the
avowedly political avant-garde (Wollen, 1982, 92) or the
European structural materialist film (Andrew, 1984, 125);
finally, the narrative avant-garde of the cinema of *écriture*
(Andrew, 1984, 126).

Where the American type is concerned, the major influences are the works of what are now called modernist painters
but which are in fact those of the avant-garde movements of
the early part of the twentieth century (see above). These
films have an abstract formalism displaying a self-reflexivity
that brings them close in their concerns to the pure cinema
of the 1920s avant-garde (as in Maya Deren's *Meshes of the
Afternoon*, 1943). As for the second type of avant-garde film,
the major influences were Bertolt Brecht and his theory of
distanciation and Sergei Eisenstein's montage theory. The
film practice invoked here is one whereby the film displays
its very structures and materiality – that is, it makes an exhibition of its signifying practices, draws attention to the
'artifice' of cinema. Point of view and narrative structure do
not exist so the spectator is under no illusion that what she
or he is watching is a two-dimensional projection of the
process of film-making. This is what Jean-Luc Godard termed
making political films politically. This cinema reflects the
revolutionary role of the avant-garde, assailing **ideology** by
revealing the structures that put it up and keep it in place (as
in Godard's *Weekend*, and *La Chinoise*, both 1967). The third
type more readily recalls the first and last stages of the 1920s
avant-garde but also has some parentage with materialist film.
Here the narrative avant-garde works with or on cinematic
codes, bringing the theory of counter-cinema into practice.

This cinema denaturalizes cinema to show that dominant cinematic language is not the only cinematic language and that new modes of subjectivity are possible, including that of the spectator as a producer of the text (see **agency**). Again, this is a predominantly European cinema and, unsurprisingly perhaps, because it addresses issues such as identification, representation, screen–spectator relations and subjectivity as well as production practices (film as work or labour) it is also a cinema associated with feminist film-makers (for example Chantal Akerman, *Jeanne Dielman, 23 Quai du Commerce, 1080 Bruxelles*, 1975; Marguerite Duras, *India Song*, 1975; Agnès Varda, *Sans toît ni loi*, 1985). (For further reading see Andrew, 1984, 119–27; Flitterman-Lewis, 1990; Gidal, 1989; Lapsley and Westlake, 1988, 181–213.)

backstage musical – see **musical**

Black cinema   This term currently tends to refer exclusively to African-American film production. Other Black cinemas are referred to as **Third cinema**. Black cinema emerged primarily from and in response to a particular brand of **Hollywood** cinema of the 1970s. Between 1971 and 1972, three films rooted in Black American urban culture all made by Black directors (*Sweet Sweetback's Baadaass Song*, Melvin Van Peebles, 1971; *Shaft*, Gordon Parks Snr, 1971; *Superfly*, Gordon Parks Jnr, 1972) were big hits, particularly with Black audiences. In the early 1970s, Hollywood was suffering financially (see **studio system**) so during the period 1971–76, with an eye to profit, it capitalized on this initial success and made a plethora of what have become known as Blaxploitation films. These films, starring Black actors, but produced by Whites and mostly directed by Whites, deliberately targeted Black audiences. This history, then, for Black cinema is not without some irony and points to the problem faced by all (so-called) minority groups – the danger of co-optation by the dominant culture.

Blaxploitation movies   Though, undoubtedly at the time (1971), Melvin Van Peebles never thought that his independently produced film *Sweet Sweetback's Baadaass Song* would be the cornerstone for some forty Blaxploitation movies, none the less his film, and the two other films mentioned, became the founding stones for a series of very profitable ventures for Hollywood. In all three films, the heroes or anti-heroes succeed against the (White) system. However, it is Van Peebles's film that remains the clearly politically motivated one; hence the irony of its co-optation by Whites. The late 1960s and early 1970s were the time of the Black Power movement in the United States; the mid-1970s the time of Blacks going to (previously) all-White Universities in significant numbers. In Black history this was a time of politicized opposition to the dominant ideology, opposition that did not seek integration in the way that, arguably, Martin Luther King had done and the 1960s civil liberties movement had advocated. Van Peebles's film reflects this politicization. *Song* is about the Black community, more specifically about the law as an enemy of Black people. The eponymous anti-hero, Sweetback, is a pimp (and a stud) who gets elevated to cult hero when he kills two White policemen who have acted abusively within the Black community. He then escapes to Mexico. This film, which was independently produced and cost $500,000 to make, grossed $20 m in the first few months of its release. Similarly *Shaft* and *Superfly*, produced by Hollywood, made tidy profits. These three films represented a positive moment in Black cultural history. Blacks, who hitherto had remained asexualized on the screen, now expressed their **sexuality**. Blacks were given strong heroes who do not get dragged down but who actually escape from the ghetto. Aggressive and rugged individualism was put up on screen and undoubtedly provided Black audiences with images that did articulate their anger.

For Hollywood the success of *Shaft* (which won an Oscar for Isaac Hayes's music score) and *Superfly* meant cheap products bringing in high returns. Now Black actors became the flavour of the month, provided they were not expensive. However, if they were inexpensive (that is, not Sidney Poitier), generally speaking they were not known by the public at large. So Hollywood turned to musicians and sportsmen (*sic*) to find its stars (thereby guaranteeing further White-audience interest as well). White directors and producers pumped out sequels to these original hits – all much of a muchness (pimp or private eye beating the system) and simplistically racist (the White as the fat villain). The success of these mix and match, push-button formulaic films led Hollywood to cast its net a bit wider, generically speaking, with monster movies (*Blacula*, William Crain, 1972) and **westerns** (*Boss Nigger*, Jack Arnold, 1974).

Then, in 1976, this movie craze crashed, for predominantly two reasons: one economic, the other political. Although Blacks were by far the greatest audiences for these movies, they represented 'only' 12 per cent of the population. Demographically speaking they are not, then, a large target audience, something that Hollywood requires to make profit. Cynically, now that (in the late 1980s and early 1990s) cable and syndicated television and video sales have increased the demand for all sorts of films and made targeting 'small' audiences a profitable concern, Hollywood is back in there making Black-cast movies. The fading of the Blaxploitation boom was also politically motivated. In the late 1970s, as a result of the politicizing effects of the Black Power movement – at least as far as the representation of Black men was concerned – images of Blacks as pimps, junkies, dealers, thieves ran counter to the new images Black men had of themselves. If, however, in the Black cinema of the 1980s and 1990s Black male images have become more diversified, this is not the case for Black women. Images of Black women as 'bitch' or 'ho' (whore) still prevail (see below).

After 1976 – towards a new Black aesthetic and a Black cinema
The new Black aesthetic has impacted on only a part of Black cinema. In the late 1970s Black students, writers and film-makers (most famously perhaps the UCLA group) got together on American campuses and sought to broaden the frame of reference of Black experiences in the United States – including that of Black women – and to challenge the stereotypes surrounding their representation. The heritage of this aesthetic is to be found primarily in just one of the three styles or traditions of Black cinema that emerged in the 1980s.

The socio-realist or ethnographic tradition hits out against **stereotypes** (including those that Blacks produce of themselves) and does not conform to the image of 'Black hero as oppressed' but offers images of self-determination for both men and women. This cinema looks at traditions of Black cultures. Equally, it also addresses issues of White post-colonialism and neo-colonialism. Of this category, the films of Charles Burnett and Julie Dash are perhaps the best known (for example, respectively, *Killer of Sheep*, 1977, and *Daughters of the Dust*, 1991).

The other discernible styles are the populist tradition, which comes down to a revival of the Blaxploitation movie (for example, the Eddie Murphy films) which, at its best, is parodied; and the urban Black-American street-life hip-hop-rap movie (Spike Lee's films are exemplary of this tradition).

Of the populist or post-Blaxploitation category, Keenan Ivory Wayans's *I'm Gonna Git You Sucka* (1988) was the first Blaxploitation parody and is, arguably, one of the best. Playfully **intertextual**, it not only sends up the clothes worn during the 1970s (as 'funny to look at now') but exposes their original parodic or ironic value. That is, the clothes-chic of flares, tight polyester shirts, platform shoes, hot pants so preponderant in Whites' dress-code of the 1970s was none other than a recuperation into mainstream culture of the dress-code of double-marginals – Black pimps and prostitutes! Wayans also brought back in the **stars** and the music from the earlier films: we all remember the music of *Shaft* – nostalgia for all, including the stars who were willing to come back and make fun of their previous selves.

If Black cinema became a visible phenomenon in the 1980s, it was thanks partly to the success of the star Eddie Murphy – an exemplar of the populist tradition (and great puller of White audiences) and, also to the success of early-1980s hip-hop-rap films. This category of Black cinema, though perhaps not ideological, does represent the revival of a specific cultural nationalism: Black urban street life – mainly as it concerns men. Thus, for feminists, Black feminists, it is not an unproblematized revival, nor is it an unproblematic representation of Black culture (see below). However, these films are compositions that do go counter to **classic narrative cinema** in their syncopated jazz-like structure and their strong reliance on the rhythm of rap music. They are low-budget products all made for under $10 m and grossing up to five times that figure. Lee's *She's Gotta Have It*, 1986, was made for $175,000 and grossed $8.5 m; *Do the Right Thing*, 1989, cost $6.5 and grossed over $27.5 m. Lee's success has opened the door for others, which is a positive outcome. For example, 1991 saw nineteen Black-cast and Black-directed films. However, as Jacquie Jones (1991) says, Hollywood still holds the purse strings – it chooses the Black directors, actors and the storyline. And, these films represent a cinema that does not threaten existing conventions. Citing numerous films, but focusing on Mario Van Peebles's *New Jack City*, 1991, Jones claims that this cinema proffers a new ghetto aesthetic that magnifies the grim realities of Black urban life, plays on the 'Black on Black crime' **myth** and, finally, serves to illuminate the image of the Black male for the American audience. At best, then, Blacks become sociologically interesting.

The reappropriation of Black women by Black male filmmakers has not represented a sign of liberation for women either (Jones, 1991). So far they occupy two positions: 'bitch', the wilful woman ripe for being brought down, or 'ho', the sexually demanding and not easily satisfied woman. Woman is usually defined in relation to the other male characters, she has no narrative of her own. Misogyny also hits out at the mother, who is often seen as ineffectual, and in return patriarchy is valorized. This is particularly the case in the films of two young film-makers, John Singleton (*Boyz'n the Hood*, 1991) and Matty Rich (*Straight Out of Brooklyn*, 1991).

Who is the speaking subject? These three categories of films all raise the question of who is the speaking **subject**? Is it 'just' Black? Is it 'just' male and Black? What, in the United States, is its originating space (that is, East or West Coast, North or South)? How is it situated in time and space (that is, in relation to its history)? Speaking the Black subject raises further questions. For whom are these images destined? What about the danger of becoming the voice of the Black cause? Of speaking about the Black condition rather than from it? Of setting in place a new set of stereotypes (for example 'Black as victim')? What, in the final analysis, is to be the relationship with Hollywood? Can Black cinema co-exist with Hollywood in the same time and space?

Blacks represent 12 per cent of the American population, they currently make up 25 per cent of the cinemagoing audience, and Black culture permeates American society, particularly the youth class. This should make Black cinema an attractive proposition for Black investment. As yet, however, this has not happened. The emergence of Black cinema is a result not of Black financing but of Hollywood's economic policy which has co-opted Black cinema into its industrial monopoly. There are kicks against this, which may herald change. First, there was Spike Lee's much-publicized defiance over the financing of *Malcolm X* (1992). Warners produced it but would put up only $28 m; Lee needed $34 m. He publicly exposed Warners when he named the Black celebrities who helped to make up the $6 m shortfall. Second, Lee and other film-makers have set up an association based in New York, the Black Filmmakers Foundation, to counter Hollywood's control and to help finance Black film-makers' work (founding members include Charles Burnett, Julie Dash, Reginald and Warrington Hudlin, Charles Lane). Third, Black film-makers have refused, through their film practices, to be measured by the two key modalities usually imposed by critics on films coming from the margins: authenticity and **realism** (Kennedy, 1993). Thus, although critics may decry the failure of films that refer to rap culture both texturally (through their structures) and intertextually (through the presence of rap artists and their songs within the film) to convey the authenticity of the concerns of rap lyrics, they are missing the point that this cinema is not one that is seeking to marginalize itself as **avant-garde** but one that is seeking to deconstruct **hegemonic** practices from within (Kennedy, 1993). Similarly, why must realism mean one thing only – ghetto-black-violence – and not middle-class success? Finally, there is another voice from the margins that is at last getting heard – that of the Black female and Black-American female film-maker (currently there are twenty Black female film-makers in the United States). This is a voice that gives an image of Black womanhood different from that offered by Black male cinema. To the misogynistic and homophobic images of Lee, Singleton and Mario Van Peebles, Kathleen Collins counters with images of middle-class professional womanhood (*Losing Ground*, 1982) and Heather Foxworth with images that expose Black male sexism within the Black community (*Trouble I've Seen*, 1988). (For further reading see Bakari, 1993; Bogle, 1988; Bogle, 1994; Diawara, 1993; Givanni and Reynaud, 1993; Hooks, 1992; Taylor, 1986; Wilkins, 1989; Reid, 1993. Finally *Black Film Bulletin* is the standard journal in this area.)

B-movies (*see also* **studio system**)   Cheap, quickly made movies first came into prominence in the United States during the depression (early 1930s) when audiences demanded more for their money – a double bill: two films for the price of one. So a B-movie was screened as a second feature alongside a major feature film (called an A-movie). Monogram and Republic made B-movies only, mostly **thrillers** and **westerns**; the major studios also had to turn some of their studios over to B-movie production and some of their productions met with astonishing success (for example RKO's *Cat People*, Val Lewton, 1942). The Supreme Court decision in 1948 to end the major studios' cartel over distribution and exhibition opened the screens to independently produced films. The impact of this decision on the Hollywood studios was to recreate fierce competition among the majors. As a result the cost of making films in and for Hollywood went sky-high. The effect was to put an end to the production of B-movies and to the double bill.

body horror films – *see* **horror films**

British New Wave (*see also* **Free British Cinema**)   The British New Wave, like its French counterpart, was quite short-lived: 1958–64. As a movement, it coincided with the social and cultural changes occurring in Britain largely as a result of the emergence during the 1950s of a youth class. This was a period marked by radical change in music, fashion and sexual mores – this was the era of the 'swinging sixties'. It was also the era of 'kitchen-sink' drama, of a gritty new **realism** on stage starting with John Osborne's play *Look Back in Anger* (1956).

The legacy of the British New Wave is both that particular kitchen-sink theatre of realism and the radicalized **documentary** tradition of the **Free British Cinema**. Given that the film-makers who dominated the New Wave – Lindsay Anderson, Karel Reisz and Tony Richardson – were the same as those of the Free British Cinema group, this part of the heritage is hardly surprising. The Free British Cinema group's work had focused on the youth and working classes at work and in leisure; the New Wave was one that focused on contemporary social issues of youth growing up in a culture of increasing mass communication. Prostitution, abortion, homosexuality, alienation caused by mass communication culture, failures in couples' relationships – these were some of the dominant 'social problems' dealt with. The documentary-realist style is everywhere in evidence in this cinema of the New Wave, with the predilection for location shooting, particularly in northern industrial cities, the use of black and white fast stock film (which gave a grainy, newsreel look to the images), and natural **lighting**. **Stars** were not used, although actors who were used, such as Alan Bates, Albert Finney, Richard Burton and Michael Caine, soon found star status thanks to their roles in these films. It is noteworthy that the two women actors most associated with the films of this movement, Rachel Roberts and Rita Tushingham, never gained such status. The majority of the films were based on books or plays written by authors who had first-hand experience of working-class life: Alan Sillitoe, John Braine, David Storey, Shelagh Delaney.

31

Although some film historians nominate *Room at the Top* (Jack Clayton, 1959) as the first New Wave film, it would be more accurate to say that that film was a precursor to the movement and that Richardson's adaptation for the screen (1959) of Osborne's *Look Back in Anger* is in fact the real beginning of this movement. Osborne and Richardson were also flag-bearers in that they were the first to form an independent production company, Woodfall Films, to finance their projects. This was swiftly followed by Joseph Janni's Vic Films, then Bryanston – a subsidiary of British Lion and made up of a consortium of sixteen independent producers – and, finally, Beaver Films, formed by Richard Attenborough and Bryan Forbes. Soon after being established, Woodfall Films sought financial backing from Bryanston to produce Shelagh Delaney's *A Taste of Honey* (Richardson, 1961). This link-up with the British Lion subsidiary would in part seal the fate of this movement in 1964.

Look Back in Anger with Richard Burton in the protagonist's role as Jimmy Porter was the first of the so-called 'angry young men' films, shortly followed by Albert Finney in *Saturday Night and Sunday Morning* (Reisz, 1960) and Alan Bates in *A Kind of Loving* (John Schlesinger, 1962). The real difficulties of single motherhood and the loneliness that social marginalization imposes on homosexuals are central themes to *A Taste of Honey*. The hypocrisy of authoritarian institutions such as the Borstal comes under fire in *The Loneliness of the Long Distance Runner* (Richardson, 1962). *This Sporting Life* (Anderson, 1963) exposes the corruption and commercialism of the Rugby League business and the brutality to which lovers can be pushed by a lack of communication.

By 1963, over a third of film production was New Wave. The movement was riding high and proving that the British film industry could resist **Hollywood** domination. It was, however, this very success, in particular of Woodfall Films which produced the majority of the New Wave films, that brought about the movement's – and thereby the British film industry's – demise. Richardson wanted to make a film adaptation of the novel *Tom Jones*. He wanted to shoot it in **colour** and full costume. This required a considerably larger budget than was typical for a New Wave production. British Lion refused to back the project and so Richardson turned to the American production company United Artists. At this time Hollywood was experiencing severe financial difficulties and was only too pleased to turn its attention to Britain and invest money where overheads and talent were cheap. United Artists' agreement to finance the production of *Tom Jones* (1963) was the thin edge of the wedge that broke the back of the British independent companies and, ultimately, British Lion. Taken by the British success, the major Hollywood **studios** invested in British production projects and by 1966 75 per cent of British films were American-financed. By 1967 this figure grew to 90 per cent. By the end of the 1960s, when Hollywood began to experience an upswing in its fortunes, the American companies had upped stakes and gone home, leaving the British film industry virtually incapable of financing itself. Add to this the selling-off in 1964 of British Lion, which had released the majority of the New Wave films, and the picture of the industry's demise is complete. (For further reading see Hill, 1986.)

buddy films Traditionally buddy films are for the boys. That is, the **narrative** centres on the friendship between two male protagonists. This **genre** was very much in vogue in the 1960s and 1970s, perhaps as a response to the dehumanizing effects of the Vietnam War in which the United States became heavily entangled after 1962. Paul Newman and Robert Redford are the icons of this genre, often appearing together (*Butch Cassidy and the Sundance Kid*, 1969; *The Sting*, 1973, both George Roy Hill). This friendship is totally heterosexualized, there is no possible misreading since the heroes are always doing action-packed things together (shooting themselves out of trouble, primarily) – 'boys will be boys' – and a woman will be 'around' even if very marginal to the narrative (she guarantees the heroes' heterosexuality, just in case). The buddy genre has now developed, in the 1980s and 1990s,

33

to include a proto-father–son friendship, again with the icon Newman but accompanied this time by a younger alter-ego, Tom Cruise (*The Colour of Money*, Vincent Lauria, 1986) – signifying a restoration of family values or at least of the value of the father ('every boy needs a man to show him how to be a man'). Though considered a male genre, recently this phallocentrism has been called into question, in some instances to hilarious effect, as in the film *Thelma and Louise* (Ridley Scott, 1991) in which two women buddies hit the road. Another 'inverted' buddy movie is the very camp and funny Australian–British co-production *The Adventures of Priscilla, Queen of the Desert* (Stephen Elliot, 1994). Buddy films have also, in the light of AIDS, stretched in meaning and produced a sub-genre that addresses gay male friendship (for example *Longtime Companion*, Norman René, 1990). In this manifestation the buddy film has come to represent what it most eschewed or feared in its earliest manifestations.

C

Cahiers du cinéma group – *see* **auteur/auteur theory, French New Wave**

castration/decapitation – *see* **psychoanalysis**

censorship   In some countries censorship is quite benign and limited to a rating system to protect minors and to inform audiences of the content of films. Other countries still pursue a very strong line in censorship, banning films in their entirety or insisting on cuts being made. Censorship tends to be imposed in three main areas: sex, violence and politics. The first two have been of primary concern to groups lobbying for the welfare of minors; the third more clearly has been the concern of state institutions and governments. Relaxation of censorship laws is very recent: late 1960s for the United States; mid-1970s for the United Kingdom, France and Spain – and so on. In some countries, the United States and Germany for example, it is constitutionally illegal to censor films, even though censorship may be maintained. Generally a country that is more assured in its political culture and does not feel its **hegemony** to be under threat is less inclined to draconian censorship. However, that fact that this is not always the case points to the notion that consensuality is not always a

35

given. Recent incidents in France around Scorsese's film *The Last Temptation of Christ* (1988) show that the Catholic lobby still has a strong foothold within smaller communities. Although there is supposed to be a separation between church and state in France, the Catholic lobby obliged mayors to cancel screenings. Similarly in this seemingly contradictory vein, repressive regimes have enacted sensible censorship laws. During the Nazi regime and also during the occupation of France, the Germans imposed strict regulations to protect minors, so that certain films were forbidden to those under sixteen.

Because the United States' film industry is dominant, the American **Hays** Office/Code is the best-known censoring body. Its official title is the Motion Picture Producers and Distributors of America, popularly renamed the Hays Office after its first president, William H. Hays (serving from 1922–45). The Hays Office was established in 1922 in response to public furore over the morality of some of Hollywood's **stars**. However, the point should be made that this office was established by the film industry itself, which thought it in its own interests to set it up as a way of protecting itself against federal intervention. It is curious that sex scandals off-screen should bring about censorship of **narratives** on-screen. But that's what happened – and many careers were broken, even if the scandals were not proved or indeed if a star was acquitted in a trial, as was the case, most notoriously, for Fatty Arbuckle. Hays wanted Hollywood to act as self-censors rather than let state or federal censorship intervene. This meant of course that stars were even more in the pocket of the production companies, thereby finding themselves in the paradoxical position of having simultaneously to be larger than life and yet also totally 'normal' and ordinary – a schizoid conflict that killed some of them (for example James Dean, Marilyn Monroe, Judy Garland, River Phoenix).

While the film industry may have been reasonably successful in watching over its stars, it did not fare so well in self-censoring its own product. Movies privileging the underworld and gangsters, for example, were severely condemned by critics. So in 1934 a production code (based on the Ten Commandments) was published to which all companies had to adhere. In 1968 the code was discarded in favour of a ratings system which still prevails. The office is now the MPAA: Motion Picture Association of America. (For further reading see Kuhn, 1988 (cinema of the silent period); Black, 1994 (Hollywood in the 1930s); Matthews, 1994 (censorship in the United Kingdom).)

cinema nôvo   A cinema that emerged in Brazil in the early 1950s and was at first influenced by the **Italian neo-realist** movement. Films of this period were primarily **documentary** in style and portrayed the lives of ordinary people. Later, in the 1960s, this movement became more radicalized and a cinema co-operative was formed that sought to renovate a film aesthetic appropriate to contemporary Brazil where poverty, starvation and violence were the daily diet of most and concentrated wealth the good fortune of the very few. Film-makers in this co-operative included Glauber Rocha, Nelson Pereira dos Santos and Ruy Guerra. This cinema was populist and revolutionary: populist because of its blend of history, **myth** and popular culture; revolutionary because, if in its populism it could advocate rights for the disenfranchised and landless peasants (for example Rocha's *Antonio das Mortes*, 1969), none the less, it made clear that such populist advocacy could do nothing against the harsh conditions in which most Brazilians lived. By the early 1970s the group's activities had been suppressed by the junta government that had taken power in 1969.

cinemascope   (*see also* **anamorphic lens**)   Cinemascope and **colour** were introduced in the early 1950s by the American film industry in an attempt to stem the commercial decline of its cinema due to falling audience numbers. Cinemascope is a wide-screen effect made possible through the use of the anamorphic lens.

37

In **film theory**, cinemascope was welcomed by the **Cahiers du cinéma** group primarily because it extended the possibilities for **mise-en-scène**. For some critics in this group, it also represented the death of **montage**. Montage for the *Cahiers* group, but most especially for Bazin (1967), was an anti-realistic film-making practice that manipulated the audience through its juxtapositioning of **shots** and the carving-up of reality. **Realism** and objectivity could be assured only by the predominance of **depth of field/deep focus** with its long takes and implicit unimpeded vision. Cinemascope, the *Cahiers* group argued, would privilege mise-en-scène and extend the merits of depth of field – meaning would be produced through the framing of shots and movement within the shots. Cinemascope implied a number of things for the *Cahiers* group. First, it gave breadth (that is, space) and thereby created a frieze effect on the screen. In so doing, it recognized the sculptural nature of cinema's **narrative** (*Cahiers du cinéma*, no. 25, 1953). Second, cinema should not try to create depth but should suggest depth through breadth. Cinema is about lateral movements and space, and cinemascope allowed for a freer expression of those two concepts (*Cahiers*, no. 31, 1954). Third, cinemascope implied location shooting and the definitive arrival of colour (*Cahiers*, no. 31, 1954). Finally, because cinemascope provided the **spectator** with almost panoramic vision (that is, virtually consonant with the way human vision functions), it was the perfect solution to the arbitrary divide between **audience** and screen.

Although in the 1950s and 1960s Hollywood perceived cinemascope as appropriate to certain **genres** (such as **westerns** and **epics**), European cinemas – starting with the **French New Wave** – used it to a subversive effect for intimist films about the failure of human relationships (as for example in Jean-Luc Godard's *Le Mépris*, 1963, or *Pierrot le fou*, 1965).

cinéma-vérité   Initially the title of a Soviet newsreel – *Kino-Pravda* ('film-truth') – which was the filmed edition of the

Soviet newspaper *Pravda*, the term was not used to describe a particular **documentary** style until Dziga Vertov (the documentarist who in the 1920s shot this newsreel/newsreal for the paper) coined it in 1940 in reference to his own work. Vertov characterized this cinema as one where there were no actors, no décors, no script and no acting. The French ethnographic documentarist Jean Rouch followed in this tradition, at first quite stringently. His earlier 1950s documentary work was an 'objective' filming of the activities of indigenous people in Francophone Africa – what was termed *cinéma direct*. There was no staging, no **mise-en-scène** and no **editing** – so these documentaries were as close to authentic as they could be. Later, in the 1960s, Rouch moved away from this very purist *cinéma direct* to a more sociological investigation where he did intervene in the staging of **shots** and put his footage through the editing process – what has come to be termed *cinéma-vérité*. Less objective but no less real, this *cinéma-vérité* attempted to catch reality on film. Ordinary people testified to their experiences, answered questions put by Rouch or his colleagues. A handful of French or French-based filmmakers followed in Rouch's tradition (Joris Ivens, Chris Marker, Mario Ruspoli, François Reichenbach, Jacques Panijel and Jean Eustache). *Cinéma-vérité* is unstaged, non-dramatized, non-**narrative** cinema. It puts forward an alternative version to **hegemonic** and institutionalized history by offering a plurality of histories told by non-elites. As such, it is quite a politicized cinema, although Gidal (1989, 129) challenges this reading and sees *cinéma-vérité* as espousing a crude **ideology**. In any event, *cinéma-vérité* impacted on the radical collectives which formed in the immediate aftermath of May 1968 in France – including Godard and Guérin's Dziga-Vertov group.

class Because film is a system of representation that both produces and reproduces cultural signification, it will ineluctably be tied up with questions of class. Because the film industry is a mode of production in itself, based in capitalism and geared to profit, it is necessarily bound up with considerations of power relations which are also related to issues of class. In both these aspects, clearly, the questions of **gender** and race will also be of significance. Debate around class in film **theory** has been mostly inflected by Karl Marx's definitions of class and by subsequent rethinkings of those definitions first by Antonio Gramsci, Louis Althusser and Herbert Marcuse and then by **post–structuralist** theorists.

The Marxian definition of class and its rethinking According to Marx, class refers to groups of people who have similar relations to the means of production. That is, they get their living in the same way. Thus, the working class works the modes of production (mines, factories, etc.), the capitalist class owns the means of production. In between these two distinct classes are others: the middle and lower middle classes who can be for example small business owners or management or trained professionals. Marx also recognized that there can be fractures within each class (for example between skilled and unskilled workers or between trained professionals (i.e., diploma-holders) and those who have made it to the same status through work on the ground, and so on). Class is based on objective differences among sets of people and defined, quite negatively, as in opposition to other sets of people: a set of people will forge a class identity to protect its interests against another class. Therefore class is about not just economic relations but also power relations (O'Sullivan *et al.*, 1992, 39–42).

The conflict of ideas is secondary to this first set of conflicts and normally occurs when new material modes of production come into being. However, because new modes of production will cause new ways of thinking about production, the dominant class will endeavour to prevent new thinking by advocating ideas based on the previous order (Burns, 1983). A contiguous way of controlling potential class conflict and maintaining the status quo is through the fracturing of the productive labour force. The worker is alienated from the total means of production in that she or he is only a part of it (on a production line doing assembly work): mass production and technology cause work to be fragmented. The worker is also alienated from the commodity produced which is destined to the market and for profit. Her or his work is built into that profit, she or he pays for it – that is, the exchange value of the commodity is based in part on the repression within the worker's wage of the profit margin (for example, a worker gets paid the real equivalent of four hours although she or he has worked for eight).

Given that class difference is predominantly based in power relations, it follows that different classes are characterized by divergent **ideologies**. This is the most evident site for the making visible of class conflict. Marx, and Gramsci after him, argue how cultural artefacts manifest these differences (think of punk as opposed to *Vogue* dress-codes). They also make the point that culture functions to make sense of those differences (for example, early **melodrama** 'explains' class difference between the bourgeoisie and the proletariat). Thus, in Marxist thinking, cultural aesthetics is very bound up with the concept of class.

Later Marxists, Marcuse and Althusser, thought that by the 1960s it was less a bourgeois/proletariat divide and more an impersonal power that dominated: 'The System' (Marcuse) or 'ideological state apparatuses' (Althusser). This idea, that there was no longer a dominant class, was taken further by French thinkers. On the one hand it was argued that there was in the post-industrial society, with its new wealth and cheaper products, an emergence of a new middle class and the obliteration of major class differences. Others maintained that class differences had become internalized in new kinds of conflict (for example, around race issues). To Althusser's and Marcuse's anti-humanist position (man (*sic*) as subject-effect of the system/state), Alain Touraine argued that the old class divide had been replaced by different sets of people: those who are in control of the structures of political and economic decision-making, and, conversely, those who are reduced to the condition of dependent participation (Bottomore, 1984).

Although it was grounded in Saussurean structural linguistics and **semiotics**, the **structuralist** debate of the 1960s also embraced Marxist thinking. Of particular interest and

41

relevance to film studies was Marx's cultural aesthetic, which determined that an art object should not be considered outside or as separate from both its mode and its historical moment of production. Marxist aesthetics necessitates a move away from textual analysis as a be-all and end-all of aesthetic evaluation and demands contextual analysis – an examination of the underlying structures (labour, finance, manufacture, etc.) that went into the making of the aesthetic text.

Relevance to film studies and film theory The Marxist theory of class and cultural aesthetics found its way into film studies and theory in predominantly four ways: analysis of class relations within the text; the historical and cultural contexts of the production; modes and practices of production, and, finally, the ideological effect of the cinematic apparatus upon spectator–text relations (see **apparatus**, **ideology** and **spectator** for discussion of this last point).

On the first point, it is clear that certain **genres** yield more readily to class analysis than others: **comedy**, melodrama and social problem films (that are a sub-genre of **social realism**) are perhaps the most obvious. To illustrate the point let's take melodrama. One of the earliest traditions in this genre was to pitch the bourgeoisie against the proletariat. Most often, that conflict was also gendered. Here are a few sample scenarios: poor young girl or fallen woman (*sic*) at the mercies of rich fat bourgeois male; poor young man (often an artist . . .) at the mercies of some rich, upper-class vamp or female (often she is married, so it is not her money – but never mind since she still represents her husband's wealth); wealthy widow falls for proletarian hero; professional woman falls for proletarian criminal (and so on). Melodramas of the 1930s and 1940s centred on social mobility (for example the self-sacrificing or scheming mother trying to better her offspring's (usually the daughter's) future).

Given Western governments' policies to get women out of the factories and back into the kitchen, melodramas from 1945 centred more on the family – particularly the middle-class family. This was especially the case in the United States, where there was a concerted mediation of the desirability of a return to the hearth (desirable for economic reasons for the government, but not for the woman). In Marxist terms, whatever the **narrative** context, clearly the bourgeoisie is the class vested with capital power. In some film narratives capital is corrupt so must be resisted. However, since that representation is often caricatural, capital as a bad thing is not being targeted but rather abuse of capital power, for which an individual will be punished. Capital in and of itself, according to the narrative, still remains intact as a good thing. Film, in this instance, **naturalizes** capital and power. In the later melodramas the family under capitalism comes to be unquestioningly represented. The father is the head of the household and wage-earner, the wife the agreeing consensual woman who will produce children. In Marxist terms, the bourgeois family is a product and thereby a representer of patriarchy and capitalism and of course a reproduction and reproducer of that system. In these melodramas, although class is there, implicitly, as an issue, class struggle is not. But because these films deal with family structures, issues of dominance have now become gendered (see Cook, 1985, 76ff.).

As this starts to make clear, historical and cultural contexts of the production (the second of our four points) yield readings in relation to capital as well as class and gender. The overdetermination or valorization of the family, that is, over-investment in its importance in 1950s melodramas and, incidentally, comedy – the Doris Day factor: the squeaky-clean girl next door – is a case in point. The modes and practices of production (the third point) also yield readings. For example, the film industry functions in exactly the same way as the class system described above. There is the same dynamic of the owning and producing classes, the same principle of alienation through fragmentation in that each worker does her or his part of the production process. The traces of manufacture (such as make-up) are elided by the camera-work, the **lighting** and the **editing**. Thus, the mark of the worker is not present in the final commodity which is produced not for her or his pleasure but for profit. The real value, labour, gets lost in the exchange value, the film as a saleable commodity. **Stars**

43

have an exchange value in much the same way as commodities in any marketplace do – they too must make profit: they are the form of value, not value itself. That is, they are not stars as persons but star images as exchange-value or capital exchange (we pay to see them, agree to the price of the ticket).

Class in cinema is iconographically denoted, is signified by certain referents (clothes, language-register, environment, and so on). Film presents itself as real, places before the spectator the illusion of reality (see **iconography**, **spectator** and **suture**). So these icons serve to naturalize class, as does the homogeneity of **classical narrative cinema**, structured around the order–disorder–order nexus (similar to the Victorian novel that has a beginning, middle and end, where end means marriage). No matter that there may be new production practices, the film industry will continue to advocate the earlier ideas rather than allow the promotion of new ones. Film-makers attempting innovative ideas quickly find themselves marginalized by the Hollywood studios – as indeed was the case at different times in their careers for Orson Welles, Francis Ford Coppola and Martin Scorsese. In this respect, mainstream cinema represents only the thinkable, that which does not challenge our sense of identity, which, as cinema constantly tells us, however subliminally, is ultimately determined through our gender, and more pervasively our presumed heterosexuality – not through our class or race. In other words, because self-identity or **spectator identification** is the constant 'reality-effect' of mainstream cinema – we look into the screen-mirror. Our first priority is with whom (not what) we identify. Our first identification is with a person as gender, not a person as class, age or race. In this respect, cinema as a cultural artefact serves hegemonic purposes. The dominant ideology is structured in such a way – at its simplest level because there must be (re)production – that we necessarily think of ourselves as gendered subjects. To think otherwise would be unthinkable (think about the still predominantly negative, even hostile, attitudes to transsexuals, transvestites, same-sex love, etc.). Viewed in this light, representations of class might appear to be a sort of red herring.

Far from it. As part of the representation of 'reality' or dominant ideology, they serve to reinforce the belief that the unthinkable is just that, unthinkable – which is of course what keeps patriarchy, class and hegemonic structures in general in place. (For further reading see Hill, 1986; Stead, 1989.)

classic canons – *see* **codes and conventions/classic canons**

classic Hollywood cinema/classic narrative cinema (*see also* **narrative**)   So-called to refer to a cinema tradition that dominated Hollywood production from the 1930s to the 1960s but which also pervaded mainstream western cinema. Its heritage goes back to earlier European and American cinema **melodrama** and to theatrical melodrama before that. This tradition is still present in mainstream or **dominant cinema** in some or all of its parts.

Classic narrative cinema is what David Bordwell (in Bordwell, Staiger and Thompson, 1985, 1) calls an 'excessively obvious cinema' in which cinematic style serves to explain, and not obscure, the narrative. This cinema, then, is one that is made up of motivated **signs** that lead the **spectator** through the story to its inevitable conclusion. The name of the game is verisimilitude, 'reality'. However, an examination of what gets put up on screen in the name of reality makes clear how contrived and limited it is and yet how ideologically useful that reality none the less remains (see **ideology**). The narrative of this cinema reposes upon the triad 'order/disorder/order-restored'. The beginning of the film puts in place an event that disrupts an apparently harmonious order (marriage, small town neighbourliness, etc.) which in turn sets in motion a chain of events that are causally linked. Cause and effect serve to move the narrative along. At the end the disorder is resolved and order once again in place.

The plot is character-led, which means that the narrative is psychologically and, therefore, individually motivated (see **motivation**). Thus, by implication, if the initial event is not

45

individually or psychologically motivated it is more than likely that it will be left without explanation. Bordwell (Bordwell, Staiger and Thompson, 1985, 13) citing Sorlin, makes the point that this is particularly evident when it is an historical event that is supposed to have initiated the narrative line. The event happens 'just like that'. An exemplary film is *Gone With the Wind* (Fleming, 1939). Hyped as 'the greatest love story ever told', it gets told against the backdrop of the American civil war which gets represented duopolistically as a clash between the southern states' traditions and the northern states' ideological conviction that slavery must be abolished. In this respect, history becomes ahistorical (events have no past, no explanation, no cause). As such, history is eternally fixed, naturalized (in a not dissimilar way to the way in which woman in this cinema gets naturalized (see **counter-cinema**)). For example, in a **war movie** we might see that war is bad, but only because of the effects it has on the characters – we do not learn about the causes of the war, nor do they get examined. Think of the Vietnam War films made by Hollywood – even if the representation of that war is harrowing to watch and war, thereby, is not glamorized (as it was in films about the Second World War), the complex set of historical circumstances whereby the United States got enmeshed in that war is not touched upon – rather it is the psychological effect of the war on GI Joe that we see. If a cause is given at all then it is in the form of an individual (as with Hitler and the Second World War).

Classic narrative cinema, no matter what **genre**, must have closure, that is, the narrative must come to a completion (whether a happy ending or not). Any ambiguity within the plot must be resolved. For example, in *Psycho* (Alfred Hitchcock, 1960), Norman Bates may still remain psychotic, but in terms of the narrative or plot-line he has been caught for his murderous activities, so there is closure. Whatever form the closure takes, almost without exception it will offer or **enunciate** a message that is central to dominant **ideology**: the law successfully apprehending criminals, good gunmen of the Wild West routing the baddies, and so on. What is interesting, however, is which ideological message supersedes all others. In his study of classic Hollywood cinema, Bordwell (1985, 16) notes that of the sample of a hundred randomly chosen films he examined, ninety-five involved heterosexual romance in part of the action and eighty-five had romance as central to the action. Closure mostly means marriage (as with Victorian novels, incidentally), with all that that entails: family, reproduction, property. That is, the representation of the successful completion of the **Oedipal trajectory** is central to the classic narrative cinema. Such a high percentage of romance films points again to the ideological effects of dominant cinema and to its motivated function as **myth**-maker. However, in its **naturalizing** heterosexual coupledom and family it also makes the point that all else must (potentially) be read as deviancy. To return to the example of *Psycho*: Marion Crane is murdered by psychotic Bates, but we know from the narrative that she would never have ended up in his motel and therefore been murdered if she had not stolen money from her male boss in order to buy or lure her lover away from his wife (ex-wife, really, but he is paying alimony to her and so cannot afford to 'leave' for Marion). Double-theft. Man as exchange commodity. So Marion is 'punished' for transgressing the patriarchal order: stealing money (from one man) and trying to 'break' up a marriage (by stealing another man and ending his ties with his wife). Why else at the end of the film does her sister do the right thing (and not get killed), do coupledom the right way – and get her man (the same one her sister failed to purchase)?

In this cinema, style is subordinate to narrative: **shots**, **lighting**, **colour** must not draw attention to themselves any more than the **editing**, the **mise–en–scène** or **sound**. All must function to manufacture **realism**. **Ambiguity** must be dissolved through the provision of **spatial and temporal contiguity** – the spectator must know where she or he is in time and space and in relation to the logic and chronology of the narrative. Reality is ordered, naturalized: 'life's just like that'. The narrative is goal-orientated and so, naturally, are the characters. This mythico-realistic storyline reflects the

47

other great American myth: that of upward mobility and success. The dream factory makes the American dream come true.

Let's show how this is done. Bordwell (Bordwell, Staiger and Thompson, 1985, 5) makes the point that this classic cinema is normative not formulaic (which implies fixity). This normativity is, presumably, what enables it to be affected by the force of other cinemas and to integrate or co-opt some of their practices, notably those of the **avant-garde** and European **art cinema**. But back to the reality-effect. To achieve the fundamental principle of realism, editing must function to move the narrative on logically and, predominantly but not exclusively, chronologically (even a flashback will, in the main, be narrated chronologically – or the causal chain will be clear). However, editing must not call attention to itself, so continuity is essential. To achieve this, generally speaking, a whole scene is shot in one take – usually in a long shot – called a master shot or master scene. After this, parts of the same scene will be reshot, this time in close-ups and medium shots. These are then edited into the master scene and redundant parts of the master scene are cut. To ensure continuity, **match cuts** and **eyeline** cuts need to be consistently observed. Match cuts link two shots – one in long the other in medium shot, for example, but related in form, subject or action – creating a **seamless** continuity (we do not 'see' the cut). The eyeline match allows us to see the direction of the character's **gaze**: we move, unobtrusively, from watching the character watching, to watching what she or he is watching (see **continuity editing**).

There are other aspects of editing that might seem not to have reality inherent in them. **Cross-cutting** is an example of how, despite its lack of realism, the reality-effect works. Cross-cutting allows us to see two separate sets of action in different spaces but juxtaposed in time – normally with a view to creating suspense. However, since we have been stitched into the narrative as omniscient spectator we do not question our ability to be in two places at once, in fact we expect to 'see it all' (see **suture**). The camera also has a vital role in this reality-effect. The **shot/reverse-angle shot** used for dialogue establishes a realistic set of exchanging looks – again stitching us into a particular character's point of view. Where necessary, establishing shots are used to orientate the spectator, after which the camera can hone in on the character or part of the setting. Because the plot is character-led there is an excess of close-ups, not just on the face but on other parts of the body, thus fragmenting the body – which would seem to fly in the face of reality. However, because such shots offer us greater access to the body, they function to reinforce the **myth** of intimacy. We are the **subject** of the gaze and simultaneously identify with the character in the film looking at those parts of the body. The natural effect produced by three-point lighting (see **lighting**) furthers the naturalness of this realism. Colour must suit the emotional or psychological mood of the sequence, setting and/or entire film. Music serves only to reinforce meaning (danger, romance, and so on).

These audio-visual cinematic norms are just as ideologically inflected as the classic narrative norms which they serve. Feminists have pointed out how, with its representations of romantic love, the family, and male–female work relations, classic cinema perpetuates and so normalizes patriarchal ideologies which assume the naturalness of unequal relationships – predominantly those of **class**, race and **gender**. The reality-effect means 'It is just like life, just like that'. (For further reading see Bordwell, Staiger and Thompson, 1985; Cook, 1985.)

codes and conventions/classic canons (*see also* **classic Hollywood cinema**, and **narrative**) All **genres** have their codes and conventions (rules by which the **narrative** is governed). These are alternatively referred to as classic canons or canonic laws. For example, a **road movie** implies discovery, obtaining some self-knowledge; conventionally the roadster is male and it is his point of view that we see. The narrative follows an ordered sequence of events which lead either inexorably to a bad end (*Easy Rider*, Dennis Hopper, 1969) or to a reasonable outcome (*Paris Texas*, Wim Wenders, 1984). These canonic laws can of course be subverted as they usually are in **art cinema** or **counter-cinema**. Codes and conventions should not be viewed just within their textual or generic context but also within their social and historical contexts. Codes and conventions change over time and according to the ideological climate of the time – compare any John Wayne **western** with Clint Eastwood's characterization of the gunman as a problematic hero or anti-hero; or again compare **science fiction** films of the 1950s with those of the 1980s and 1990s. These shifts may not represent real social change (how many men really question their machismo?), but they reflect, however indirectly, changes in social attitudes (for example, the effect of the women's movement has rendered unequal power relations between men and women less desirable than before).

colour The history of colour in cinema is a more chequered one than that of **sound**. It was not until the advent of colour television in the 1960s and 1970s (first in the United States, later in Europe) that it became fully dominant. Until that date its only peak period had been the early 1950s and even then accounted for only 50 per cent of the production (Cook, 1985, 29).

History As an idea, colour had been thought of as early as the first days of cinema. By 1896, the American Edison was employing teams of women to hand-paint images in the whole or part of the frame. In France, Méliès was doing much the same thing – single-handedly. A little later, as films got longer and therefore more expensive to paint, Pathé Frères invested in stencil painting – again carried out by women (who incidentally also did the **editing** for these longer films) – a process which the American industry also adopted. By the 1920s, Hollywood had moved on from stencil coloration and was tinting or toning films that were for major release.

The first experimentation with colour film itself came about in 1912 in the United Kingdom when it was used for

documentaries. Colour film was produced by an additive process, that is, by filming through colour filters and subsequently projecting through the same colour filters. But this process did not prevail. Instead, modern colour technology was based on the subtractive process (eliminating unwanted colours from the spectrum). This was first done in the 1920s by Technicolor Motion Pictures Corporation (a company set up in 1915).

The principle of technicolour is that of a dye transfer. Technicolor first used two-strip cameras and negatives quite successfully in the 1920s until, in 1932, it perfected three-strip cameras and negatives. After shooting, these negatives were processed through an optical printer on to three separate positives through a filter for one of the primary colours. These positives were then individually imbibed with the appropriate complementary colour (also known as the subtractive colour). Thus the original image when projected would have the appropriate colour gradations. Since this colour system could be achieved only through using three-strip cameras and since they had been patented by Technicolor, the company by 1935 had complete control of its product in relation to Hollywood – control that would last almost twenty years. It hired out its cameras and its technicians, and processed and printed the film. Technicolor supplied its own colour consultant, Natalie Kalmus (ex-wife of one of the founders of the company), whose job it was to fit the technology to **Hollywood**'s needs – a factor that would considerably affect the **ideology** surrounding colour (see below).

In 1947 the US government's anti-trust law started the process of erosion on Technicolor's monopoly of 35 mm colour film. At that time, Eastman-Kodak, in a mutual agreement, was not in competition with Technicolor. It had a cross-licensing agreement with the company to use colour for its smaller gauge, 16 mm, film – and in any event colour film was still not the dominant factor in film production in the 1930s and 1940s. Colour was mostly used for **musicals**, **costume dramas** and cartoons – often with great success (*A Star Is Born*, George Cukor, 1937, *Gone With the Wind*,

51

Victor Fleming, 1939). Incidentally, Walt Disney, who was the first to use technicolour, was so pleased with his short colour cartoons' success that he acquired exclusive rights for colour cartoons. However, by the early 1950s the two companies had rescinded their agreement since the anti-trust law had charged both companies with monopolistic practices. Eastman-Kodak now went on to develop its own technology and produced an integral tripack colour film that could be used in any camera and was cheaper and easier to use than Technicolor. It was also cheaper to process because it was a single negative. Technicolor's demise in the film industry was further accelerated by the fact that its dye process did not adapt well to **cinemascope**. Although Technicolor finally resolved those problems, it was not before Eastman had garnered most of the market. The Technicolor company is still involved in feature films but to a small degree and focuses more on research and laboratory processing.

Colour and theory Colour film is an ambiguously positioned concept. On the one hand it can reproduce reality more naturally than black and white film. However, it can also draw attention to itself and, indeed, have symbolic value. Hollywood had a double response to this. At first, in the 1930s and 1940s, it decreed that colour should be reserved for certain genres that in themselves were not particularly realistic – stylized and spectacle genres (musical, **fantasy**, **epics**). Later, in the 1950s, when colour was more widely used, Hollywood concurred with Natalie Kalmus's dictat that all colour films should endeavour to use colour to underscore mood and meaning. To that effect bright and saturated colours were discouraged (Bordwell, in Bordwell, Staiger and Thompson, 1985, 356).

But colour also has value and functions in relation to the **scopophilic drive**. Steve Neale's (1985) analysis of the value of colour in film representation makes three essential points. First, colour has a dialectical (that is, a dual conflictual) function. This came about because colour was initially associated with spectacle and, therefore, was not seen as realist. Subsequently, however, following the advent of colour television

– with its documentary and news or current affairs programmes – colour also obtained the cachet of **realism** (thus, incidentally, going back to one of its original meanings in the earliest experiments). Henceforth, the key terms centring the **discourse** about colour became nature/realism on the one side and, on the other, spectacle/art – two contradictory sets of terms. Simply expressed, if colour is used as spectacle it cannot refer to its realist function, any more than if its aesthetic mode prevails. If the realist mode is invoked, then the film must reflect nature (the colour on screen is the colour 'out there' in the real world) and, thereby, deny its function as spectacle and/or art.

Neale's second point about colour is possibly the most important (certainly for **feminist film theory**). Referring to the contradiction between the two sets of terms, Neale (1985, 152) says that it is at this point that another element enters into consideration: the female body. Women already occupy, within patriarchal ideology, the 'contradictory spaces both of nature and culture' (that is, nature and artifice) and they are also the 'socially sanctioned objects of erotic looking' (i.e., spectacle). For these reasons, women 'naturally' function as the 'source of the spectacle of colour in practice' (colour within the film will be determined by the female star's colouring, that is, what colour most complements her (but why so much orange for Rita Hayworth and Deborah Kerr, and so much yellow for Doris Day?)). Women also function as 'a reference point for the use and promotion of colour in theory' (the female **star** is an essential vehicle for colour, she gives pleasure in her look-at-able-ness). Neale concludes, first of all, that 'the female body . . . bridges the ideological gap between nature and cultural artifice', that is, she bridges the gap caused by colour's **ambiguity** – so she is both real(ism) and spectacle. But the female body simultaneously marks and focuses 'the scopophilic pleasures involved in and engaged by the use of colour in film'. Colour positions her as the site of pleasurable viewing *and* makes the **spectator** want to look at her.

53

What is significant in this reading, at least for feminists, is that, in being the embodiment of the dialectical function of colour, the female figure must implicitly be placed in other sets of dialectical functions. Thus at the same time as the female body bridges the gap between the two sets of terms within the discourse on colour (realism and spectacle), she both *marks* and *contains* 'the erotic component involved in the desire to look at the coloured image' (Neale, 1985, 155). That is, in relation to the erotic, she is simultaneously positioned as **subject** (she contains, she is the holder of the erotic) and as object (she marks, she is the site of the erotic, the 'to be looked-at-ness'). Even though in mainstream or **dominant cinema** it is doubtful that this double positioning (subject and object) leads the female body, through its visual treatment, to assume **agency** (to become subject), it is clear that in non-mainstream cinema such agencing could occur. In this respect colour could be used **counter-cinematically** to subvert the canonical **codes and conventions**.

Neale's third point develops further this potential for colour to subvert. Referring to Kristeva's writings on colour, Neale (1985, 156) argues that, because colour is so closely associated with the psychic and erotic pulsions, it is capable of escaping, subverting and shattering the symbolic organization (i.e., colour subordinated to the narrative) to which it is subject. According to Kristeva, colour operates on three levels simultaneously: the objective, the subjective and the cultural. Within the domain of visual perception, the objective level refers to an outside whereby an instinctual pressure is articulated in relation to external objects. In the case of cinema this 'outside' would be the images up on screen at which the spectator looks (instinctual pressure). This same pressure motivates the subjective level and causes the eroticization of the body proper ('seeing is responding'). Finally, the cultural level functions to insert this pressure under the impact of **censorship** as a **sign** in a system of representation. That is, the cultural operates to contain what happens between the objective and the subjective. It is a form of censorship in that the cultural's intentionality is containment of the subjective and erotic processes ('seeing is responding but watch it does not go too far'). The cultural is not always successful in its purpose of course. Pornographic films are an easy example of this. However, certain scenes in un-X-rated movies can be so erotically charged as to catch the spectator by surprise! (For further reading on colour technology see Bordwell, Staiger and Thompson, 1985; Konigsberg, 1993; on colour and theory see Neale, 1985.)

comedy (*see also* **genre**)   In film history comedy is one of the very earliest genres. This is not surprising, given that the first actors to come on to the screen were predominantly comedians from vaudeville and music-hall theatres. Early exhibition practices also explain this phenomenon. The first films were short one-reelers and were included in a mixed-media show presented by a compère in a vaudeville theatre, a music-hall or a tent at a fair. At that time, then, cinema catered for popular taste and the humour on screen tended to reflect popular comedy – as opposed to comedy of manners or social comedy. The early silent tradition of comedy was gag-based (as indeed was the very first comic film, Louis Lumière's *Arroseur arrosé*, 1895). This developed into routine comedy (Mack Sennett's *Keystone Kops* comedy series, of the 1910s, with their inevitable chase sequences) and into the emergence of the comic hero (*sic*) as, for example, Charlie Chaplin, Buster Keaton and Fatty Arbuckle. This primarily gestural tradition was, in its later manifestations, especially in **sound** cinema, closely allied to farce. Gestural gags now became verbal gags in comedies by the Marx brothers and W. C. Fields. But, as with the earlier tradition, violence was never far from the surface and this comic tradition is noteworthy for its aggressive humour.

As a genre, comedy deliberately goes against the demands of **realism** – hardly surprising given film comedy's heritage. Yet it is a genre that is perceived as serving a useful social and psychological function in that it is an arena, or provides an arena, where repressed tensions can be released in a safe manner. Apart from the gag-based comic tradition, the other

55

dominant style of comedy comes from the more 'polished' comic theatre tradition. The plot-line is less anarchic than in the earlier vaudevillesque tradition and therefore less ostensibly aggressive until one examines characterization. **Stereotypes** are far more foregrounded in this comedy, starting with **gender** (screwball comedies, as we all know, are about 'the battle of the sexes'), but including race, national prejudice and so on. Some comedy parodies this stereotyping. For example, Marilyn Monroe is much smarter than the dumb blonde she is purported to be in *Gentlemen Prefer Blondes* (Howard Hawks, 1953), *The Seven Year Itch* (Billy Wilder, 1955) and *Some Like it Hot* (Billy Wilder, 1959). Or again, Katherine Hepburn may have to comply with Hollywood's insistence on closure meaning marriage but she'll choose her man, she'll whip him into shape before she's at all prepared to consider him as a suitable partner (*Philadelphia Story*, George Cukor, 1940; *The African Queen*, 1951, and the innumerable combinations with Spencer Tracey).

Comedy is still a big tradition in Europe, especially in France where half the film industry's production is comedy. Britain has a strong tradition with its Ealing Comedies and Carry-On movies. But these are past history (1940–50s and 1958–78 respectively) – as indeed is the British film industry itself. In the United States comedy is no longer the big audience puller it used to be. Production tends to target youth audiences, which means action-packed narratives, not sassy talk. For this reason, the comedy that is produced tends to be more in the farce and gag tradition than the supposedly more sophisticated talk-humour (note the popularity of the *Wayne's World* movies of the 1990s). Certain film-makers, notably women, have taken the genre on board to explore its subversive potential. Susan Seidleman's *Desperately Seeking Susan* (1985) is exemplary in this respect. (For further reading see Brunovska Karnick and Jenkins, 1995.)

connotation – *see* **denotation/connotation**

content – *see* **form/content**

continuity editing (*see also* **seamlessness** and **spatial and temporal contiguity**) This is a strategy in film practice that ensures **narrative** continuity. The film does not draw attention to the way in which the story gets told. The editing is invisible, and as such offers a seamless, spatially and temporally coherent narrative. Spatial continuity is maintained by strict adherence to the **180-degree rule**, temporal continuity by observing the chronology of the narrative. The only disruption of this temporal continuity in mainstream cinema comes in the form of a **flashback**.

However, theoreticians have made the point that this seamlessness masks the labour that goes into manufacturing the film and as such has an **ideological** effect. This cinema gives the **spectator** the impression of reality, presents as natural what is in fact an idealistic reality (no 'fault-lines' can be perceived). The spectator has a sense of unitary vision ('it's all there, before me') over which she or he believes she or he has supremacy ('it's all there, so I know everything that's going on'). In this respect, the spectator colludes with the idealism of the cinematic reality-effect (for further discussion see **apparatus** and **spectator**). (Bordwell and Thompson (1980) provide a very full and useful introduction to the concepts and strategies of continuity editing, and also to alternatives. For more detail on the continuity system within classical Hollywood cinema see Bordwell, Staiger and Thompson (1985, chapter 16).)

costume dramas (*see also* **genre**) Not to be confused with **historical films** or with period films, costume dramas are set in an historical period but do not, like historical films, purport to treat actual events. They refer in general terms to the time in history through the costumes which, by convention, should be in keeping with the time. A period film is a different, looser term in that it can be used to refer to costume dramas and also to more contemporary times but where dress–codes and **setting** are clearly of another period (for example period films could be set in the 1910s, 1920s or 1930s but a film shot in the 1990s and set in the 1980s is not a period film – the time-lapse is not long enough). Thus, the Merchant–Ivory adaptations of E. M. Forster's novels, because they are set in the 1910s, are more readily period films than costume dramas. However, in that they refer to earlier times, Roman Polanski's adaptation of Hardy's *Tess of the D'Urbervilles* (*Tess*, 1979) is a costume drama, as is Martin Scorsese's *Age of Innocence* (1993), a film based on Edith Wharton's novel of the same name. Many costume dramas are literary adaptations (the French film industry is particularly strong in this tradition). Arguably, the most famous of them all is Victor Fleming's *Gone With the Wind* (1939). (For further reading see Harper, 1994.)

counter–cinema/oppositional cinema (*see also* **deconstruction, feminist film theory** and **naturalizing**)   This type of cinema can be found in a variety of cinemas: experimental, **avant-garde** and **art cinema**. At its simplest it is a cinema that, through its own cinematic practices, questions and subverts existing cinematic **codes and conventions**. In its aesthetic and often political concerns with the how and the why of film-making, it is a cinema that can be quite formalist and materialist and, therefore, very discontinuous in its look. That is, the structure and texture of film will be visible on screen. For example, **spatial and temporal contiguity** will be deconstructed, the security of the **setting** offered by a logical **mise-en-scène** will be decomposed and all other elements of **seamlessness** and compositional continuity will be exposed. This is then a cinema that draws attention to itself, its man/u/facture and the production of meaning. There is no safe **narrative**, no beginning, middle and end, no closure or resolution. Needless to say, spectators are not stitched into counter–cinematic films but are intentionally distanced by these practices so they 'can see what is really there', and reflect upon it rather than be seduced into a false illusionism.

Although as a practice this questioning and, potentially,

self-reflexive cinema goes back to the 1920s, it was in the early 1970s that the term *counter-cinema* was coined – largely because film theorists and some film-makers (notably Jean-Luc Godard and Agnès Varda in France and the **underground** film movement in the United States) began to question **Hollywood**'s hegemony and **dominant cinema**'s system of representation. It is in this latter respect that feminist film theorists first took an interest in the possibilities of counter-cinema to do more than just retransmit women's issues by doing it politically – by exposing the way in which dominant cinema has represented as natural woman's position as object and not **subject** of the **gaze**, as object and not agent of desire (see **agency**). Women film-makers, in subverting cinematic codes, not only denaturalized dominant film **hegemony** in so far as verisimilitude is concerned. Through their films they also made visible the meaning of phallocentric fetishization of women as spectacle and receptacle. By denormalizing dominant practices, they made visible what was made invisible: woman's **subjectivity** and difference – which fetishism denies (see **subjectivity**). An example is Sally Potter's *Thriller* (1979), which rejects the male gaze and seeks to find and assert woman's right to her own subjectivity.

Counter-cinema, then, is oppositional, exposes hegemonic practices, unfixes – renders unstable – **stereotypes**, makes visible what has been normalized or invisibilized. (For further reading see Johnston, 1976; Kaplan, 1983, 142ff.; Gidal, 1989.)

crime thriller, criminal films – *see* **film noir, gangster/criminal/detective-thriller/private-eye films**, **thriller**

cross-cutting Literally, cutting between different sets of action that can be occurring simultaneously or at different times, this term is used synonymously but somewhat incorrectly with *parallel editing*. Cross-cutting is used to build suspense, or to show the relationship between the different sets of action. (For further discussion see **cut** and **editing**.)

cut (*see also* **sequencing**)   The splicing of two shots together. This cut is made by the film editor at the **editing** stage of a film. Between sequences the cut marks a rapid transition between one time and space and another, but depending on the nature of the cut it will have different meanings.

jump cuts, continuity cuts, match cuts and cross-cuts   These are the four types of cut typically used for cutting between one sequence or scene and another, although jump cuts are also used within a sequence or scene.

Jump cuts   Cuts where there is no match between the two spliced **shots**. Within a sequence, or more particularly a scene, jump cuts give the effect of bad editing, of a camera that, literally, is jumping about without any desire to orientate the **spectator**, or of jolting the spectator along. Spatially, therefore, the jump cut has a confusing effect. Between sequences the jump cut disorientates not only spatially but also temporally. The most quoted film which exemplifies all of these uses of the jump cut is Jean-Luc Godard's *A bout de souffle* (1959). The most famous jump cut of all comes between sequences 1 and 2: in a countryside lane the protagonist shoots a motorcycle cop dead, runs across a field – cut – to the protagonist in a Paris telephone booth. Within sequences, jump cuts around enclosed spaces particularly make those spaces unfamiliar. Most unusual of all is the use of jump cuts within dialogue. In the same film the two protagonists (Michel and Patricia) at one point are sitting talking in a car. However, we never fully decipher what they are saying because of the numerous jump cuts inserted into the dialogue. Godard (1982) claimed that he had to insert these jump cuts because he had made his film (his first) far too long, by an hour. He may be pulling our leg. However it does go to show how economies of scale force decisions that eventually become canonized as art (see **30-degree rule**).

Continuity cuts   These are cuts that take us **seamlessly** and logically from one sequence or scene to another. This is an unobtrusive cut that serves to move the **narrative** along.

Match cuts   The exact opposite to jump cuts within a scene.

These cuts make sure that there is a spatial–visual logic between the differently positioned shots within a scene. Thus where the camera moves to, and the angle of the camera, make visual sense to the spectator. **Eyeline matching** is part of the same visual logic: the first shot shows a character looking at something off-screen, the second shot shows what is being looked at. Match cuts then are also part of the seamlessness, the reality-effect, so much favoured by **Hollywood**.

Cross cuts These are cuts used to alternate between two sequences or scenes that are occurring in the same time but in different spaces. Generally they are used to create suspense, so they are quite commonly found in **westerns**, **thrillers** and **gangster** movies. These cuts also serve to speed up the narrative.

montage cuts, compilation shots and cutaways These are all used within sequences or scenes, although montage cuts can in fact compose a whole film (see **editing**).

Montage cuts A rapid succession of cuts splicing different shots together to make a particular meaning or indeed create a feeling (such as vertigo, fear, etc.). First employed by the **Soviet school**, they have become incorporated into **avant-garde** or **art cinema**. They can be used to deconstruct one set of meanings and put in place another (for example the slow pomp of a funeral procession can be deconstructed and reconstructed by a rapid montage of shots into an indictment against the bourgeoisie, as in René Clair's *Entr'acte*, 1926).

Compilation shots Series of shots spliced together to give a quick impression of a place (shots of Paris, London or New York to establish the city) or a quick explanation of a situation (police arriving at a murder scene: shots of the crowd, journalists, police, detectives, finally the corpse) or a character's impression of an event (watching the highlights of a sporting event, or a performance of some sort).

Cutaways Shots that take the spectator away from the main action or scene. Often used as a transition before cutting into the next sequence or scene. For example: inside a court scene the day's proceedings are coming to an end, cutaway shot to the outside of the courthouse then cut to the next day in the lawyer's or solicitor's office.

Cuts give rhythm to the film, so getting that tempo right is essential. A film, therefore, goes through several cuts before the editor – usually working in tandem with the director – comes up with what is known as the rough cut or director's cut. Adjustments and changes are then made to produce a fine cut before the final cut is made and the film is ready for the post-synchronized **sound** mix to be transferred on to its optical track.

decapitation – *see* **castration/decapitation**

deconstruction   Although the term originates with the French
philosopher Jacques Derrida in the late 1960s and is seen as
co-terminous with **post-structuralism**, in terms of film history deconstruction was being practised and deconstructive
films were being made as early as the 1920s. Noël Burch (1973)
argues that the first deconstructive film was the **German
expressionist** film *The Cabinet of Dr Caligari* (Robert Wiene,
1919), an interesting claim given that the **codes and conventions** of **dominant cinema**, which this film contested,
were barely in place. But this claim also suggests that any
new cultural **discourse**, once it assumes a dominant status,
will bring in its wake an oppositional cultural discourse. In
film theory the term *deconstruction* is largely perceived as
synonymous with **counter-cinema**. Deconstructive film does
what the term implies: it deconstructs and makes visible
through that deconstruction the codes and conventions of
dominant cinema; it exposes the function of the cinematic
apparatus as an instrument of illusionist representation and
attacks the **ideological** values inherent in that representation. It refuses the logic of a homogenous filmic space and
narrative closure. Deconstructive films are counter-cinematic
in both aesthetic and political terms. However, politics and

63

aesthetics until recently have rarely meant sexual politics. With the exception of Germaine Dulac's and Maya Deren's **surrealist** films of, respectively, the 1920s and the 1940s, feminine **subjectivity** had hardly been addressed at all until the impact of the women's movement of the 1970s brought in its wake **feminist theory** and feminist films. (For further reading see Gidal, 1989; Kuhn, 1982.)

deep focus/depth of field (*see also* **editing**)   These two terms are not interchangeable but they are interconnected. Depth of field refers to the focal length any particular lens can provide. Greater depth of field is achieved by a wide-angle lens and it is this type of lens that achieves deep focus. With deep focus, all planes within the lens's focus are in sharp focus – thus background and foreground are both in focus. Although some critics have credited the film-maker Jean Renoir with first using this type of focus so that he could make long takes and not have to edit to create movement (movement of course occurring within the frame), it is traditionally Orson Welles who is credited as the first to use the effect in *Citizen Kane* (1941). Because deep focus requires a small aperture, it also requires fast film stock and this was not available until the late 1930s. Renoir created the illusion of deep focus by creating depth of space through staging in depth and adjusting the focus according to what was of main interest. Staging in depth is a perspectival strategy that dates back to the 1910s in cinema history. It is a system whereby the illusion of depth is created by characters moving from the back to the foreground or by the **mise-en-scène** privileging the background or middle-ground characters. The background could be brought ('pulled') into sharp focus and the foreground would be slightly out of focus (Salt, 1983, 269). However, as David Bordwell (in Bordwell, Staiger and Thompson, 1985, 344) makes clear, neither Renoir nor Welles was in fact the first to achieve deep focus. Bordwell (Bordwell, Staiger and Thompson, 344–6) lists several examples of its use in 1940s films and points also to the work of the US cinematographer Gregg Toland (who, incidentally, shot *Citizen Kane*), where it is already in evidence as early as 1937 (*Dead End*).

The debate around the merits of deep focus over **montage** was first launched by André Bazin in the 1950s. For him deep focus made a greater objective **realism** possible. Since use of deep focus, contrary to the fast editing style of montage, usually implies long takes and less editing from **shot** to shot, this style of shooting is one that draws least attention to itself and, therefore, allows for a more open reading. Deep focus's great virtue for Bazin was that the **spectator** was not subjected to the ideological nature of montage – resting as it does on *a priori* knowledge, that is, that montage will produce x meaning – but was presented, rather, with a **naturalism** of the image that refuses all *a priori* analysis of the world (see **ambiguity** and **ideology**).

denotation/connotation Two key terms in **semiotics**. Following on from Ferdinand de Saussure's work on signification (see **semiology/semiotics**), Roland Barthes coined these two terms to give greater clarity to the way in which **signs** work in any given culture. They are what Barthes termed the two orders of signification. Thus there is a first order of signification (denotation) and a second order (connotation). These in turn produce a third order: **myth**. Denotation means the literal relationship between sign and referent; thus, *three* denotes the object referred to. In film terms, this first order of meaning would refer to what is on the screen, that is, the mechanical (re)production of an image: for example, three people in a frame (a three-**shot**), two men and a woman. The second order of meaning, connotation, adds values that are culturally encoded to that first order of meaning. And it is at this second order of signification that we can see how signs operate as myth-makers. That is, they function as crystallizers of abstract concepts or concepts that are difficult to conceptualize – they make sense of the culture (for example, institutional, social) in which individuals or communities find themselves.

Returning, by way of illustration, to this three-shot. At the denotative level, the two men are standing either side of the woman. The main source of **lighting** is coming from the side, casting one of the men into the shadows. The camera is at a slight low angle, thereby slightly distorting the features of the characters. At the connotative level of meaning, the reading produced is as follows: this image is signifying the dangers of a triangular relationship. In **classic narrative cinema** – which reposes on the triad order/disorder/order-restored – convention has it that a triangular relationship must end with the demise of one character (the man in the shadows), so that order can be re-established. Within that cultural convention we can also see how the third order of signification, myth, gets produced and feeds into **ideology**. The myth that triangular relationships are doomed, and cause disruption to order, implicitly makes clear that heterosexual coupledom is the only ideologically acceptable face of sexuality.

depth of field – *see* **deep focus**

desire – *see* **fantasy**, **flashbacks**, **narrative**, **spectator**, **stars**, **subjectivity**

detective thriller – *see* **gangster films**

diachronic/synchronic These terms are taken from linguistics, where they refer to two different approaches to language study. Diachronic linguistics is the study of language over time, its history. Synchronic linguistics studies language in a specific moment in time. The former examines language as an evolving process; the latter as a structured whole whose internal relations must be examined. Applied to film studies, a diachronic approach would examine film as an evolving language and industry, from its beginnings in 1895 to the present day. It would also examine any individual film in terms of its chronological linear **narrative** movement in time from one point to another (that is, basically, the development of the film's story through the typical narrative triad order/disorder/order-restored). A synchronic approach would examine a particular film in relation to its contemporary cultural context and would also view the film as a structural entity whose internal relations must be analysed (see **theory**). Film studies now tends to see these two approaches not as mutually exclusive but indeed as well worth combining to give a fuller reading of the film as text and context.

diegesis/diegetic/non-diegetic/extra- and intra-diegetic
Diegesis refers to **narration**, the content of the narrative, the fictional world as described inside the story. In film it refers to all that is really going on on-screen, that is, to fictional reality. Characters' words and gestures, all action as enacted within the screen constitute the diegesis. Hence the term diegetic **sound**, which is sound that 'naturally' occurs within the screen space (such as an actor speaking, singing or playing an instrument on screen). The term *non-diegetic sound* refers to sound that clearly is not being produced within the on-screen space (such as voice-over or added music). Of course film is about the illusion of reality into which the spectator gets comfortably stitched (see **suture**). And to a degree even diegetic sound and space are totally illusory and falsely constructed: the sound because with most films it is post-synchronized; the space because the actual images and **shots** we see are the result of countless takes – so neither is ultimately 'naturally' there (see **naturalizing**). Certain film-makers will play on or with this illusory nature of cinema through the use of extra-diegetic sounds. Extra-diegetic sounds or shots apply to sounds or shots that come into screen space but have no logical reason for being there. They are inserted as a form of **counter-cinematic** practice or **deconstruction** to draw the **spectator**'s attention to the fact that she or he is watching a film. Jean-Luc Godard is a famed practitioner of this.

67

The term diegetic also refers to **audiences**, so that there are diegetic audiences: audiences within the film. These are often used to draw attention to the **star** in the film or to act as a backdrop to display the star. These diegetic audiences also serve to draw us, the extra-diegetic audience, into the screen and thereby into the illusion that we too are part of the diegetic audience. **Musicals** very commonly use diegetic audiences, dancing and singing around the main protagonist(s) – usually a couple – just to show off how brilliant they are in performing their song and dance. **Westerns** also use the diegetic audience to show off the bravery of the hero in contrast with their own cowardice (see, for example, Gary Cooper in *High Noon*, Fred Zinnemann, 1952).

Finally, intra-diegetic sound. This refers to sound whose source we do not see but whose presence we 'know' to exist within the story: for example, the voice-over of a narrator whose story we are being told and who is also portrayed in the film, that is, who exists on the same level of reality as the story and characters in the film. Michael Curtiz's *Mildred Pierce* (1945) is a classic in this domain. At times we only hear the heroine's disembodied voice recalling moments of her past in voice-over as we **flashback** to images of her in the frame, but we know the voice belongs to her and that she is a character in the story. She recalls in voice-over in the first flashback: 'I felt all alone . . . lonely' after her husband, Bert, had left her. Another classic example of this use of intra-diegetic sound is *Rebecca* (Alfred Hitchcock, 1940). At the very beginning we hear the disembodied voice of a woman say: 'Last night I dreamt I went to Manderley'. A little later in the film we realize that that 'I' and the 'I' of the female protagonist are one and the same. At that moment we realize the earlier sound was intra-diegetic – an interesting way of creating suspense. The voice-over of a protagonist who is announcing a flashback in her or his life, then, is intra-diegetic. Most typically the protagonist's face will dissolve into an image of an earlier time as we hear the voice-over say 'and yet it was only yesterday . . . .' (as in *Le Jour se lève*, Morcel Carné, 1939). In fact flashbacks themselves could be seen as intra-diegetic because although they are part of the **narrative** they none the less interrupt the narrative flow in the present. Interior monologue is also intra-diegetic and is quite distinct from the non-diegetic voice-over of an omniscient narrator who gives information about the story but is not personally part of the story. Intra-diegetic sound, then, at its simplest refers to the inner thoughts or voices of a narrator whose story we are witnessing. It also creates a different order of audience **identification**. During those intra-diegetic moments the character's **subjectivity** becomes ours: there is a double privileging – we are positioned not only physically but also psychically as the **subject**.

discourse This term is enjoying great currency, replacing the more imprecise word 'language'. Discourse refers to the way in which texts are **enunciated**. For example, cinematic discourse differs from that of a novel or a play, for it tells the story through **image** and **sound**. Discourse also refers to the social process of making sense of and reproducing reality, and thereby of fixing meanings. Cinematic discourse reproduces 'reality' and tells stories about love and marriage, war and peace, and so on.

In that discourses are simultaneously the product and the constituter of reality (they speak for and speak as the **hegemonic** voice), they both reflect and reinforce **ideology** and in this respect they reflect power relations – that is, there will be dominant and marginal discourses. In cinema, for example, there is mainstream/**dominant cinema** which is the dominant discourse and then the marginal discourses of, say, Black, Third World and women's cinemas (for example, Latino women's cinemas: Black, Asian, White).

Discourses 'differ with the kinds of institutions and social practices in which they take shape, and with the positions of those who speak and those whom they address' (Macdonell, 1986, 1). Thus, there are different types of discourses: institutionalized discourses (law, medicine, science); media discourses (television, newspapers); popular discourses (pop music, rap, comic strips, slang). These discourses, although they fix meaning, do not fix them as eternal. Thus, discourses cannot be separated from history any more than they can be disassociated from ideology since they serve to make sense of the culture in which we live. For example, legal or medicinal discourses fix the way in which the treatment of crimes or illnesses are dealt with at a particular time in history. It is clear that seventeenth- and eighteenth-century legal and medicinal practices are not the same as today (we do not use the stocks for punishment of petty crime nor leeches for curing ailments).

Discourses, then, are social productions of meaning and as such are wide-ranging: political, institutional, cultural and so on. Although film is predominantly perceived as a cultural discourse, social and political discourses are, of course, equally present. And dominant film discourse both reflects and reinforces dominant ideology (starting with heterosexuality and marriage). Furthermore, as with other discursive texts, there are discourses not just within film but also around it. Discourses around cinema attempt to fix its meaning, and these can range from theoretical discourses on cinema (**auteurism**, **spectator**–film relations, **sexuality**, etc.) to more popular discourses such as film reviews, trade journals and articles in fanzines. Or these discourses can be based in other discourses not necessarily related to cinema (such as **psychoanalysis** and feminism). Or, finally they can be either critical discourses (for example film reviews, students' essays) or populist ones (as in fanzines, popular press). (To illustrate how film discourses within a film operate in relation to history, ideology and reality construction, see the discussion of the shift in meanings in the entries on **horror** and **science fiction** movies.)

dissolve/lap–dissolve These terms are used interchangeably to refer to a transition between two **sequences** or scenes, generally associated with earlier cinema (until the late 1940s) but still used on occasion. In a dissolve a first **image** gradually dissolves and is replaced by another. This type of transition, which is known also as a soft transition (as opposed to the **cut**), suggests a longer passage of time than a cut and is often used to signal a forthcoming **flashback**. If it is not used for a flashback but as a transition between two sequences or scenes then it usually connotes a similarity between the two spaces or events – even though that similarity may not at first be apparent.

distanciation (*see also* **naturalizing**, and **spectator-identification**)
A term first coined in relation to theatre, specifically by Bertolt Brecht in relation to his own theatre production in the 1920s and 1930s, although the principle on which it is based, alienation, comes from the **Soviet cinema/school** of the 1920s. Brecht's purpose was to distance the **audience**, through numerous strategies, so that it could adopt a critical stance and perceive how theatre practices and characterization serve to reproduce society as it is ideologically and institutionally constructed (see **ideology**). By denormalizing theatre, by showing its artifice (staging and acting), he wanted to politicize his audience into thinking that society itself could be denormalized and therefore changed. Distanciation in film is an integral part of **avant-garde** films and **counter-cinema** and is achieved in a number of ways. First, on a visual level, fast **editing**, **jump cuts**, **unmatched** shots, characters speaking out of the screen to the audience, unexplained intertitles (written or printed words on a blank screen between shots to explain the action or supply dialogue, common in silent films), non-**diegetic** inserts – all serve to distance and indeed disorientate the **spectator** (as in Jean-Luc Godard's films). Second, on the **narrative** level, distanciation is achieved by either over-filling or under-filling the narrative with meaning (Chantal Akerman's films are exemplary of the latter, Godard's of the former). Finally, characterization: distanciation occurs here through the anonymity of the character, her or his two-dimensionality and inscrutable physiognomy (Robert Bresson's and Alain Resnais's films are good illustrations of this practice).

documentary The first film-makers to make what were in essence travelogues and called *documentaires* were the Lumière brothers in the 1890s. Thirty years later the British film-maker and critic John Grierson reappropriated the word to apply to Robert Flaherty's *Moana* (1926). Grierson was the founder of the 1930s documentary group in Britain and was one of the theorists influential in determining the nature of documentary. According to Grierson, documentary should be an instrument of information, education and propaganda as well as a creative treatment of reality. In the late 1940s, the academicism of Grierson's position was severely criticized by Lindsay Anderson and other founder members of **Free British Cinema**. According to these critics the use of the documentary as a means of social propaganda took away the aesthetic value of documentary film and, on an ideological level, normalized intellectual condescension and social elitism (see **naturalizing** and **ideology**). Although Grierson's position, with hindsight, does appear elitist, if we examine the climate of the times in the late 1920s, the reasons for that position do at least become clear. In the United Kingdom (as in the United States) after 1918 there began a progressive development in popular democracy. By 1928 both men and women in the United Kingdom had equal rights to vote. Grierson, who had worked in the United States during the period 1924–7, was struck by the intellectual concerns about mass democracy – such as lack of education among the electorate, making the ordinary voter uninformed when making choices – and was determined to do something about it. This feeling of the need to educate was held by other members of the British establishment who, like Grierson, saw cinema as an excellent means of education. So he worked between 1930 and 1939, first with the Empire Marketing Board and subsequently with the GPO, as producer of some forty-two documentaries on aspects of British life, institutions, governmental agencies and social problems – all with the intention of involving citizens in their society. *Coalface* (1935), about the miners and their labour, and *Night Mail* (1936), about the Post Office workers are exemplary films in this regard.

An alternative voice in documentary work emerged a little later, during the Second World War primarily, in the films of Humphrey Jennings. Jennings was a poet and a painter, interested in **surrealism** and Marxism, in literature and science. Unlike Grierson's liberal elitism, which focused on the dignity of labour but as divorced from the social context, Jennings's films focused on the everyday life and sounds of ordinary men and women (as in *Spare Time*, 1939). He was the first documentarist to go outside London into the northern parts of the UK and to make films about industrial workers. A great concern of his was the Industrial Revolution and its effects on Britain and British people. Many of Jennings's films were made, appropriately, for the Mass Observation Unit – a unit set up by left-wing thinkers to observe ordinary people through registering accounts of their lives and feelings. Jennings's intimate observation of the ordinary also had a poetic, surreal quality to it, shown in the way he framed his images of industrial Britain and juxtaposed images of the ordinary with those out of the ordinary.

Although the tradition of recording other cultures dates back to the travelogues made by the Lumière brothers, it is really Robert Flaherty who was the first documentarist in that tradition. The first so-called documentary is his *Nanook of the North* (1922), about Eskimo life. Flaherty also directed a film for Grierson, *Industrial Britain* (1931–2) – surprisingly given Flaherty's romantic world-view. In the Soviet Union during the 1920s Dziga Vertov recorded Soviet progress in his documentaries made for *Kino-Pravda* 'Film-Truth'. Interestingly, in his work we can trace the possible heritage of the two British tendencies mentioned above. Vertov, like Grierson, saw documentary as an educative tool, but his style – an **avant-garde** formalism, achieved by **montage**, to the point of **deconstruction** – showed an aesthetic preoccupation with the image that we find in Jennings's work. During the 1930s the Soviet film-maker Medvedkin took the possibilities of documentary on to a new stage: he shot, developed and projected filmed documentation on the spot to workers as he travelled around the Soviet Union by train – this work became known as *ciné-train*.

Owing to lack of financial resources following the Second World War, many aspiring film-makers in Europe had to turn to documentary work before they could go on to make feature films (Alain Resnais, Georges Franju and Agnès Varda in France and Ken Russell in the United Kingdom spring to mind). Although some of these directors, especially those mentioned, made important politicized documentaries they hardly constituted a movement. The next important development to occur was in the 1960s with the rise of the **cinéma-vérité** group in France and the direct cinema in the United States. Two new technological developments contributed to this documentary style – television and the lightweight camera. Television news had the appearance of live images. The lightweight camera made it possible to be unobtrusive and mobile and to catch reality on film. Certain earlier documentary traditions also inflected their work: ordinary people testified to their experiences whether, for example, it was the everyday experience of Parisians in the summer of 1961 (Jean Rouch and Edgar Morin's *Chronique d'un été*, 1961), the French people's experience of the German Occupation (Marcel Ophuls, *Le Chagrin et la pitié*, 1970) or the miners' strike in the United States (Barbara Kopple's *Harlan County USA*, 1976).

In the liberal climate of the 1970s in western society, many film-making collectives and independent film-makers made documentaries challenging the establishment. Feminist films were much in evidence and were about individual women's lives, motherhood, prostitution. Black women and women of colour also got their first foothold in the film-making process. Lesbian and gay film-makers found a voice through the documentary and dealt with their lifestyles as well as gay politics. During this period some of the major themes tackled were abortion (even in France, where it was then still illegal: see *Histoire d'A*, Charles Belmont and Marielle Issartel, 1973), sexual identity, racism and economic exploitation.

More recently in the 1980s, the advent of video technology has led to the emergence of numerous collectives and workshops in Europe and the United States. It has also led to a further and a still greater democratization of the camera and to more voices from the margins finding a mode of expression. Changes in television broadcasting have also helped to raise the visibility of the documentary. With the advent of cable and satellite television there is a need for more programmes, including ones that target specific audiences. (For further reading see Barsam, 1992, for a general history; Nichols, 1991; Renov, 1993, for theory on the documentary; Lovell and Hillier, 1972 and Winston, 1995, for the British documentary.)

dollying shot – *see* **tracking shot**

dominant/mainstream cinema   Dominant cinema is generally associated with **Hollywood**, but its characteristics are not restricted to Hollywood. As Annette Kuhn says (1982, 22), it is in the relationship between 'the economic and the ideological [that] dominant cinema takes its concrete form'. Thus all countries with a film industry have their own dominant cinema and this cinema constantly evolves depending on the economic and ideological relations in which it finds itself. Given the economic situation, the film industry of a particular country will favour certain production practices over others. For example, the assembly-line system and vertical integration of Hollywood's **studios** in the 1930s and 1940s have now given way to a fragmentation of the industry and to the rise of independent film-makers whom Hollywood studio companies now commission to make films. On the ideological front, the dominant filmic text in western society revolves round the standardized plot of order/disorder/order-restored. The action focuses on central characters and so the plot is character-driven. **Narrative** closure occurs with the completion of the **Oedipal trajectory** through either marriage or a refusal of coupledom. In any event closure means a resolution of the heterosexual courtship (Kuhn, 1982, 34). This resolution often takes the form of the recuperation of a transgressive female into the (social) order (Kuhn, 1982,

34). Visually, this **ideological** relation is represented through the 'reality' effect – the illusion of reality. The **continuity** of the film is **seamless**, **editing** does not draw attention to itself. The **mise-en-scène**, **lighting** and **colour** are appropriate to the **genre**. **Shots** conform to the **codes and conventions** dictated by the generic type. (For further reading see Bordwell, Staiger and Thompson, 1985.)

editing/Soviet montage (*see also* **sequencing, spatial and temporal contiguity**) Editing refers literally to how **shots** are put together to make up a film. Traditionally a film is made up of sequences or in some cases, as with **avant-garde** or **art cinema**, episodes, or, again, of successive shots that are assembled in what is known as collision editing or montage. At its simplest there are four categories of editing: (1) chronological editing (2) **cross-cutting or parallel** editing (3) **deep focus** and (4) montage.

A film can be constructed entirely using one category (as for example Sergei Eisenstein's montage films of the 1920s); generally speaking, however, it tends to be made up out of two if not all categories. Each category has different implications in terms of temporal relations. Time can seem long or short. Time can have an interior or an exterior reality. Interior temporality is suggested by the sequence and is fictional. Exterior temporality occurs when there is a direct correspondence between sequence time and time within the **narrative**: reel time equals real time (in its most extreme manifestation see Andy Warhol's 1960s films). Again, generally speaking, a film will use both kinds of temporality.

Chronological editing As the term implies, this type of editing follows the logic of a chronological narrative, and is very close in spirit to **continuity editing**. One event follows 'naturally' on from another. Time and space are therefore logically and unproblematically represented. Beginnings and endings of sequences are clearly demarcated, shots throughout the sequence orientate the spectator in time and space and the end of a sequence safely indicates where and when the narrative will get picked up in the following sequence. This type of editing is one most readily associated with **classic Hollywood cinema** and is one which produces a very linear text. This linearity or chronological order gets broken only when there is a **flashback** or a cross-cutting to a parallel sequence. In both instances this break with linearity is signalled: a fade or dissolve with a voice-over ('and yet it was only yesterday . . . ') for example, to signify that a flashback is coming; a quick series of cuts between two locales at the beginning of a parallel sequence to link them up logically for the spectator. (For detailed discussion, see Bordwell, 1985, 60–9.)

Cross-cutting editing   **Cross-cutting** is limited as a term to the linking-up of two sets of action that are running concurrently and which are interdependent within the narrative. The term *parallel editing* has been used incorrectly to refer to the same effect, probably because it is a literal way of explaining the effect of cross-cutting: putting in parallel two contiguous events that are occurring at the same time but which are occurring in two different spaces. However, as a term, parallel editing actually refers to the paralleling of two related actions that are occurring at different times (a classic example is Alain Resnais's *Hiroshima mon amour*, 1959). Both styles of editing are used for reasons of narrative economy (they speed it up) and of course suspense. They also assume that there will be a resolution in one space and time of these two sets of action. Unsurprisingly, **Hollywood**, with its love of linearity and safe chronology, makes little use of real parallel editing and primarily uses cross-cutting. Commonly cross-cutting is used in **westerns** (John Wayne or Clint Eastwood on the way to rescue some damsel or town in distress) and **gangster** or **thriller** movies (cuts between the goodies and the baddies, victim and killer for example). Jean Cocteau makes imaginative use of parallel editing in his fantasy fairy tale *La Belle* *et la Bête* (1946) – real and fantasy time and space are in inverted order to each other and yet they run in parallel.

Deep focus editing   André Bazin was the first to qualify this style of editing as objective **realism**, although the United States cinematographer Gregg Toland was arguing as early as the mid-1930s for the realism of **deep focus**. Shooting in deep focus means that less cutting within a sequence is necessary so the spectator is less manipulated, less stitched into the narrative and more free to read the set of shots before her or him. Ideologically, then, as an editing style it can be considered counter-Hollywood, or at least counter to **seamlessness** (see **ideology** and **suture**). Certainly Hollywood, at different times in its history, used deep-focus photography, that is, shots staged in depth; it did not, however, use deep-focus editing – clearly, with its emphasis on stardom, cuts to the close-up are inevitable. (For detailed analysis see Bordwell, in Bordwell, Staiger and Thompson, 1985, 341–52.)

[Soviet] montage (see also **Soviet cinema***)*   Montage editing came out of the Soviet experimental cinema of the 1920s and, although it was Lev Kuleshov who first thought of the concept of montage, it is primarily associated with Sergei Eisenstein (director of *Strike, Battleship Potemkin,* both 1925, and *October,* 1928). In his films of the 1920s, Eisenstein adapted Kuleshov's fundamental theory that collision or conflict must be inherent to all visual **signs** (see **semiology**) in film. Juxtaposing shots makes them collide or conflict and it is from the collision that meaning is produced. A simple illustrative example, provided by Eisenstein himself: the first set of shots depicts a poor woman and her undernourished child seated at a table upon which there is an empty bowl; cut to the second set of shots depicting an overweight man with a golden watch and chain stretched over his fat belly; he is seated at a table groaning with food – the rapid juxtaposition of these two sets of images through fast editing cause a collision that in turn creates a third set of images (construed in the **spectator**'s mind), that of the oppression of the proletariat by the bourgeoisie. A first principle of **montage** editing, then, is a rapid alteration between sets of shots whose signification occurs at the point

79

of their collision. Fast editing and unusual camera angles serve also to denaturalize **classic narrative cinema**, and this is a second principle of montage editing. In fact, as far as narration goes, given Einsenstein's revolutionary task (to present the proletarian story), it is unsurprising that his editing style indicated a privileging of the image over narrative and characterization (that is, there is no single hero, only the proletariat as hero). Montage is largely used by art and avant-garde cinemas, but mainstream cinema has also incorporated it to spectacular effect (as in *Jaws*, Steven Spielberg, 1975). Perhaps the most ironic of all recuperations of montage editing, though, must be the use of these principles in film and television advertisements.

It is obvious that montage and deep-focus editing are diametrically opposed. Montage takes over the spectator's **agency**: the choice of images to be juxtaposed encodes a **preferred reading**. Meaning and therefore interpretation are imposed by the film-maker. On the other hand, this style of editing is one that works towards **deconstruction** because it draws attention to itself, and that is certainly a major way in which it has been used by art and avant-garde film-makers, even though the closed reading effect never in fact disappears. A good illustration is Luis Buñuel's surrealist film *Un Chien andalou* (1929). The montage editing of this film gives an aesthetic plasticity to it, pushing the film form forward. However, the juxtaposition of images clearly produces anti-clericalism and anti-bourgeoisie meanings (as well as profound misogyny).

It is also evident that these two editing styles create opposite rhythms through their visual impact. Montage editing is fast, jerky and abrupt; deep focus quite slow and uniformly even. An alternation of these two styles in a film would create two very distinct times, either juxtaposed or contradictory. In other words, the temporal exteriority (that is, real time) and objectivity of deep-focus editing would juxtapose or indeed be contradicted by the temporal interiority and subjectivity of montage editing. Perhaps one of the most extreme examples of this incorporation of both styles into film is Alain

Resnais's *L'Année dernière à Marienbad* (1961), where time is completely destroyed by the juxtaposition, particularly within sequences, of these two styles.

ellipsis A term that refers to periods of time that have been left out of the **narrative**. The ellipsis is marked by an editing transition which, while it leaves out a section of the action, none the less signifies that something has been elided. Thus, the **fade** or **dissolve** could indicate a passage of time, a **wipe**, a change of scene and so on. A **jump cut** transports the spectator from one action and time to another, giving the impression of rapid action or of disorientation if it is not matched (that is, if the **spectator** does not know where she or he has 'jumped' to). **Cross-cutting** and parallel editing also imply ellipsis.

emblematic shot A procedure in early cinema, introduced in 1903 by the film-maker Edwin S. Porter in his film *The Great Train Robbery* (in this case a medium close-up of the mustachioed gang-leader holding a gun and poised to shoot). Porter recognized the need to situate the **genre** and **narrative** for the **spectator**, hence the use of the emblematic shot. The **shot**, usually placed at the beginning of the film, was to act as a **metonymy** for the whole film, that is, it would sum up the **diegesis** of the film. This shot could also be placed at the end of the film to sum up what had been seen. Noël Burch (1990, 193) describes this use of the shot at the beginning as the earliest attempt to establish the narrative – acting, therefore, much as establishing shots in current mainstream or **dominant cinema** (shots at the beginning of a film or sequence that serve to orientate the spectator in time and space). It also serves to create ocular contact between actor and spectator and so represents an early form of **suture**. When placed at the end, such emblematic shots constitute the first attempts at narrative closure – that is, the film has a meaningful, constructed and signalled ending – it is no longer a case of the film just having run out, as with the earliest cinema.

enunciation   Film theorists have adapted this term into discussions of modes of cinematic address. As a concept it was first developed by the French semiotician Emile Benveniste (1971) in an attempt to study the operation of **discourse** within specific social contexts. It is more specifically the three key terms that come under the general rubric of *énonciation* that are particularly helpful to discussions of modes of cinematic address and **subjectivity**. The key terms are: *énonciation*/enunciation: the time-bound act of making a speech act; *énonciateur*/enunciator: the person responsible for making the speech act; *énoncé*/enounced: the verbal result of that act (that is, what is spoken).

The first important point is the distinction between enunciation and enounced: the enunciation is a time-bound speech act (the speech act as it is happening); the enounced is the result of that act, so it is now out of time, out of the time at which it was uttered. Thus, on a time scale, they are not one and the same. The next point concerns the terms enunciator and enounced. These two terms allowed Benveniste to make a distinction between two types of **subject**: the subject of the enunciation, as opposed to the subject of the enounced. The subject of the enunciation is the enunciator (the one who utters). But who is the subject of the enounced? Who is represented within that utterance? The enunciator? Are they necessarily one and the same? We may think so but this it not always the case, says Benveniste. And to illustrate his point he gives the paradox of the 'liar'. If the enunciator says 'I am lying', to which subject is she or he referring? Who is telling the truth? If the subject of the enunciation is telling the truth ('I am lying') then the subject of the enounced is lying. They cannot both be lying because they are not one and the same. The subject of the enunciation (the one who utters) has already moved on. If the subject of the enounced is telling the truth, then the reverse is true and the subject of the enunciation is lying (the one who utters is lying). Therefore to the earlier temporal difference of the two speech acts (enunciation and enounced) is added the idea of subject difference (see Lapsley and Westlake, 1988, 50). The following diagram illustrates this.

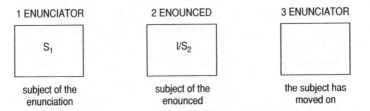

1 ENUNCIATOR	2 ENOUNCED	3 ENUNCIATOR
S_1	I/S_2	
subject of the enunciation	subject of the enounced	the subject has moved on

It is not difficult to see how this reasoning fits in with Jacques Lacan's concept of the divided subject and misrecognition (for a fuller discussion, see **subjectivity** and **suture**). Lacan (1977) points to the crucial nature of the unconscious in this process of enunciation. The subject of the enunciation is both the conscious and the unconscious subject. Thus, as the conscious subject seeks to represent itself in language, it does so at the expense of coming after the word, by which time the unconscious subject is already not there but becoming something else, a situation Lacan refers to as 'future anterior'. In other words, the conscious subject of the enunciation utters 'I' and in becoming situated as 'I' becomes the subject of the enounced (see above, diagram 2). The spoken subject becomes presence. However, the unconscious subject is already beyond that 'I' and becoming something else. The spoken subject, subject of the enunciation, now becomes absence. To say 'I', therefore, is not to be it, because the subject of the enunciation (who in enunciating is making a *time-bound* speech act) has already gone past it and is saying and being something else. What is absent for the subject of the enounced, then, is the unconscious – it is outside the unconscious subject and fixed in language. The belief that both subjects are one and the same, whereas they are not, is to misrecognize the self. That is, the mirrored 'I' (this time in language) is not the same as the one standing before the mirror – that one has already gone on (see above, diagrams 2 and 3).

Relevance to film theory/cinematic address   In terms of **spec-tator**–film relations, the spectator-as-subject is both consti-tuting and constituted through the process of 'reading' the film text. In terms of cinematic address (that is, the interaction or interrelatedness of film as text and the spectator), the specta-tor is, therefore, both the enunciator (the subject–spectator making sense of the text) and the enunciated (the spectator-subject being situated by the text). The self-reflexivity of **art**, **avant-garde** and **counter-cinema** keeps those two subjects distinct. However, **dominant cinema** produces films that are **seamless** and do not draw attention to the **apparatus** (that is, the way films are made): the story 'naturally' unfolds, the text makes sense of itself so the constituting subject-spectator, because she or he has no role to play, is no differ-ent from the constituted spectator-subject. And this leads to the illusion of unity between the two subjects, in other words, to misrecognition.

Although not referring to film *per se*, Benveniste makes a clear and useful distinction with regard to these two implicit modalities of enunciation. According to Benveniste, enuncia-tion is articulated in one of two registers: *histoire* (meaning story) and *discours* (meaning discourse). Story, or better *histoire* since it connotes both story-telling and history, indicates the enunciation of past events by a dissimulated author (authors in this register do not announce their presence – they are not there). *Discours*, however, implies that active ongoing social production of meaning and the subject of enunciation in this register is ever present and so too is the receiver (since discourse implies dialogue and therefore an interlocutor). As Kuhn (1982, 49) clearly puts it: '*discours* foregrounds subjectivity in its address, while in *histoire* address is more impersonal'. We can see here the usefulness of these registers in relation to cinematic address. The more impersonal regis-ter of *histoire* means that the actual process of story-telling – the authorial voice or point of view – is absent. All markers of subjectivity are hidden. The story unfolds 'naturally', as 'always there', complete, with no hint as to how it got there. In mainstream and **classic narrative cinema**, the **narrative** itself – through the effects of **continuity editing** and its ensuing seamless appearance – does precisely the same. As *histoire*, the narrative represents itself, because complete, as reality. And the spectator, confronted with this completeness, gets positioned as the all-knowing subject. Since sexual identity (read: heterosexuality) is **Hollywood**'s great subject, it is not difficult to see the ideological resonances of this reality-effect.

Of course mainstream cinema is not devoid of *discours*. Character subjectivity within the **diegesis** occurs, for example through point-of-view **shots**, dialogue, **flashbacks**. But, as Lapsley and Westlake (1988, 51) make clear, such 'explicit instances of enunciation are [still] contained within a supervening narrative that specifies who is speaking and looking'. However, I would tend to nuance this and concur with Kuhn (1982, 53) that *histoire* 'is a defining feature of dominant cinema' but that that is not the end of it. By very dint of the presence of discursive elements it 'might be possible to envisage modes of address which, in mobilising the discursive, constitute viewing subjects rather differently' (Kuhn, 1982, 53). This point relating to positioning is developed in the **spectator** entry. But Kuhn's other point, that narrative point of view as an element of cinematic address 'is worth examining for what it reveals about the place of women as enunciator' (1982, 52) is one I would now like to examine in relation to the flashback.

In terms of modes of address within film, Benveniste's concept of enunciation does seem particularly useful when discussing flashbacks. It would seem to be able to show what is going on in terms of subjectivity. As Turim (1989) makes clear, there are several types of **flashbacks**. I only want to deal next with the broad concept of flashback and enunciation and then see how it relates to the female protagonist as enunciator. The first point to make is that the protagonist-as-subject, like the spectator, is a constituting and constituted subject. The subject both performs the text, that is, plays her or his part in the narrative, and is performed by it, is placed *in* it. The protagonist is, then, simultaneously subject of the enunciation and subject of the enounced. A first 'mirroring'

85

occurs: let us call it A_1. A_1 then goes into flashback mode through a dissolve and possibly a voice-over. The subject of enunciation is now signifying that she or he is becoming the subject of the enounced – a 'past-interior' to rephrase Lacan's term. The subject of the enounced is about to be re-enounced. A second mirroring occurs: A_2. In the flashback proper, the subject of the enounced, A_2 (that which has already been spoken and so is past-anterior) is now masquerading as the subject of the enunciation. Masquerading because there is a reperformance of the past, a making over again, in a time-based speech act, which has already occurred. So there is an apparent subject reversal. But there is also a double-mirroring: first, the subject of the enounced in relation to the subject of enunciation (which the former is pretending to be, hence the 'abnormal' subject reversal) *and*, second, the subject of the enunciation in its 'normal' relation to the subject of the enounced (but in the past). So now we are confronted with a third and fourth order mirroring: A_3 (the subject reversal, the masquerading subject) and A_4 (the subject of the enunciation set in the past). It is A_3 which points to the most intriguing effect of the flashback. All others of course point to the narcissism inherent in this cinematic trope or figure of speech, but A_3 suggests the distorting effect of the flashback on time and memory (both are back to front). Because there is a double agencing of subjectivity (the subject of the enounced and the subject of the enunciation are both at work here), it also suggests a **mise-en-scène** of the relationship between the conscious and the unconscious. In this respect, absence (the unconscious) is made presence – almost as if the 'I' of the subject of the enounced is looking back and catching the 'I' of the subject of enunciation.

Given this parametric reading, using variables on a constant, the flashback, then, can be the moment when the psyche has control of its unconscious. So flashbacks for whatever **gender** should represent an ideal moment of empowerment. But is this the case? Leaving **avant-garde** and **counter-cinema** aside, if we look at classical narrative cinema it is with little surprise that we find that male flashbacks dominate, including male flashbacks narrating a woman's story – as is ultimately the case in *Mildred Pierce* (Michael Curtiz, 1945). In this film, of the three flashbacks it is the last one, the detective's flashback, that in essence rewrites/interprets Mildred's two preceding ones. It is his flashback that resolves the enigma around the murder and Mildred's role in it (Kuhn, 1982, 50–2). Women's flashbacks in the films of the 1940s and 1950s, which are often triggered off by a male 'expert' (doctor, detective), are used to 'explain away' their psych(ot)ic disorders (suicide attempts or just plain insanity). In other words, they tend to be frameworked by the male protagonist, so that it is he who is reaching into the unconscious of the woman, not the woman herself. In these instances, clearly the female protagonist remains the subject of the enounced – her unconscious is therefore 'beyond' her (read: her comprehension). (Maureen Turim (1989, 117) looks at the issue of women's flashbacks in mainstream and art cinema, and attempts to read against the grain of some of the 1940s and 1950s obvious readings of mainstream films' use of flashbacks.)

epics (*see also* **genre**) In the beginning there was *The Ten Commandments* (1923) and *Ben Hur* (1926), and they were so successful they went forth and multiplied and, born anew in **sound**, there was *The Ten Commandments* (1956), *Ben Hur* (1959), but then there was *Cleopatra* (1963) and she was so wilful and costly she ruined **Hollywood** and did the epic in. . . . So one official version of this genre's rise and fall might have it. And of course, because epics cost so much to make, it is a case of economies of scale. Epics not only cost a monumental amount of money, they require huge sets, casts of thousands and, above all, a monumental hero (*sic*) played – at least since the advent of sound – by a monumental **star**. And as for topic, it is usually taken from history: Biblical or 'factual'; certainly most preferably from a distant past so that the ideological message of national greatness would pass unremittingly. Generally speaking, in western society, *the* nation is the United States because the epic is predominantly an American genre, Hollywood having the resources necessary to produce it.

Arguably D. W. Griffith's *Birth of a Nation* (1915) was the first great epic and David Lean's *Lawrence of Arabia* (1962) the last. The heyday of the sound epic was the 1950s, starting with *The Robe* (Henry Koster) in 1953, the first film to be made in **cinemascope**. The major reason for a resurgence in production of this genre was of course economic. Hollywood's popularity was on the decline. Home leisure, especially television, was keeping **audiences** away from the movies. To attract them, film studios were having to produce big spectacles that no television set could muster. So **colour**, 'scope and epics seemed a surefire cocktail to seduce audiences back in. Another factor in their appeal was the grandeur of the themes based in heroic action and moral values which of course fed into the dominant cultural climate of the time: the United States as a superpower, the need to be cleaner than clean in the face of McCarthyism and the need for clearly defined **gender** roles in the economic restructuring of the nation's post-war job market (that is that women should relinquish jobs they had taken up during the war period and go back into the domestic sphere).

From this, it might seem easy to see why an epic based on Cleopatra might sound the death-knell for the genre. After all, it was about a woman, a leader, a queen (even) who picked and chose her men and spat them out (that is, had them killed) when she had had enough. Strong, self-assertive women were not the norm on screen and the feminist movement had yet to come to the United States. In any case this brand of 'Hollywood feminism' (to use Thomas Elsaesser's term, 1987, 69) was far removed from any feminist **ideology**. So that was not the reason why this film was the swan-song for Hollywood and its epic tradition. This was the period of John F. Kennedy (the youngest president of the United States), of optimism, change and collectivism. As a topic, *Cleopatra* was out of date – even though in terms of fashion the creations designed for Elizabeth Taylor's Cleopatra had a profound influence on women's garments, hairstyle and make-up well into the late 1960s. None the less, the cost and the epic grandeur on and off screen, the numerous changes of directors, locations, scripts, Taylor's illness, her affair with Burton, represented a type of **excess** that was out of touch with the spirit of the age. And so it was that *Cleopatra* marked the end of Hollywood's movie imperialism, old-style.

European cinema   Entries in this book have been made on various individual European cinemas when, at a point in history, they could be said to constitute either a movement or a school (for a list, see the end of this entry). When talking about European cinema it must be borne in mind that political **ideologies** have meant that Europe has never been a stable unified entity. For example, from the Second World War until very recently (1990) there were two Europes, as is best exemplified by the former division of Germany into two Germanies (East and West). So clearly it is impossible to talk about *a* European cinema – at least from this side of the Atlantic. Viewed from the United States, more particularly **Hollywood**, European cinema since 1920 has been construed as a global concept and perceived as meaning two distinct things (at least). First, European cinema is predominantly **art cinema** and is often more sexually explicit than the home product (see **Hays code**). Second, it is the only true rival to Hollywood and must at all costs be infiltrated and dominated. The most recent trade agreements between the United States and Europe are but the latest in a series of attempts of the American film industry to secure favourable deals for the export of its products into Europe – an attempt which France, as the only European country still to possess a viable film industry, has robustly resisted. (The agreements included, at France's insistence, a quota limitation on the number of films to be imported into France annually from the United States. The United States wanted unlimited access to the screens; France kept the quota to around 180–200 films a year.) Although the United States is a very dominant presence in the share of the film market in

Europe, if we compare the United Kingdom with France it is clear how much of a resistance France has put up. In 1981 the US share of the film market in the UK was 80 per cent, in France 35 per cent. In 1991 the figures were 80 per cent and 59 per cent. But these figures also show how, over the last decade, protectionism notwithstanding, the United States has eroded that resistance.

Because Hollywood is still so dominant in western culture, it continues to be the point of reference. Thus in western Europe a nation's cinema is defined, in part, in relation to what it is not (that is, 'not-Hollywood'), in relation to an 'other'. This in turn produces two strategies. First, European countries produce films with the intention of intruding into that 'other's' territory. France and the United Kingdom in particular have done this with some degree of success with their heritage films (such as *Manon des sources*, Claude Berri, 1985; *Cyrano de Bergerac*, Jean-Paul Rappeneau, 1990; *A Room with a View*, 1985; *Howards End*, 1992 both Merchant/Ivory). Second, with a view to protecting its own financial interests, an indigenous industry makes products specifically for the national **audience**, thereby drawing on its nation's cultural specificities, something which Hollywood of course cannot do. France, Germany and Spain in particular follow this practice. (For an interesting example of an attempt to bring some cohesion to bear when talking about European cinema see Sorlin, 1991. See (listed chronologically) **German Expressionism**, **Soviet cinema**, **French poetic realism**, **Italian neo-realism**, **Free British Cinema**, **French New Wave**, **British New Wave**, **Germany and New German cinema**.)

eyeline matching (*see also* **editing, 180-degree rule**) A term used to point to the **continuity editing** practice ensuring the logic of the look (see **gaze**). In other words, eyeline matching is based on the belief in mainstream cinema that when a character looks into off-screen space the **spectator** expects to see what she or he is looking at. Thus there will be a **cut** to show what is being looked at: object, view or another character. Eyeline then refers to the trajectory of the looking eye. The eyeline match creates order and meaning in cinematic space. Thus, for example, character *A* will look off-screen at character *B*. Cut to character *B*, who – if she or he is in the same room and engaged in an exchange either of glances or words with character *A* – will return that look and so 'certify' that character *A* is indeed in the space from which we first saw her or him look. This 'stabilizing' (Bordwell and Thompson, 1980, 167) is true in the other primary use of the eyeline match which is the **shot/reverse-angle shot**, also known as the reverse angle shot, commonly used in close-up dialogue scenes. The camera adopts the eyeline trajectory of the interlocutor looking at the other person as she or he speaks, then switches to the other person's position and does the same.

excess   Usually used in terms of performance (see **stars**) but also for certain **genres**. In terms of performance, excess points to a highly stylized performance through gesture (as with the mannered style of Bette Davis) or to a contrast in actorly style when the whole performance is minimalist bar a momentary outburst of verbal and gestural excess (Robert De Niro, Jeremy Irons and Meryl Streep are actors in this vein). In the first instance, the star is drawing attention to herself or himself as star – as being more than the part – and as such is pointing to her or his authenticity as star persona (that is, we expect Jack Nicholson to 'act like that'). In the second, the star points to her or his authenticity as actor. And by being both less than the part (minimalist) and more in a moment of excess (such as an outburst of anger) the star proves that she or he can impersonate a role, and yet be more of a star than one who merely personifies a role.

Other aspects of excess can be found in **narrative** and **mise-en-scène**. **Classic narrative cinema** contains and does not expose its **signs** of production. However, there are certain genres, such as the **epic**, **musical**, **science fiction** movies, that are readily associated with excess by **Hollywood**.

With others, the excess is not deliberately on display but may be uncovered through a reading against the grain or close textual analysis. As Kuhn (1982, 35) says, narrative excess can be found in the **film noir** genre of the 1940s. Not only is the detective or private eye investigating a murder or a crime of some order or another, he (*sic*) is also involved in investigating and scrutinizing the female protagonist. To the solution of the crime is added the 'woman question' – and as such the narrative is in excess. In terms of mise-en-scène and excess, **melodrama**, with its obsessive attention to décor within the domestic sphere, is a genre that comes to mind. Part of the reason for excessive mise-en-scène has to do with consumerism and targeting the female **audience**. But a more subversive reading can be made of melodrama's highly stylized look. Elsaesser (1987, 53) points out that this is to do with the effects of **censorship** and morality codes – very much in effect until the 1960s. In this regard, style becomes used as meaning. In order to convey what cannot be said, primarily on the level of sexual and repressed desire, décor and mise-en-scène had to stand in for meaning (see **melodrama**).

fade   A transition between sequences or scenes generally associated with earlier cinema – up until the late 1940s – but still used on occasion. In this transition an **image** fades out and then another image fades in. In use from 1899, the fade was one of the first forms of transition that could be edited within the camera, so its historical importance resides in the fact that earliest film-makers realized they could now make films that were composed of more than just a single action taken in one take. The **cut** as a transition came a little later, in 1901. The use of the fade suggests a lapse of time and possibly a change of space (for example, if a character gets knocked out she or he may go out with a fade and come back 'some time later' through a fade-in in the same room).

fantasy/fantasy films   Generically speaking, fantasy films englobe four basic categories: **horror**, **science fiction**, fairy tales and a certain type of adventure movie (journeys to improbable places and meetings with implausible 'creatures', such as *Planet of the Apes*, Franklin Schaffner, 1967). Fantasy films are about areas 'we don't really know about' and, therefore, areas we do not see as real. However, fantasy is the expression of our unconscious, and it is these films in particular that most readily reflect areas we repress or suppress – namely, the realms of our unconscious and the world of our dreams. It is also true that these films, as indeed with other genres, act **metonymically** as **enunciators** of dominant **ideology** and social **myths**. As we know, mainstream **Hollywood** cinema's great subject is not sexual identity but heterosexuality and more precisely the family. When this dream is threatened, the 'threat' must be removed. The doubly deviant woman in *Fatal Attraction* (Adrian Lyne, 1987) – she is not a mother but a career woman and she is sexually voracious – must be removed so that family life can go on. Norman Bates's victim in *Psycho* (Alfred Hitchcock, 1960), was a deserving one because she was a double thief: stealing her boss's money *and* stealing another woman's husband. The fairly recent spate of cyborg movies (the artificial reproduction of humans), as Kaplan (1992, 211) argues, are clearly related to the issue of reproduction rights and who controls them. (It is noteworthy that probably the first cyborg novel was written by a woman. Why did Mary Wollstonecraft Shelley first dream of (1816) and then write (1818) *Frankenstein*?) It is also noteworthy that the number of these films has increased since the legalization of abortion in many countries in the western world. Men are wanting either to have control over reproduction, as in *The Fly* (David Cronenberg, 1986) and *Alien³* (David Fincher, 1992) or to destroy the reproductive organism, as in *Dead Ringers* (Cronenberg, 1988).

Fantasy is inextricably linked with desire, which, according to Lacan, is located in the Imaginary (see **Imaginary/Symoblic** and **suture**) – that is, the unconscious. Fantasy, then, is the conscious articulation of desire, through either **images** or stories – it is, then, the **mise-en-scène** of desire. In this context, film puts desire up on screen. The film industry *is* the industry of desire, Hollywood *is* the dream factory. But film is not just film, it is also a nexus of text relations which function as fantasy structures enunciating unconscious desire. Film–text relations can best be described as a series of overlaying triangles of equal importance that are enclosed within the desire/fantasy parameter – as the diagram opposite illustrates.

There is no single set or level of fantasy (just as there is no one desire). In the first instance, each triangle in the diagram

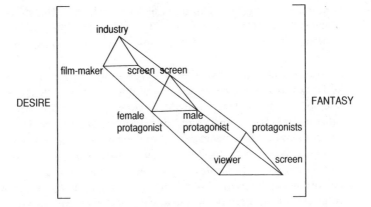

generates a set of fantasies that are both interrelated and yet distinct from each other. Just to illustrate: the fantasy created by the film-maker is in relation to but distinct from the fantasy perceived by the **spectator** as constituted subject; and, as constituting subject the spectator creates yet another fantasy; but, given that fantasy structures are multiple, spectator identification is equally multiplicitous. For example (but of course by way of fantasy!), with *Rebel Without a Cause* (1955) the film-maker Nicholas Ray could have fantasized that his film was about teenage malaise and alienation in 1950s America and that James Dean was an archetypal anti-hero. Given Ray's own background – as a loner, something of a drifter and misfit – he could also have fantasized Dean as his alter ego. A male teenage spectator, seeing the film when it was released, would identify with Dean which, as constituted subject, he is supposed to do, but in this context he would fantasize Dean as *his* alter ego. As constituting subject, his reading of the film and the character portrayed by Dean could concur with the **documentary** realism created by Ray, but not necessarily read the film as a 'problem film' *per se* in which, as Dean exclaims, 'we are all involved'. He could read it instead as a realistic portrayal of youth culture and, too, its embattlement against uncomprehending adults or parents. The film becomes appropriated, encultured – a 'cult film' of the spectator's life (as he fantasizes it). Finally, given the multiplicity of identificatory

95

positions, this spectator can identify with both Sal Mineo and Natalie Wood (Dean's friends) as Dean's **diegetically** adoring audience – thus satisfying both homoerotic and heteroerotic desire.

The second point to make in relation to these structures of fantasy is that, since fantasy is the mise-en-scène of desire and since desire is located in the unconscious, it follows that cinema, in creating images that we as spectators wish to look at, calls upon the structures of our own unconscious and makes us privy to them. The cinematic **apparatus** functions in this respect to position us as voyeurs to our own fantasies. According to Sigmund Freud, storytelling is a child's way of dealing with its anxiety around sexual differences and dependencies, most particularly on its mother. Storytelling, then, is creating fantasies that emerge from our unconscious desires and fears. Cinema narratives relay these fantasies before our eyes, the primary ones being as follows: the fear of abandonment by and desire for unity with the mother/([m]other); the fear of castration (Freud) or the fear of being devoured by the mother (Melanie Klein); the bastard and foundling fantasies; the desire for illicit viewing (of parental coitus) – the primal scene.

Let's take *Jurassic Park* (Steven Spielberg, 1993) to explore this set of fantastic mise-en-scènes. The devouring mother(s) are of course the recreated dinosaurs – all female (at least at birth) and the result of genetic engineering (men tinkering with reproductive rights). These dinosaurs who become sexually ambiguous after birth – they are able to change sex – are also the attacking father and terrifying parents illicitly viewed/fantasized as copulating. The children, Lex and Tim, fear abandonment, and this is fulfilled when they are separated from their 'parents', the two palaeontologists Ellie Sattler and Alan Grant, in whose care they have been placed. Incidentally, it is this same 'father' (Grant) who poses the threat of castration in the opening sequence when he draws the talon of a dinosaur over a young boy's stomach in reply to his persistent questions about dinosaurs – no child-liker he. Father as life-giver and life-destroyer is also exemplified in the role of this reluctant 'father': when Lex and Tim are being attacked in the Land-rover, Grant eventually has to try to rescue the life-threatened children.

In this film the foundling fantasy, whereby the child can reject the family because the parents are not her or his and are too lowly, is inverted. The foundlings, Lex and Tim, are eventually accepted by Grant when, at the end of the film, he fulfils the **Oedipal trajectory** by saving his 'family'. He even feels protective to the point that the boy ends up cradled asleep in his arms. The only 'bastards' in this movie are the illegitimate dinosaurs. They are the illegitimate children of the billionaire entrepreneur John Hammond – their 'mother'. Again an inversion, this time sexual. In the bastard fantasy, the mother is perceived by the child as not being possessed by the father – because of her illicit liaisons with other men. She is also perceived as lowly and immoral – a prostitute. This fantasy then breaks up the notion of the family unit: the child sides with the real mother against the father and, moreover, because of her status, the child can even possess her. In the film, as a result of Hammond's illicit reproductive practices, the dinosaurs do break up the 'family' unit; and they unite with Hammond as mother against the father (all the people they kill are men); they also leave Isla Nublar (!) with Hammond in the form of the blood in the amber on his stick – but now Hammond is a fallen (wo)man, exposed for his immorality, a potential prey to be possessed by his dinosauric children. (For further reading see Donald, 1989.)

female spectator – *see* **spectator**

feminist film theory (*see also* **theory**)   Although there were women film-makers back in the 1920s and even earlier (see Hayward, 1992) making statements about the suitability of the camera to a woman's expression of her own **subjectivity**, feminist film theory did not come about fully until the late 1960s as a result of the second wave of feminism – the first being the Suffragists and Suffragette movement of the early 1900s. This second wave took the world of academia and journalism in the western world and Australia by storm and very quickly began to generate texts related to women's issues and, just as importantly, to disciplines taught within academia – including film studies. Indeed, no discussion of film (or television for that matter) can ignore feminist film theory which, since the early 1970s, has so strongly impacted on film studies – starting with the issue of **gender** representation. Essentially, to date, we can distinguish three periods in the evolution of this theory: the early 1970s; the mid-1970s to the early 1980s; the mid-1980s to the present. The following three sections set out the history and the debates of those periods and look at the impact of each period as well as the problems and outcomes each generated, thus pushing the debate along.

Feminist film theory 1968–74   Although we use the term 'feminist film theory', Annette Kuhn (1982, 72) rightly points out that there does not exist one single theory, rather a series of 'perspectives'. The logic for this can be found in two occurrences directly linked to the second wave of feminism. The first is a contemporary occurrence, an effect of the 1960s. The second is based in a longer look at history. Women (mostly students), radicalized during the 1960s by political debate and so-called sexual liberation, reacted against being placed second after men in the intellectual – and at times violent (as in the United States) – pursuit of political change. The failure of radicalism, which culminated and then crashed in 1968, to produce any substantive change for women led them to form consciousness-raising groups that effectively galvanized women into forming a women's movement. This rejection of male radicalism in intellectual terms can be interpreted also as a rejection of the pursuit of 'total theory' as exemplified by the totalizing effect of **structuralism** (*the* debate of the 1960s) – although, as we shall see, feminists did not reject some of the fundamental principles of structuralism. Indeed they were party to moving that debate on to the more pluralistic one of **post-structuralism**.

The second occurrence was in some ways an outcome of the first. Looking at what had happened to them in recent history, women saw the need to look longer and further at woman's history and from a number of perspectives. Annette Kuhn's definition of feminism, in this instance, most aptly sums up how feminism and feminist film theory after it are composed of a number of tendencies, so resisting the fixity of one 'single theory': '[feminism is] a set of political practices founded in analyses of the social/historical position of women as subordinated, oppressed or exploited either within dominant modes of production (such as capitalism) and/or by the social relations of patriarchy or male domination' (1982, 4). By extension, feminist film theory, then, is political. And as early as its first period it set about analysing, from different perspectives, **dominant cinema**'s construction of women. As we shall see, at this juncture, the differences in perspectives were particularly marked between feminists on either side of the Atlantic.

The effect of this first period of feminist film theory was to shift the debate in film theory from **class** to gender. Feminist film critics examined the question of feminine identity and the representation of women in film images as the site/sight or object of exchange between men. At this point the focus of these analyses was exclusively **Hollywood** cinema and had the sobering effect of dismissing films, which previously had been elevated to **auteur** status, for their male-centred point of view and objectification of women. Exemplary of this approach was Molly Haskell's book *From Reverence to Rape: The Treatment of Women in the Movies* (1974). (It is noteworthy that the person to coin the term *auteur theory* was Andrew Sarris, Haskell's husband – see **Auteur**.) In her book Haskell, an American journalist, made two very important points. First, she suggested that film reflects society and vice versa and in so doing reflects the **ideological** and social construction of women who are either to be revered (as the Virgin) or reviled (as the whore). Second, in her analyses of the 1930s and 1940s Hollywood cinema she made the important distinction between **melodrama** and women's films – the latter, as she pointed out, being made specifically to address women. This second point, that of the central role of the female protagonist *and* female spectator, led to a renewed and different focus on **genre** and the possible aesthetic and political consequences of gender difference. This very crucial point was one which was developed in the second period of feminist film theory. For the moment, however, let's focus on the first point, since this was the one that revealed differences in perspectives held by feminists on either side of the Atlantic.

In the United States in the early 1970s, Molly Haskell, Marjorie Rosen (1973) and Joan Mellen (1974), were the three leading feminists writing on the representations of women in cinema. The approach they adopted was sociological and empirical – which was consonant with the state of the art in film criticism in the United States at that time. Their critical approach was intended to expose the misrepresentation of women in film, which it did, but in a specific way. Consistently with a sociological-empirical approach, which aims to ascribe – to fix meanings based on fact – they also assumed a presumed feminine essence repressed by patriarchy. That is, their analyses presumed a predetermined sexual identity, difference. In simple terms what was being said was 'the facts show that women get represented in images as Virgin or whore because that's how patriarchal society represents women to itself'.

With hindsight this conclusion now seems quite reductionist. But the fact remains that these findings constituted a first important stage. Meantime in Europe (particularly in the United Kingdom) this essentialist debate represented three major problems for feminist film theorists, who included Claire Johnston, Laura Mulvey, Pam Cook and Annette Kuhn. These feminists were influenced by the more scientific and definitely anti-empirical approach offered by **semiotics** and structuralism. They argued that the essentialist debate assumed, first, that all women possessed an innate ability to judge the authenticity of the representation of women in film, and, second, that all women film-makers were feminists. Most critically of all, they pointed out that a belief in a fixed feminine

100

essence meant legitimating patriarchy through the back door. By accepting the fixed essence of woman as a predetermined, 'given order of things', implicitly what was also being accepted was the 'naturalness' of the patriarchal order (Lapsley and Westlake, 1988, 25). The British feminists, arguing along Althusserian lines, also pointed out that film was as much productive of as it was a product of ideology, and, furthermore, that – in the same way that Althusser theorized that the **subject** was a construct of material structures – so too was the **spectator** a constituted subject when watching the film. The time was ripe for a moving on from a causal and reductionist debate. Historical materialism (an analysis of the material conditions within historical contexts that placed women where they were), semiotics and **psychoanalysis** were the tools invoked to investigate beyond the currently superficial findings and reflectionist statements produced by the American authors.

These criticisms notwithstanding, Haskell's, Mellen's and Rosen's work represented a significant first benchmark that had important outcomes. Their 'saying that it was there' made it clear that the next step was to find out 'how it got there', the better to change 'it'. Their work led to the definition of three basic approaches to achieve this uncovering and subsequent changing of the way women are constructed in film. There was a need for, first, a theoretical analysis of the way in which mainstream cinema constructs women and the place of women; second, a critical analysis of the work of women film-makers; and, third – as a conjuncture of these two points – the establishing and implementation of feminist film practices.

The final point that needs to be made about this period is that women were becoming a presence in all areas of the cinematic institution. The year 1972 witnessed the first feminist film festivals in the United States and the United Kingdom. Women film-makers formed collectives to encourage women into film-making (for example the London Women's Film Group, formed in 1972). *Women and Film*, the first feminist film journal, was also published in the United States between

1972 and 1975. The next period then had a powerful heritage already as it set to its own trail-blazing practices.

Feminist film theory 1975–83   In 1972 Claire Johnston, Laura Mulvey and Linda Myles organized the Women's Event at the Edinburgh Film Festival. To accompany the Event Johnston edited a pamphlet, *Notes on Women's Cinema*, published in 1973, which contained her own ground-breaking essay: 'Women's Cinema as **Counter-Cinema**'. This text was one of the first to make clear that cinematic textual operations could not be ignored. To change cinema, to make women's cinema, Johnston argued, you had first to understand the ideological operations present in actual mainstream film practices. The task was to determine both the 'how' of female representation and the 'effect' of female positioning in the process of meaning construction. Under the 'how', of first importance was a reading of the **iconography** of the **image**. How was the female framed, lit, dressed, and so on? Under the 'effect', of primary significance was the female's positioning within the structure of the **narrative**. In the first instance what was required was a reading of the image as **sign**, a need to understand the **denotation and connotations** of the image. In the second instance the psychology of the narrative had to come under scrutiny: why, repeatedly, do so many narratives in mainstream cinema depict the woman as the object of desire of the male character embarked upon his **Oedipal trajectory**? Camera-work and **lighting** make it clear that she is a figure upon whom he can fix his fantasies. These, then, are the textual operations constructing ideology which, argues Johnston, we must come to understand through a **deconstruction** of the modes of production, which in turn leads to an exposing of the cinematic and narrative codes at work. Only then can an oppositional counter-cinema become a possibility. It is worth quoting from her conclusion to make the point that the cinema she envisaged was *not* one that relied on self-reflexivity or **foregrounding** the conditions of film production alone (what she refers to here as political film) but one that would draw on female **fantasy** and **desire**:

a strategy should be developed which embraces both the notion of films as a political tool and film as entertainment. For too long these have been regarded as two opposing poles with little common ground. In order to counter our objectification in cinema, our collective fantasies must be released: women's cinema must embody the working through of desire: such an objective demands the use of entertainment film. Ideas derived from the entertainment film, then, should inform the political film, and political ideas should inform the entertainment cinema: a two way process. (Johnston, 1976, 217)

This formidable recipe of foregrounding film practices and female **subjectivity** would, Johnston believed, effect a break between ideology and text – a dislocation that would create a space for women's cinema to emerge.

The other ground-breaking essay of this period was Laura Mulvey's 'Visual Pleasure and Narrative Cinema' (1975). Mulvey's focus was less on textual operations within the film and more on the textual relations between screen and **spectator**. This important text is perceived as *the* key founding document of psychoanalytic feminist film theory. Since this issue is discussed in much greater detail under **spectator**, I will confine myself to a brief summary here. In this essay, Mulvey seeks to address the issue of female spectatorship within the cinematic **apparatus**. She examines the way in which cinema functions, through its **codes and conventions**, to construct the way in which woman is to be looked at, starting with the male point of view within the film and, subsequently, the spectator who identifies with the male protagonist. She describes this process of viewing as **scopophilia** – pleasure in viewing. However, she also asks what happens to the female spectator, given that the narrative of **classic narrative cinema** is predominantly that of the Oedipal trajectory and since that trajectory is tightly bound up with male perceptions and fantasies about women? How does she derive visual pleasure? Mulvey can conclude only that she must either identify with the passive position of the female character on screen, or, if she is to derive pleasure, she must assume a male positioning. This deliberately

103

polemical essay met with strong response by feminist critics. The next section details the development of that debate. For now let's examine the third aspect of theoretical work during this period: textual analysis. But first a brief synopsis of the relevance of psychoanalysis to feminist film theory.

The introduction into feminist film theory of psychoanalysis represented a major departure from the first, sociologically based period. It made it possible to address feminist issues such as identity and memory; it also led to the discussion of femininity and masculinity as socially constructed entities as opposed to the more simplified binary divide along biological lines into female and male. This important distinction meant that it was now possible to analyse sexual difference rather than just assume it as a predetermined reality. If it was socially constructed, then that construct could be deconstructed and changed. Difference could be analysed in terms of language rather than in terms of biologism. Until Jacques Lacan's analysis insisted on the importance of the Symbolic (that is, language) in the construction of subjectivity, feminine **sexuality** had languished under the Freudian principle of penis envy – that is, of lack. Given that Sigmund Freud privileged the penis, it is hardly surprising that he never managed to theorize the female **Oedipal trajectory** satisfactorily. Why should he, since it would mean a loss of power? According to a Freudian analysis, then, power relations are based in sexual difference. This ignores the social and material conditions that construct human sexuality. This is why the shift from sex to language, which Lacan's approach did much to assist, meant that the ideological operations of language (patriarchal language) could come under scrutiny. By bringing structuralism and psychoanalysis together, feminist film theorists had at their disposition an incisive analytical tool. The text was ready for deconstruction!

In the United States particularly, feminists turned their attention to analyses of the textual operations in film and their role in constructing ideology. Essays in the influential journal *Camera Obscura* – launched in 1976 by a breakaway group from the earlier *Women and Film* collective – were instrumental in revealing the ideological operations of patri-archy; and through applications of structural–psychoanalytic theories they demonstrated how narrative codes and conven-tions sustain patriarchal ideology in its conditioning and control of women. Note that, for the moment, historical materialism has disappeared from the theoretical triumvirate. That was to go on the back-burner until the third period. Currently, textual analysis focused on narrative strategies and, in particular, picked up the question of genre and its role in structuring subjectivity – a point which, as we have seen, Molly Haskell had raised in drawing the distinction between melodrama and women's films.

The intervention of psychoanalysis and feminism now brought melodrama and women's films into the critical lime-light, focusing on the **discourses** that construct the symbolic place of 'woman and the maternal'. The **western** too was investigated. The dominance of male-defined problematics within the narrative, the role of women as mere triggers (*sic*) to male action and choice and, finally, the counter-Oedipal trajectory of so many of its heroes – all these narrative strate-gies are exposed. Why indeed do so many gunmen ride off into the sunset leaving 'the woman' behind? **Film noir** was another genre which under scrutiny could not hide the domi-nance of a male subjectivity whose **gaze**, motivated by the fear of castration, either fetishizes the 'threatening', dangerous woman into the phallic and therefore unthreatening other or seeks to control and punish the perceived source of this fear. (See **melodrama**, **western** and **film noir** for a full discussion; and for more detail on these points see **psychoanalysis**.)

Another part of the feminists' strategy in their textual analyses was to read against the grain and, in particular, to foreground sexual difference. **Horror** and film noir, because of their voyeuristic 'essence', were prime targets of investi-gation, but so too were melodrama and women's film because of their focus on the family and the so-called 'woman's space'. Thus, for example, in a film noir or horror film a woman's annihilation, which on the surface might appear as a result of her own actions, may in fact be read as the male repressing

105

the feminine side of his self by projecting it on to the woman and then killing her. Alfred Hitchcock's *Psycho* (1960), for example, plays on this sexual identity in crisis in a number of very complex ways. Norman Bates adopts numerous positions: that of his 'castrating phallic mother' who constantly reminds him that women are filth; so in disguising or dressing himself up as her, he becomes that filth – which, of course he must eradicate; he is also the voyeuristic gaze of mainstream cinema looking through numerous holes (peeping Tom) at the woman's body and, finally, the male gaze that must annihilate that which he must not become – woman and filth.

Melodrama is historically perceived as a theatre form that reflects nineteenth-century bourgeois values whereby the family at all costs will prevail, remain united and in order. When the genre was taken up by early cinema this reflection continued. Superficially, by the 1930s and 1940s, melodrama and women's films appeared not to challenge the patriarchal order. However, in their narrative construction these films gave space for a woman's point of view. And it was in this respect that a reading against the grain was possible. Closure for these films meant that order and, if possible, harmony in the family had to be restored. But what caused the initial disorder? Most often conflict between the two sexes. As Laura Mulvey (1977, reprinted 1989, 39) points out, melodrama is the one genre where ideological contradiction is allowed centre screen: 'Ideological contradiction is actually the overt mainspring and specific content of melodrama. . . . No ideology can ever pretend to totality: it searches for safety-valves for its own inconsistencies'. And melodrama is just one of those safety-valves. But what are interesting in this context are the implications of the **setting** specific to melodrama: the domestic sphere, the woman's space or place and the family. The male character at the centre of the conflict has to resolve it within that sphere. 'If the family is to survive, a compromise has to be reached, sexual difference softened, and the male brought to see the value of domestic life. . . . The phallocentric, misogynist fantasies of patriarchal culture are shown here to be in contradiction with the ideology of the family' (Mulvey, 40). And because it is the female character's subjectivity to which we are privy, it is her emotions with which we first identify. Unlike the western or gangster movie and the dominance of male-defined problematics which only the hero's action can resolve, here we are confronted with 'the way in which sexual difference under patriarchy is fraught, explosive and erupts dramatically into violence within its own private stamping ground, the family' (Mulvey, 39). There is something tantalizing in the implications of this reading against the grain that goes something like this: 'If melodrama and women's films are the only sites where narrative strategies expose the contradictions in patriarchal ideology, and if the domestic sphere is the private stamping-ground of patriarchy, then how much indeed the rest of mainstream cinema must work to assert in public spaces that patriarchal ideology is without contradiction. *And* how 'dangerous' it would be if female subjectivity crept out of the private domestic sphere and exposed those contradictions'. If melodrama did not exist, Hollywood would have had to invent it.

Feminist film theory 1984–90s   The revalorizing of certain genres that previously had been dismissed, scorned even, was an important accomplishment, as was the opening up of the debate around female spectatorship. However, by the mid-1980s feminists felt that the focus on the textual operations of films was too narrow and that a film needed to be examined within its various contexts – that is, the historical and social contexts of its production and reception. Clearly this move broadens the debate around spectatorship and reintroduces the question of class, which had been superseded during the last two periods by questions of gender. Since Mulvey's 1975 essay on female spectator positioning as male, the debate had moved on to consider her as masochistic (Silverman, 1981), or as either masochistic or transvestite (Doane, 1984). But the significant breakthrough came in De Lauretis's (1984, 152) rereading of an earlier essay by Modleski (1982) from which she deduced that the female spectator enjoyed a double desiring position. As a result of the mother/ daughter relationship, in which the daughter never fully relinquishes her desire for her mother, the female spectator is positioned bisexually. And it is her constant shifting back and forth between the two positions that creates woman's enigma (Modleski, 1988, 99). This shifting means also that women can never become fully socialized into patriarchy – which in turn causes men to fear women and leads them, on the one hand, to establish very strict boundaries between their own sex and the female sex and, on the other, to the need to 'kill off' the woman, either literally or by subjugation.

Explicit within Modleski and De Lauretis's arguments is that there is a female **Oedipal trajectory** and that the notion of lack and penis envy is a patriarchal construct designed to preserve the status quo of male dominance and to side-step the issue of sexual difference. Williams (1984, 89), arguing against Stephen Heath's reading (1978) of horror films as a **mise-en-scène** of sexual difference where the woman represents castration, draws on Susan Lurie's challenge (1980) to Freud's notion of the male child's perception of the mother's body as castrated. Williams (1984) resumes Lurie's argument: 'The notion of the woman as a castrated version of a man is, according to Lurie, a comforting, wishful fantasy intended to combat the child's imagined dread of what his mother's very real power could do to him'. The fact that texts have been constructed around the castration myth does not, argue these feminists, make it any more real but merely points to the lengths to which patriarchal ideology will go out of its fear of the (m)other. Modleski and De Lauretis single out women's films as rare exceptions to this neglect or disavowal of a female Oedipal trajectory in cinema. But this does not necessarily make them a 'good thing'. In this genre, that is deliberately woman-centred (the story is apparently told from the woman's point of view) to attract female audiences, the narrative often plays on the 'two positionalities of desire [male and female] that define the female's Oedipal situation.' (De Lauretis, 1984, 153). By the end of the film, however, this shifting back and forth will and must be brought to an end and desire for the female suppressed in favour of desire for the male. Moreover, even when the mother or surrogate mother is represented as quite monstrous, as the phallic mother, the Oedipal trajectory is still there and is completed. Hitchcock's *Rebecca* (1940) is one such film where the heroine eventually turns away from her evil set of surrogate mothers (especially Mrs Danvers) and enters into maturity (that is, a full relationship with her father-figure husband).

This revelation of a female Oedipal trajectory, according to De Lauretis (1984), is not where feminist film theory must stop. After all 'the cinema works for Oedipus', which means that the heroine's double desiring within the film narrative is eventually resolved along Oedipal lines. She will 'kill off' the mother and marry her father. The ideological operations of patriarchy cannot tolerate women sustaining their double desire. Why else in both *Now Voyager* (Irving Rapper, 1942) and (although a thriller and not a women's film *per se*) *Marnie* (Alfred Hitchcock, 1964) is it a male – more specifically with *Now Voyager* a psychiatrist – who 'rescues' the heroine away the (phallic) mother? (For discussion of *Rebecca* see Modleski, 1988; for *Now Voyager* and *Marnie*, Kaplan, 1990.)

In this analysis we can see one of the ways in which women's cinema can foreground woman's own construction of meaning: that is, by constructing differently a different social subject, a double-desiring subject whose duplicity need never be resolved. Not a counter-Oedipus, but, as De Lauretis (1985) so felicitously puts it, an 'Oedipus Interruptus'. What is extraordinary (but maybe not) is that women film-makers from cinema's earliest days were constructing differently desiring subjects, as Sandy Flitterman-Lewis's study (1990) so admirably demonstrates.

So far so good. However, feminist thinking by now was also perceiving the limitations of psychoanalysis. Although Lacan's notion of the construction of the subject through language/discourse opened up the debate on sexual differ-ence, there still remained the problem that femininity was still defined in relation to masculinity – the feminine other to the masculine subject. Power relations were also seen in that light. The limit of this approach was to create an ideology of gender: that is, to construct the concept 'Man'/'Woman' (or if you prefer: patriarchal-subject-man/patriarchal-object-woman), in the end to essentialize Woman, and in the final analysis Man (as the subject of the gaze, power, etc.). It was not so much that the issue of gender had been done to death, but that, in focusing their attention in this way, critics had neglected issues around Woman and women – or that through such an approach women could not be talked about. There was a need to move on from questions of gender and to broaden the debate to include questions of class and power relations between women, of differences among the spectating female subjects, of the film industry as more than just an ideological institution or apparatus of patriarchy that renders women invisible and constructs Woman – and also to see these questions in relation to history. Only after this broadening of the debate could gender be reintroduced – because, as we shall explain, it had been relocated.

In the United Kingdom, feminists began to incorporate the historical-materialist approach of work done in cultural studies – which examined popular culture within the sphere of class, gender and race and in relation to power and resistances to that power. In the United States, feminists more specifically turned their attention to the French philosopher Michel Foucault and his theory of power as well as his 'notion of the social as a practical field in which technologies and discourses are deployed' (De Lauretis, 1984, 84). By technologies Foucault meant the conjuncture of power (*technos*) and knowledge (*logos*). *Logos* also means *discourse*. Thus *technologies* means *discourses of power*. This last point will be discussed more fully when we examine the effect of another of Foucault's theories, the technology of sex, on feminist theory. But first to power theory.

Since Foucault also had an impact on cultural studies debates, what follows is a brief explanation of how his writings influenced both American feminists and cultural studies and how this influence in turn affected feminist film theory. There are certain problems with adapting Foucauldian

110

theory to film theory (see De Lauretis, 1984, 84–102), but, in the sense that he more or less evacuates gendered subjectivity, it makes it easier to see what else is there. In arguing, in relation to power, that 'discourses produce domains of objects and modes of subjection' (Lapsley and Westlake, 1988, 101), Foucault points to a multiplicity of positionings; some where individuals have power, others where they do not. Foucault's statement (1977, 194) that 'power produces; in fact it produces reality' means that, as a product and producer of power, the individual is both a producer and a product of reality. But it also means that reality is produced from a multiplicity of positions within the power network. It is for this reason that Foucault argues that power comes from below. It is useful, he states, to see power not as hierarchized from the top down but rather as being omnipresent (1978, 93) since all social relations are power relations. Domination evolves from a complex set of power strategies or investments, so it is possible to pinpoint not one source but, rather, several. Foucault also makes the point that, at all stratifications of power, there are resistances to those power relations and that these resistances, far from being in a position of 'exteriority in relation to power', coexist alongside the nexus of power relations (1978, 94–6). Finally, within the context of this synopsis, Foucault insists that power, in and of itself, is neither negative nor positive and that what does matter is how it gets exercised (1977, 194). That is, power in its exercise is a 'silent, secret civil war that re-inscribes conflict in various "social institutions, in economic inequalities, in language, in the bodies themselves of each and everyone of us"' (Merquior, 1985, 110–11).

In terms of feminist film theory, there are two main points of application of Foucault's thinking on power. First, the notion of cinema or the film industry (particularly Hollywood) as unique producer of the reality-effect no longer holds. The multiplicity of positions that produce the reality-effect include not just the textual operations of the film products themselves but also the conditions or (im)positions of production and reception. Thus the social relations of power between the different parts of the industry (that is, scriptwriter(s), continuity and location assistants, camera and lighting crew, editor(s), director(s), producer(s), distributor(s), exhibitor(s), and so on) are as much parts of the reality-effect as the spectators. (The use of the plural here draws attention to the fact that several scriptwriters, directors, etc. may be involved in the making of a single film, thus increasing the notion of a plurality of producers of meaning.) How that reality is produced is as much an effect of the power relations and resistances within the industry as it is within the **audiences**. The spectator can no longer be seen as the single construct of an ideological apparatus. Audiences are multi-plicitous. There is not a 'female' or 'male' spectator but different socio-cultural individuals all busy producing reality as the film rolls by. Age, gender, race, class, sexuality affect reception and meaning production. This broadening of the context in which a film is analysed has enabled feminist film theorists to move away from the male-centred effects of psychoanalytic readings, but without necessarily having to throw out psychoanalysis itself, which could be refocused within this context. In other words, femininity no longer needs to be defined in relation to masculinity; nor does it have to be perceived as a single construct, Woman. As Doane (1982, 87) says, femininity can now be seen as a position constructed 'within a network of power relations'. So femininity becomes more than *just* a male construct. Femininity can be viewed as multiform and pluralistically positioned: women. By implication femininity can be viewed, as De Lauretis says (1989, 25), from 'elsewhere' – from women's points of view.

This point leads on to the second, which concerns resistances. Resistances, as Foucault says, exist alongside the nexus of power relations. As always present, they filter through social and institutional strata – they leave their traces. This means also that they get caught up at some point within power relations, even though as resistances themselves they have moved on. I am talking here about counter-cinema. Interestingly, Foucault talks about resistances as counter-investments

(1978, 97) – that is, counter-investments are the opposite of what occurs with power, whereby individuals have vested interests in adopting one discursive practice over another. In this light, counter-cinema counters the workings of power relations in mainstream cinema but does not stand as exterior to them. It gives voice to a multiplicity of discourses that are in contradiction or counterpoint, thus simultaneously exposing the complex set of stratifications and power strategies that lead to domination (**hegemony**) and proposing a making visible of what is so palpably dissimulated by hegemonic investment (that is, the discourses that get dropped). This means that patriarchal hegemony is revealed as no more of a fixed essence or totality than femininity. Rather, what this counter-cinema discloses is that patriarchy has come about as a result of investments in certain discourses over others (including psychoanalysis). By extension these counter-cinematic practices expose the silent civil war mentioned earlier that reinscribes conflict into institutions, language and individuals. In this respect, women's counter-cinema is about discursive disclosure, that is, the expression of other knowledges normally passed over in silence. Moreover, because counter-cinema is not exterior to power relations, those practices of exposure and disclosure get recuperated to some degree into dominant cinema. In the meantime new resistances are in formation. Although recuperation into the mainstream does serve to normalize resistance, recuperation in Foucauldian terms means also to choose to invest in a discourse until now ignored and unpractised. Vested interests change as we know; so too then must the present hegemony, however slowly. As Claire Johnston (1976, 217) said two decades ago: 'we should seek to operate at all levels: within male-dominated cinema and outside of it'. The fact that women currently do this, although the numbers are still quite small, attests to that possibility for change.

If we bear this in mind, it should become clear why gender could be reintroduced into the debate. In his first volume of *The History of Sexuality* (1978), Foucault talks of the technologies of sex, by which he means the way in which sexuality

113

is constructed by discourses that are in the culture's vested interests. In her brilliant and ground-breaking essay 'Technology of Gender', Teresa De Lauretis (1989, 2) argues that gender is also a product of various social technologies, including cinema. Foucault's discussion of the technology of sex, just like his theory of power, evacuates the idea of gendered subjectivity. But to do this De Lauretis asserts, is to ignore the 'differential solicitation of male and female subjects' and 'the conflicting investments of men and women in the discourses and practices of sexuality' (1989, 3), which is why she insists on a technology of gender. In the first instance, De Lauretis is referring to the ways in which the technologies of gender construct gender in terms of sexual difference – in this respect institutional discourses, which are 'implemented through pedagogy, medicine, demography, and economics' (1989, 12), are the power/knowledge investments producing 'meanings, values, knowledges and practices' as they concern or interpellate or solicit the male and female subject differently (1989, 16). Division of 'labour' (*sic*) is a prime example: Man as producer, Woman as reproducer. As far as cinema is concerned, we have seen (above) how feminist theory was already focusing on how discourses construct the symbolic place of Woman. So the institutional representation of femininity was, as De Lauretis acknowledges, already under scrutiny. What is different about this way of looking is that male and female subjects are viewed not in relation to masculinity but in relation to different power strategies.

In the second instance, De Lauretis is signalling that men and women do not have the same investments in terms of discourses and practices of sexuality. How could they, given their different histories? Women 'have historically made different investments and thus have taken up different positions in gender and sexual practices and identities' (1989, 16). And it is at this point that De Lauretis starts to 'rough-map' (her term) the possibilities for changes or dislocations in the social – that is, power-relations of gender. She goes on to argue that the 'female-gendered subject [is] one that is at once inside and outside the ideology of gender' (1989, ix).

We saw earlier how the ideology of gender fixes Woman (as feminine, maternal or eternal): that is, Woman fixed on-screen inside the ideology of gender – not woman as a multiplicity of discourses, nor the multiplicity of women. This multiplicitous woman is the female-gendered subject outside the ideology of gender, the one that is not represented, the one that is off-screen and yet by being off-screen, as off-screen space implies, is inferred on-screen (1989, 26).

the movement in and out of gender as ideological representation, which I propose characterises the subject of feminism, is a movement back and forth between the representation of gender (in its male-centred frame of reference) and what that representation leaves out, or, more pointedly, makes unrepresentable. . . . These two kinds of spaces are neither in opposition to one another nor strung along a chain of signification, but they co-exist concurrently and in contradiction (1989, 26).

Even if mainstream cinema through its textual operations and industrial practices tries to conceal the off-screen space, it no longer can, says De Lauretis, because the 'practices of feminism have shown them to be separate and heteronomous [subject to different laws] spaces' (1989, 26).

Feminist film theory over the past two decades has exercised considerable influence over film theory in general. But the debates have to broaden further still. It has not yet, as Black feminists have said, dealt with the social and cultural experiences of all women. And the feminist voices have been predominantly White and middle-class. The effects of cultural studies in the United Kingdom since the early 1980s have caused change in this respect. The study of popular culture has not been a White-only area of investigation. Blacks and Asians are writing about and creating their own experiences. Increasingly Black women are entering into the academy, particularly in the United States. The voices of Latin American women, Asian women and Asiatic women as well as those of Black and White women are being heard and seen on the screen – and in growing numbers. The debates

115

move on, as the reading list makes clear. (For readings on feminist film theory see Kuhn, 1982; Kaplan, 1983 and 1990; De Lauretis, 1984 and 1989; Doane, Mellencamp and Williams (eds), 1984; Penley, 1985 and 1988; Mulvey, 1989. For readings against the grain see Kaplan, 1980; Mayne, 1984; Williams, 1984; Kuhn, 1985; Modleski, 1988; Penley, 1989; Doane, 1992; Creed, 1993. For profiles on women film-makers see Kuhn and Radstone, 1990. On female spectatorship see Pribham (ed.), 1988; Mayne, 1993; Stacey, 1993. On Black feminism see Davis, 1981; hooks, 1981; Moraga and Anzaldúa (eds), 1981; Hull, Scott and Smith (eds), 1982; Attille and Blackwood, 1986; Davies, Dickey and Stratford (eds), 1987.)

fetishism – *see* **film noir, voyeurism/fetishism**

film industry – *see* **Hollywood, studio system**

film noir (*see also* **genre**)　　This is a term coined by French film critics in 1946 to designate a particular type of American **thriller** film. After the liberation of France in 1944, which saw the lifting of the ban (imposed by the occupying Germans) of the importation of American films, French screens were inundated with Hollywood products, including a new type of thriller. By analogy with the label given by the French to categorize hard-boiled detective novels – *roman noir* – the term film noir was coined to define this new-looking film. The film noir, predominantly a **B movie**, is often referred to as a sub-**genre** of the crime **thriller** or **gangster** movie – although as a style it can also be found in other genres (for example, **melodrama, western**). This is why other critics see film noir as a movement rather than a genre. These critics point to the fact that, like all other film movements, film noir emerged from a period of political instability: 1941–58, the time of the Second World War and the Cold War. In the United States this was a time of repressed insecurity and paranoia: the American dream seemed in tatters and American

116

national identity under severe strain. As a result of the war women had moved into the workforce and had expanded their horizons beyond the domestic sphere; at the same time men were removed from that sphere – which they had controlled – to go and fight. The men's return to peacetime was a period of maladjustment: what had 'their' women been up to? where was their role at work and in the political culture generally? and what had they fought the war for, only to find the United States involved in a new kind of hostility based in suspicion and paranoia? So the question of national identity was also bound up with the question of masculine identity.

Rather than a genre or movement it might be safer to say that film noir is above all a visual style which came about as a result of political circumstance and cross-fertilization. The various claims, therefore, to a single heritage are not really in order. The French claimed a first with Marcel Carné's *Le Jour se lève* (1939) – a very dark film; the Americans believed they had strong claims to the honour with their thriller films of the 1940s (for example, arguably the first one, John Huston's *Maltese Falcon*, 1941). Certainly the visual **codes** given to express the deep pessimism of the **French poetic realist** films of the latter part of the 1930s (exemplified by the work of Carné, Julien Duvivier and Jean Renoir) were in part antecedents to the film noir. But so too was the 1920s **German expressionist** style in so far as the distorted effects created by **lighting**, **setting** and use of shadows reflected inner turmoil and alienation so associated with film noir. However, it would be political events that would complete the cross-fertilization. In the late 1930s and early 1940s, as the threat of war increased and anti-Semitic pogroms continued, a considerable number of European film-makers and technicians fled to America, more particularly Hollywood. The most significant impact was made by the émigré film-makers who had worked in Germany and who were associated in one way or another with German expressionism. Fritz Lang, Josef von Sternberg, Billy Wilder, Richard Siodmark, Otto Preminger, Douglas Sirk, Max Ophuls are but the most famous names.

117

There are three main characteristics of the film noir which emanate from its primary founding on the principle of contrastive lighting: *chiaroscuro* (*clair–obscur*/light–dark) – the highly stylized visual style which is matched by the stylized narrative which is matched in turn by the stylized **stereotypes** – particularly of women. The essential ingredients of a film noir are its specific location or setting, its low-key lighting, a particular kind of psychology associated with the protagonist, and a sense of social malaise, pessimism, suspicion and gloom (not surprising given the political conjuncture of the time). The setting is city-bound and generally a composite of rain-washed streets and interiors (both dimly lit), tightly framed shots often with extreme camera angles – all reminiscent of German expressionism. The cityscape is fraught with danger and corruption, the shadowy, ill-lit streets reflecting the blurred moral and intellectual values as well as the difficulty in discerning truth. Characters are similarly unclear, as is evidenced by the way their bodies are lit and framed: half in the shadows, fragmented. The net effect is one of claustrophobia, underscoring the sense of malaise and tension. The protagonist (according to classic canons the 'hero' is a male) is often side-lighted to enhance the profile from one side and leaving the other half of the face in the dark, thus pointing to the moral **ambiguity** of this main character who is neither a knight in shining armour nor completely bad (interestingly the prototype for this characterization goes back at least as far as Edward G. Robinson's gangster portrayal in *Little Caesar*, Mervyn LeRoy, 1930). He usually mistreats or ignores his 'woman' (either the wife, very much tucked away out of the city, or the moll with the golden heart who invariably sees the 'truth') and gets hooked on a *femme fatale* who, more often than not according to the **preferred reading**, is the perpetrator of all his troubles (see *Double Indemnity*, Billy Wilder, and *Murder My Sweet*, Edward Dmytryk, both 1944). This 'hero' is often obsessive and neurotic and equally capable of betrayal of his *femme fatale*. The ambiguity of his character is paralleled by the contortions of the plot, whose complexities seem unresolvable, particularly by the hero, who, until the very end, seems confused and unclear about what is happening. In this respect, film noir is about power relations and sexual identity. The power the *femme fatale* exerts over the hero is his own doing, because he has over-invested in his construction of her **sexuality** at the expense of his own **subjectivity**. He has allowed her to be on top because of his own insecurities about who he is. (For a full discussion of this crisis in masculinity see Krutnik, 1991.)

But that's only half the story, because film noir is not so clear-cut in its misogyny. Film noir gives a very central role to the *femme fatale* and privileges her as active, intelligent, powerful, dominant and in charge of her own sexuality – at least until the end of the film when she pays for it (through death or submission to the patriarchal system). In this respect, she constitutes a break with **classic Hollywood cinema**'s representation of woman (as mother/whore, wife/mistress – passive). These women are interested only in themselves (as the frequent reflections of them in mirrors attest) and in getting enough money, by all means foul, to guarantee their independence. By being in contradiction with the ideological construct of women, such an image construction makes readings against the grain eminently possible. As Janey Place (1980, 37) says, as far as these women are concerned, 'It is not their inevitable demise we remember but rather their strong, dangerous and above all, exciting sexuality'. These women are symbols of 'unnatural' phallic power: toting guns and cigarette holders like the best of the men – to get what they want. They move about easily in traditionally male spaces, bars, etc. They might even dress like men with their very tailored suits with broad shoulder-pads; or they might slink out of the shadows, thigh-first, dressed in clinging sequinned evening gowns – either way they are mysterious, ambiguous and deadly (guns and looks can kill). In both instances they are empowered by their sexuality. (Examples are *Woman in the Window*, Fritz Lang, 1944; *Gilda*, Charles Vidor, 1946; *Kiss Me Deadly*, Robert Aldrich, 1955.)

Ultimately film noir is not about investigating a murder, although it might at first appear to be. Generally speaking, in the film noir the woman is central to the intrigue and it is therefore she who becomes the object of the male's investigation. But, as you will have guessed, it is less her role in the intrigue that is under investigation, much more her sexuality because it is that which threatens the male quest for resolution. The ideological contradiction she opens up by being a strong, active, sexually expressive female must be closed off, contained. That is the **diegetic** trajectory and visual strategy of film noir. However, there are obvious difficulties in containing this woman. And this is reflected by the **narrative** strategies inherent in film noir. There is, as Gledhill (1980, 14) points out, a proliferation of points of view. Whose voice do we hear through these multiple **discourses** each telling a story? Who has the voice of author/ity? The devices used in film noir – voice-over and **flashback**s (which primarily privilege the male point of view), diegetic narratives issued by different characters (the woman, the police, the private eye) – are just so many discourses vying for dominance. In the end, film noir is about which voice is going to gain control over the storytelling and – in the end – control over the image of the woman (Gledhill, 1980, 17). This struggle occurs both between men and between the man and the woman, but, more importantly what this struggle foregrounds is the fact that the woman's image is just that: a male construct – which 'suggests another place behind the image where woman might be' (Gledhill, 1980, 17). Food for feminist thought, but not the director's cut! There has to be closure – which means implicitly a closing-off of the ideological contradictions that such a suggestion makes plain. And in the end, closure does occur, but at a price. It is the male voice (that of the Symbolic Order, the Law of the Father) that completes the investigation (see **Imaginary/Symbolic**). However, as the multiplicity of points of view that prevailed until the closing moments show, guilt is not easily ascribed to only one person. Because of the lack of clarity it is not quite so easy to 'Put the blame on Mame, boys'. (For an interesting play on female/male subjectivities see *Mildred Pierce*, Michael Curtiz, 1945. Of the three flashbacks, the first two are hers, the last and 'truthful' one is that of the male and representative of the law, the police detective.)

There are contextual reasons for this struggle for dominance. As Janey Place (1980, 36) says, **myths** do not only mediate dominant **ideology**, they are also 'responsive to the *repressed* needs of culture'. Thus, in film noir this construction and subsequent destruction of the sexually assertive woman must be viewed within the economic and political climate of the 1940s and 1950s. I have already mentioned the repressed insecurity and paranoia respective to the political climate of those two decades. On the economic front, thanks to the Second World War, women went into work in the 1940s in huge numbers to help the war effort – and in many cases did so by replacing 'their' men who were at war. By the end of the war, these formerly independent women were being pushed back into the family and the domestic sphere. The film noir challenged the family by its absence and so did the film noir woman who, as sexually independent, contributed to the instability of the world in which the male protagonist found himself. The 1940s film noir was, then, an expression of male concern at women's growing economic and sexual independence and a fear of the men's own place in society once they returned from war. The 1950s film noir functioned to reassert the value of family life not just so that the men could get their jobs back but so that national identity, so much under siege in postwar United States, could be reasserted. We see here how film noir articulated the repressed needs of American culture. Furthermore, the masochistic sexual fantasies implicit in the threat the *femme fatale* poses for the male protagonist are, in this respect, tied up with questions of (male) identity. But they are 'nothing' really in relation to the sadistic closures designed for the woman: death, being outcast or being reintegrated into the family. (For further reading see Cameron, 1992; Copjec, 1993; Kaplan, 1980; Krutnik, 1991; Modleski, 1988); Stephens, 1995.)

121

film theory – *see* **theory**

flashback   A **narrative** device used in film (as in literature) to go back in time to an earlier moment in a character's life and/or history, and to narrate that moment. Flashbacks, then, are most clearly marked as **subjective** moments within that narrative. Flashbacks are a cinematic representation of memory and of history and, ultimately, of subjective truth. Interestingly, flashbacks date back to the very beginnings of film history – at least as early as 1901 with Ferdinand Zecca's *Histoire d'un crime* – thus coinciding with the birth and burgeoning of psychoanalysis. In this respect flashbacks are closely aligned therefore with the workings of the psyche and an individual's interpretation of history. Furthermore, because flashbacks almost always serve to resolve an enigma (a murder, a state of mental disorder, etc.) they are by nature investigative or confessional narrative **codes**, which again brings them close to the process of **psychoanalysis**. Finally, because they also reconstruct history, flashbacks can serve nationalistic purposes or conversely can be used to question certain social values.

Let's now unpick this. Most of what follows is very largely based on Maureen Turim's excellent and thorough analysis: *Flashbacks in Film: Memory and History* (1989). First we'll look at the codes of the flashback; second, flashbacks and history; third, flashbacks and the psyche.

Flashback codes   In the first instance the spectator is given visual and aural codes to signify the beginning and ending of a flashback. Normally there is a **fade** or **dissolve**, often on the face of the person whose flashback we are about to witness, and generally a voice-over by a narrator (again usually, but not always, the person whose flashback it is). The **image** shifts from the present to the past. However, although there is a shift in temporal and spatial reality, that shift does not undermine the narrative logic. Already then the flashback is exposing itself as a double-edged code. There is an assumption of temporality and order in the flashback but simultaneously – by its very nature – it is patently calling

122

into question our assumptions about chronological time. Time is carved up and layered. It is both the past and the present, the past made present visibly before our very eyes. We are watching the flashback, so the assumed time is the past. However, we 'understand' cinema in the present (the reel/real is unreeling before our eyes in the always present). The **spectator** is doubly positioned in relation to time. She or he is aware, thanks to the visual and aural codes that mark out the flashback, that she or he is in the past; but also unaware of being in the past because of the '**naturalising** processes within the fiction' (Turim, 1989, 17) – naturalized, that is, because the shift in time and space does not disrupt the narrative logic, rather it keeps it safely in place (see **enunciation** and **spatial and temporal contiguity**).

Part of this naturalizing process can be pointed at by the fact that the spectator is rarely in a position, thanks to the **seamless** codes, to question whose **subjectivity** the flashback might represent, whose truth it is and whether or not it is truth (see Kuhn's discussion (1982, 50–3) of *Mildred Pierce*, Michael Curtiz, 1945). If we do believe that flashbacks are more authentic than a chronological tale it is because of their confessional nature and also because they are supposed to be answering an enigma. In both instances there is an implicit truth, even if it is one-sided.

Flashbacks are hermeneutically determined: that is, they will yield a solution to an enigma in the end. So flashbacks come to a 'natural' end when the past has either caught up with the present or has explained the present state of affairs. They can also be seen in this light as a retardation device creating suspense and delaying the answer to the enigma. Alfred Hitchcock's films are notorious for this; he even went so far as to hold the flashback back to keep the enigma alive (as in *Marnie*, 1956, when a last-minute flashback tells us the reasons for Marnie's psychological disorders).

Flashbacks and history Flashbacks are 'naturally' aligned with history since they make the spectator aware of the past. They are both history and story (the French word *histoire* usefully encapsulates this double nature of the flashback). But they

are a particular representation of the past because it is subjec-
tivized through one or several people's memories. History/
story becomes personalized and is narrated through the
heroics or eyes of the individual. The ideological, and indeed
nationalistic, implications of this are clear. By framing history
as an individual experience and because a film in flashback is
based on the premise that cause and effect are reversed (we
know the result before we know the cause), history can become
didactic: a moral lesson is to be learnt – alternatively, as in times
of war, it can lead to patriotic identification (Turim, 17). To
illustrate these two possible outcomes I quote the disastrous
effects of Hollywood and stardom on a woman's psyche as in
Sunset Boulevard (Billy Wilder, 1950), the inadvisability of a wife
and mother having too much socio-economic and class ambition for her family, especially an ungrateful daughter as in
Mildred Pierce, and, as a classic example of the displacement of
the meaning of war on to personal relationships (which makes
identification possible), *Casablanca* (Curtiz, 1942) with its call
to American patriotism and engagement in the Second World
War (see Turim, 1989, 126ff. and 133ff.).

In the framework of history, biographical flashbacks are also
redolent with ideological connotations. Because they represent an evaluation of a life, but through a subjective framing
of history, they tend to mythologize the 'great man' (*sic*): as,
for example, in Abel Gance's *Napoléon vu par Abel Gance*
(1927). In this film there are various levels of ideological and
nationalistic readings to be made. First, of course, is the might
and intellect of Napoleon – the brilliant battle strategist since
early boyhood when he had to prove against bullying school-
boys that, although from Corsica, he was just as good if not
a better Frenchman than they. There is also the man of destiny
and vision: *l'homme providentiel* who can help France to find
national coherence *and* assert its greatness in the world. His
success in war and his emblematic eagle reflect the glory and
the stability of France's First Empire under his emperorship
as opposed to the factionalism and instability of France's
republican periods (a clear pointing to Gance's own political
dissatisfaction with the then Third Republic).

124

Only occasionally do biographical flashbacks put in question a nation's power structures and its belief in the legitimacy of capitalism. *Citizen Kane* (Orson Welles, 1941) is a classic in this respect in its demythologizing the American way of life and the **myth** of capitalism that allows men to become tycoons. This is a film that deconstructs larger-than-life ideological statements on class and power in American society (see **deconstruction** and **ideology**). This deconstruction is achieved by the fact that the flashbacks are not those of the dead Kane. They are a third-person compendium-narrative, put together by a journalist, of other people's subjective readings of him (see Turim, 1989, 112–17). The trial testimonies that make up the flashbacks in this film do more than expose Kane and American societal values, they also put journalism on trial (to make the Kane story sellable, truth must be compromised). Last but not least, *Citizen Kane* exposes Hollywood's cinematic practices of seamlessness that produce the reality effect (that is, film's ability to dissimulate that it is only a representation of reality up on screen, not reality itself).

Flashbacks and the psyche   The flashback is a mimetic representation of thought processes looking to the past, whether they be dreams, confessions or memories. They are then subjective truths, an explanation of the present through the past. Flashbacks show how memories are stored and repressed. They also function on an associative level with memory (the protagonist might see something that reminds her or him of a similar sight in the past that has deep resonances for her or him). Because we are positioned as witnesses to these divulgences of the past we become the proto-analyst, and the protagonist our analysand. Often this spectator positioning is strengthened by the presence of an actual psychiatrist or confessor within the film. Flashbacks that deal with psychological motivation were particularly popular in American cinema during the 1940s and 1950s when popularizing Sigmund Freud was very much the order of the day. This popularization must be seen in the context of the very deep malaise felt during the 1940s at the relinquishing of isolationism and entering the Second World War and then, in the

1950s, the aura of suspicion generated by the Cold War and the deep cynicism of the younger generation in relation to their elders' values and beliefs. Freud did not necessarily offer easy solutions, but at least popular Freudianism resolved enigmas or provided simple explanations as to why a character was as she or he was.

What is interesting first of all about flashbacks in this context is that they tend to predominate in two **genres** – **film noir** and psychological **melodrama** – and that they tend to be gendered (see **gender**). But before explaining this statement it should first be said that both genres start from a similar positioning in relation to the representation of the past. The past is seen as an object of nostalgia, therefore of desire or as an object of despair. In both cases this object of fascination is also frightening and dangerous because of the nostalgic desire to repeat (Turim, 1989, 12). This desire to repeat is of course deeply atavistic and masochistic, but it is also bound up with the notion of fate – this notion of fatalism is particularly evident in the film noir genre. Patterns of repetition generated by flashbacks point to psychotic fears that are acted out in the present. Such patterns as the abandoned child syndrome, the rejected child, the controlled/(s)mothered child, the abused child are just some of the psychoses that motivate the flashbacks particularly in the psychological melodrama. However, they are also present in film noir, especially (but by no means exclusively) if the victim of the psychosis is a woman.

This brings us to the issue of the gendered nature of these flashbacks. Predominantly, in these films of the 1940s and 1950s the film noir focuses on the male protagonist, the psychological melodrama on the female. What is surprising is that the flashbacks do not break down into such neat genderized categories. In the psychological melodramas, which often represent the woman as disfunctional, over-ambitious, mad or making repeated suicide attempts, the flashback functions as an exploration of the woman's psyche, not necessarily by the woman herself, but rather by her analyst, doctor, enquiring detective, and so on. Furthermore, when necessary, women are given truth serums and electric shock treatment in order to 'get at the truth'. So the flashback is not their subjectivity but others' subjective view of them – a return to the past provoked by a probing or electrifying of the female psyche. Implicitly the ideological purpose being served here is the message that women do not control their unconscious, but men do (control the women's and of course their own). Women are stripped of their own narration and, therefore, subjectivity (Turim, 1989, 160). Given that during the war women had been able to enter the workforce and 'do men's jobs' and that they were separated from their men who were at war and very far away, the independence they had gained would 'naturally' unsettle the returning servicemen. Viewed in this context such films as *Mildred Pierce*, *The Locket* (John Brahms, 1946) and *Possessed* (Curtis Bernhardt, 1946) say more about masculinity in crisis than they do about the female psyche – particularly when one considers that in all three of these films it is the investigator (doctor or detective) who resolves the enigma to the woman's disturbed psyche, not the woman herself. (For further reading on these films see Cook, 1980; Turim, 1989, 157–64.)

What of the male protagonist in the film noir? The flash-backs are clearly inscribed as his and are most generally marked by his voice-over. They are either investigative or confessional and unlike the flashbacks in psychological melodrama, with their redemptive quality, they are strongly inscribed with fatalism. They are also more retrospective than introspective: a summing up or evaluative judgment of the past events (Turim, 1989, 172). The flashbacks serve to underscore the profound ambiguity of the male protagonist. As Turim says (171), the voice-over bridges the gap between the past and the present, the present is speaking about the past and as such the voice-over represents a subjectivity that is a controlling of the past 'exhibiting a self-reliant masculinity'. The protagonist is also streetwise. However, he is driven by a fatal neurosis, a fatal compulsion that is triggered off by an 'evil' woman to whom he is fatally attracted, but who is forbidden to him (because either she or he is married). The fact that

127

he is attracted to the 'evil' woman and will transgress to 'get her' reveals his desire to play the death scenario. The fact that he repeats the scenario through his confessional or investigative flashbacks shows also how compelling the masochistic scenario is – the past as object of desire.

Turim (1989, 175) describes the film noir as 'a romance of the death drive', but such a romance cannot be accomplished without the inscription of the evil female protagonist. In other words, the male protagonist cannot fulfil his masochistic fantasy without the woman. The woman stands as a projection of the protagonist's psyche, and as such she is the agent of evil, forcing him into a cycle of repetition that can be stopped only with death (his or hers). This projection, however, does make clear just how alluring the wish to transgress is to the protagonist. The forbidden woman in this respect becomes that which is forbidden to him by patriarchal law: namely, the mother. So now the masochism inherent in the fatal compulsion of repetition and death also points to a refusal to complete the **Oedipal trajectory**. Rather than enter into the Law of the Father, the male protagonist chooses to transgress it (see **Imaginary/Symbolic**).

A brief analysis of *Double Indemnity* (Billy Wilder, 1944) will serve to make these points clear. In this film the protagonist, Walter Neff, is an insurance broker. He is the site of exchange between client and his company and is directly answerable to the claims-investigator Barton Keyes. In this respect he is doubly inscribed into the Law of the Father: the company and more specifically his boss – who 'locks' him into it, even (through his name, Keyes). He is also quite 'feminized': as site of exchange for money which he never gets to handle. The film opens with Neff (a weak name suggesting naff, inept) stumbling into his office, fatally wounded. What has happened? Through his confessional flashback, which he records for Keyes to hear – presumably after he dies – we learn that, in an attempt to get his hands on insurance money fraudulently, by killing off a client to whom he had sold a double indemnity package, he has ended up getting himself shot by the client's wife to whom he had become fatally attracted and with whom he had dreamt up the fraudulent scheme. During his whole confession, Keyes is standing listening, unnoticed, by Neff's office doorway.

The confessional flashback is doubly confessional: the tape and the listening Keyes. The nature of the confession shows how desperately Neff wanted to procure the money, that is to pull off the fraud successfully. In other words, in his transgression, Neff was willing himself to defy Keyes (the claims-investigator/defrauder). In so doing, he was defying the Law of the Father as represented by Keyes – testing his masculinity against Keyes's. The transgression marks, then, a desire to assert his masculinity over his 'feminized' position – which of course in and through his confession he makes clear he failed to do. During this confession his 'father' is listening; the father listening to the 'feminized' son who cannot assert his masculinity over his father. Furthermore, we discover during the confession that his fatal wounding is at the hands of his desired forbidden woman/other/mother, Phyllis Dietrichson. Although he kills her before he returns to his office (site of the patriarchal law, the company) to make his confession, she – as fetishized woman, therefore phallic mother – is the one to shoot first.

Let's tie this all up. The double confession points to an atavism around his 'feminized' self and to a masochistic desire to repeat the failure either to usurp the father or to fulfil successfully the Oedipal trajectory. Although Neff does not know Keyes is listening, he intends him to listen eventually. So he clearly wishes to display his 'feminized' self to Keyes as well as his failure to assert his masculinity. Counterpointed to this homoerotic display of Neff's desire for the father is the father witnessing, unseen: a reversal of the primal scene with the father watching the son desiring. Absent from this scene is the mother: she has already been killed by the son but not before she let loose the fatal (castrating) shot. Because she is forbidden, she represents fascination and danger, the very qualities that make her desirable. In this respect she functions on two levels. First, she embodies the very nature of the flashback in relation to the past as object of desire but also frightening and dangerous. The nostalgic desire to repeat, which is an inherent code of the flashback and which we know is redolent with masochism, is exemplified by her dual gendering as fetishized object of desire and as phallic mother who actually carries a gun. Since he cannot assert his masculinity over the father, his masochistic scenario must lead him to death. The 'feminized' son is shot by the 'phallicized' mother – death at the hands of the father. Second, by shooting the son, she forces him to return to the father and to expiate his transgression, first through confession and then through death. True to the Oedipus myth, Neff confesses and then dies, thereby reasserting the primacy of patriarchal law as ultimately unviolable.

foregrounding Bringing to the fore or front, in this instance, the front of the screen. Formal elements of a film may function to show that it is a particular character's story that is being foregrounded: subjective camera **shots**, medium close-ups of the character in the foreground, voice-over. By extension, but also by analogy with linguistics, foregrounding means drawing the **spectator**'s attention to a particular element in a film through the use of an unusual filmic device. Because foregrounding can be used to draw attention to the practices of film-making itself, clearly it is much in evidence in **counter-cinema**. But mainstream cinema makes use of it as well. For example, Alfred Hitchcock foregrounded his 'self-as-auteur' by making a brief appearance in most of his films.

Michael Powell's *Peeping Tom* (1960) is arguably the best example of foregrounding. Starting with foregrounding film-making itself, this film is a film about movies *and* about the spectators who watch them and their (in this case morbid) urge to gaze (that is, **scopophilia**). It foregrounds the three looks that characterize the cinema: the look of the camera; that of the character; that of the spectator. It foregrounds the power of the film-maker: Mark Lewis, the protagonist. He is a compulsive film-maker who, by the time the film picks up with him, has taken to murdering the women he is filming by pointing a spiked leg of his camera tripod at their throats and stabbing them to death. The spectator is positioned behind the camera (foregrounding her or him as director or murderer or voyeur). But she or he also, in a complex set of shots towards the end of the film, gets doubly positioned behind and in front of the camera (foregrounding her/him as voyeur or victim). This latter instance deserves some further elaboration because of the density of the **mise-en-abîme** of foregrounding. This series of shots occurs towards the end of the film when Mark, returning home, finds his lodger sitting in the dark watching one of his 'murder' films. He confesses his crimes and then sets the scene to show her 'fear itself' (let us not forget that in **horror** and **thriller** films abject fear is gendered feminine). He approaches her with his camera, spiked leg pointed at her throat and with a mirror fixed to the camera so that she can see her face reflected in it. The spectator sees the shots from behind the camera and, in a **reverse-angle shot**, those of the face reflected in the mirror. The first set of shots foregrounds the role of the director/spectator/voyeur; the second set foregrounds the victim, not *as* victim but as voyeur of her victimness. The chilling effect for the spectator, first of all, is the double foregrounding both of woman-as-victim and of fear (the spectator becomes the woman-as-victim in fear watching her own fear). The second effect is equally unnerving. As the mirrored image looks out to the spectator she or he is caught in the co-conspiratorial role as accomplice to the director/murderer. In other words, the film is watching the spectator watching the film.

form/content   In film studies form and content are seen as inextricably linked. The form of a film emerges out of the content and the content is created by the formal elements of the film. Thus the contents of a character's memories are given form through the use of a series of **flashbacks** which, in turn, are formally signalled by a **dissolve** or a **fade** (the **spectator** would not expect to sit through an hour and a half of watching the character, seated in a chair, recalling her or his memories). Film form guides the spectator's expectations. Thus if the content is about a triangular love relationship, the film form will follow the **classic narrative** plot structure of 'order/disorder/order-restored', **shots** will frame the threesome in different readable ways to show who in the end 'will have to go'.

framing (*see also* **mise-en-scène, shots**) The way in which subjects and objects are framed within a shot produces specific readings. Size and volume within the frame speak as much as dialogue. So too do camera angles. Thus, for example, a high-angle extreme long shot of two men walking away in the distance (as at the end of Jean Renoir's *La Grande Illusion*, 1937) points to their vulnerability – they are about to disappear, possibly die. Low-angle shots in medium close-up on a person can point to their power, but it can also point to ridicule because of the distortion factor. (For a more detailed discussion see Bordwell and Thompson, 1980, 104–36.)

Free British Cinema According to Lindsay Anderson, one of the founders of Free Cinema, this movement coincided with the explosion on to the theatre boards of John Osborne's *Look Back in Anger* (1956). Free Cinema was a term Anderson coined in 1956 to designate a series of documentaries and shorts he was putting together for screenings at the National Film Theatre. There were six programmes (from 1956 to 1959) and the basic ethos linking the films, which included the work of French and Polish film-makers, was that the films were free because they were made outside the framework of the film industry and because their statements, which were commentaries on contemporary society, were entirely personal. Although these films were personal statements, none the less there was a strong emphasis on the relationship between art and society and an insistence that the film-makers were committed to the values expressed in their work.

Rather than a movement, however, we should speak of a tendency in cinema. First, because the Free Cinema programme itself was international and made up of an eclectic grouping of films made by young contemporary film-makers – and as such represented the deep-felt need for new voices to be heard: but that constitutes an appeal not a movement. Second, because, on a national scale, Free Cinema films were produced by only a handful of film-makers, and while they may have shared common ideals, they had no style in common with the exception of the work of the three film-makers who founded this so-called movement: Lindsay Anderson, Karel Reisz and Tony Richardson. As Richardson himself stated, in an interview in *The Listener* (2 May 1968), Free Cinema was a label invented to designate a number of **documentary** films made by the three film-makers during the 1950s; it was not a case of a movement but a sharing of common ideals where cinema was concerned. In any event, the legacy of Free Cinema is closely related to the work of these three film-makers and it is on this that the rest of this entry will focus. (For a wider debate see Lovell and Hillier, 1972.)

Among the common ideals held by these film-makers, two stand out as most significant: first, documentary films should be made free from all commercial pressures and, second, they need to be inflected with a more humanist and poetic approach. In this respect, Free Cinema was born out of the 1930s documentary tradition of Humphrey Jennings rather than John Grierson (whom this group of film-makers criticized). A third important point in relation to the emergence of this cinema is that both Anderson and Reisz were critics for the film review *Sequence*, which was launched by Anderson in 1946, and that it is out of writings for this review that the ethos of Free Cinema was born. This review criticized the British documentary for its conformity and apathy and feature film for its conventionality and lack of aesthetic experimentation. *Sequence* was a new departure in film criticism. In their articles Anderson and Reisz examined the style rather than the content of a film and deplored British cinema's adherence to **classic narrative cinema**. They denounced

133

the bourgeois, suburban tradition inherent in this cinema and accused it, through its lack of **transparence** on the working **class**, of avoiding reality.

These three Free Cinema film-makers were unanimous in their condemnation of the monopolizing practices of the British film industry. In the 1950s full feature films were produced by only two companies: Rank Organisation and ABC (a branch of Warner Brothers). And the films that predominated were, according to Anderson *et al.*, insipid comedies or war films that glorified the British fighters, trivialized the horrors of war and, last but not least, perpetuated the tradition of the class system (*The Dam Busters*, Michael Anderson, 1955, being exemplary of this second type of film). Needless to say financing for their own film projects was not forthcoming from those two giants. On the whole they had to self-finance, which is why their first films were shorts or documentaries. They did, however, manage to obtain some resourcing from the British Film Institute's Experimental Film Fund and the giant industrial company Ford of Dagenham. In the event, Ford was a 'greater' patron of Free Cinema than the British Film Institute, which helped to finance only one film: *Momma Don't Allow* (Richardson and Reisz, 1956). Ford commissioned a series of documentaries – entitled *Look at Britain* – of which Free Cinema were responsible for two: Anderson's *Every Day Except Christmas*, 1957, and Reisz's *We are the Lambeth Boys*, 1959.

The primary characteristic of these film-makers' documentaries and shorts was their belief in the importance of everyday life and people. They were committed to representing working-class life as it was lived, not as it was imagined. In their images nothing is forced, giving an authenticity that makes their films close in spirit to the humanism of Jennings's documentaries (what Anderson (1954) terms 'public poetry'). What links the three film-makers is the fact that their work focuses on the individual and the collective; that, in terms of editing, they use juxtaposing rhythms (slow or fast). Indeed, their rhythmic editing had strong connotations with jazz – deliberately, since jazz was part of the working-class subculture

(*Momma Don't Allow* deals explicitly with jazz and dancing as a social and sexual liberation for the working-class youth). The other important link between the three is the continuity in the style of their films, undoubtedly due to the presence on four out of their six Free Cinema films of the cameraman Walter Lassally. Finally, a contributing factor to the continuity in their style was the homage their films paid to those film-makers they considered constituted their own heritage: John Ford, Marcel Carné, Jean Cocteau, Robert Flaherty, Jean Grémillon, Humphrey Jennings, Jean Renoir, Vittorio de Sica, Arne Sucksdorff and Vigo.

What of the legacy of the Free Cinema? Certain critics claim that it left very little trace at all, and that the **British New Wave Cinema** of the late 1950s (of which *Look Back in Anger*, Richardson, 1959, was the first film) was not, as other critics claimed, a direct outcome of Free Cinema but of the literature and theatre of the time. The 'truth' of course lies somewhere in between: the New Wave movement came out of the conjuncture of literary trends and the Free Cinema documentary tendency. This argument is sustained by the fact that the names of these three film-makers reappear as directors of these New Wave films. In 1959 Tony Richardson founded a production company with John Osborne, Woodfall Films (with financial support from Bryanston Films, a subsidiary of British Lion!). This company produced most of the New Wave films. Richardson, who had earlier directed the stage performance of *Look Back in Anger,* now made it into a film. Reisz made *Saturday Night and Sunday Morning* (1960) and Anderson *This Sporting Life* (1963) – two key films for British cinema. (For more details of this legacy see **British New Wave** cinema).

French New Wave/*Nouvelle Vague* (*see also* **auteur/auteur theory**)   Not really a movement, but certainly an important moment in film history. The French New Wave came about in the late 1950s, although, as we shall see, it did have precursors. The term refers to films made, on the whole, by

135

a new generation of French film-makers which were low-budget and, most importantly, went against the prevailing trends in 1950s cinema of literary adaptations, costume dramas and massive co-productions – a cinema which had been labelled by the *Cahiers du cinéma group* as the *'cinéma de papa'* (old fogeys' cinema; see **auteur**).

The term *Nouvelle vague* was not in the first instance associated with these film-makers. Indeed it was originally coined in the late 1950s by Françoise Giroud, editor of the then centre-left weekly *L'Express*, to refer to the new socially active youth class. However, the term very quickly became associated with current trends in cinema because of the appeal of the youthful actor Gérard Philipe and, more especially, the tremendous success of twenty-eight-year old Roger Vadim's *Et Dieu créa la femme* (1956) and the mythologizing effect it had on Brigitte Bardot. This meant that producers in the late 1950s wanted work made by 'young ones' – both on screen and behind the camera. This demand helped to propel a new wave of film-makers on to the screen. This was not the exclusive reason, however, for this 'new' cinema. In demographic terms the older guard of film-makers, who had held the reins from the 1930s through to the 1950s, were ageing fast or dying off. This created a gap for a new wave of film-makers (some 170 in the period 1959–63) who in turn became associated in people's minds with the *Nouvelle Vague*. In the collective memory, all that remains of *La Nouvelle Vague* today is this group of film-makers – not the new youth class. A misnomer made **myth**.

Misnomer or not, an important effect of this demand for a *jeune cinéma* was that it created the myth that those making it were all young. There was also a commonly held belief that, because some of the more notorious first films of the New Wave to hit the screens were made by critics from the influential *Cahiers du cinéma* group (Claude Chabrol, Jean-Luc Godard, Jacques Rivette, Eric Rohmer, François Truffaut), all of this cinema came from film-makers who had not been through the normal circuit of assistantship to established directors. The facts attest differently. The film-makers loosely grouped into this so-called '*jeune cinéma*' was were in their early thirties. During the period 1959–60, of the sixty-seven film-makers making their first feature film, only 55 per cent came from backgrounds not directly attached to film-making, and the remaining 45 per cent was made up of short-film directors (like Alain Resnais or Agnès Varda) and film assistants.

Another myth perpetuated was that this cinema coincided with the birth, in 1958, of the Fifth Republic. Two films, *Le Beau Serge* (Chabrol, 1958) and *Les 400 Coups* (Truffaut, 1959), were seen as the trail-blazers of this New Wave, shortly followed by Godard's *A bout de souffle* (1959) and Resnais's *Hiroshima mon amour* (1959). History is not so convenient. There were of course precursors. On the one hand, there was the influence on film-making practices of the theoretical writing, primarily emanating from the *Cahiers du cinéma* journals of the 1950s, which advocated the primacy of the **auteur** and **mise-en-scène**. And, on the other, there were film-makers who were already making films that went counter to dominant cinematic practices of the 1950s. They were just not associated with any group. Low-budget, non-studio films were being made. In fact Agnès Varda's 1954 film *La Pointe courte* is often cited as the herald of this movement. The modes of production and the **counter-cinema** practices she put in place became commonplace by the late 1950s. Location shooting, use of non-professional actors (or unknown ones from the theatre, such as the young Philippe Noiret in Varda's film), a deliberate **distanciation** so that **spectator identification** cannot occur, no necessary sense of chronology or **classic narrative** are a first set of hallmarks of Varda's style that are recognizable in the New Wave films. Her subversion of genres, her use of counterpoint, of juxtaposing two stories – one based in the personal, the other in the social – and her deliberately disorienting **editing** style are other important features of her cinematic style which Resnais for one has acknowledged as influencing his own film-making practices.

Another, last myth that needs examining is the belief that because this cinema was controversial or different in style it was also a radical and political cinema. This is predominantly not true: the New Wave film-makers were largely non-politicized. If their films had any political aura it came down to the fact that some film-makers carried on the 1930s tradition of criticizing the bourgeoisie, but now placed their narratives in contemporary **discourses** – that is, viewing the bourgeoisie from the youth point of view. The other reason why the New Wave might have been perceived as political, or a reason *post facto*, is that there were in fact two New Waves. The first occurred in the period 1958–62, the other during 1966–68. The first New Wave was anarchic, but only in relation to what preceded it: the *cinéma de papa*. As we shall see, the second New Wave was more clearly a politicized cinema. Hindsight may have conflated the two moments into one and perceived it as political. Politicized or not, both were to inform and have an impact on future cinemas.

1958–62 As we already know, the New Wave film-makers rejected the cinema of the 1950s and focused their attention on the auteur and mise-en-scène. The individual film-maker and his (*sic*) signature was all. Paradoxically, given their so-called modernity and innovativeness, this was rather a romantic ideal and conservative aesthetic. But it must be reiterated that they were not a politicized group. Their cinema marked a complete rupture with the 1950s cinematic codes and conventions on both the narrative and the visual level. In terms of **narrative**, there was often no *récit*, no completed or necessarily realistic story as such; there was no beginning, middle and end – more often it was a slice of life; gone were the literary adaptations of the 1950s, no 'high art' literature but rather pulp or popular fiction if adaptations were being made (with a particular liking for American detective pulp fiction). There were no **stars**. The time was the 'now-ever-present' of the 1960s. Discourses were contemporary and about young people. Taboos around sexuality were 'destroyed' (partly the effects of the so-called 'free-love' phenomenon) and the couple was represented as a complex entity with issues centring on power relations, lack of communication and questions of identity. The representation of women was more positive, women became more central to the narrative, and more **agencing** of their desire.

On the visual side, the institutional **iconography** was **deconstructed**. The establishing **shots**, which safely orientate the spectator in terms of **space and time**, were excised. A fast **editing** style, achieved by **jump cuts** and **unmatched** shots, replaced the **seamless** editing style that had prevailed before. The newly adopted lightweight camera, more commonly used for television, abandoned the **studios** and went out into the streets and suburbs of Paris (Paris was the one icon that did not disappear). Film stock was fast and cheap. These two latter aspects of technology gave this cinema a sense of spontaneity and **cinéma-vérité** more readily associated at the time with television production, which was mostly live at that time.

1966–68 By the time of this second New Wave, the contemporary discourses of the earlier New Wave had generally become more politicized and there was no positive reflection of the dominant **ideology**. Godard's films are particularly exemplary in this context (*Deux ou trois choses que je sais d'elle*, 1966; *La Chinoise* and *Weekend*, both 1967). Bourgeois myths (especially those surrounding marriage, family and consumption practices) were taken to bits and denormalized. The consumer boom, nuclear war, Vietnam, student politics, adolescence – all were subjects for treatment. By now the consumer boom (already criticized in the first New Wave) was not about comfort and a better way of life but about prostituting the self in order to be better able to consume. The most important consumer durable of that time, the car, was exposed as the machine of violence and death into which our covetousness had transformed it – a minotaur of our age (*la déesse*), the consumer durable that consumes us.

This cinema then was as much about the process of film-making as it was about denormalizing the sacred cows of the bourgeoisie. Film-making practice, the technology of the media, exposed social practice, consumption. It was also a counter-**Hollywood** cinema that did not seek to emulate the

139

American giant, as the 1950s products had done, but addressed first the personal and later the political tensions that the younger generations were experiencing during the 1960s. Both New Waves put in place a counter-cinema to the standardization effects of American technology (hand-held camera, no studio, editing practices that drew attention to themselves, no star-system). It did not de-Parisianize itself, but it did secure a social sphere for the youth class, for both men and women. The first New Wave was not politically engaged but it was anti-bourgeois in sentiment (especially Chabrol's films). And it was motivated by a desire to present the point of view of the individual in society. Moreover, the themes it treated filtered into mainstream cinema as early as the mid-1960s. In the late 1960s, by the time of the second New Wave, this cinema had become politicized, questioning institutions and their power effects over individuals – questions which filtered into the more evidently political cinema of the 1970s (the exemplary director being Constantin Costa-Gavras, but also Louis Malle).

It is worth noting that the brief popularity of both New Waves coincided with the political culture in which they found themselves and with the most politically tense moments in France's history of that period. The first period of popularity, 1958–62, coincided with the radical effect on institutions of the advent of the Fifth Republic and its new constitution which invested the presidency with executive powers – giving the president virtually supreme power over the parliament. This period also marked the bloody decolonization of Algeria. In this light it is easy to see why the disruptive anarchy of the first New Wave was seen as political. The second period of popularity, 1966–8, coincided with the progressive disenchantment with de Gaulle's authoritarian presidential style, unrest on social and educational levels owing to lack of resources to accommodate the expanding urban society and student university numbers, workers' concern at their conditions, and concern with unemployment – all of which culminated in the events of May 1968.

Although this cinema was criticized for its focus on the individual – its emphasis on auteur and the confessional style of the films – it left one very important legacy. Thanks to the huge influx of film-makers into the industry (around 170), production practices had to be reconsidered. For money to be spread around, films had to be low-budget. Given the number of film-makers, the cheaper, lightweight camera came into its own. As a result there was a democratization of the camera. This pioneering effect was to make the camera more accessible to voices formerly marginalized and by the 1970s and 1980s women, Blacks and Beurs (the Arab community in France) were entering into film-making.

French poetic realism   In the mid-1930s the liquidation of the two major film trusts in France, Pathé and Gaumont, meant that the small independent producer could take up pole position. Whereas before 1935, the two majors had dominated production, after 1935 and until 1939 on average 90 per cent of the French films produced were by small independent film companies. This had a fortunate effect on the French film industry. The collapse of the major commercial **studios** facilitated France's **art cinema**. Independent producer-directors were, for a while, free to make their films, and moreover could access the majors' studios and technical services, as well as their cinema circuits. A small faction of these independents, most famously Yves Allégret, Marcel Carné, Julien Duvivier, Jean Grémillon and Jean Renoir, became loosely banded under the label of the Poetic Realist school. But, despite their small number, they none the less re-established France's ailing international cinematic reputation which had been on the decline ever since the First World War, by which time the **Hollywood** majors had completely cornered the international market.

Poetic realism has been seen in relation to its historical context as shadowing the rise and fall of the Popular Front – a consolidated party of the left which eventually came to power in 1936. The party was voted in on a wave of optimism for its platform of social reforms. However, because of the economic climate and the threat of war these were never

141

fully implemented. The party was in power for a thousand days, but after only six months in office it was obvious that little or no change was going to be possible given the political and economic climate. To the optimism of its advance come the filmic echoes of working-class solidarity as exemplified in Renoir's *Le Crime de M. Lange* (1935) and the optimistic title of his *La Vie est à nous* (1936). As markers of the decline of the Popular Front and of the desperation felt at the ineluctability of war come deeply pessimistic films like Marcel Carné's *Quai des brumes* (1938), *Le Jour se lève* (1939) and Renoir's *La Règle du jeu* (1939).

This simplistic reflection needs nuancing however, since not all the films in this grouping necessarily gave this straightforward early-optimism, later-pessimism message. Furthermore, not all the film-makers in this school were sympathetic to the left. At least two 1936 films are undyingly pessimistic in their message. These are Julien Duvivier's *Pépé le Moko* and *La Belle Équipe* (both starring the poetic realist fetish star, Jean Gabin). In the first, Pépé dies at his own hands. Wanted by the police, he holes up in the Casbah in Algiers where he is surrounded by an adoring gang and mistress; but all he can dream of is returning to Paris – the price for fulfilling that desire is death. In *La Belle équipe* male working-class solidarity is exposed for its weakness as it swiftly becomes eroded by the alluring presence of a woman. Duvivier was certainly not a man of the left, which might explain his dark films in this euphoric period of the early Popular Front. However, another film-maker, Jean Grémillon, this time of the left, was making similarly bleak films around the same time. His *Gueule d'amour* (1937) portrays the destruction of a man who forgoes his duties (as a soldier) for his passion for a 'heartless' woman (whom he eventually murders).

In poetic realist films there is a strong emphasis on **mise-en-scène**: décor, **setting** and **lighting** receive minute attention and owe not a little to the influence of **German expressionism**. Poetic realism is a recreated **realism**, not the socio-realism of the **documentary**. In this respect the realism is very studio-bound and stylized. For example, parts of Paris are studiously reproduced in the studio – an almost inauthentic realism. This stylized realism of the mise-en-scène is matched by the poetic symbolism within the **narrative**. The narrative is heavily imbued with the notion of fatalism. The male protagonist is generally doomed and the film's **diegesis** is so constructed as to put the degeneration in his mood on display. This is the mise-en-scène of male suffering par excellence. Setting, gestures, movement (or lack of it), verbal and non-verbal communication are all markers for this degeneration and so too are the lighting effects. To this effect side-lighting, for example, is used on the protagonist's face, or part lighting of the space in which he finds himself, or highlighting objects that are of symbolic value to him. Indeed objects are endowed with symbolism to quite a degree of abstraction and resonate throughout the film, measuring the state of degeneration as the protagonist responds to their recurrence in the film.

A major reason why all aspects of the film process function so intensely to create this aura of poetic realism is that these films are, in the final analysis, the result of team work. There is the director, but there are also – of major importance – the scriptwriter, the designer for the sets, the lighting expert and the composer of the music soundtrack. Carné for example worked with the poet Jacques Prévert who scripted several of his films, he had Alexander Trauner as his set designer and Joseph Kosma was a frequent composer to his films. (For further reading see Andrew, 1995.)

futurism (*see also* **Soviet Cinema**)   A revolutionary modernist movement, founded in Italy at the beginning of the twentieth century when in 1909 the poet Filippo Tommasso Marinetti published a literary manifesto calling for the obliteration of past Italian culture and the creation of a new society, literature and art extolling the virtues of modern mechanization. Although short-lived in Italy, this movement had considerable impact on several aesthetic movements: the vorticists in the United Kingdom (inaugurated 1913) and

143

the Russian futurists (1912). The Russian futurists adopted an experimental and innovatory approach to language that was to filter through into the post-Revolutionary movement of constructivism. The pre-Revolutionary movement, influenced as it was by the abstract forms of European **modernist** art, primarily exemplified by cubism and futurism, believed in technique and the evacuation of fixed meanings. After the Revolution, the constructivists, seeing in technology the huge potential for social change, advocated a new order in which workers, artists and intellectuals would work together to produce a new vision of society – art and labour were' seen as one. This notion of art as production was eagerly embraced by the newly emergent Soviet Cinema of the 1920s – and also admirably suited the political exigencies of post-Revolutionary Russia of the 1920s who needed the propagandizing effect of cinema to spread the message that all workers were pulling together to secure the national identity of the new Soviet republics.

gangster/criminal/detective thriller/private-eye films (*see* **film noir** and the separate entry for **thriller**; *see also* **psychoanalysis**) These different titles point to the difficulty of allocating a single generic name to a set of types of film – a difficulty due primarily, as we shall see, to the shifting contexts in which a particular **genre** finds itself and which dictate that it must change its system of signification.

The gangster film is the one most readily identified as an American genre even though the French film-maker Louis Feuillade's *Fantômas* (1913–14) is one of the earliest prototypes. It is in the contemporaneity of its **discourses** that the gangster film has been so widely perceived as an American genre. This genre, which dates from the late 1920s, came into its own with the introduction of **sound** and fully blossomed with three classics in the early 1930s: *Little Caesar* (Melvyn LeRoy, 1930), *The Public Enemy* (William A. Wellman, 1931) and *Scarface* (Howard Hawks, 1932). In the United States this was the period of Prohibition (1919–33), during which the manufacture, sale and transportation of alcoholic drinks was forbidden, and the Depression (1929–34), when worldwide economic collapse precipitated commercial failure and mass unemployment.

These two major events in the United States's socio-economic history helped to frame the mythical value of the gangster in movies. Prohibition proved impossible to enforce

145

because gangsters far outnumbered the law enforcers. Prohibition, however, brought gangsters and their lifestyle into the limelight as never before. Gang warfare and criminal acts became part of the popular press's daily diet and soon became transferred on to film. In fact, many of the gangster films of that period were based on real life. Gangsterism viewed from this standpoint was about greed and brutal acts of violence – in summary about aggression in urban society. But the gangster movies were not as straightforwardly black and white as that. The male protagonist embodied numerous contradictions that made **spectator identification** possible. If we look to the second socio-economic factor mentioned above, we can find a possible reason for the complex and nuanced characterization of the gangster-hero.

The Depression exposed the American dream which said that success, in the democratic and classless society guaranteed by the American Constitution, was within the reach of everyone. How could this be so when the society was so evidently hierarchized into the haves and have-nots – as the effects of the Depression made so blatantly clear? According to the American Dream, success meant material wealth and, implicit within that, the assertion of the individual. The gangster was associated with the proletarian **class**, not the rich and moneyed classes of the United States. Therefore the only way he (sic) could access wealth and thereby self-assertion – that is success, the American Dream – was by stealing it. Accruing capital meant accruing power over others. In this respect, the gangster embodies the contradictions inherent in the American Dream: success comes, but only at the expense of others. And because the gangster points up these contradictions, his death at the end of the film is an ideological necessity. He must ultimately fail because the American Dream cannot be fulfilled in this cynical way; and he must also fail because he may not show up the Dream's contradictions.

The classic gangster film came into its own with the advent of sound, which reinforced the realism of this genre. Warner Brothers (see **studio system**) was the first studio to launch this genre in a big way with *Little Caesar* and *The Public*

Enemy, and their films are seen as the precursors to the film noir. By 1928 this production company had finally become vertically integrated and entered into full competition with the other majors. It was the first company to introduce sound (1927, *The Jazz Singer*, Alan Crosland) and was now poised, as a major in its own right, to outstrip the other four. Warner Bros became associated with the genre because its production practices had set a certain house style of low-budget movies and short shooting schedules. Cheap-to-make films influenced the product, and so **backstage musicals** and gangster films were the genres to prevail. Warners were also very much associated with social content films, and indeed after the launch of Roosevelt's New Deal (1933–4) became identified with the new president's politics of social and economic reform. **Social realism** and political relevance combined with a downbeat image endowed Warners' films with a populism that made their products particularly attractive to working-class audiences, a major source of revenue for film companies.

The gangster movie, in its naked exposure of male heroics, has been likened to an urban **western**. But unlike the western, where rules are observed, the gangster movie knows no rules, other than death. Central to the gangster film is the antagonism between the desire for success and social constraint. The gangster will choose to live a shorter life rather than submit to constraints. Hence the aura of fatalism that runs through the film. But, as far as the spectator is concerned, for the duration of the film, where violence is countered with violence, where there are no rules, she or he is witnessing an urban nightmare as the **narrative** brings the plot to the brink of a social breakdown.

The gangster film is highly stylized with its recurrent **iconography** of urban **settings**, clothes, cars, gun technology and violence. (In recent years, the film that most fulsomely parodies and yet pays homage to this genre and its iconicity is Quentin Tarantino's *Reservoir Dogs*, 1992.) The narrative follows the rise and fall of a gangster; a learning curve that of course has **ideological** resonances for the spectator – but not before there has been a first pleasure in identifying with

147

the lawlessness of the 'hero'. During his (fated) trajectory towards death, the protagonist's coming to self-awareness – rather than self-assertion, which is what he initially sought through success – functions cathartically for the spectator: we 'learn' from his mistakes. Furthermore, the use of the woman who is romantically involved with the protagonist and in whose arms he (often) dies – as the law enforcers stand menacingly around the prostrate couple, armed to the teeth – positions the spectator like her and therefore as sympathetic, understanding even, to the gangster. And thus, although the 'message' of the film – 'the gangster must die for his violent endangering of American society' – intends to provide the spectator with a sense of moral justification, there is none the less an inherent criticism of American society which says that ultimately the 'little guy' must fail.

The classic age of the gangster movie (1930–4) was brought to a swift halt in an ambience of moral panic. Pressure was put on the **Hays** office to do more than ask the film industry to apply self-**censorship**. In 1934 the Production Code (see **Hays code**), which condemned among other things films glorifying gangsters, became mandatory. Given the popularity of the genre, film companies were not going to give up such a lucrative scenario. Forced to water down the violence, they produced a set of sub-genres: private-eye films and detective thrillers. That is, without dropping much of the violence, they now **foregrounded** the side of law and order resolving disorder. Told to put a stop to the heroization of gangsters and violence, they simply shifted the role of hero from gangster to cop or private eye. Thanks to the Hays code intervention, the seeds for the film noir were sown. The sadism of the gangster became transformed into the guilt and angst of masculinity in crisis of the film noir protagonist. Against the ambiguous urban landscape of some modern American city, the hard-boiled detective seeks justice. The **ambiguity** of the city reflects the ambiguity and complexity of a society where corruption reigns and law cannot easily bring the guilty to justice. Thus the detective is often a private eye, outside 'official' law, a law unto himself. As a marginal, by being outside he can solve the crime and bring the perpetrators to justice (Cawelti, 1992). Traditionally the detective is male; however, recent hard-boiled detective novels written by women (such as Sara Paretsky) have introduced the phenomenon of the woman private-eye detective, who has subsequently found her place on the screen – they are 'just as tough' and as equally poor as their male counterparts. Being poor is part of the construct of the private-eye, pointing to the fact that, even though their methods may be outside the law, none the less they are not in the job for the money. Women in the detective thriller, on the whole, have a more central role than in the earlier gangster movies. They are beautiful and dangerous, often the murderess and therefore subjected to investigation by the detective. (For more on this sub-genre, see **film noir**.)

gaze/look (*see also* **apparatus, psychoanalysis, scopophilia, spectator**)   This term refers to the exchange of looks that takes place in cinema. But it was not until the 1970s that it was written about and theorized. In the early 1970s, first French and then British and American film theorists began applying psychoanalysis to film in an attempt to discuss the spectator–screen relationship as well as the textual relationships within the film. Drawing in particular on Freud's theory of libido drives and Lacan's theory of the mirror stage, they sought to explain how cinema works at the level of the unconscious. Indeed they maintained that the processes of the cinema mimic the workings of the unconscious. The spectator sits in a darkened room, desiring to look at the screen and deriving visual pleasure from what she or he sees. Part of that pleasure is also derived from the narcissistic identification she or he feels with the person on screen. But there is more; the spectator also has the illusion of controlling that image. First, because the Renaissance perspective which the cinematic **image** provides ensures that the spectator is **subject** of the gaze. And, second, given that the projector is positioned behind the spectator's head, this means that it is as if

149

those images are the spectator's own imaginings on screen. Let's see what the theorists have to say about all of this.

Christian Metz (1975) draws on the analogy of the screen with the mirror as a way of talking about spectator positioning and the voyeuristic aspect of film viewing whereby the spectator is identified with the gaze (since the gaze cannot be returned, the spectator is voyeuristically positioned). However, Metz argues, because he (*sic*) is identified with the gaze, this also means that he is looking at the mirror. In other words, through the look, the spectator is re-enacting the mirror stage. In this respect, this identification is a regression to childhood. Raymond Bellour (1975), for his part, talks about the cinema as functioning simultaneously for the **Imaginary** (that is, as the reflection, the mirror) and as the **Symbolic** (that is, as language through its film **discourses**). In both instances, these two theorists assert, the spectator is at the mirror stage and about to acquire sexual difference (in looking into the mirror the boy child sees his sexual difference from his mother). You will note that the female spectator got left out of this debate. It would take the work of the British feminists Laura Mulvey (1975) and Claire Johnston (1976) to take this debate further, closely followed by American feminists. But by the early 1970s the debate around the gaze had got as far as saying that at every film viewing there occurs a re-enactment of the boy child's unconscious processes involved in the acquisition of sexual difference (mirror stage), of language (entry of the Symbolic) and of autonomous selfhood or **subjectivity** (entry into the Symbolic order and, thereby, the Law of the Father, and, consequently, rupture with the mother as object of identification). Thus the spectator is constructed as subject, derives visual pleasure from seeing his self as having an identity separate from his mother, and – aligned with his father whose patriarchal law he has entered – he can now derive sexual pleasure in looking at the (m)other; that is, woman – the female (m)other. (For greater detail see **Imaginary/Symbolic** entry.)

It is not difficult to see that Oedipal desire is indeed a male reality (as opposed to **fantasy**). In fact, Bellour (1975)

150

particularly draws attention to the notion of male representation or characterization in cinema as a reiteration of the Oedipus story (see **Oedipal trajectory**). Cinema actively encourages Oedipal desire. **Hollywood**'s great subject is heterosexuality, the plot resolution 'requires' the heterosexual couple formation. Cinematic practices, then, are a perfect simile for Oedipal desire in that their looking relations structure woman as object and man as **subject** of desire. In so far as the exchange of looks is concerned, in **dominant cinema**, it comes from three directions – all of which are 'naturally' assumed as male. First, there is the pro–filmic event – the look of the camera, with behind it the cameraman (*sic*). Then there is the **diegetic** gaze: the man gazing at the woman, a gaze she may return but is not able to act upon (see **agency**). Finally there is the spectator's gaze which imitates the other two looks. The spectator is positioned as the camera's eye and also, because as spectator he (sic) is subject of the gaze, as the eye of the beholding male on screen. A nice **naturalizing** of Oedipal desire if ever there was one!

Small wonder feminists took up this concept of the gaze and submitted it to some more rigour. As E. Ann Kaplan (1983, 30) says: 'Dominant Hollywood cinema . . . is constructed according to the unconscious of patriarchy; film **narratives** are organized by means of a male-based language and discourse which parallels the language of the unconscious'. And it is for this reason that she makes such a strong plea for feminists not to reject psychoanalysis as a male construct, which it is, but to examine it and by exploring it learn how to counter its effects. The first step was to expose the naturalization of the triple position of the look. Laura Mulvey's vital and deliberately polemical article 'Visual Pleasure and Narrative Cinema' (1975) started the debate by demonstrating the domination of the male gaze, within and without the screen, at the expense of the woman's; so much so that the female spectator had little to gaze upon or identify with (for greater detail, see **scopophilia** and **spectatorship**). The exchange or relay of looks (as it is also known) within film reproduces the **voyeuristic** pleasure of the cinematic

151

apparatus, with all that that connotes of the male child viewing, unseen, his parents copulating (what in psychoanalytic terms is called the primal scene). Visual pleasure equals sexual pleasure, yes, but for the male.

Kaplan (1983) asks 'Is the gaze male?' She comes up with an answer that opens a door for readings against the grain, for readings that do not necessarily show the woman as object of the gaze. While conceding that in mainstream Hollywood cinema it is men on the whole who can act on the desiring gaze, she none the less makes the point that to own and activate the gaze is to be in the 'masculine' position, that is to be dominant. She then goes on to argue that both men and women can adopt dominant or submissive roles. But of course this does not mean any real change, the same binary opposition (masculine/feminine) is still in place. And as Linda Williams (1984) cautions 'When the Woman Looks' (that is, becomes 'dominant') she usually pays for it, often with her life. 'The woman's gaze is punished . . . by narrative processes that transform curiosity and desire into masochistic fantasy' (1984, 85). So this ability to switch roles is not necessarily fortunate – it is even potentially dangerous.

Having recognized the existence of the dominance/submission structure, the next stage, Kaplan (1983) argues, is to question why it is there. What need, whose need does it fulfil? If cinema does mimic the unconscious, then it must reflect what is repressed – latent fears around sexuality and sexual difference. It is for this reason that she advocates investigating film through psychoanalytic methodology as a first step towards 'understanding our socialization in patriarchy' (1984, 34). It is here that the readings against the grain become possible. By exposing how woman is constructed cinematically, this reading refuses to accept the normalizing or naturalizing process of patriarchal socialization (for further detail see **feminist film theory**).

gender (*see also* **feminist film theory**, **Oedipal trajectory**, **sexuality**, **stereotypes**, **subject/subjectivity**) Gender has a socio-cultural origin that is **ideological** in purpose and must be seen as quite distinct from the notions of biological sex and sexuality. Part of the ideological function of gender has been to dissimulate this difference and to see sex and gender as the same. This in turn, as we shall see, makes possible numerous slippages, including the notion of a fixed sexuality. The ideological function of gender 'has been to set up a heterogeneous and determinate set of biological, physical, social, psychological and psychic constructs as a unitary, *fixed* and unproblematic attribute of human subjectivity' (Kuhn, 1985, 52, my emphasis). The ideological function of gender is to fix us as either male or female and is the first in a series of binary oppositions that serve to construct us as male or female. As Kuhn points out, these binary oppositions are socially, psychologically, physically and biologically grounded. Thus the female is economically inferior to the male, is associated more with the domestic than the public sphere, is more emotional, less strong than the male. She is the site of reproduction and not production which is the male domain, and so on. It is clear how this essentialist approach (woman is this/man is that) fixes gender and leads to a **naturalizing** of gender difference (we accept it as 'natural').

During the 1980s, feminist critics marshalled gender relations into the centre of the debate around sexuality. In so doing they sought to problematize gender relations which up until then had not been considered as problematic. In western culture, masculinity had not been seen by men as determined by gender relations. It was free from such considerations, natural and therefore unproblematic. In language, the masculine is the linguistic norm and the female is defined in relation to it (for example, actor/actress). During the 1970s the focus of feminist thinking had been on issues of femininity. But it became clear that, in order to challenge any essentialist reading of the female, gender relations would have to come under scrutiny. Femininity could not be seen in isolation but as part of other categories of difference starting with the vexed issue of gender difference. This, in turn, would finally place scrutiny of masculinity on the agenda.

153

There are, arguably, two dominant debates surrounding gender relations, both of which found a voice first within feminist theory, and subsequently within cultural studies, gay studies, literary and film theory. These debates are rooted in **psychoanalysis** and Marxist materialism. Both debates have contributed significantly in moving the whole question of gender relations into wider arenas and in so doing have helped, rather than hindered, an understanding of how gender is not a simple case of sexual difference as ideology would have us believe, but a series of hierarchical power relations cleverly disguised so as to hide the way in which gender is imposed by force. Furthermore, these debates have shown the importance of historical and social processes with regard to gender relations and have stressed the way in which they can occlude other forms of social determination such as race, **class** and sexuality. These debates have examined how cultural practices reproduce gender ideology and have demonstrated the importance of understanding how the inscription of gender and renditions of sexual difference operate in dominant culture. To understand the construction of gender and how gender ideology functions are vital first steps to countering them, to the uncovering of alternative readings (see **ideology**).

The psychoanalytic debate draws largely on Jacques Lacan's rooting of subjectivity in language (see **Imaginary/Symbolic**). The child, in order to complete its socio-sexual trajectory, must move from the Imaginary illusion of unity with the self and desire of the mother into the Symbolic Order. This order is the patriarchal order and represents social stability, and is governed by the Law of the Father. The father prohibits his son from incest with the mother and the male child obeys for fear of castration by the father. This order, then, is also determined as phallic since sexual difference is marked by the possession or lack of a penis. This approach shows how patriarchal language serves to perpetuate gendered subjectivity and how it is hierarchically deterministic. The male is fixed in language as 'he', but he is also subject of that language since, in entering the Symbolic Order, he joins ranks with his father to perpetuate the Law of the Father.

Conversely, the female in entering the Symbolic Order is fixed by language as 'she'. But because she is not *of* the patriarchal language she is not subject but object. This approach, then, makes it possible to see how sexual relations are rooted in power relations that are linguistically based and as such does expose the ideological functions of gender relations. It does not go far enough, however, for two reasons. First, it smacks of a self-fulfilling essentialism: 'it will always be like this'. Thus psychoanalysis explains subject construction and so to a degree sanctions it. Second, if it does show a way to challenge gender ideology it assumes that it will take place at the level of language. But this is to ignore the other forms of social determination such as history, class and race.

This was the objection of the Marxist materialists. And it is their debate that has served both to balance the psychoanalytical approach and to broaden further the frame of investigation. They see gender ideology as a social and cultural construction that attempts to construct gender upon purely binary lines. The notion of a fixed and gendered subjectivity becomes impossible as a concept, they argue, since it assumes that only one category of difference exists: masculinity and femininity. The impossibility of such an ideological stance becomes clear if one considers that power relations also affect gender relations. Because masculine is the linguistic norm, a first hierarchy imposes itself. In the western world we live not only in a patriarchal world but also a homosocial world. Power is invested in the masculine and, in order for it to stay there, men bond (the political and economic establishment, military forces, just to mention two obvious instances). Why is there such a prevalence of homophobia in society if it does not bespeak this desire to conceal that we live in a homosocial environment? And how far removed is the homosocial relation from the homoerotic one? Racial and class difference are other categories that gender ideology seeks to dissimulate. Why otherwise the prurience with the potency of the Black male or the working-class hero? They are perceived first as their sex and sexuality.

This fixing of a gendered subjectivity attempts to disguise the fact that gender is not as stable as ideology would have it. And it is here that we understand why gender ideology seems so necessary to the safe functioning of a patriarchal world. Gender is constructed not just through language but through social ascriptions and cultural practice. Thus, gender ideology is represented in a variety of cultural practices: literature, mass media, cinema and so on. However, it is the examination of the inscriptions of gender into cultural practices that allows not only for a **deconstruction** of gender ideology to take place but also for other differences to emerge. Where to situate cross-dressing, transsexualism and transvestism if gender is so fixed? What to do with lesbians and gay men? What about masquerade and metaphorical transvestism? The sexual subject or subjectivity here is 'defined' in terms of either otherness (transvestism, etc.) or sameness (homosexuality, etc.) but not difference. Clearly, the binary oppositions start to collapse under such questions.

A film which poses these questions and remarkably exposes the problems inherent in gender ideology is Neil Jordan's *The Crying Game* (1992). Here no sexual identity is fixed. A Black soldier, Jody, posted in Northern Ireland, falls into an IRA trap by letting a woman seduce him. Taken captive, he shows a photograph of his lover, Dil, to his captor, Fergus, with whom he has established a rapport. His lover, also Black, lives in London and works as a hairdresser. After Jody dies, Fergus, who is on the run from his IRA masters, goes to London and seeks her out. He goes to the salon where she works and has her cut his hair. He has already changed his name to Jimmy so the haircut completes the disguise. He is immediately attracted to Dil. However, Dil is a transvestite. But her/his cross-dressing is so successful that she/he dupes all, including Fergus/Jimmy. Only when their relationship gets to the point of making love does Jimmy 'discover the truth'. At first he is horrified and runs away. But Dil seeks him out and their relationship resumes. The IRA masters are closing in on Jimmy, but they also 'know' about his relationship with Dil so her life is in danger. In order to save her, Jimmy disguises Dil into a slimmer version of her/his dead lover Jody by cutting her hair and making her dress in Jody's cricket whites (!).

The point here is that no sexuality, no gender identity is fixed. Jody, it now transpires, was bisexual – the name Jody itself is sexually unidentifiable. Dil (an equally ungendered name) can assume any gender and so is completely unfixable. All is in a fair state of flux. Indeed, the mirroring of the double disguise of Fergus/Jimmy and Dil/Jody makes this point clear. Fergus, until meeting Dil, thought of himself as heterosexual. His attraction to Dil changes his perceptions of his identity. When he transforms Dil into Jody he assumes Dil's earlier role when she completed his disguise as Jimmy. All sorts of levels of play around Fergus/Jimmy's sexuality are encoded into this: metaphorical transvestism (becoming 'Dil'), homoeroticism (fabricating 'Jody'), homosexuality (loving Dil).

Mainstream cinema does not function, however, to undermine dominant ideology. Quite the reverse. But this does not mean that its own functioning as an ideological **apparatus** cannot be unpicked nor that alternative readings to the **preferred reading** cannot be given. Conventional signs of gender fixity can come under scrutiny. **Lighting** and **colour** are but two primary and evident areas for this scrutiny. Lighting, particularly with black and white films, was used differently for male and female stars to point to their gender difference and to a set of binary oppositions. The use of back-lighting to give the heroine a halo effect and front-lighting to bring out the whiteness of her skin was intended to point to the virginal and pure nature of American womanhood. It was used also to point to her fragility when contrasted with the deliberately contrastive lighting used for the hero. This lighting brought out his handsome dark looks, pointing to his strength and manliness. Colour is also used to point to gender difference. Indeed, since the introduction of colour it is noteworthy how the female and male protagonists are shot differently. As Neale (1985, 152) makes clear, colour is used to signify woman's look-at-able-ness, woman as the 'source of the spectacle of colour'. And since the advent of colour there has been an even greater emphasis on the fragmentation of the female body (Turner, 1988, 81). Other conventions play into this strategy of gender differentiation.

Thus **mise-en-scène**, the **iconography** of the **image**, **gesturality** in performance styles, the function of the **gaze**, just as much as lighting and colour, are also conventions at the service of gender ideology that can be questioned. Clearly, if these can be questioned then so too can the idea of a fixed gendered spectator (see **spectator**).

By way of illustrating this notion of questioning, let us take a fairly extreme example, that of cross-dressing. As we shall see, the function of cross-dressing in mainstream cinema can be critically examined in the light of the debates around gender. For a start, why is it that we must not be allowed to be completely duped by cross-dressing? Why in the film *Tootsie* (Sydney Pollack, 1982) must we always be aware of the phallus under Tootsie's dress? How come neither Jack Lemmon nor Tony Curtis is allowed to convince fully as a woman in *Some Like it Hot* (Billy Wilder, 1959)? In other words, why is it that male sexuality must not be completely repressed? What occurs to women who cross-dress? Annette Kuhn's brilliant essay on cross-dressing (1985, 48-73) addresses these questions and provides some illuminating answers. Cross-dressing, she argues, **foregrounds** the performance aspect of dress and problematizes gender identity and sexual difference (1985, 49). Clothing as performance threatens to undermine the ideological fixity of the human subject: change your clothes and you change your sex (1985, 53). Cross-dressing plays with the distance between the outer-clothed self (gendered clothing) and the self underneath (the gendered body). Thus sexual disguise plays on gender fixity, makes it possible to think about it as fluid (1985, 56). With its potential to denaturalize sexual difference (1985, 55), it is small wonder that cross-dressing is so contained in mainstream cinema. Thus we are always in the know. We derive pleasure from knowing/not-knowing: *we* know it is a masquerade but we do not know if or how it will be found out (see **naturalizing**).

It is probably because of its potential to threaten ideological fixity that for the most part cross-dressing occurs only in **comedies** or **musicals** (**genres** that operate in fairly asexual and unrealistic spaces). Given that Hollywood is obsessed with selling gender difference and particularly heterosexuality, it is naturally wary of destabilizing cultural stability. Not surprisingly, then, cross-dressed women for the most part have to suppress desire, or suspend it until their 'true identity' comes out. Not so the male cross-dresser. He can make clear his desire for the woman – indeed it is an essential ingredient to the comedy. What this tells us is that 'lesbianism', as evinced by a male cross-dresser attracted to a woman, is safe. The joke is at the lesbian's expense – because the cross-dresser is so evidently straight. If, however, he is not straight, he threatens the status quo – and for this reason is unlikely to be seen in mainstream cinema (compare for example *Tootsie* with *The Kiss of the Spiderwoman*, Hector Babenco, 1985). A female cross-dresser must suppress her sexuality if she wants to occupy a central position. No other comportment can be countenanced, otherwise she implicitly masquerades as homosexual – which as we have already discussed is one of the greatest taboos of all, and is no position for a woman to play with. To make this cross-dressing completely safe, even though she is cross-dressed, the male protagonist continues to probe and seek to assure himself of her sex. Unlike the male cross-dresser whose disguise within the **diegesis** is taken as a given, the female cross-dresser's disguise then is not. In either case, male or female cross-dresser, it is not gender-bending but gender-pastiche that is on offer. (For further reading, see Butler, 1990; De Lauretis, 1989; Showalter, 1989; Tasker, 1993.)

genre/sub-genre (*see also* **specific genres**) As a term genre goes back to earliest cinema and was seen as a way of organizing films according to type. But it was not until the late 1960s that genre was introduced as a key concept into Anglo-Saxon film theory, even though the French critic André Bazin was already talking of it in the 1950s with reference to the **western**. The debate around genre at that time served to displace the earlier debate around **auteur theory** – even though, in more recent times, genre and auteur theory have become reconciled.

Genre is more than mere generic cataloguing. As Neale (1990, 46 and 48) points out, genre does not refer just to film type but to **spectator** expectation and hypothesis (speculation as to how the film will end). It also refers to the role of specific institutional **discourses** that feed into and form generic structures. In other words, genre must be seen also as part of a tripartite process of production, marketing (including distribution and exhibition) and consumption. Generic marketing includes posters, souvenirs, film press releases, hyperbolic statements: 'the *greatest* war movie ever!' – all the different discourses of 'hype' that surround the launching of a film product on to the market (think of the tremendous marketing strategy surrounding *Jurassic Park*, Steven Spielberg, 1993). Consumption refers not only to audience practices but also to practices of critics and reviewers. Clearly, genres are not static, they evolve with the times, even disappear. Generic conventions as much as genres themselves 'evolve', become transformed for economic, technological and consumption reasons. Thus, genres are paradoxically placed as simultaneously conservative and innovative in so far as they respond to expectations that are industry- and **audience**-based. In terms of the industry, they repeat generic formulas that 'work' and yet introduce new technologies that shift and modernize generic conventions. This same paradox holds true for audiences with their expectations of familiarity as well as change and innovation.

Some general principles   Neale (1990, 63) remarks that the term *genre* is a fairly recent one at least in its reference to popular mass entertainment. Prior to the nineteenth century it was literature or high art that was generic. But with the impact in the late 1800s of new technologies which made popular entertainment more accessible, the position has reversed. The need to commodify mass culture and target different sectors of the public has meant that it is now popular culture that is generic.

Genre is seemingly an unproblematic concept, but this is not the case. And this is particularly evident with film. First, because generally speaking a film is rarely generically pure.

This is not surprising if we consider film's heritage which is derivative of other forms of entertainment (vaudeville, music-hall, theatre, photography, the novel and so on). As Neale says (1990, 62) film constantly refers to itself as a cross-media generic formation. Thus, a clear generic definition cannot immediately be imposed on a film even if a genre can be defined by a set of **codes and conventions** (as in, say, our expectations of a **road movie** or a **musical**). But, because genres themselves are not static and because, as we have just mentioned, they are composed of several intertexts, they are, of course, mutable (see **intertexts**). They rework, extend and transform the norms that codify them (Neale, 1990, 58). As we shall see, attempts at straitjacketing a genre are virtually impossible. Neale (1990, 58) offers a term that helps to clarify this problem when he refers to 'genre texts' which could be seen as distinct from genre itself. Genre would stand for the generic norms and genre texts for the actual film products. In a similar drive for clarity Alan Williams (quoted in Neale, 1990, 62) speaks of 'principal genres' to refer to what he sees as the three main categories of film: **narrative** film, **avant-garde** film and **documentary**. He reserves the term 'sub-genres' to refer to what we term film genres.

A second problematizing factor is that genres also produce sub-genres, so again clarity is proscribed. For example, sub-genres of the **war movie** are Resistance films, certain colonial films, prisoner of war films, spy films (most of which cross boundaries with the **thriller** film genre) and so on. A third factor is that a genre cannot be seen as discrete and ideologically pure (see **ideology**). As Robin Wood (1992, 478) makes clear, genres are not 'safe' but are ideologically inflected. Ideological inflections within film genre find representation through a series of binary oppositions which, among other hegemonic 'realities', reinforce **gender** distinctions. For example, constructs of **sexuality** are based around **images** of the active male versus the passive female, independence versus entrapment (that is, marriage and family). **Sexuality** is constructed also as good/bad, pure/perverse. Furthermore, these are attributes which are most commonly attached to

161

women – thus reinforcing the virgin/whore **myth** of woman. Constructs of society, beyond heterosexuality and the 'desirability' of marriage and reproduction, posit the evils of city versus rural or small town life, the work ethic and capitalism versus fraudulent attempts to get rich quick (that is, good capitalism versus bad capitalism).

Although it is important to be aware of the ideological function of a genre, it is equally important to be aware of the dangers of reductionism inherent in an ideological approach to genre. As we shall make clear in the next section, genres are inflected as much by the capitalist imperatives of the film industry as they are by audience preference and the socio-historical realities of any given period. And, as we have already mentioned, genres evolve and change over the years, some even disappear. This would indicate, as Leo Baudry (1992, 431) believes, that genre serves as a barometer of the social and cultural concerns of cinema-going audiences. Genres have codes and conventions with which the audience is as familiar as the director (if not more so). Therefore, some genre films 'fail' because the audience feels that they have not adhered to their generic conventions sufficiently or because they are out of touch with contemporary times – see what has happened to the **epic**. Alternatively, the nonconformity of a film to its generic conventions can lead an audience to make it into a cult film. Film genre, therefore, is not as conservative a concept as might at first appear: it can switch, change, be imbricated (an overlapping of genres), subverted. Indeed, in terms of product, genre films do get parodied (Mel Brooks's *Blazing Saddles*, 1974, for example). And also, films are read against the grain by spectators.

Some approaches: structuralism, economies of desire and history
Mention was made at the beginning of this entry of the genre debate displacing the **auteur** debate. You will note from the auteur entry, however, that the auteur debate did not disappear. Indeed, it went through several phases, much like the genre debate itself. Gledhill (in Cook, 1985, 58–68) gives a superb synopsis of the debates so I will make only brief mention of the impact of the structuralist debate on genre

theory (see **structuralism**). This debate made two things possible. First, it relocated genre in a much wider set of structures (after it had been through the 'total structure' rites of passage in the 1970s). Second, it reconciled the auteur/genre debates and dissipated the misconception that the two concepts are mutually exclusive.

Until the late 1960s genre had been considered only in terms of codes and conventions and as a system for codifying films. However, it is easy to perceive why such a reading of genre made it a prime site for **structuralist** practice. Metz (1975) argued that genres go through a cycle of changes: 'a classic stage, to a self-parody of the classics, to a period where films contest the proposition that they are part of a genre, and finally to a critique of the genre itself' (Turner, 1988, 86). Although not all genres necessarily follow this dynamic, some do seem to (for example, the western). Most helpful in examining the dynamic nature of genre, however, was the application to genre of Vladimir Propp's description of the narrative as a set of oppositions. An analysis, over a period of time, of the structure of a genre through a set of oppositions made it possible to see where change had taken place – even to the point of being able to discern where inversion occurred. The classic example of this Proppian approach is Wright's (1975) investigation of the western. Wright demonstrates how a first set of oppositions established in the classic western evolves over time so that in more recent westerns there is a completely inverted set of oppositions. For example, what was valued in the earlier western was civilization and strong socialization. It was the hero's function to ensure that those outside society, the bad, weak–willed villains, remained out in the wilderness. Having saved a situation, the hero might well move on, but society and order had been made secure and were seen to be good – so the hero has upheld the values of civil society. In later westerns, the hero is no longer inside society as an upholder of civilization. Rather, civilization is now seen as corrupt and weak. And it is the villains who now live inside society, the hero outside, in the wilderness.

163

Wright makes the point also that these changes reflect social change and audience expectations. Thus, for example, *Butch Cassidy and the Sundance Kid* (George Roy Hill, 1969) says much about the young generation of that time and their desire to be free and on the road. Wright's analysis serves, usefully, to make the point that genres are less about ritual than we might at first believe. As Neale (1990, 58) puts it, conventions of a genre 'are always *in* play rather than being, simply, *re*-played'. Moreover, since genres are about **spectator**–text relations as well as socio–historic relations, it becomes evident that genre must be discussed in relation to the numerous structures that serve not to fix it but to sustain it. The value of structuralism in relation to genre history is, then, that it broke the hold auteurism had on critical thinking about film and showed how structures other than that of the auteur had to be taken into consideration in so far as the production of meaning was concerned.

In an earlier informative essay on genre, Neale (1980, 19) argues that genres are a fundamental part of cinema's machinery. The cinema machinery or **apparatus** regulates the different orders of **subjectivity** including that of the spectator (1980, 19). This means that a genre, just like the apparatus of which it is a part, becomes part of a system that regulates desire, memory and expectation (1980, 55). Neale draws a useful conclusion on the strategies that genres fulfil in relation to the economies of desire (1980, 55). First, genres operate over a series of textual typologies (that is, **war movies**, **westerns**, etc.), what Neale calls 'instances', and so offer the possibility of regulating desire over a determined number of genre texts (that is, there are only so many textual instances possible). In this way they help the industry to control demand and, therefore, production. Second, genres contain the possibilities of reading. That is, generic codes and conventions give a **preferred reading**, thus regulating memory and expectation. This provides the industry with the wherewithal to control 'the effects that its products produce' (1980, 55).

The idea of generic limitation is clear enough: we can actually see how that worked during the heyday of the **studio**

164

system when studios specialized in the production of certain genres and not others – in other words, economies of scale dictated that their production machine was geared to specific output. The second point needs further clarification and can best be explained in relation to four essential component parts of genre: technology, narrative, **iconography** and **stars**. Genres exhibit the technology of cinema. Depending on the genre, different aspects of cinema's technology are put on display. For example, colour and **cinemascope** or wide screen are important technological devices for the western; **science fiction** requires special effects. Not to use them could be to frustrate spectator expectations and therefore not to regulate desire. Indeed the voyeuristic and fetishistic (see **voyeurism/ fetishism**) nature of film technology – the camera as probe and as container of the image – makes possible the fusion of desire and technology into an eroticization of technology (for example, Stanley Kubrick's *2001: A Space Odyssey*, 1968; David Cronenberg's *Dead Ringers*, 1988). Genres also act as vehicles for stars. But stars, too, act as vehicles for genres. As we know, narrative structures and iconography are two functions whereby the audience recognizes the genre. Thus, the star becomes the site of generic **enunciation** – that is, the star now becomes a vehicle for the genre. In this light, genres are the discursive or narrative site in which the star can exhibit her/his potential to fulfil the demands, codes and conventions of a particular genre and perhaps even surpass them (take any Robert De Niro film as an example). Genres are also the iconographic site in which the star can display the body, or have it displayed. On these two counts (narrative and iconography), memory, expectation and desire are all activated within the spectator and regulated by the strategies of performance: we recall the genre and the star and we expect certain things of them and are gratified.

Genres refer to others of their own type and so are both inter-referential and intertextual. This means also that they are inscribed in history. The latest western refers back generically to the other westerns made since the very first one. But there are also social motivations behind the making of a genre: why do westerns or **gangster** movies exist? what needs do they fulfil? So genres are therefore motivated by history and society even though they are not simple reflectors of society (Neale, 1980, 16). For example the Cold War films of the 1950s made on both sides of the 'Iron Curtain' were an attempt to allay fears of insecurity in the face of techno-logical advancement (atomic bombs, space exploration), and to vindicate the merits of either western or eastern block ideologies (capitalism and communism). **Film noir**, as a sub-genre of the thriller, had its heyday in the 1940s, a time when the United States was at war and immediately after-wards. During that time, the role of women had fundamentally changed. They were now at work, part of the social and public sphere. But what of 'their men' over 'there' fighting? What could they expect to find once they got 'home'? Home, the United States, was no longer the safe patriarchal regime they had left behind them. Nor did peace hold much promise given the apparent threat of communism. Film noir, viewed in this light, has been seen as an expres-sion of male insecurity in the face of social change and a growing disillusionment with the lasting efficacy of peace. (For further reading see Grant, 1986; Schatz, 1981.)

German expressionism A film movement (1919–31) so-called after the movement in modern art whose aim was to convey the crude force of human emotion. Edward Munch and Vincent Van Gogh are exemplary forerunners of this movement with their distorted figures and bright colours. It was a deliberately anti-bourgeois movement, challenging the bourgeoisie's concepts of reality and conventional art and was manifested in literature, theatre and architecture as well as painting in Germany and the other German-speaking coun-tries. In film this expressionism produced a highly stylized type of film. Oblique camera angles distorted bodies, shapes and sets. **Settings** were bizarre and incongruous, almost gothic in their look and framing. **Lighting** was similarly highly stylized in its use of heavy contrast creating dramatic

166

shadows. The subject matter was equally surreal and gothic and about unnatural acts or realities – a projection on screen of a character's subjective, and often mad, world. The film that launched the movement was the Austrian Robert Wiene's *The Cabinet of Dr Caligari* (1919). This **horror** film tells the story of a mad and sinister psychiatric doctor who has joined a fair and uses his somnambulist sidekick (played by Conrad Veidt, *the* fetish **star** of this movement) to murder people who cross his path. Although the look of the film is definitely expressionistic (the sets were painted and designed by the expressionist artists Hermann Warm, Walter Reiman and Walter Röhrig), in terms of the **narrative**, with its themes of death, tyranny, fate and disorder, this film continues the long line of German romanticism (as exemplified by the Brothers Grimm and Friedrich Schiller).

This particular film met with huge success upon its release and became an international hit. Germany dreamt that it could revitalize its ailing film industry by capitalizing on this success and set to with earnest fervour to make expressionist films that would export well. *Destiny* (Fritz Lang, 1921), *Dr Mabuse, the Gambler* (Lang, 1922), and *Nosferatu* (Friedrich Murnau, 1922) were hugely successful and allowed Germany to enter foreign markets in a way unknown before. Added to this financial success story was the cultural respect these films obtained for a country that had lost a war and with it considerable international prestige. Fortunes soon waned, however, and by 1924 this type of film was not gaining the recognition and plaudits of its predecessors. Thus, the movement itself more or less came to an end in 1924 although the style lived on for a while in Lang's *Metropolis* (1926) – which, amazingly, was a box-office failure – *M* (Lang, 1931) and Georg Pabst's *Kameradschaft* (1931).

Critics of different generations have tried to read different things into this movement. Some have seen it as reflecting a German mentality on the brink of madness, obsessed with death and ready to encompass fascism. More realistically, these films reflect a desire to escape, even into horror, from the dreadful effects of the economic crisis and inflation. They did leave an important legacy not just in themselves but in the influence they had, particularly in matters of style, on the horror film and the **film noir**. Cross-fertilization with Hollywood came about in part because a number of the German directors, for example Lang and Murnau, went to Hollywood, particularly during the late 1920s and early 1930s.

Germany/New German cinema A movement that had come into forceful being by the early 1970s although its roots go back to the early 1960s when, inspired by the **French New' Wave**, twenty-six young film-makers signed the Oberhausen Manifesto in 1962. Among its proposals it swore a death to the established film industry (*Papas Kino*, daddy's cinema) and the birth of a new cinema that would be international. By 1971, after several years of making short films and some feature films under considerable hardship and resistance from the established film industry, some of the film-makers decided to take on board the distribution and international sales of their films. They formed the Authors' Film Publishers and were particularly successful in selling films outside West Germany (as it then was) but less so within the country.

The names most famously associated with this movement are the film-makers Rainer Werner Fassbinder, Wim Wenders, Werner Herzog, Volker Schlöndorff, Jean-Marie Straub, Hans Jürgen Syberberg and Alexander Kluge – and the fetish film **stars** Hanna Schygulla and Klaus Kinski. Mostly the films are socially and politically motivated as they examine the German-speaking countries' recent past or contemporary scene, and as such are quite influenced by the work of Jean-Luc Godard. Fassbinder's *Fear Eats the Soul* (1974), Kluge's *Strongman Ferdinand* (1976) and the collectively directed film *Germany in Autumn* (1978) take a hard look at contemporary Germany from the point of view, respectively, of racism, fascism and the state of the nation in general including political **censorship**. Herzog's films stand out as different within this movement in that they tend to be in the romantic tradition and historical in their setting (as with *Aguirre, Wrath of God*, 1973).

But that's not the whole story. Also part of the New German Cinema was an important group of women directors, mostly overlooked by histories of cinema – the exceptions being Thomas Elsaesser's book (1989), a special *Jump Cut* issue (no. 27, 1982) and more recently Julia Knight's book (1992). Some fifty-six women directors have contributed films (shorts, experimental video or feature length) to this movement. They, like their male counterparts were in the 1960s part of the new generation of film-makers, mostly born after the Second World War. If the male film-makers encountered difficulties with the establishment, at least not so many doors were closed to them as to the women. In the 1960s it was difficult for women to get into film schools and mostly, if they did get in, they received very little by way of technical training. Unlike their male counterparts they did not 'burst on to the scene' in the 1960s. Perhaps it is their later start that has made them less 'notice-able' to historians than the men. Primarily their output started in the 1970s – a significant date since their emergence coin-cided with the feminist movement in Germany (as elsewhere in the world) – a movement to which many were firmly committed. Jutta Bruckner, Margarethe von Trotta, Doris Dörie, Helke Sander and Helma Sanders-Brahms are just some of the film-makers better-known abroad. The 1970s films tended to focus on real-life issues such as abortion (illegal in West Germany), domestic violence, working conditions and the possibilities of social change. Sabine Eckhard's *Paragraph 218* and *What We Have Against It* (1976–7), Cristina Perincioli's *The Power of Men is the Patience of Women* (1978) and Barbara Kasper's *Equal Wages for Men and Women* (1971) are examples of these tendencies in the women's cinema of the 1970s. Later, in the 1980s, the tendency was to explore the issue of whether there is a feminine aesthetic and a different, even disruptive, way of viewing the world (as in von Trotta's *The German Sisters*, 1981, or Sanders-Brahms's *Germany, Pale Mother*, 1979–80). In any event, by the 1980s, West Germany, as Knight (1992, 13) points out, 'boasted a highly acclaimed women's cinema and a vibrant feminist film culture as part of its new cinema'. (For further reading see Rentschler, 1988.)

gesturality (*see also* **stars**) Stars are **signs** of indigenous cultural codes. Gestures, words, intonations, attitudes, postures – all of these separate one nation's stars from another's, thus affirming the plurality of the cultures. Indeed, it could be argued that the gestural codes, even more so than the **narrative** codes, are deeply rooted in a nation's culture – which is why some stars do not export well. Traditions of performance, then, have national as well as individual resonances and need to be borne in mind when analysing a star's performative style. Gesturality is also tied up with the question of authenticity. We expect certain rituals of performance from our stars, indeed the camera colludes with this process of recognition by giving us close-ups of the particular gesture that authenticates the star in question (*the* Garbo smile, *the* Bette Davis wringing of hands, *the* Clint Eastwood side-mouth delivery of the few lines he ever utters, and so on).

gothic horror – *see* **horror**

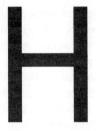

H

Hammer horror – *see* **horror**

Hays code (*see also* **censorship**) In 1922, the Motion Picture Producers and Distributors of America (MPPDA) was established. It quickly became more popularly known as the Hays Office – after the MPPDA's first president, Will H. Hays (1922–45). The MPPDA (later to become the Motion Picture Association of America) was established in response to public outrage at the sex scandals in **Hollywood** and the sexual contents of films. The MPPDA was a bulwark between state and federal governments on the one hand and the film industry on the other. Hays was politically powerful and had a strong moral reputation and his job was to prevent intervention and **censorship** being governmentally imposed. The MPPDA applied pressure on the film companies to control their **stars** and the content of their films – a form of self-censorship which more or less worked until 1930. In 1934, under renewed pressure from the general public (and the moral brigades), the MPPDA produced the Motion Picture Production Code which was to act as a guideline for the industry on taste and decency. However, by 1934 public reaction to the industry's products again became vociferous, particularly at the violence portrayed in **gangster** films, and so the production code became mandatory.

Hegemony (*see also* **ideology**)   A concept devised by the Italian political thinker Antonio Gramsci to describe the winning of consent to unequal class relations. It is a more succinct term for the expression often used in its place: dominant ideology, which within the western world, is taken to be a white, middle-class, male construct. That particular socio-economic group exercises leadership in such a way that the subordinate groups see that it is in the general interest to collude with that construct. The dominant groups (elites) make sense of the institutions through which they govern those not in power by showing that they (as elites) are but representatives of those institutions that govern us all. Thus they use consensual terms such as 'our government, our economy, our educational system'. Those who are subordinate to it, then, are not 'coerced' but their consent and collusion in being so dominated emanates from a desire to belong to a social–political–cultural system, to a nation – to have a sense of nationhood. Mainstream or **dominant cinema** functions consensually in its mediation of hegemonic values (the family, social mobility, etc.) and as such is inscribed within that hegemony. In its **transparency** on the class interests of the dominant group, cinema reveals them as 'natural', therefore unquestionable and desirable.

historical films/reconstructions (*see also* **epics, genre, costume drama**)   Authenticity is the key term where historical films are concerned, at least in terms of the production practices. From **setting**, costumes, objects to use of **colour** (once it was finally introduced in 1952), every detail must appear authentic. Hence the very high costs of producing such films. The **narrative** focuses on a real event in the past, or the life of a real person. Often highly fictionalized, the historical film invests the moment or person with 'greatness'. 'Authenticity' serves a different purpose in this context. In this respect, historical films have an **ideological** function: they are serving up the country's national history before the eyes of the indigenous people, teaching us our history according to the 'great

moments' and 'great men or women' in our collective past
– our heritage on screen.

Hollywood (*see also* **classic Hollywood cinema, studio system, stars**)   Known as the 'dream factory', Hollywood was originally an escape route from the controlling powers over film companies of the Eastern Trust (1909). The climate, the mountains and plains and low land prices of California made Hollywood an ideal and profitable place to set up film studios. Huge studios were built in the Hollywood neighbourhood as well as extravagant mansions for the stars in nearby Beverly Hills. Production techniques were unique. By the 1920s Hollywood was producing 90 per cent of the American film product, and exporting massively abroad so that it was the most important film industry world-wide. By the 1930s the Hollywood studios were totally vertically integrated (controlling production, distribution and exhibition). In the same period, Hollywood was making around six hundred films a year (six times the number of most western nations at that time) and exercised a major influence over American **audiences**. All changed in 1948 when a Supreme Court decision put an end to the vertical integration of the Hollywood studios. Then came television, destined to be Hollywood's major rival. Thought of as an intrinsically American phenomenon, Hollywood is presently losing its all-American status and being bought up by multinational, primarily Japanese, companies. (For details on all these issues see **studio system**.)

Hollywood blacklist   As a reaction to the Cold War, the United States was extremely preoccupied with the Red Scare ('Reds under the beds'), and the fear that its institutions were in grave danger of infiltration from communists or subversives. To track down subversives the House Un-American Activities Committee (HUAC) was established in 1947 and, under the leadership of Senator McCarthy, a witch-hunt was led to unearth people who had associations in any way with communism or subversive activities. People denounced people, people tried to protect people. And Hollywood was no different. It too came under HUAC's scrutiny and Hollywood, to protect itself against government intervention, blacklisted numerous people in the industry who had been accused or denounced as communists or subversives. Hollywood wanted to show that it was patriotic, but many careers were destroyed. Only ten members of the industry (known as the Hollywood Ten) refused to testify before HUAC and were sent to prison for their courage.

Hollywood majors – *see* **classic Hollywood cinema, studio system**

horror/gothic horror/Hammer horror/horror thriller/ body horror/vampire movies (*see also* **genre**, **science fiction films**) This genre has its origins in the late nineteenth-century Victorian gothic novel although it does have earlier antecedents, most famously Mary Shelley's *Frankenstein* (1818), and Dr Polidori's lesser-known *The Vampyre* (1819). It is for reasons of its English and European heritage that this genre is not considered a particularly Hollywoodian one (unlike the **westerns** which are based on and in US history). Even so, Hollywood has a long track record with this genre dating back to 1931, in terms of **sound** movies, like *Dracula* (Tod Browning,) and *Frankenstein* (James Whale). The earliest prototype is Feuillade's *Les Vampires* series (1915–16), starring the music-hall actress Musidora as the notorious Irma Vep (anagram of Vampire). Feuillade's series picked up on the earliest tradition of vampire stories which had women as the predatory beasts. Lesbian desire is **foregrounded** in this series (women/virgins swoon under Vep's advances before succumbing to her) rather than the more stereotypical representation of woman as vamp, the bloodsucking killer of men. This is not, however, the dominant tendency of the vampire film, which tends to centre on the male. There are literary reasons for this male predominance since the earlier vampire stories themselves underwent a regendering. The vampire was last 'seen' as a woman in Sheridan Le Fanu's novel *Carmilla* (1871) and was superseded some twenty years later by Bram Stoker's *Dracula* (1897). The rest is history. With one or two rare exceptions, the agent of vampirism is male (see Kuhn and Radstone, 1990, 243).

The vampire film had its heyday in Hollywood during the 1930s. The **mise-en-scène** at that time was influenced by **German expressionism** – more particularly by the **lighting** and sets of two German silent horror movies, Robert Wiene's *The Cabinet of Dr Caligari* (1919) and Friedrich Murnau's *Nosferatu: A Symphony of Terror* (1922). After the Second World War the vampire film tended to disappear – being replaced by other sorts of alien 'unnaturalness'. However, it made a brilliant and vigorous comeback in the United Kingdom under the name of Hammer Horror films (produced by Hammer Production Limited). These were made from the late 1950s to the late 1960s and starred Christopher Lee and Peter Cushing (for Hammer's policy and strategy see Cook, 1985, 44–7). During the 1970s, the acid-cold dinner-suited vampire hitherto so much in evidence gave way to the acceptable face of vampirism: the vampire became more romantic to the point of deserving love (flower-vampire) and the female vampire made a brief reappearance (as in *Vampire Lovers*, Roy Ward Baker, 1970, *Le Rouge aux lèvres*, 1970, *Vampyres*, 1974, and as late as Tony Scott's *The Hunger*, 1983). By the early 1980s vampire films all but disappeared doubtless due to their unsuitability in the face of AIDS. But Francis Ford Coppola has come back with a *Dracula* (1992) supposedly faithfully based on Bram Stoker's original. And in 1994 Neil Jordan's *Interview with the Vampire* transformed vampirism into a sexual aesthetic not without homosocial/sexual overtones.

Vampire films, however, are not the whole or even the main canon of horror movies. Essentially horror is composed of three major categories: the 'unnatural' (which includes vampires, ghosts, demonology, witchcraft, body horror); psychological horror (for example *Peeping Tom*, Michael

Powell, 1959; *Psycho*, Alfred Hitchcock, 1960); and massacre movies (for example *The Texas Chainsaw Massacre*, Tobe Hooper, 1974). These last two categories (which are also loosely labelled horror-thrillers) are a distinctly post-Second-World-War phenomenon. As for the first category, it is pre-eminently the body-horror movie that is associated with post–1950s, post-nuclear mentalities. Bodily mutation from man (*sic*) to beast and back again had a forerunner in the 1920 film *Dr Jekyll and Mr Hyde* (John Robertson). But by the 1950s mutilation, destruction or disintegration of the body was at the core of horror films conscious of the effects on the human body of real science (the dropping of the atom bomb on Hiroshima and Nagasaki). The Japanese produced holocaust films of these effects (for example *Godzilla*, Inoshiro Honda, 1955), and the Americans did not neglect them either (as with *Them*, Gordon Douglas, 1954). After this incursion into horror-realism this mutation/mutilation re-entered the realms of fiction, though not necessarily losing its political edge, particularly during the 1970s, starting with *The Night of the Living Dead* (George Romero, 1969) and culminating in David Cronenberg's 'body-as-host-to-mutants' films of the late 1970s (*Shivers*, 1976; *Rabid*, 1977; *The Brood*, 1979). During the 1980s and 1990s this type of film has continued to express anxiety of the body (often, but not always male) as a diseased space (*The Thing*, John Carpenter, 1981; *Alien³*, Ridley Scott, 1992). And it is not difficult to read into these films of the last three decades a preoccupation with the politics of health, a fear of invasion of un(fore)see-able substances (cancer, AIDS). This represents quite a shift from the earlier 'unnatural' category of films – especially the vampire films that were so clearly about sexuality and bourgeois conformity.

The psychological horror film and the massacre movies (also known as slasher movies) reveal, albeit in very different ways, a particularly vicious normalizing of misogyny (see **naturalizing** and **psychoanalysis**). Very few fall short of being 'hate-women-movies'. By way of understanding this quite dominant trend in this cinema it is useful to look at what

Richard Dyer has to say, in an article on Coppola's *Dracula* (*Sight and Sound*, January 1993, vol. 3, 1), about vampirism. He makes the point that nineteenth-century vampirism originates in a bourgeois society that had become aware that its concealed dependency on the working **class**, which came about as a result of the industrial capitalist democracy, is now being uncovered. In other words dependence of the stronger on the weaker *as it is about to be exposed* breeds an almost irrational fear which is registered through the body. The vampire assails bourgeois morality by seducing its virgins and drinking their life blood (what chance the bourgeoise surviving the attacks of the mob?). Class issues are sexualized: the brute force of the working class (bestiality) will undo (deflower or destroy) the future of middle-class capitalism. Similarly, in the psychological horror films and massacre movies, male dependence on the female for his **subjectivity** (sense of identity derived from his difference from the female) again becomes registered through the body. Female presence exposes the dependency. Thus penile instruments (phallus replacements or substitutes) such as knives or chainsaws are used to recastrate the phallic woman. Although the woman is hierarchically positioned as weaker, as is the working class, none the less she is finally stronger since she holds the key to male identity through her difference. The killing therefore is an irrational response to the fear of exposure. He must kill her before the dependency is exposed.

Cook (1985, 99) explains that, despite its popularity as a genre, the horror film did not achieve respectability in critics' circles until the 1970s. She attributes this change to the impact of **psychoanalysis** on film **theory**. To have taken the genre seriously prior to this time would have meant dealing with the suppression of the id, a repression of certain unspeakable desires (sexual and psychological). It is instructive that until the psychological thriller of the 1960s, which suggested that the monster is repressed in us and not external to us (although Cocteau's *La Belle et la Bête*, 1946, certainly makes this point), our id, our own Other, took the form of an alien or monster outside of us – as if the genre itself could not face up to the

177

suppression of the id either. This would suggest that the **spectator**, beyond the thrill of being frightened by the terror and violence made visible before her or him, is also attracted by the implicit ambivalence inherent in the genre as to where it should locate sexual and psychological 'abnormalities'. (For further reading see Creed, 1993; Hardy, 1993; Jancovich, 1992; Kuhn, 1990; Paul, 1994; Tudor, 1989.)

iconography A means whereby visual motifs and style in films can be categorized and analysed. Iconography can study the smallest unit of meaning of a film, the **image**, as well as the largest: the generic qualities of the whole film. Iconography then stresses both **mise-en-scène** and **genre**. Iconography also refers to the dress-codes of characters in the film. Iconography is then historically marked – the icons of one period will not be icons for another – and so it points to the shift over time of the look of a particular genre. It also points to social and sexual changes. If there appears to be no change, that too merits investigation.

For illustrative purposes let's take the iconography of the **western** and the **gangster** film. Both genres have their dress-codes and their 'tools of the trade' (Cook, 1985, 60). The horse, the six-shooter, the spurs, boots, waistcoat, neckerchief (etc.) for the western; fast cars, automatic rifles, flashy suits for the gangster film. The western's hero smokes a cheroot, the gangster a cigar. The gangster lives in urban spaces, mostly in dark enclosed environments – at least in the gangster movies of the 1930s and 1940s. Action takes place at night. In more contemporary gangster films action takes place day or night. In the western the hero is mostly moving across vast plains or desert land, arriving in small towns, tying his horse up to the inevitable cross-bar in front of the saloon (or wherever else he is headed). What differentiates these genres primarily is that the western almost 'never changes' – the iconography remains almost the same, even in Clint Eastwood's late films where he does challenge the ideological message of westerns (as in *Pale Rider*, 1985; *Unforgiven*, 1992 – both directed by and starring Eastwood). Gangster movies' iconography does shift with the times. The special **lighting** effects of the 1930s and then 1940s **films noir** are no longer present in gangster films. Even the iconography of violence has 'evolved' – nothing is spared in its mise-en-scène. Part of the reason for this absence of change for westerns has to do with **audience** expectation. The western refers to a time gone by, but it is still part of the United States' cultural history and, as part of the currency for the society for which it works, it must perpetuate the existing iconography. If it does not, it disturbs. Such is not the case for the gangster film. Audience expectation is quite the opposite. Urban violence is very much an everyday preoccupation in the United States, as is gang warfare. This might explain why a new form of the gangster genre, Black gangster films, is currently so popular – speaking as it does to both the reality and the **myth** of Black urban violence (for example *New Jack City*, Mario Van Peebles; *Boyz 'n the Hood*, John Singleton, both 1991).

Iconography has connotative powers beyond the visual imagery. For example, dress-codes reflect more than just the historical period. Gangsters in 1930s films wear very flashy suits as opposed to the detective in his sober suit, connoting **excess** versus order. Women, in particular, 'say' a lot through their clothes: the power-dressing woman, almost masculinized in her shoulder-padded tailored suit (as in 1940 movies); the untrustworthy *femme fatale* in a long slinky gown – preferably with a slit thigh-high – and so on.

identification *see* **distanciation, spectator-identification**

identity *see* **psychoanalysis, spectator-identification, subjectivity**

ideology (*see also* **hegemony** and **class**) Ideology as a theoretical term comes from Marxism. Ideology is the **discourse** that invests a nation or society with meaning. And, since it reflects the way in which a nation is signified, it is closely aligned to **myth**. Ideology, then, is at the interface of language and political organization (the discourse, *logos*, of or on ideas). It is a system of ideas that explains, makes sense of, society. But the 'making sense', as Karl Marx points out, is predominantly the domain of the ruling classes, who assume their right to rule as natural. Thus, according to Marx, ideology is the practice of reproducing social relations of inequality. The ruling classes not only rule, they rule as thinkers and producers of ideas and so control the way the nation perceives itself and, just as importantly, they regulate the way other classes are perceived or represented. From this 'misrepresentation' (that is, the ruling classes' assumption of their natural right to govern and to determine the status of other classes) comes Marx's idea of ideology as false consciousness. But the subordinate classes also act with false consciousness, says Marx, if they accept that their position is natural, that is, if they accept the prevailing ideology as it makes sense of their subordination (see **naturalizing**).

Louis Althusser (1984, 37) takes issue with Marx's notion of false consciousness and makes the point that ideology is not just a case of a controlling few imposing an interpretation of the nation upon the subjects of the state. He suggests that, in ideology, the subjects also represent to themselves 'their relation to those conditions of existence which is represented to them there' (1984, 37). In other words, they make ideology have meaning by colluding with and acting according to it. Why this consensuality? Because of the reassuring nature of national identity. The nation state gives people a sense of identity, status and pride. The state is *their* state, the governing body is *their* indigenous governing body, not some foreign ruler's, and so on. Ideology, then, is a necessity and it is produced 'by the **subject** for the subjects' (1984, 44). Thus society renders ideology material (gives it a reality) and so too do the subjects. Individuals recognize and identify

181

themselves as subjects of ideology. Althusser's central thesis that 'ideology interpellates individuals as subjects' (1984, 44) – that is that ideology constructs the subject, that the subject is an effect of ideology – has had profound implications for the theorizing of **spectator**–text relations. As we shall see, this recognition and identification process by which ideology functions is one that film readily re-enacts.

Ideology infiltrates everyday life and serves the ruling classes, collusion notwithstanding. The rulers are after all those who have produced and control the institutions in which we as subjects function and by which we understand our society. School, the family, the media, are obvious institutions that are permeated by ideology. However, even though dominant ideology serves the ruling classes (who put it there in the first place), ideology is not a static thing nor is it immutable. Within dominant ideology, because it is composed of so many diverse institutions and institutional practices, there are bound to be contradictions. So while ideology is dominant (and despite its 'naturalness') it is also contradictory, therefore fragmented, inconsistent and incoherent. Moreover it is constantly being challenged by resistances from those it purports to govern: groups such as the Black Power movement in the United States, the feminist movement in the western world and some parts of the eastern world, subculture groups like the punk movement – these are just some of the most obvious examples.

Where does ideology fit into a discussion of cinema? Cinema is an ideological **apparatus** by nature of its very **seamlessness**. We do not see how it produces meaning – it renders it invisible, **naturalizes** it. Mainstream or **dominant cinema**, in **Hollywood** and elsewhere, puts ideology up on screen. Hollywood's great subject, heterosexuality, is inscribed into almost every **genre**. So genre is a first place to examine the workings of ideology. The other area is, of course, that of representation (class, race, **gender**, age and so on). Genres function ideologically to reproduce the capitalist system. They are hermeneutically determined, that is, there will always be closure, a resolution at the end. In this respect they provide simple common-sense answers to very complex issues, the difficulties of which get repressed. Already, however, we can see how generic convention is opening itself up as ideologically contradictory. Even though it is seemingly producing meanings that support the status quo, none the less, generic convention is quite distinct from the social reality which it purports to reflect. Social reality does not present easy solutions, life is not 'order/disorder/order restored' as the **classic narrative** would have us believe. But because of the reality-effect which seamlessness produces, the spectator is easily stitched into the narrative (see **suture**), the process of recognition and identification is under way and so too the ideological function of film – which is why generic repetition works so well and we go back again and again to the movies.

Because ideology is contradictory, some films unintentionally show 'disjunctures in their relation to ideology' (Kuhn, 1982, 86), what Kuhn calls structuring absences (1982, 87). In other words, what gets repressed, left out, draws attention to itself by its absence. The much-quoted example is the **historical** biopic film *Young Mr Lincoln* (John Ford, 1939) which the *Cahiers du cinéma* group subjected to a detailed textual analysis (*Screen*, Vol. 15, No. 3, 1972). Although supposedly a historical film about a man of enormous political importance, it is precisely history and politics that are the structuring absences of that film. The question then becomes why? To 'imbue the figure of Lincoln with qualities of universalism – precisely to represent the man as outside history, and thus to elevate him to the ahistorical status of myth' (Kuhn, 1982, 87). Another reason could be the historical context. At the time of its release (1939), the United States was maintaining an isolationist policy as Germany began its war on Europe. It was choosing to stand out of history. So this was not the time for political history lessons, nor for statements (good or bad) about the nation state. As ahistorically positioned, the United States could not 'show' history, the 'reality' of Lincoln's time. Thus, it could not proselytize about the abolition of slavery or show the nation

183

as politically divided (the Civil War). The need for a man (*sic*) of mythic status also points to a nation facing a contradiction or dilemma which it seeks to resolve through the very creation of that myth. Universalism implies being above all conflict. Finally, still within the historical context, the *Cahiers* group's reading examined the film within its domestic political sphere and claimed that it mediated Republican values to counter Roosevelt's Democratic New Deal measures (1933–41) and to promote a Republican victory in the presidential election of 1940 (see **auteur**; and Cook, 1985, 189).

There are, then, films which show the contradictions inherent in ideology. Two of the earliest advocates of applying symptomatic readings to expose the ideological operations in film, Comolli and Narboni, put it succinctly when they say that such films contain an 'internal criticism . . . which cracks the film apart at the seams. If one reads the film obliquely, looking for symptoms, if one looks beyond its apparent formal coherence, one can see that it is riddled with cracks: it is splitting under an internal tension which is simply not there in ideologically innocuous film' (1969/1977, 7). **Melodrama** and **women's films** would seem to be just such innocuous films with their ideologies of romantic love, the family and maternity. But feminist readings against the grain have rendered visible the patriarchal ideology upon which these films feed and exposed the ideological contradictions inherent in that ideology (see **feminist film theory**).

image (*see also* **shots**, **denotation/connotation**, **iconography**) As a basic definition, the image is the smallest unit of meaning in a filmic text in the sense that it is composed of a single shot. The image lends itself to a series of readings depending on the type of **shot**. Volume and size of objects within the shot give a first **denotative** reading; the angle of the camera further informs the meaning or **preferred reading** at a denotative level. When one is considering the image, considerable importance must be given to what is called the **iconography** of the image, for this will yield a second-order or connotative reading.

Imaginary/Symbolic (*see also* **psychoanalysis**, **Oedipal trajectory**, **suture**, **apparatus**, **sexuality**, **spectator**, **subject/subjectivity**) These two key psychoanalytical concepts were first devised by Jacques Lacan to refine Sigmund Freud's theory on the child's unconscious and conscious drives in the development of its subjectivity (sense of identity). Freud described these drives in sexual terms, referring to them as the mirror phase followed by the Oedipal phase. The merit of Lacan's theory was to place the discussion of this development more evidently in a linguistic rather than a purely sexual domain. And, although he focused primarily on the male and paid less attention to the female child, none the less, by frameworking subjectivity within language his theory greatly facilitated feminist theory in general and feminist film theorists in particular when discussing sexual difference and subjectivity (see **feminist film theory**). What follows is a brief outline of the earlier Freudian theory and the nuances brought to it by Lacan – after which its relevance to film theory will be explained.

According to Freud, there is a stage at which the child goes through the mirror phase. The mirror phase is, of course, an abstract concept and it is used to describe a first part of the process of achieving sexual and (for Lacan) social identity. The mirror phase normally occurs when the child is weaned from the mother (so the age of the child varies). Until that moment the child has had an illusory notion of unity with the mother – it feels as one with the mother. In Lacan's terminology this identification with the mother is the first stage of the Imaginary. Subsequently, the mother holds the child up to the mirror. The child now has an illusory sense of identification and unity with that image of her or his self in the mirror. This is the second stage of Lacan's Imaginary and what Freud referred to as the narcissistic moment in the child's development towards a subjectivity (sense of identity). It is at this juncture that the male child perceives his sexual difference from his mother, or the girl child her sameness with the mother. The child becomes aware of the illusory nature of his or her sense of unity with the reflected image in the mirror – it is not one and the same.

185

Simultaneously, it senses the loss/absence of the mother (the loss of the breast, and the ensuing loss of a sense of unity with her).

The male child perceives that he is sexually different from his mother: that he has a penis and she does not (remember she is in the mirror too, holding him up to look at his reflection). According to Freud, the male child perceives the mother as lacking a penis and, as Freud explains, it is that lack that fills the male child with the fear of castration. The mother represents what he could lose. So she is potentially, in Freudian terms, a castrating mother. The female child meanwhile, says Freud, perceiving her sameness with her mother, wishes she had a penis – the notorious penis-envy **myth**. Lacanian psychoanalysis does not challenge the idea of the castrating mother but does make the point that the child's subjectivity is dependent on the presence of the mother, the female other. Lacan is, of course, referring to the male child; he is less clear where the female child is concerned. Thus, male subjectivity is dependent on the (m)other. Without her, the sense of self as subject is not secure.

At this stage, the mirror phase, or the Imaginary, draws to a close. The male child now moves on to the next stage in his development: the Oedipal phase. Sensing his difference from his mother, but still desiring unity with her to assert his identity (that is, his difference, his subjectivity), the male child now wishes to bond sexually with his mother. According to Freud, the father must impose the sexual taboo – forbidding intercourse with the mother. The male child must seek to bond with a female who is not his mother. If he disobeys, the punishment he risks is castration, this time by the father. That is, he could realize his worst fear and become like his mother – what then of his identity?

Lacan gives a different emphasis to this stage, which he refers to as the Symbolic, by situating it in language. At the moment that the male child recognizes his desire for his mother, the father intercedes and imposes the patriarchal law. The father is the third member to enter the reflecting mirror. It is he who represents to the child the authoritative figure in the family. So the child imagines what the authoritative figurehead would say – the father is, therefore, a symbolic father. The father proscribes incest. This taboo is imposed linguistically through the 'No' that is defined by Lacan as the Law of the Father. Because it is based in language, patriarchal law is a Symbolic Order. The male child must then decide whether to obey. To obey means to repress desire. This repression founds the unconscious. However, in exchange for this repression, the male child enters into the Symbolic Order, becomes part of the patriarchal law, joins forces with the father and so perpetuates the Law of the Father (for more detail see **psychoanalysis**). By entering into the Symbolic Order the male child enters into language and becomes subject to it. Where he was prelinguistic in the Imaginary he is now subject of language – patriarchal language. By entering into the Symbolic Order the male child conforms to the Law of the Father, acknowledges his misrecognition of the object of his desire, the mother, and seeks now to fulfil his Oedipal trajectory not through his mother but through a female other. His sexual security depends on it as does his subjectivity (remember that Freud and Lacan concur that the male child's sexual identity is reliant on his sense of difference from his mother, the female (m)other).

The whole notion of identity for the male child is then bound up with the question of sexual difference and language. What of the female child? First, she will never fully relinquish her desire for her mother because there is no recognition of it within the Law of the Father. Second, she will never fully enter into the Symbolic Order because the Law of the Father does not apply to her. She is then doubly poised both sexually and in relation to language. With regard to the first point, we recall that her subjectivity is determined by her sameness with her mother. She is then doubly desiring, first, of her own sex (the mother) and also the male sex (her natural trajectory is to desire the father, and, forbidden that desire by the father, she will then seek to fulfil it by finding a male other). In terms of language, again she is doubly positioned.

187

On the one hand, she is prelinguistic: because she can never be subject *of* patriarchal language she is always outside it. On the other hand, however, she is also *in* the Symbolic Order. Even though she is not subject of language (unlike the male child) but object of the Symbolic Order, she must be there in the patriarchal constructs of sexual identity: her reflection as (m)other must be in the mirror for the male to recognize his difference.

Relevance to film theory These concepts can serve to illuminate, first the **ideological** operations at work within the film **diegesis** and, second, those taking place at the level of the spectator–text relationship. I will deal only with the first point here since the second is amply discussed in the entries on **spectator** positioning and **suture**.

Cinema has been widely acknowledged as revelatory of psychological states and mental experiences since before 1914 by film-makers and some critics. However, prior to the impact on film **theory** of Lacan's re-thinking of Freud, prevailing readings of films tended to be based not so much in psychoanalysis as in sociological and aesthetic interpretations. If psychoanalysis did motivate reading and theorizing on film – as it did in the 1920s and again in the 1940s and 1950s – then the focus, in the earlier period, was on film's ability to translate the workings of the unconscious on to the screen and, in the later period, on the **mise-en-scène** of a populist interpretation of Freud. The 1920s films of the **avant-garde** certainly addressed questions of subjectivity and male dependence on woman to provide that sense of sexual identity, and in that respect predate Lacan. Conversely, the 1940s and 1950s films – many coming from **Hollywood** in the light of the popularization of Freud – produced **narratives** of mother/daughter relationships which portrayed the mother as either self-sacrificing or as controlling and repressive (see Kaplan, 1992, for detailed analyses of mother/daughter relationships). Otherwise film narratives gave potted versions of (usually male) youth's dysfunctionality in the contemporary United States. In this instance it is the neglect of the father or the overpowering nature of the mother which brings about their offspring's tormented state.

However, it is in the new readings of film through Lacan and post-Lacanians (including Lacanian feminists) that we can begin to measure the helpfulness of these key concepts of the Imaginary and the Symbolic. This is particularly the case with recent readings of **film noir** and women's films (see **melodrama** and **women's films**). These readings have been able to demonstrate that the ideological operations at work, for example in the film noir, seek to disguise the fact that the *femme fatale* or 'woman who knows too much' must be punished because she is 'bad'. These new readings suggest also that she ends up victim, not only because she is 'bad' but because the male protagonist has been unable to assert his difference in relation to the female other and has failed therefore to complete his Oedipal trajectory satisfactorily. Woman threatens the male's sense of subjectivity because the assertion of his difference depends on the presence of the woman, of the (m)other reflected in the mirror. Indeed, she may refuse to be in the mirror. In this case the male protagonist often feels obliged to spy on her and follow her in a desperate attempt to make her comply with her assigned role in patriarchy. But that is not the only way in which woman threatens. She also threatens because she is the 'mother'. And the male knows he must move on to the Symbolic Order or face castration, because he may not make his mother the object of his desire. Because that threat points to the instability of his dependence on the 'other', and brings in its wake the apparently concomitant threat of castration, the male adopts two strategies: **voyeurism** and **fetishism**. Voyeurism places the woman under constant surveillance and is a way of controlling her (to the point of sadistic murder, as in *Psycho*, Alfred Hitchcock, 1960). Fetishism commodifies the woman's body by over-investing parts of the body with meaning (breasts, legs, torso in slinky dresses) and thereby denies its difference: the male produces a masculinized female image that is phallic and therefore reassuring. In both instances, he neutralizes the threat. In both, however, we are in the presence of masculinity in crisis and the projection of the male's fears on to women – a **mise-en-scène** of a profoundly

189

ambivalent attitude towards femininity. And it is in this respect that the perceived misogyny of film-makers (most notoriously Hitchcock but there are plenty of others) can be seen in a far more complex and indeed more interesting light. (For further reading on Lacan see Benvenuto and Kennedy, 1986; Grosz, 1990. For psychoanalysis and film see Kaplan, 1990; Penley, 1988 and 1989. For film readings see Fischer, 1989; Kaplan, 1980 and 1992; Kuhn, 1985; Modleski, 1988; Mulvey, 1989.)

independent cinema (*see also* **avant-garde**, **counter-cinema**, **underground film**) This term refers to films made by film-makers independently of the dominant, established film industry. Because they are made outside mainstream cinema practices they tend to be avant-garde and counter-cinematic, and, even if not experimental, they all tend to give an alternative voice to dominant **ideology**. They are mostly low-budget films either privately financed or subsidized by government.

intertextuality Literally this expression means texts referring to texts, or texts citing past texts. Intertextuality is a relation between two or more texts which influences the reading of the intertext. This latter term refers to the present existing text which, in some part, is made up by reference to other texts. Most films are intertextual to some degree – a text referring to other texts, an intertext in whose presence other texts reside. For example, a film may be based on an original text, a novel or play. The shooting style of the film may be painterly, suggesting painted texts to which it might be referring. **Shots** or combinations of shots might refer back to earlier films (by way of a homage to earlier directors). Songs within a film are an intertext. Thus, if the **star** playing the central protagonist is also a well-known singer the **audience** will expect a song. That performance refers to another part of the star persona that has been developed outside of film-making and so refers to another text: the star as singer.

Italian neo-realism   A film movement that lasted from 1942 to 1952. Even though critics credit Roberto Rossellini's 1945 *Roma Città Aperta* (*Rome Open City*) as being the first truly neo-realist film, Luchino Visconti's *Ossessione* (1942, *Obsession*) was really the herald of this movement. And in fact the scriptwriter of Visconti's film, Antonio Pietrangeli, coined the term *neo-realism* in 1943 when talking about *Ossessione*. The main exponents of this movement are Visconti, Rossellini and Vittorio De Sica.

Rossellini called neo-realism both a moral and an aesthetic cinema, and in order to understand what he meant we need to look at the historical context in which that cinema emerged. During the period of fascist rule under Mussolini the type of cinema that was being produced was divorced from reality and concerned only with promoting a good image of Italy. The government had decreed that crime and immorality should not be put on screen. The films primarily produced were slick middle-class **melodramas**, disparagingly called (after fascism) 'white telephone movies'. During the fascist government's control of the film industry, some 'good' did come about: the famous Cinecittà studios (Italy's answer to **Hollywood**) were built and the Italian Film School was established. And, perhaps more significantly, some film-makers took a moral and aesthetic stance against fascism.

Neo-realism, then, owes its existence in part to these film-makers' displeasure at the restrictions placed on their freedom of expression. And it is in this light that Visconti's 1942 film can be seen as the harbinger of neo-realism. But he too had precedents to his own film style. During the 1930s Visconti worked as an assistant with the French film-maker Jean Renoir: a significant apprenticeship, first, because of Renoir's association with the **French poetic realist** movement and, second, because he worked with Renoir on a film that historians perceive as the precursor to the Italian neo-realist movement, *Toni* (1934). Undoubtedly the social and pessimistic realism of poetic realism did cross-fertilize into neo-realism, but the point to make about *Toni* is that it was a film based on a true story of an Italian immigrant worker in France whose passion for a woman led him to murder. Renoir used non-professional actors, shot the film on location and kept to the original **soundtrack**. The film has a grainy, realistic look which the crackling sound-track reinforces in its **documentary** verisimilitude. Visconti's *Ossessione*, while not a true story, was loosely based on an American pulp fiction novel, James M. Cain's *The Postman Always Rings Twice*. The film was shot on location in northern Italy and tells the story of a labourer who becomes obsessed by a woman and agrees to her plan to murder her husband. Having accomplished the deed, she gets killed in a car crash ('naturally'!). With this tale of sordid obsessions and shots redolent with lust and sensuality, Visconti was deliberately defying governmental decrees of cleanliness and propriety on screen. The film was released, but in a heavily censored cut and Visconti did not make another film until 1948, *La terra trema (The Earth Trembles)*. However, the seeds for neo-realism were sown.

By 1943 fascist rule in Italy was coming to an end and in 1944 Italy was occupied by the Allies. The fall of fascism allowed for the truth to be told about the impoverished conditions of the working **classes** and of urban life. And this is precisely what a small group of film-makers did. They rejected the old cinema and its codes and conventions and went for the gritty reality. The basic tenets of this movement were that cinema should focus its own nature and its role in society and that it should confront audiences with their own reality. These principles had implications for the style and content of this cinema. First, it should project a slice of life, it should appear to enter and then leave everyday life. As 'reality' it should not use literary adaptations but go for the real. Second, it should focus on social reality: on the poverty and unemployment so rampant in post-war Italy. Third, in order to guarantee this **realism**, dialogue and language should be natural – even to the point of keeping to the regional dialects. To this effect also, preferably non-professional actors should be used. Fourth, location shooting rather than studio should prevail. And, finally, the shooting should be documentary in style, shot in natural light, with a hand-held camera and using observation and analysis. These are very exacting demands, and in fact only one film meets with all these tenets: De Sica's *Ladri di bicicletti* (1948, *Bicycle Thieves*), although Visconti's *Terra trema* comes very close (it falls short because it is a literary adaptation) as does *Roma città aperta* (which used a mixture of professional and non-professional actors, including *the* fetish star Anna Magnani, and used three small studio sets).

Roma città aperta was based on real events that Romans lived through during the period 1943–4. This was before the Allied forces had arrived in the city and the Germans were still in control. The **narrative** is focused on the goings-on of the Italian Resistance during a three-day period. Money and film stock were extremely difficult to come by; however, it is the difficulties of the production that give this film its authenticity. Rossellini had to use newsreel stock, which gave the images their grainy realistic look. Virtually the whole film was shot in Rome. Resistance fighters die during this three-day period, but the impression given is that we have picked up on their story and that of others in the film and that these people's lives go on once the film has ended.

As film movements go, neo-realism was not particularly short-lived. It lasted ten years, even fourteen if we take into consideration that the last neo-realist film was De Sica's *Il tetto* (1956, *The Roof*). In a sense, neo-realism was officially 'demised' in the early 1950s by the government when it appointed Giulio Andreotti as Director of Performing Arts and gave him extensive powers. Any films giving a bad image of Italy were denied screening rights in Italy and, because he controlled bank loans, Andreotti could go so far as to withhold money from films he considered too neo-realist in **motivation**. The Cold War mood of the early 1950s also contributed to governmental dislike of the **social realism** inherent in these films, which they perceived as politicized and of the left – even though of the film-makers concerned only Visconti was avowedly a Marxist.

Despite its demise, neo-realism had a huge impact on future film-making practices in Europe, the United States and India.

The **French New Wave** widely acknowledged its debt to this movement, and resonances of its style are clearly in evidence in the **British New Wave**. A younger generation of Italian film-makers was also much influenced by the neo-realists' work, in particular Emmanuel Olmi, Michelangelo Antonioni and Federico Fellini. And in India Satyajit Ray's films of the late 1950s are strongly marked with the tenets of neo-realism.

J

jouissance – *see* **psychoanalysis**

jump cut (*see also* **cut**, **match cutting**, **spatial and temporal contiguity**)   The opposite of a match cut, the jump cut is an abrupt cut between two **shots** that calls attention to itself because it does not match the shots **seamlessly**. It marks a transition in time and space but is called a jump cut because it jars the sensibilities; it makes the **spectator** jump and wonder where the **narrative** has got to. Between sequences, the jump cut has quite the reverse effect of the standard cut. The narrative is transposed from one time and space to another without any explanation such as a shot or voice-over. This fragmentation of time and space can either produce a disorientation effect (within the **diegesis** and for the spectator) or put in question the idea that all lived experience can be explained by the comforting cause–effect theory. Those two effects can coexist. Jean-Luc Godard is undoubtedly one of the best exponents of this use of the jump cut (especially in his 1960s films). His characters appear disoriented in a world where reason seems incapable of imposing a logical order on events. Equally, the spectator is disoriented and troubled by the non–causality of the **images** and the narrative.

Within a sequence, the jump cut cuts two shots of the same person together, but neither the **30–degree rule** nor the **reverse angle shot** is observed. Thus, the impression of fragmentation is even more strongly felt, to the point where the brutality of this transition can suggest madness or, at the least, a state of extreme instability (as in Alain Resnais's films – for example *Hiroshima mon amour*, 1959; *L'Année dernière à Marienbad*, 1961). Certain sequences in Godard's *A bout de souffle* (1959) are quoted as illustrations of this disorientation effect. However, Godard (1980, 34) himself puts a question mark on the aesthetic intentionality of his use of the jump cut when he states (but is he pulling our leg?) that his film was an hour too long (as are all first films he adds) and he had to cut. The cuts included a lengthy dialogue scene between the two main characters, Patricia and Michel, as they drive through Paris. The dialogue scene was cut in such a way that one of the interlocutors was cut out and only one remained. The decision whom to cut was taken by tossing a coin (in the end it was Michel, played by Jean-Paul Belmondo, who was cut). Thus, we see and hear only Patricia (played by Jean Seberg) at four different junctures in time and space as this scene unfolds. We first see and hear her and the back-drop is one part of Paris. Then there is a cut, we see and hear her speak again but what she says bears little to no rela-tion to what she said before. Similarly, the backdrop of Paris has changed, showing some other part of the city. We are aware that time and space have moved on and that we have made a jump in time and space. However, nothing in the diegesis serves to explain how we have got there. The shots are edited together without a change in the camera position (the camera is in the back of the car focused on Patricia). Thus, each time we 'come back' to Patricia via the cut, we experience it as a jerky movement – as if the camera has jumped.

lap dissolve – *see* **dissolve**

lighting   In the earliest cinema only natural lighting was used, so most shooting was done in exteriors or in **studios** that had glass roofs or roofs that would open to the sunlight. As **narratives** became more complex (early 1900s) and as increased demand for products meant working to tight shooting schedules, artificial lighting was introduced to supplement existing light. As far as **Hollywood** was concerned, lighting should not draw attention to itself. In some countries, however, lighting was used to aesthetic effect quite early in cinema history. For example, the low-angle and low-key lighting effects so closely identified with **German expressionist** cinema of the 1920s had already been used for emotional effect in Danish films as early as 1910. Lighting for dramatic effect became quite generalized by 1915 for probably two reasons: the predominance of studio shooting, on the one hand, and the advent of the **star** system (both in Europe and the United States), on the other. Lighting was a tripartite affair: key lighting (hard lighting focused on a particular subject), fill lighting (extra lights to illuminate the overall framed space fully) and back-lighting. In a close-up the key-lighting would outpower the effect of fill-lighting. Hence the white highlighting (garish to our contemporary eyes) of the physiognomy of the stars.

197

On the whole **classic Hollywood cinema** frowns upon lighting that is not subordinate to the demands of the narrative, and adheres therefore to quite strict rules of dramatic lighting: the lighting should fit the situation but never supersede it to the point of artificiality or extreme abstraction which, it was believed, would create unease in the audience. A combination of frontal, side- and back-lighting creates a 'natural' light effect. Any one of these types on its own has a distorting effect on 'realism'. They are therefore crucial in considerations of the **mise-en-scène** because they draw attention to themselves. Frontal lighting on its own flattens the image and removes the illusion of three-dimensionality. Side-lighting highlights objects or people in a distorting way, catching only one side of their volume. Back-lighting also distorts, bringing out menacing silhouettes, and is a favourite in **horror** movies. Because they do draw attention to themselves, these different types of distorting lighting are seen as **codes** of certain film styles or **genres** such as **film noir**, German expressionism or **French poetic realism**.

look – *see* **gaze/look, imaginary/symbolic, scopophilia, suture**

M

mainstream cinema *—see* **dominant/mainstream cinema**

matchcutting (*see also* **cut, editing** and **eyeline match**) A cut from one **shot** to another where the two shots are matched by the action or subject and subject matter. For example, in a duel a shot can go from a long shot on both contestants via a cut to a medium close-up shot of one of the duellists. The cut matches the two shots, is consistent with the logic of the action. This is a standard practice in **Hollywood** film-making, to produce a **seamless** reality-effect.

mediation Literally, acting as an agent for conveying information or meaning. Thus a film mediates, but so too do the characters mediate meaning. It is not, of course, a direct transferral of meaning. Meaning is encoded to give a **preferred reading**. Thus films have an **ideological** function in their act of mediation, as do the characters (as an extreme case, think of John Wayne, the **western** and what those two media together mediate about America).

melodrama and women's films (*see also* **genre**) (Major references for this entry include Elsaesser, Mulvey, Nowell-Smith, Harper and Gledhill, all in: Gledhill (ed.) 1987; Feuer, 1982; Kaplan, 1983 and 1992; Cook, 1985; Doane 1982, 1984 and 1987; Modleski, 1988 and 1992) Melodrama's earliest roots are in medieval morality plays and the oral tradition. Subsequently the tradition found renewed favour in the French romantic drama of the eighteenth and nineteenth centuries and the English and French sentimental novel of the same period. These dramas and novels based in codes of morality and good conscience were about familial relations, thwarted love and forced marriages (Elsaesser, 1987, 45). The melodrama coincides, then, with the rise of **modernism** and can be seen as a response to the French Revolution, the Industrial Revolution and modernization. In the early 1800s the post-Revolutionary bourgeoisie sought to defend its newly acquired rights against the autocratic aristocracy – including the *droits de seigneur*. According to Peter Brooks (quoted in Kaplan, 1992, 60), with the emergence of the bourgeoisie as a propertied **class** 'the ethical imperative replaces the tragic vision'. The melodrama focus is essentially on the family and moral values and not the dynastic and mythic deities (as it was in Greek tragedy). Thus, the melodrama – at least in these earliest stages – pitted bourgeoisie against feudalism. Many a tale related the ravishment of the middle-class maiden by the villainous rich aristocrat. In this respect, **class** conflict was repressed sexually and manifested itself via sexual exploitation or rape.

It is important to remember that, as a genre, melodrama also developed alongside nineteenth-century capitalism – and that capitalism gave rise to the *need* of the family to protect, through the inheritance system, the bourgeoisie's newly acquired possessions (including property). The family becomes the site of patriarchy and capitalism – and, therefore, reproduces it. The Industrial Revolution, for its part, placed the family under new and different kinds of pressures. It brought about the separation of the work from the home environment. Middle-class women withdrew from the labour market and working-class women and children entered the factories – leading to an increased urbanization of the proletariat

(Gledhill, 1987, 20–1). This in turn led to the fear of the mob. The middle class felt assailed on both sides, by the aristocracy and the working class. In Europe, in particular, classes became increasingly polarized as opposed to hierarchized as they had formerly been. Since the United States denies, constitutionally, that it has a class structure, it would be fairer to say that its citizens were socio-economically constituted into different groupings. The early melodrama reflects these preoccupations. However, it is noteworthy that the cinematic melodrama, until the Second World War and in some isolated cases until the 1950s, also reflected class concerns.

The end of the nineteenth century marked the birth of the consumer culture. It should be recalled that, prior to the existence of cinema theatres (the first appearing in 1906), one of the venues for cinema was the department store (both in Europe and the United States). The idea was that the film screenings would attract not just **audiences** but also customers. Film, then, was very early identified with consumerism. Because it was seen as an integral part of selling consumer culture, it quickly became evident that it was necessary to address a female audience as much as a male one since the woman is supposedly the arbiter of taste in the home – as opposed to the male who is the arbiter of justice outside the home (as in **westerns** for example). A legacy of this targeting women through the melodrama is the high investment, if not over-investment, in **mise-en-scène** – a surplus of objects and interior décor. But this is not the only reason for excessive mise-en-scène (see below).

It is in its relationship to social change and upheaval that melodrama is such an interesting genre to investigate, particularly since it does not marginalize the woman (as do so many other genres). Having been derided for years, in the early 1970s melodrama finally became recognized, in terms of cultural history alone, as an important generic type to examine. Peter Brooks and Thomas Elsaesser, closely followed by Geoffrey Nowell-Smith, were pioneers, examining the genre from both a Marxist and a psychoanalytic point of view. By the late 1970s, given that it primarily foregrounded the female character, it was also taken on as a genre for investigation by feminist film critics (see **feminist film theory**). Laura Mulvey and Mary Ann Doane led the way, shortly followed by a host of feminist theorists (Kaplan, Mellencamp, Williams, Cook, Gledhill, LeSage, Kuhn, Brunsdon to name just a few).

Melodrama does two things in relation to the social changes and advent of modernization. It attempts to make sense of modernism, and of the family. To take the first point, modernism exposed the reality of the decentred **subject** caused by alienation under capitalism and technological depersonalization (see **modernism**). Melodrama becomes an attempt to counter anxieties produced by this decentring and the massive scale of urban change – hence the 'moral polarisation and dramatic reversals' that structure this genre (Gledhill, 1987, 30). Bourgeois values are felt to be under threat – perhaps because they never had time to become fully established (unlike feudalism) – and, viewed in this light, the melodrama is quite paranoid. Thus, for the bourgeoisie the social, which to them means firstly Victorian morality and what assails it, must be expressed through the personal (Elsaesser, 1987, 29). The everyday life of the individual must be invested with significance and justification (1987, 29). The melodrama as a popular cultural form takes this notion of social crisis and mediates it within a private context, the home (1987, 47). Melodrama, then, reflects the bourgeois desire for social order to be expressed through the personal. In this respect, we can also see how there is an over-investment in the family, how its starting point is in **excess** (Gledhill, 1987, 38). Because the social is internalized, there follows an externalization of the psychic states (Gledhill, 1991, 210). In the process of internalizing the former, the latter are pushed out into the open. And because the melodrama is focused on the family, its conflicts and related issues of duty and love, characters adopt primary psychic roles. They are more ciphers than developed personalities, they lack depth. As Gledhill (quoting Brooks) puts it, 'melodrama of psychology' is what you get (1987, 210). Dramatic action takes place between and not within the characters (210).

Melodrama serves to make sense of the family and in so doing perpetuates it, including the continuation of the subordination of the woman. However, there is a twist. In the melodrama, the male finds himself in the domestic sphere (home). So he is in the site no longer of production but of reproduction. The home represents **metonymically** the site for the **ideological** confrontation between production and reproduction. The alienation of the labour process becomes displaced (the man brings the experience of alienation home with him) and the family – especially the woman and children – is supposed to fulfil what capitalist relations of production cannot (Cook, 1985, 77). The cost of this displacement is repression (sexual) and woman's self-sacrifice. If, for the bourgeoisie of the nineteenth century, melodrama's ideological function was to disguise the socio-economic contradictions of capitalism, then in the final analysis it failed. Because it reproduces the family and within it the displaced sense of alienation, the melodrama makes visible, in the form of familial tensions, the exploitation and oppression differingly experienced by members of the family. Laura Mulvey (1987, 75) argues that 'ideological contradiction is the overt mainspring and specific content of melodrama . . . its excitement comes from conflict not between enemies, but between people tied by blood or love'. Mulvey goes on to say 'there is a dizzy satisfaction in witnessing the way that sexual difference under patriarchy is fraught, explosive and erupts dramatically into violence within its own private stomping ground, the family'. Finally on this point Mulvey (1987, 76) states that for 'family life to survive, a compromise has to be reached, sexual difference softened, and the male brought to see the value of domestic life'. The male is not in his typically ascribed space, in the work sphere, the sphere of action. He is in the domestic, female sphere which is the non-active, even passive sphere. In order to achieve a successful resolution to the conflict the male has to function on terms that are appropriate to the domestic sphere. In this way he becomes less male and in the process more feminized. And this is undoubtedly one of the reasons why the melodrama appeals

203

to the female **spectator**. The female spectator also derives pleasure from seeing the ideological contradictions exposed on screen – they provide her with a mise-en-scène of her own experience. As for the male spectator, pleasure is derived from seeing the contradictions 'resolved'.

In this same essay, Mulvey develops these points by relocating melodrama in relation to sexual difference. She distinguishes between the masculine melodrama and its function of reconciliation and the female melodrama and its function of excess and unresolved contradictions. Because patriarchal culture, in its over-evaluation of virility, is in contradiction with the ideology of the family, the male in the masculine melodrama has to achieve a compromise between the male and female sphere. In female melodramas there is not necessarily a resolution or reconciliation. Indeed it is 'as though the fact of having a female point of view dominating the **narrative** produces an excess that precludes satisfaction' (77). What Mulvey is arguing is that the female point of view often projects a **fantasy** that is, in patriarchal terms, transgressive – and so cannot be fulfilled. Despite the fact that in the end the female protagonist loses out, the female spectator identifies with and gains pleasure from her behaviour during the unfolding of the narrative. The example Mulvey quotes is *All that Heaven Allows* (Douglas Sirk, 1955). A middle-class widowed mother ('past' the age of child-bearing, we are informed) falls in love with her younger male employee, a gardener. But she is only allowed to 'unite' with him once he has been rendered impotent (and bedridden!) by a car accident. For fantasizing too far, she gets only half her man.

Codes, conventions and structures   A first point is that whilst there are arguably two dominant categories of melodrama, (masculine and feminine), none the less as a genre it remains remarkably unfixed in that traces of its generic make-up can be found in many other genres or sub-genres (such as the **musical**, the **thriller** – especially the **film noir** when the hero is pushed to wish his own death – and the gothic thriller of which Hitchcock's work is exemplary). This section makes

204

some general points about melodrama; the next deals specifically with the woman's film and female melodrama.

The melodrama focuses on the victim. The earliest scenarios staged persecuted innocence and the drive to identify the good and the evil. Alternatively, the melodrama offers a triangular set-up, with the male tempted away from his family and all that is 'good' (and usually rural) by an 'evil' temptress or vamp living in a sumptuous city apartment. Variations include the 'fallen' woman, the single or abandoned mother, the innocent orphan, the male head of household as ineluctable victim of modernization. The two main driving forces behind the genre are Victorian morality and modern psychology (Gledhill, 1987, 33). For the most part, melodrama is nostalgic: it looks back at what is dreamt of as an ideal time of respectability and no anti-social behaviour. It dreams of the unobtainable – emotions, including hope, rise only to be dashed, and for this reason the melodrama is ultimately masochistic. Melodrama plays out forbidden longings, symptomatic illness and renunciation (*Imitation of Life*, John Stahl, 1934 has all of these). Before the advent of Freud in a popularized form to the cinematic melodrama in the late 1940s, masochism was displayed in the form of inner violence, the self-sacrificing mother or wife (*Stella Dallas*, King Vidor, 1937; *Mildred Pierce*, Michael Curtiz, 1945). In male melodramas the focus was less on masochism – unless the film was in the **gangster** and subsequently film noir tradition. In the 1930s they focused on the protagonist's unwillingness or inability to fulfil the **Oedipal trajectory**. French male melodramas of that period, in particular, exemplify this, especially the films starring Jean Gabin. The characters played by James Dean in his films of the 1950s certainly reflect an unwillingness to fulfil society's expectations of male adulthood.

The heyday of the melodrama as far as **sound** cinema and **Hollywood** are concerned is from 1930 to 1960. In the period after the Second World War, the genre became revitalized, thanks to the introduction of a popularized reading of Sigmund Freud. Interestingly, by the early 1950s the male weepie really came into its own and the focus now became either the father–son relationship as conflict, or the middle-class husband or lover or father who has succumbed to social pressures. Nicholas Ray's *Rebel Without a Cause* (1955), and *Bigger than Life* (1956), respectively illustrate these representations. In male weepies, through a portrayal of masculinity in crisis, melodrama exposes masculinity's contradictions. The male either suffers from the inadequacies of his father (*Rebel Without a Cause*), or is in danger of extinction from his murderous or castrating father (as in *Home from the Hill*, Vincente Minnelli, 1959), or, finally, he fails in his duty to reproduce (the family), or simply fails his family (*Bigger than Life*; *The Cobweb*, Minnelli, 1955). (For more detail on male weepies see Grant, 1986; Schatz, 1981.) Numerous readings can be offered for this development. First, the change in women's lives that resulted from their entry into the workforce during the war gave them an unprecedented economic independence and created great unease for the returning menfolk after the war. Second, the feeling of paranoia generated by the Cold War, and the failure of post-war American ideology to deliver promises, left veterans wondering why they had fought the war after all. And, finally, the fairly dominant presence in the production of this genre of European immigrant film-makers (Sirk, Max Ophuls, George Cukor, Minnelli) and those outside the Hollywood system (Ray) meant that the contemporary United States, and American masculinity in crisis, could be viewed from a distance.

Ideas about **psychoanalysis** were introduced into film melodrama, where they made women 'safe': women's behaviour was easily explained away through psychology so their psychosis was not a threat. They explained the newly emerging youth culture and revealed the male as victim, trapped in late capitalism. It did not vastly alter the narratives of this genre (so earlier prototypes can always be found), it simply provided open psychological interpretations and **discourses** to explain why clashes, conflicts and ruptures occur in the family. Thus, the father-figure is marked as more dysfunctional than in the earlier melodrama, he becomes

206

transgressive as in madness (*Home from the Hill*) or completely ineffectual and unable to uphold authority (*Rebel without a Cause*). The female is also represented as transgressive, but mostly quite differently from her male counterpart. She puts on display the conflicts at the heart of feminine identity between female desire and socially sanctioned femininity (Kuhn, 1990, 426). Socially sanctioned femininity – that is, motherhood, and integration into the family – means that she has in the end to resume that position or disappear (*All that Heaven Allows*; *Imitation of Life*, Sirk's 1959 remake of Stahl's 1934 film; and, as an earlier example of the disappearing woman, *Christopher Strong*, Dorothy Arzner, 1932). The female rejoins her male counterpart in the melodramas that position her as suffering from some psychotic malaise: the major difference being that only a doctor – or at least a man – can help her resolve it (as in *Marnie*, Alfred Hitchcock, 1956 – with an earlier prototype, *Now Voyager*, Irving Rapper, 1942).

The melodrama is an oxymoronic product in that it has to produce dramatic action whilst staying firmly in place; this gives it an inherently circular thematic structure, hence often the recourse to **flashbacks** (Cook, 1985, 80). This circularity also signals claustrophobia. The melodrama is played out in the home or in small-town environments. Time is made to stand still, suffocating the child, teenager, young adult – especially women. Windows and objects function similarly to suffocate, entrap and oppress. The decor or mise-en-scène become an outer symbolization of inner emotions, fragility or torment (Elsaesser, 1987, 59). And the desire for the unobtainable object or other is just one final nail in the coffin of this claustrophobic atmosphere. The melodrama as a genre turns inwards for drama. So too do the characters, in the form of inner violence which can take the form of substitute acts (Elsaesser, 1987, 56). Aggressiveness by proxy or behaving in a way that is completely at odds with what is desired are forms of displacement-by-substitution (1987, 56). Elsaesser demonstrates how this principle of substitute acts is Hollywood's way of portraying the dynamics of alienation. And he cites (1987, 64) the pattern of *Written on the*

Wind (Sirk, 1956) as exemplary: 'Dorothy Malone wants Rock Hudson who wants Lauren Bacall who wants Robert Stack who just wants to die'.

Melodramas are often highly stylized. Elsaesser (1987, 53) points out that this is to do with the effects of **censorship** and morality codes – very much in effect until the 1960s. In this regard, style becomes used as meaning. In order to convey what could not be said (primarily on the level of sex and repressed desire), décor and mise-en-scène had to stand in for meaning. Curiously here, as Elsaesser (1987, 54) makes clear, the popular cultural form of melodrama has a modernist function. Given that the melodrama seeks to be grounded in **realism** and modernism does not, but wishes to signify through process and form and not content, melodrama, by signifying meaning (repressed desire) through style or form, finds itself making sense of modernism in a most unexpected way (see entry on **modernism**). On this issue of realism and stylization, Nowell-Smith (1987, 73–4) talks about the syphoning off of unrepresentable material into excessive mise-en-scène and refers to it via Freud's concept of conversion hysteria – the return of the repressed ('if I can't have a phallus, I'll have a doric column'). According to Nowell-Smith, the repressed for the woman may well be female desire, but for the male it is the fear of castration. Acceptance of that fear or possibility is repressed in melodrama at the level of the story but reappears, returns through music or mise-en-scène (Nowell-Smith, 73–4). Gledhill (1987, 9) summarizes Nowell-Smith in the following succinct terms: 'if the family melodrama's speciality is generational and **gender** conflict, verisimilitude demands that the central issues of sexual difference and identity be 'realistically' presented. But these are precisely the issues realism is designed to repress'.

The female melodrama and the woman's film   These two obviously overlapping categories of film have been subdivided by various feminists into different types. Doane (1987) defines four: the female patient, the maternal, the impossible love, and the paranoid melodrama. Kaplan (1992), focusing primarily on the mother melodrama, has three typologies:

208

the sacrifice paradigm, the phallic mother paradigm, and the resisting paradigm. Modleski (1992) speaks of hysteria, desire and muteness as behavioural comportments of women in melodrama. Masochism is everywhere, except in the resisting paradigm – and even there it comes close.

Before going into further detail on these matters, it is useful first of all to consider that most of these melodramas were adaptations of female fiction – particularly those films produced during the 1930s and 1940s. This fiction embraces stories in women's weeklies, women's romance novels and women's historical romances. Second, apart from Dorothy Arzner in the United States, most film-makers making these films were men. Given that the novels at least were often very long, scriptwriters and film-makers went for stage adaptations of the fiction if they existed, or reduced the text to a narrative that held together and lasted around ninety minutes. The point here is that this leads to a density of **motivation** which in turns feeds into this notion of melodrama and excess (Elsaesser, 1987, 52). The gender shift from female author to male film-maker or **auteur** also poses some interesting questions. Traditionally, the male is used to working in the non-domestic sphere. Here, however, the film-maker finds himself in the very sphere in which he is expected to reach compromise. Thus, not only is he reproducing the site of reproduction by the very act of filming, he is also functioning on terms that are appropriate to the domestic sphere. This potential feminization of the film-maker makes possible an unintentional opening up of gaps for moments of subversion within the filmic text and subversiveness in terms of spectator pleasure – including, of course, readings against the grain (see Modleski, 1988, and her readings of Hitchcock).

In the female melodramas, also known as weepies or tear-jerkers, the central character is female and what is privileged is a female perspective. We are in the world of emotions not action. The appeal of the woman's film for the spectator (primarily female, but also male) is the mise-en-scène of female desire. It thematizes female desire, it produces, therefore, female subjectivity. It puts woman's *jouissance* (unspeakable

209

pleasure) up on screen. Of course, the genre also destroys her for this, in the end. One way or another she is reinscribed into her 'Lawful' place as (m)other (see **psychoanalysis**). In this respect, it comes as no surprise that women's films function ideologically as repression of female desire and reassertion of the woman's role as reproducer and nurturer. Or, if she is incapable of resuming or assuming that role, then she must stand aside, disappear, not be. The tears come because of the ultimate unfulfillability of desire – the spectator sees only the dream. The dream-fantasy stands for the real (Fischer, 1989, 101).

Women's films then reproduce the scenarios of female masochism (Doane, 1984, 80). As Doane explains, female masochistic fantasies are de-eroticized. This is particularly evident in the impossible love melodrama. Lucy Fischer (1989, 101) examines Max Ophuls's *Letter from an Unknown Woman* (1948) as an example of masochistic fantasy functioning not as a vehicle 'for sexuality but *instead* of it'. The woman in the film, Lisa, is seduced as a young woman by a 'brilliant' pianist. He abandons her, she bears his child. Even though she never meets him again, at least not until it is too late, she devotes her life to him. She lives her life through her fanciful desire for him. An entire life for one night. She survives on imaginary **images** of her lover, thereby substituting fantasy for eroticism (1989, 101). Melodrama reproduces here, unquestioningly, the assumption that a woman's main concern in life is love. The woman in love is the one who waits and as she waits she fantasizes *he* who is absent (1989, 95). Desertion of the man is a frequent trope in this type of melodrama and until recently this meant being left with nothing, including financial support. However, these latter considerations seem never to enter Lisa's fanciful world.

A similar de-eroticization takes place within the paranoid woman's film, often also referred to as the gothic woman's film. This latter typology includes some Alfred Hitchcock vehicles: *Rebecca* (1940); *Gaslight* (1944). In both films the woman is entrapped in the house. Doane (1984) talks of these films as 'horror-in-the-home' melodramas where marriage and murder are brought together in the female protagonist's mind. After an often hasty marriage (why, one wonders?) the wife fears that her husband has murderous intentions – she even hallucinates them. However, because the actual narrative assumes that this fear is based in female frigidity, fear of sex or even rape, it is evidently a male fantasy that is up on screen. As Doane says (1984, 79) this has consequences for the **gaze** and **subject** positioning. She argues that a despecularization and hence de-eroticization takes place because it is supposedly the woman's point of view but it is a male fantasy. This two-way 'gazing' cancels out real **agency** and similarly empties the gaze of knowledge. A first point, then, is that what gets taken away is female desire. But the question arises: does not the female spectator identify with the female protagonist and get commodified up on screen? Thus we too get positioned masochistically. Further, the 'investigating' gaze may well be female but since we too are positioned in it there occurs a doubling of the fear factor (good suspense tactics if you are Hitchcock, though it says much about his own pathologies!). The twist of course, as we have just noted, is that even though she appears to agence the gaze, she does not really understand what she sees. She misreads the information, often because part of the picture is proscribed her. In these films the home becomes the body (Doane, 1984, 72–3) which the female investigates (remember that in film noir it is usually the male who gets to investigate the female body). This is far too dangerous for patriarchy to countenance. Thus, the male contains a secret space of his own, a final space the woman is not allowed to see (1984, 80). This space is either within the house (usually a room in the attic) or mentioned by name (so contained within patriarchal law) – as by De Winter in *Rebecca* when he talks of the boathouse. In the end, although she sees, the woman understands nothing. What she sees will only have meaning once the male respecularizes it for her – as De Winter does at the end of the film.

Women's films point to Hollywood's capacity to produce a female **subjectivity** and then destroy it. This occurs even more strikingly in patient melodramas. Here, female subjectivity, female desire, is rearticulated on to the body as a site of symptoms and illness. Conversion hysteria functions to transfer desire not on to objects or mise-en-scène but on to the body itself. Women suffer from some sort of psychosis. This is induced either by their own sense of guilt, unfulfilled love or transgressive behaviour or by the effects on the psyche of a dominating, aggressive 'phallic' mother. In the first instance, this illness is a 'punishment'. In the second, the illness so cripples the daughter that she cannot entertain 'normal' relations with men. In these films the gaze shifts away from the woman and becomes relocated in the eyes of the male, usually a medical expert who investigates the problem and, naturally, resolves it. Hysteria can cause muteness as in Joan Crawford's case in *Possessed* (Bernhardt Curtis, 1947) and she can be brought to speak only by the administration of a special drug injected (!) into her body by the doctor. We come to understand what traumatized her through the flashbacks which only the all-knowing doctor can induce. Language then is the 'gift' of the father – he *is* the **Symbolic** Order into which she may step at his say-so (see **Imaginary /Symbolic**). (See Doane's excellent analysis of muteness, 1984, 76–7 and Modleski, 1992, 536–48.)

In phallic mother scenarios, as for example in *Now Voyager*, again it is the male, a psychiatrist this time, who releases the victimized daughter and 'castigates' the bad, possessive mother for oppressing her daughter. Even untrained psychiatrists can dabble in the art, as does the rich business-man Sean Connery in *Marnie*, or the detective in *Mildred Pierce*. The point is that they represent the all-seeing, all-knowing male. The point is also that, under the medical or pseudo-medical gaze, the female body is de-eroticized. But, as Doane says (1984, 80), in patriarchal society 'to desexualise the female body is ultimately to deny its very existence'. It is of course also to deny the woman the 'epistemological gaze'; effectively 'a body-less woman cannot see' (1984, 80). The point is, finally, that in this way any threat to male dominance is safely contained.

Quantitatively speaking, the melodrama since the advent of sound cinema is not as prolific a genre as other more identifiably male genres. As we have seen, it has produced a great volume of research into its typologies and to its systems of repression. This entry ends on a brief consideration of two types of resisting paradigms to this predominantly repressive genre (primarily of women's desire, but also on occasion of male sexuality). The first type, convincingly argued and analysed in detail by Kaplan (1992, 149–79), is that of the 'modern' or 'liberated' woman. I will focus on just one of Kaplan's examples: Katherine Hepburn in *Christopher Strong* (1932). The second is that of the Gainsborough costume melodramas of the 1940s, analysed in an exemplary fashion by Harper (1987, 167–96).

The Hepburn vehicle is an Arzner film. But, as Kaplan states, Arzner should not be taken for a feminist. She was, it transpires, 'sympathetic' with her hero (rather bizarrely since he is far from 'strong' and quite a cad really). Kaplan argues that the 'film contains an ironic subversion of its surface meanings' (1992, 150). The story concerns Cynthia (Hepburn), an independent woman aviatrix who falls in love with Strong, a married man. He urges her to give up flying. She succumbs to this request; but she also becomes pregnant by him. She decides in the end not to tell him. She bases this decision mostly on his spineless behaviour towards her after their sexual encounter – basically, he gets cold feet and clings to his wife. Crucially, when she asks him 'what would you do if I were pregnant?', he answers 'it'd be my duty to marry you and take care of you first'. Duty is not the word she wants to hear. She takes the fateful decision to attempt an altitude record, thereby ensuring her death – but not without the possibility of Strong discovering the reason. She writes him a note: 'I am breaking my promise to take no more risks; you will know why when I don't come back. Courage conquers everything, even love'. Having given up her desire for self-fulfilment in the public sphere, she now resumes it and the ultimate recognition of her bravery will be the monument erected in her honour.

Cynthia never perceived love and work as a conflict, but patriarchy does. 'Patriarchy can barely permit the coexistence of female erotic desire and female achievements in the public sphere . . . but even less can it tolerate *motherhood* outside of marriage' (Kaplan, 1992, 156). Significantly, once her affair is consummated she gives up flying. But what is also significant is that both the affair and her pregnancy reduce her power. She becomes progressively silenced, a passive object to Strong's subject. Her only way to reassert her power is to refuse those positionings (so typical of patriarchy). In returning to flying she reasserts her self against the 'prevailing maternal discourse that threatens to confine and reduce her' (157). We would also add that she rejects the patriarchal discourse as well – even if to do so means death at her own hands but on her own terms.

As far as the Gainsborough costume melodramas (made in Britain in 1944–6 in the Gainsborough Studios) are concerned, the standard definitions of melodrama do not operate. There is no family melodrama – only sexual melodrama. These melodramas were based on novels originally written for the middle-class female reader. However, the films were targeted towards a working-class female audience. The timing of these dramas, during the Second World War, was also fairly crucial to their unexpected success. Beyond the attraction of the female and male stars, the costumes themselves were equally a very important factor for audience pleasure. Clothes couponing was introduced in the United Kingdom during the war (primarily to oblige the labour force to move into munitions); thus pleasure was derived from looking at the stylized, sometimes flamboyant, clothing on screen. These dramas also responded to popular taste in another way, given their historical context. They helped women to be patient about the war, gave them a form of escapism from the real conditions of that time of extreme uncertainty (Harper, 1987, 171). These films were about surplus, excess. There was excess in costume, sexual behaviour and class power, including aristocratic surplus (1987, 172). Aristocracy, gypsies, aggressive women alike all 'exhibit exotic energy' which the audience is invited to take pleasure in (1987, 172). Indeed it is primarily women who are the site for this sexual excess and, of course get punished for it in the end. But only after the audience has seen a movie full of female excess. Pleasure in identification indeed! Retribution for excess can wait until the last frames. (For further reading see: Bratton, Cook and Gledhill (eds), 1994; Brooks, 1976; Harper, 1994; Kuhn, 1982; Mayne, 1984; Rosen, 1973.)

metalanguage   *Meta* is Greek for 'with' or 'after', thus metalanguage means literally a language with or after a language, a language that refers *after* another language – that is, a language about a((n)other) language. Metalanguage is an articulated **discourse** on other discourses, that is, a speech act or text about other speech acts and texts. In this respect, film **theory** is a metalanguage: it is a language about film texts or discourses.

However, metalanguage does not refer just to languages that are outside but about another language. Texts and speech acts can produce their own metalanguage from within. An example is a **narrative** that refers to its own narrative procedures: in its self-referentiality it is producing a metalanguage. Film texts when self-referential (pointing, say, to how they are made) serve as their own metalanguage. Embedded narratives – narratives about other narratives in the text – are metalanguages, more commonly termed metanarratives. The effect is often to problematize the **spectator**'s reading of a film. The interrelatedness of the different levels of narration at work in the text function to reposition the spectator – it is not intended for there to be a 'safe' or single reading. Alain Resnais's films are remarkable exemplars of this sustaining of multiple metanarratives, but mainstream cinema of course uses these practices just as widely. A recent film starring Clint Eastwood, *In the Line of Fire* (1993) is an excellent example of embedded narratives. In the film Eastwood is responsible for the security of a presidential visit. However, Eastwood's deadly enemy, played by John Malkovich, reminds him over

215

the telephone how some thirty years earlier he failed to protect John Kennedy from being assassinated. We even see Eastwood embedded in the real footage of the Kennedy assassination (thanks to virtual technology). His enemy threatens to reproduce the same failure, and thereupon hangs the plot. The earlier narrative informs and comments upon the present one: will Eastwood catch his man this time and save the president?

metaphor – *see* **metonymy/metaphor**

method acting (*see also* **motivation**)   A style of acting that was adopted by the Actors Studio, founded in 1947 in the United States and which was derived from the Soviet actor and director Konstantin Stanislavsky. The method was to act completely naturally, to so infuse one's own self with the thoughts, emotions and personality of the character that one became that character. Simultaneously the actor must draw on her or his own experiences to understand what motivates the character she or he is to play. Often the performance is understated – certainly never in **excess**. The method is seen as totally realistic and is best exemplified by the actors Marlon Brando, Montgomery Clift, James Dean, Rod Steiger and Julie Harris (see, for example, *A Streetcar Named Desire*, Elia Kazan, 1951; *From Here to Eternity*, Fred Zinnermann, 1953; *On the Waterfront*, Kazan, 1954).

metonymy/metaphor   According to to the linguist Roman Jakobson, metonymy and metaphor are the two fundamental modes of communicating meaning. Although they are separate in function, they are examined together here as two sides of a coin.

   Metonymy From the Greek *meta*, 'change' and *onuma*, 'name'. So a first meaning is that metonymy is a substitution of the name of an attribute for that of the thing meant (for example, 'crown' for 'queen'). In speech and writing it means the application of a word or phrase that belongs to one object or subject on to another with which it is normally related (for example, the cleaning person is referred to as the 'daily'). Jakobson also includes under the heading of metonymy the term *synecdoche* – that is, the use of a part standing for the whole (for example, the 'sail' for the sailing ship). In this way, metonymy has come to mean, first, a word representing another word (that is absent but implied) and, second, a term that, although only a part of the term to which it refers, stands as meaning the whole of that term. Thus in film metonymy can be applied to an object that is visibly present but which represents another object or subject to which it is related but which is absent. Thus, in Orson Welles's *Citizen Kane* (1941) the toboggan named Rosebud functions metonymically for the mystery that surrounds Kane – an enigma which the journalist tries desperately to unravel. Or the series of objects accumulated on François's mantelpiece, in *Le Jour se lève* (Marcel Carné, 1939) act as metonyms for his past life to which they refer. They stand as substitutes for the events that have pushed him to kill a man (Valentin). The photograph of a cyclist points to the dream he will never fulfil of going with his beloved François to the sea to collect lilac and mimosas. The teddy bear, which was François's but which he took home with him after being rebuffed for his sexual advances, stands for him (François remarks on how the two resemble each other, with one sad eye and one happy). It also refers to the potential happiness (the happy eye) he could have had with François had not fate or his own melancholic defeatism (the sad eye) pushed him to destroy that happiness. Finally, the brooch, which is the token of exchange between his rival (Valentin) and the women he has seduced (among them, François), refers to the reason why he killed Valentin.

An opening or credit sequence can function metonymically for the whole of a film (the **shots** refer to the unravelling **narrative** to come) – for example, the credits and opening sequence of Alfred Hitchcock's *Vertigo* (1958). The credits come up over an extreme close-up of a woman's face. In fact

217

the credits are formed out of spirals that emanate from her eyes! In the opening sequence there is a chase over some rooftops. Two policemen, one uniformed, the other (we assume) a plain-clothes detective, are in pursuit of a third man. The detective loses his footing and holds on for grim life as the policeman returns to help him. In his attempt, the policeman falls to his death. The title of the film refers to this incident, which incapacitates the detective from properly investigating a case involving a woman who hallucinates (remember the spirals) and makes suicide attempts by running to the top of towers intent on throwing herself off. The detective's vertigo prevents him from following her.

Metaphor Literally, the transference or application of a name or descriptive term to an object to which it is not in real fact applicable (for example, to go or be green with envy). Similes are types of metaphors (for example, to run like a rabbit). The metaphor then substitutes the known for the unknown, or rather it communicates the unknown by transferring it into terms of the known. In film, metaphor applies when there are two consecutive shots and the second one functions in a comparative way with the first. Take, for example, a lovers' embrace that is followed by a shot of a train running wildly through a tunnel! The second shot communicates the meaning of the embrace – which is unknown, because unseen, at least to the **spectator** – and transfers it into known terms: speed of the train equals rush of emotion, tunnel equals excitement of penetration, and so on.

With metaphors, we come to understand the unknown through reference to the known, through associative relations. In this respect, metaphors function paradigmatically. That is, the unknown gets explained by being inserted into a paradigm – a framework or pattern, or, in the case of cinema, an image – that is new to it, but known to us. In cinema, an image when used metaphorically functions as a substitute for the real meaning.

Metaphors, then are very visible. They draw attention to themselves. Metonyms are not. And this is why the two terms can be seen as two sides of a same coin. Metaphors render the unknown visible, make the unknown have presence. Metonyms represent what is absent, stand as part of the whole story to which they refer, which is why they work invisibly. In these examples, you can see how metonyms are understood to be such only when the story to which they refer has been told. Until then they seem natural, unnoticeable (see **naturalizing**). However, they are only one part of a whole, and what if another part of the whole were given? Would the meaning of the story to which it refers change? Metonyms, then, are encoded, they organize meaning in a precise way. Metaphors have to be decoded. The juxtaposition of shots has to be read, understood by the spectator.

A useful way of distinguishing metonyms from metaphors is to understand that metonyms work syntagmatically and metaphors paradigmatically. By paradigmatically what is meant is a system of substitution: an **image** will act as a substitute for the real meaning and convey that meaning clearly even though it is a substitute (see above on metaphor). By syntagmatically what is meant is that a story is constructed from the part that is given. For example, the fact that we all experience finishing someone else's half-completed sentence; or, in Hitchcock's *Strangers on a Train* (1951) we know that the broken spectacles belong to the woman who has been murdered: we saw her wearing them earlier, they now refer to her dead body but it is we who supply that part of the story. Metonyms have syntagmatic value: there is a story to which they refer. In film, which works in ways similar to our psyche, metonyms often get the combination of meanings to which they refer played out. Thus, in the example of *Le Jour se lève*, each object gets explained, has a story woven around it through a series of **flashbacks** which the protagonist has as he looks at them, picks them up in turn.

mise-en-abîme This occurs within a text when there is a reduplication of **images** or concepts referring to the textual whole. Chinese boxes or Russian dolls are concrete examples

219

of mise-en-abîme – the outer shell being *the* full-size *real* thing, those within a constant referral to the original. Mise-en-abîme is a play of signifiers within a text, of sub-texts mirroring each other. This mirroring can get to the point where meaning can be rendered unstable and in this respect can be seen as part of the process of **deconstruction**. Some examples taken from films will make these points clear.

The film within a film is a first example of mise-en-abîme. The film being made within the film refers through its **mise-en-scène** to the 'real' film being made. The **spectator** sees film equipment, **stars** getting ready for the take, crew sorting out the various directorial needs, etc. (as in François Truffaut's *La Nuit américaine*, 1973). The **narrative** of the film within the film may directly reflect the one in the 'real' film (as in Karel Reisz's *The French Lieutenant's Woman*, 1981). **Voyeurism** gets ruthlessly mise-en-abîme in Michael Powell's *Peeping Tom*, 1960 – at the same time as it is a mise-en-abîme of cinema itself (for clarification of this point with regard to this film see **foregrounding**). Mise-en-abîme can also function at the level of characterization: objects serve to reflect the basic nature of a protagonist – for example, games or toys collected by and played with by an adult (male) protagonist point to an inherent childishness, to an unwillingness to complete the **Oedipal trajectory**.

mise-en-scène Originally a theatre term meaning 'staging', it crossed over to signify the film production practices involved in the framing of **shots**. Thus, first it connotes **setting**, **costume** and **lighting**, second, movement within the frame. It became endowed with a more specific meaning by the *Cahiers du cinéma* group (established in 1951) who used it to justify their appellation of certain American film-makers as auteurs (for further clarification see **auteur**). Given that these directors were working under the aegis of **Hollywood** they had no control over the script but they could stage their shots and so be deemed to have a discernible style. Mise-en-scène is the expressive tool at the film-maker's disposal which a

critic can read to determine the specificity of the cinematographic work. That is, the critic an identify the particular
style of a specific film-maker and thereby point to it as an
authorial sign.

misrecognition – *see* **psychoanalysis, suture**

modernism (*see also* **postmodernism**)   Modernism is most easily understood as an art movement, although it does have
socio-political resonances as explained below. You will note
from the entry on postmodernism that it is difficult to pinpoint where modernism ends and postmodernism begins. It
is better to think in terms of an overlap between the two –
an overlap that occurs, first, because not all aspects of art
became postmodern simultaneously and, second, because there
is not often full agreement, among critics and theorists, on the
categorizing of a particular cultural artefact. Thus a novel, say,
might find itself being termed a modernist text by one critic
but a postmodern text by another. This happens with the novels of Samuel Beckett. This inability to insert a dividing line
points to the fact that, to a certain – if not considerable –
extent, postmodernism reacts less against the conventions of
modernism than we might believe, even though we are aware
that it must in some way be different, because it comes after
(post)modernism. A useful analogy might be drawn with
industry. We are acutely aware that we could not now be a
post-industrial society if we had not originally possessed an
industrial one. Vestiges of our industrialization remain, but
they no longer carry the same meaning they once did. Take,
for example, the railway systems of the United Kingdom and
the United States. These were once heralded as heroic and
pioneering in their engineering exploits. Now, in the interest
of capital, they have been reduced to a shadow of their former self and face what appears to be permanent decline.
     Modernism finds its roots in the Enlightenment period of
the eighteenth century and man's (*sic*) belief in the supremacy

221

of human reason over all other considerations. It was a period that marked the end, or rather decline, in western society of a theocratic (God-centred) interpretation of the world. As evidence of this belief in the power of human reasoning to understand the world, this age was also termed the Age of Reason. This belief in human reason meant that man (*sic*) could achieve clarity or enlightenment in scientific thought and natural philosophy (that is, natural science – maths, astronomy and physics); he would come to understand the way things really are in the universe and thereby be able to have control over nature and make the world a better place. Jeremy Bentham's enlightened prison reforms came from this spirit – including his concept of the panopticon as an alternative to cell emprisonment and the cruelty of prison treatment. The panopticon was an imagined building wherein everyone could observe everyone else – a using of the **gaze** as a system of total surveillance. But, as we shall see, the outcome of total surveillance is far from benign.

As such, then, the Enlightenment represented an optimistic belief in progress. Science and technology were man's tools whereby he could implement change. Science, or scientific thought, was the only valid thought, and facts the only possible objects of knowledge. In philosophy the task was to discover the general principles common to all the sciences and to use these principles as guides to human conduct and as the basis of social organization. Man controlled nature and all procedures of investigation had to be reducible to scientific method.

Not all was optimism, however. Even during that period some philosophers expressed disquiet at the totalizing effect of this positivist philosophy of science. Thus a strain of pessimism exists alongside the waves of optimism, a pessimism with which we have to concur if we look at the end of the eighteenth century in France and its bloody Revolution, particularly during the Reign of Terror. Writers of that time pointed to the ends to which man could go. The Marquis de Sade's writings are but one extreme. But consider also the 'humane' invention devised to kill off all those who fell victim to the Revolution: the guillotine. Designed by Dr Guillotine to make death more swift and efficacious and therefore more humane, in the end it allowed for the acceleration of executions because it was so swift. In other words, it became an instrument for mass-execution.

The industrial age of the nineteenth century was a logical continuance of the Enlightenment's belief in science and technology, and represents the optimistic strain of belief in progress. Art, however, echoed the other, pessimistic, strain of the Age of Reason and signified as a counter-culture to scientific thought, producing, first, romanticism (a nostalgia for what was lost) and, second, **realism** (a desire to show the mostly negative effects of technological progress). The Enlightenment then produced two strains, and modernism, as its natural heir, continued in the same vein. Modernism perpetuates the belief in scientific research and the pursuit of knowledge. It believed in the positing of universal truths such as progress of which science and technology were its major proponents. However, it also expresses profound disquiet at those beliefs which it perpetuates.

As a movement we could loosely say that modernism begins at the end of the nineteenth century and 'ends' at the end of the 1960s, when **post-structuralism** heralded the arrival, if not the existence already, of postmodernism. Modernism was born as a reaction against realism and the tradition of romanticism. As a movement it is often also termed the **avant-garde**. However, it is truer to say that the avant-garde is part of the modernist aesthetic – not all modernist art is avant-garde, but avant-garde art is modernist. In its vanguardism and perception of itself as an adversary culture, modernism is 'relentless in its hostility to mass culture' (Huyssen, 1986, 241). It believes that only high art can sustain the role of social and aesthetic criticism. In this context, modernism's belief in progress means also a belief in modernization – including belief in the 'perpetual modernization of art' (1986, 238) – a constant renewal of that role of art as critique, therefore.

Modernism eschewed the **seamless** verisimilitude of realism and sought to reveal the process of meaning-construction in art. Formal concerns were, therefore, paramount. To give a couple of examples: with the realist novel, plot and character construction lead us through a **narrative** where the process of narration does not directly draw attention to itself – we are stitched into the narrative (see **suture**); a modernist novel, however, deliberately draws attention to its process of meaning-construction from the very first reading – compare a Jane Austen novel with one by Virginia Woolf for example. In painting, the realist aesthetic seeks to create the illusion of 'truth' before your eyes, as in a Constable painting, say. This illusion starts with the principle of perspective which gives a sense of three-dimensionality. A modernist cubist painting removes perspectival space and transposes the three-dimensions 'truthfully' on to a flat two-dimensional surface. So, in a Picasso portrait, the eyes are flattened out on to the canvas and the nose is placed to the side of the face and not between the eyes. Similarly, just as the novelist draws attention to her or his own mode of meaning-production, modernist painters draw attention to the materials they use (for example Georges Braque, Jackson Pollock). In that respect, modernism is highly self-reflexive (art referring to itself).

As we know, the modernist movement and the avant-garde are closely associated with modernization and as such espoused a belief in its tools and an investment in self-reflexivity that was deliberately counter-illusionist. None the less, not all its proponents were of the optimistic vein. Indeed, many expressed a mistrust of science and technology – even though, as we have already noted, they were inextricably part of it. This mistrust was characterized by a deep pessimism about the modern world and came about as a result of the brutal effects of science and technology on human life in the First and Second World Wars. The wanton destruction of human lives through chemical warfare, bombs of mass extinction, the using of technology and architecture to create a final solution – as in the case of the Holocaust – all these were products of man's reason. It may not be possible to see fascism purely as a formidable crisis of modernist culture (Huyssen,

224

1986, 268). However, it is not impossible to see it as a logical end to the principles of modernism taken to their extremes of anti-humanism. In this respect, then, modernism embraces the two strains evoked in the case of the Enlightenment. The tragedy, and thereby the paradox, for the modernist artist is being part of the culture and age that she or he in some regards despises: 'I am part of this age of self-reflexive formalism that can also build the technology for mass destruction'.

It is here that we can see a first set of paradoxes inherent in this movement (as we would in any movement of course). The paradox is this: in its self-reflexivity and focus on the individual, modernism seems quite anti-humanist. Yet, in its mistrust of science and technology, it has all the appearances of a relative humanism. This is further compounded when we consider that the modernist age evolved alongside, and in certain domains was part of, modern industrial technology. If we consider architecture we can make this point succinctly. Modernist architecture believed in drawing on all materials possible – especially modern materials, such as reinforced concrete – to construct buildings heretofore unimaginable. And yet – and here is the anti-humanist aspect of this movement – in its belief in the functionality of cheaply produced materials and their being put to use in the building of community spaces in a rationalized and standardized fashion (as with Le Corbusier's ideal concrete village) it has left many countries with a legacy of concrete jungles and towers which, though inhabited, are essentially uninhabitable. Belief in the unending potential of its materials led modernist architecture to profoundly anti-humanist practices.

Another, related and important, aspect of modernism that needs explaining is the mood of alienation and existential angst that pervades this movement and which comes about as a result of the climate of pessimism generated by the two World Wars. This mood of alienation emanates from a sense of fragmentation of the self in the social sphere and a concomitant inability to communicate effectively with others. This fragmentation of the self, in turn, raises the question of identity:

225

'who am I in all of this?'. In terms of its manifestation in modernist art, this tendency can best be illustrated by the novel. In the modernist novel, there is no traditional narrative of beginning, middle or end, nor is there an omniscient protagonist. Character definition is mostly, if not totally, absent. In its place, an interior monologue or stream of consciousness explores the subjective experience of an individual. The coincidence of the beginning of this movement with the emerging importance of **psychoanalysis** – especially in the work of Freud – cannot be sufficiently stressed. It is clear that it had a significant impact on modernism and made possible the exploration of the inner self as a way of, if not responding to, then at least describing the effects of alienation on human individuality. In this regard, then, modernism is again very self-reflexive.

Lastly, in its belief in a unified underlying reality modernism once more shows its debt to the Enlightenment. However, as we have already made clear, this leads to conceptual strategies that end up having **ideological** implications in that modernism can help to legitimate structures of domination and oppression – as in the use of technology in war time mentioned above. In this regard, we can perceive other structures that it has served to legitimate – structures of **class**, binary structures around sex and race, and so on. Modernism's belief in a rationalistic interpretation of the world found its acme in the 1950s within critical **theory** and philosophy. The whole concept of **structuralism** can be seen as an attempt to provide a reassuring set of underlying structures that are common to all: be it in the domain of the human brain, language, cultural artefacts, social organization and so on. Structuralism was to have an important impact on film theory and, albeit to a much lesser degree, on film itself. (For further details on this last point see Gidal, 1989.)

If we now consider cinema's place in the modernist period we come up against a first apparent contradiction. Technologically speaking, the camera, although a modernist artefact, is seen as an instrument for reproducing reality and, as such, it is more readily associated with realism than modernism. The entire cinematic **apparatus** is geared towards creating the illusion of reality and it achieves this primarily through the very **seamlessness** of its production practices. Second, as John Orr (1993, 60) points out, the camera as a technological instrument has grown up as part of the culture of surveillance. It is also part of war technology – for example the wide-angle lens, which made **cinemascope** possible, is a product of First World War technology, produced as it was for tanks' periscopes to give a 180-degree view. War technology turns the weapon, the camera, into a gaze. 'Knowledge of the image becomes a form of potential capture of the symbolic, seizure of the **image**, and as we know the human gaze is part of this quest for knowledge, including self knowledge, a form of mirroring' (Orr, 60). The camera is also extremely self-conscious, not just because it reflects itself but also because someone (film-maker, **spectator**) has to watch what the camera is watching for it to have any 'meaning'. In its self-reflexivity the camera has built into it the very essence of modernism which it could exercise provided production practices do not render its operations invisible. But, of course, this is precisely what mainstream narrative cinema does.

However, as with all other art forms, cinema also has its avant-garde – although, unlike other modernist art forms, it is not explicitly hostile to mass or popular culture. In fact, many avant-garde film-makers wanted their work to reach mass **audiences**. Modernist cinema should be seen, therefore, as a global term that includes the work of film-makers of the avant-garde – which, depending on the period in history, can mean **surrealist** cinema, **counter-cinema** and **underground cinema** (to name but the most obvious). The work of these film-makers explores and exposes the formal qualities of film. Modernist cinema, in privileging formal concerns, is one that makes visible and questions its meaning-production practices. In this regard, modernist cinema questions the technology it uses, questions its power of the gaze, questions its power to represent (among other things reality, **sexuality**, and, just occasionally, the female body).

227

It questions *how* it represents and *what* it represents. Modernist cinema turns the gaze into a critical weapon, turns the camera as an instrument of surveillance upon itself, starting with the fragmentation, destruction or **deconstruction** even of **classic narrative** structures.

Modernism focuses on questions of aesthetics and artistic construction. And much of modernist cinema follows that trend. Formal concerns are **foregrounded** over content. Certainly, the **Soviet cinema** of the mid- to late 1920s espoused the modernist principles of meaning being produced from style – principally from **editing** styles. And the **montage** effects, produced by fast editing, of Sergei Eisenstein's films (such as *Strike* and *Battleship Potemkin*, both 1925) influenced other European cinemas of the avant-garde. The avant-garde and surrealist cinema in France of the 1920s is another early manifestation of this modernist trend. Filmmakers of this generation in the early 1920s, were interested in the visual representation of the interior life of a character, that is, a formal rather than narrativized projection on to screen of the character's subjective imaginings and fantasies – dreams even (as in *Fièvre*, Louis Delluc, 1921, about female **subjectivity**, hallucination and desire). This subjective cinema gave way by the mid-1920s to a concern with the plasticity of the medium and its temporal and spatial qualities. The intention was to create a pure cinema where film signified in and of itself through its rhythms and plasticity (for example Jean Epstein's *Photogénies*, 1924; René Clair's *Entr'acte*, 1924). Later in the 1920s a third avant-garde was conceived out of the earlier two modes. Under the influence of surrealism, this avant-garde cinema became interested in how the temporal and spatial properties of film as well as its plasticity could be employed to reflect the workings of the unconscious – especially its suppression of sexual obsessions or desires. Germaine Dulac was, arguably, the first to combine surrealist and avant-garde preoccupations in her film *La Coquille et le clergyman* (1927).

The various American avant-garde movements of the 1930s and 1940s pursued the French avant-garde tradition, particularly in its latest manifestation. Maya Deren's haunting *Meshes of the Afternoon* (1943), is an exemplary film in this respect. Deren stars in this film of paranoid dream fantasies. Her experimental play with time and space is just one way by which she achieves this sense of paranoia. By using a loop system (a single piece of film that is continuously repeated) with a sequence of a young woman fearfully coming down an anonymous street, traditional notions of time and space are eroded – instead we feel the urgency and inescapability of the woman's fear as well as the timelessness in which it is felt.

The American avant-garde of the 1960s to the mid-1970s, when it more or less died out (see also **underground cinema**), tends to echo the middle period of the French avant-garde with its notion of pure cinema. It produced, among other cinemas, a minimalist cinema – where the pro-filmic event (that which the camera is aimed at) is reproduced on screen and becomes, simultaneously, the filmic event (Gidal, 1989, 16). These films were either performed events involving the film-maker or a static camera standing outside a building for hours on end. In each case, time itself is being filmed. Andy Warhol's film *Empire* (1965) is an extreme case. He left his camera running for eight hours outside the Empire State building. Generally speaking, Warhol was more contained, shooting in single takes of thirty minutes (for example *Kitchen*, 1965). The plasticity of the film was also explored by either painting on to it or scratching it and by the use of tight compositional editing (as in Carolee Schneeman's *Fuses*, 1964, which uses all three modalities to provide an intimate portrait of a couple's sexual relationship).

As we indicated above, some modernist cinema, within its formal probings and experimentation, also addressed questions of subjectivity and sexuality. However, it is not a cinema that is readily associated with politics *per se*. That being said, at certain points in history aesthetics and politics do combine to produce a political cinema, particularly in Europe. Jean-Luc Godard, in the mid- to late 1960s talked about making a political cinema politically. By that he meant making

229

political films through a political aesthetics of film. As with the other, primarily aesthetic modernist cinema, the process of meaning-production is exposed. The difference here lies with the non-subjective intentionality of this political cinema and the greater degree of fragmentation of meaning-production. In the first instance we are privy no longer to the inner workings of the mind but, rather, as to how ideology constructs us. In the second instance, fragmentation, the gaps between signifier (the meanings produced) and the signified (the modes and means of production) are opened up and the relationship between the two is exposed. The illusion of realism and its ideological resonances are made transparent. The film as **sign** and as **myth** is deconstructed before our eyes. Godard, Agnès Varda and Margarethe von Trotta are exemplary film-makers of this second tendency of modernist cinema – a political aesthetic cinema, what is also known as counter-cinema.

A summary of episodes in Godard's film *Pierrot le fou* (1965) can serve as an illustration. Near the beginning of the film Ferdinand (alias Pierrot), who is in the advertising business, is obliged by his Italian wife to attend a cocktail party. He turns up with her, an unwilling guest. This seemingly 'innocent' beginning is in fact a reference to the state of the French film industry which, in order to compete against **Hollywood** products, had found itself since the mid-1950s obliged to make co-productions with Italy. At the party, the entire shooting of which is through a pink filter, women and men talk to each other in advertising-speak – but this advertising-speak is also **gendered**: women, therefore, talk in advertising-speak about bras and hair products, men about cars and the like. At one point Ferdinand asks an American film-maker, Sam Fuller, 'what is cinema?' To which he gets the answer: 'film is like a battleground: love, hate, action, violence, death, in a word, emotions'. At the end of this sequence, Ferdinand picks up a huge piece of angel cake and throws it at a woman's face. He then runs out of the party and dashes home only to elope with his former lover of five years past, Marianne, who just 'happened' to be the babysitter for the evening.

Sam Fuller, then, speaks in the same clichés as the rest of the guests. Hollywood is as empty and full of air as the advertising-speak and the angel cake (a cake that is particularly American). Marianne, the symbolic name of France, might just rescue Ferdinand/Pierrot from the 'hell' in which he finds himself. In other words, the French film industry might just be able avoid going under as an indigenous industry in its own right not only by foregoing co-productions with Italy but also by refusing to follow the candy-floss practices of Hollywood (hence the pink filter) and refusing to opt for the safe classic Hollywood narrative (as exemplified by Fuller's clichés) but choosing to run with its own talent (the eloping with Marianne). Of course the ending of the film, where both protagonists die, makes it clear that this is ultimately a utopian scenario. And, as recent figures show, Hollywood is in an even more dominant position in France than it was at the time of the making of this film (in a ten-year period, 1981–91 the American share of the market in France has grown from 35 to 59 per cent).

But Godard does not confine his political statements to the celluloid war. *Pierrot le fou* is his first ostensibly political film and several international crises get similar parodic treatment, namely, the Algerian crisis and the Vietnam War. Let's take a look at the latter. Much later in the film, Ferdinand and Marianne – who have escaped Paris to some idyllic island in the sun – find themselves strapped for cash. They take a boat over to the mainland where they know they will encounter some American tourists and be able to fleece them thanks to their brilliant storytelling skills (incidentally, we have already seen that Ferdinand, at least, is not particularly successful at this). Marianne 'disguises' herself as a Vietnamese woman (she actually looks more like a geisha girl) and Ferdinand dons an American sailor's cap and blazer. Their audience is composed of two or three American sailors. Ferdinand and Marianne then act out a sketch, in a Punch and Judy style, that purports to reflect the United States/Vietnamese conflict. The actual filming of the sketch is very flat, giving the screen a comic-strip appearance and the colour is extremely hard (during his

231

1960s period Godard almost invariably used Eastman Kodak colour, which allows, in its processing, for the primary colours to be singled out, thus giving a harshness and violence to the image). The sketch shows Ferdinand/'Uncle Sam' dominating Marianne/'Uncle Ho' through brutal if senseless words: 'Hollywood, YAH! New York, YAH!' he yells as he swigs at a bottle of American whiskey – Marianne/'Uncle Ho' meantime crouches, cowed, mumbling in pseudo-Vietnamese. Ferdinand/'Uncle Sam' also holds a 'pretend' pistol which he continuously aims at Marianne's/'Uncle Ho's' head.

Godard's prescience is extraordinary here. It is noteworthy that in the mid-1960s, American opinion was very much behind the sending of its troops to Vietnam. By the late 1960s and early 1970s, however, opinion was wavering and was in the end radically changed thanks in part to television coverage. The then president, Richard Nixon, believed that television coverage might galvanize waning support for the war effort. It did precisely the opposite. One image in particular – the holding of a gun to a Vietnamese civilian's head and blowing his brains out – was crucial in turning public opinion against American intervention in Vietnam. The sketch in Godard's film ends with a matchbook made into an aircraft which is on fire and about to crash. Ferdinand holds the matchbook in his hand so that it also looks as if his hand is on fire – a clear allusion to the use of napalm in the war (recalling another image of a little Vietnamese girl running down a road with her back on fire). The Americans, throughout the sketch, respond with stupid, vapid comments: 'Hey, I like that!', 'It's really good' – when the sketch is patently not good but embarrassingly crude.

By placing such an internationally crucial issue within the context of evidently inappropriate cultural texts, the comic strip and Punch-and-Judy vaudeville, and filming it in elemental and violent colour while simultaneously flattening the image, Godard achieves, through visual parody and irony, a far more virulent satire than he would have done through a straightforward polemic. Nor should it be forgotten that the presence of Sam Fuller at the beginning of the film now has a further resonance: Fuller is *the* American film-maker most associated with the spate of Cold War movies made during the 1950s and his films, set in Korea, were notorious for their extreme violence (see **war films**). Viewed in this light, Fuller's words uttered at the beginning of the film now take on different dimensions.

montage – *see* **editing, Soviet cinema**

motivation   Motivation functions on a number of levels within a film to give the **diegesis** verisimilitude; it is a cinematic convention designed to create **naturalism**. David Bordwell (in Bordwell, Staiger and Thompson, 1985, 19) defines four types of motivation which serve to give a film unity and make the film's causality seem natural (see **naturalizing**): compositional, realistic, **intertextual** or generic, and artistic. Compositional motivation means the arrangements of props and specific use of **lighting** if necessary as well as the establishing of a cause for impending actions so that the story can proceed. For example, a dimly lit room in which only one object, the telephone, is highlighted suggests that the phone will ring and the protagonist will answer it and take action as a result. Realistic motivation concerns **setting**. The decor must be motivated realistically. So, in an **historical reconstruction** attention goes into every detail (costumes, sets, objects, etc.) to ensure that verisimilitude prevails. Realistic motivation also includes **narrative** plausibility. Motivation for actions must appear realistic. Generic motivation means that all **genres** have **codes and conventions** which they follow. Thus, although a **musical** is intrinsically not compositionally or realistically motivated, within its own specificity the singing and dancing are entirely justified. Intertextual motivation, the complement to generic motivation, refers to the justification of the story as it relates to the conventions of other similar texts. Bordwell (1985, 19) quotes the **Hollywood** film narrative: 'we often assume that a Hollywood film

233

will end happily simply because it *is* a Hollywood film'. Or the **star** can be the source of intertextual motivation: if she or he is a singer as well, the audience will expect a song. If she or he leads in real life the life she or he is portraying on screen, that again is a form of intertextual motivation (guaranteeing authenticity as well as **realism**). Finally artistic motivation appears when the film calls attention to its own aesthetics. With Hollywood this happens particularly when the technical virtuosity of film-making practices is highlighted, as in the studio spectacular. (For more detail see Bordwell in Bordwell, Thompson and Staiger 1985, 12–23 and 70–84.)

musical (*see also* **genre**, **studio system**) This entry is in two parts: a schematic history of the genre and an overview of its structures and strategies.

History The musical is seen as a quintessentially American or **Hollywood** genre, in much the same way as the **western**. Unlike the western, however, it is a hybrid genre given its descent from the European operetta (particularly Austrian) and American vaudeville and the music-hall. Although Alan Crosland's *The Jazz Singer* (1927) is generally accepted as the first **sound** film, the first all-talking, all-singing, all-dancing musical was the *The Broadway Melody* (1929, directed by Harry Beaumont). It is a noteworthy musical for a number of reasons, not least its title, which generated three further *Broadway Melodies* in the 1930s alone. Noteworthy too because its title refers topographically to a major source of Hollywood musicals, New York's Broadway. Furthermore, it established the tradition of the backstage story as an integral part of the musical. This tradition developed also into the sub-genre of the backstage musical – of which *Singin' in the Rain* (Stanley Donen, 1952) is arguably the best exemplar. *The Broadway Melody* also brought the lyricist Arthur Freed to the attention of the MGM mogul Louis B. Mayer who by the mid-1930s had finally agreed to give him a relatively free rein as producer. Freed was responsible for a major shift in the conventions of the musical, which during the late 1920s and early 1930s had been fairly conservative. He was also responsible for convincing MGM of the need for a stable of musical **stars**.

MGM is the studio most readily associated with this genre. However, one of the first all-time great musical pairings – Fred Astaire and Ginger Rogers – was with RKO. In 1933 Astaire and Rogers were paired up as a supporting team to the main story in *Flying Down to Rio*. **Audience** response was such that they became an overnight success, and during the 1930s they were regularly RKO's best box-office hit and the ideal romance couple (at least on screen). Traditionally they played the roles of the man-about-town sophisticate and the girl next door and their story was set in contemporary times. The other famous romance pair of that period, Jeannette MacDonald and Nelson Eddy, figured for the first time together in 1935 in an MGM production, *Naughty Marietta* (directed by Woody Van Dyke). This romantic couple appeared mostly in costume operettas and often the roles were reversed, MacDonald being the woman with **class** and Eddy the penniless prisoner (as in their first film) or in the role of some kind of out-of-society type (as in *New Moon*, 1940).

Musicals at this time had a fairly naive plot and were primarily perceived as vehicles for song and dance. However, it is worth considering just what this means. First of all, the **narrative** did incline towards simplicity – and was based on the Cinderella/Prince Charming **myth**. Often it was a case of 'boy meets girl, boy hates girl/girl hates boy', but because there was such an undoubted attraction they come together in the end: 'boy gets girl'. It is in this respect that, as Richard Dyer (*The Movie 75*, 1981, 1484) says, the musical points to its generic and **ideological** function as a 'gospel of happiness'. But, as far as the singing and dancing were concerned, routines and performance were a far more complex affair. Some of the greatest names from Broadway – lyricists and composers – were brought in by Hollywood: Cole Porter, Irving Berlin, Ira and George Gershwin, Jerome Kern, Rodgers and Hart, a bit later Oscar Hammerstein. The reason for bringing such talent in was twofold. In the early 1930s

235

the musical genre was experiencing a slump, much like the rest of Hollywood, because of the Depression. To bring some excitement and panache into the musical and thereby attract audiences, Hollywood decided to buy in Broadway hits. In referring to Broadway, Hollywood also sought to bring artistic clout to its own productions.

These great names of American popular music did much in the 1930s to shape the look of the musical. At first, because they were commissioned to package songs for the films, the song and dance routines were worked through more like items in a review show. The songs paid little attention to plot and characterization. Indeed, characters seemed to burst into song and dance in an artificial and arbitrary way. Alternatively, the breaking into song and dance was given a rational explanation – for example, tapping a rhythm or something tapping a rhythm, or using a specific word or expression that necessarily introduces a song. However, once Fred Astaire had broken into the big time this changed and, because of his meticulous planning of his dance routines, composers were brought into closer alliance with the actual production practices. For example, Astaire's work in collaboration with Irving Berlin and Jerome Kern certainly produced some of the best musicals of the late 1930s. Astaire insisted on full **shot** photography with no cutting away for his dance routines, whether solo or with Ginger Rogers (with whom he made nine films during the period 1933–9). This meant that music and choreography had to be worked out in the minutest detail. Music and dance informed each other (as for example in *Top Hat*, 1935; *Follow the Fleet*, 1936; *Carefree*, 1938).

The other move in the 1930s to counter the slump brought on by the Depression came with the highly stylized films of Busby Berkeley – the master of drill precision with his fanciful and abstract approach to dance routines using hundreds of chorus 'girls' to create geometrical patterns through their movements under the eye of the camera. His 1930s films (made for Warner Brothers) were almost pure spectacle with little attention to narrative but full focus on the capacity of the human form to exude an erotic sensuality. To this effect he used a single camera that roved over the human formations through either tracking or crane shots. Berkeley was the first to put female nudity into the musical (*Roman Scandals* 1933); he is equally famous for his 'crotch shots' (*Gold Diggers of 1933*). As Altman (1989, 257) puts it, Berkeley offered sex through the **gaze** – with the camera acting as the eye – in his spectacles 'the show's power (was mainly) identified with the woman's lure'.

By the end of the 1930s the musical was on the wane again. Ginger Rogers had split from Fred; MacDonald and Eddy were very faded stars indeed. Several strategies were adopted. At MGM, thanks to Freed's insistence that talent should be nurtured amongst the contract actors and thanks too to his success in producing *The Wizard of Oz* (Victor Fleming, 1939), a new musical formula was introduced. This combined youth and music in the form of the 'kids putting on a show' musical. The star vehicles were Judy Garland (launched by *The Wizard of Oz*) and Mickey Rooney (already a star for his Andy Hardy series). Together they made four musicals in this vein (*Babes in Arms*, 1939; *Strike up the Band*, 1940; *Babes on Broadway*, 1941; *Girl Crazy*, 1943). At Universal, child actors were used as well, but this time as a vehicle for bringing popular classics into the musical arena. Thus Deanna Durbin sang her way through *One Hundred Men and a Girl* (1937) and managed to persuade the great conductor Stokowski to conduct an out-of-work orchestra. By the 1940s other, new formulas were introduced. To the classic musicals and putting-on-a-show musicals were added composer biographies (*Yankee Doodle Dandy*, 1942; *Rhapsody in Blue*, 1945; *Till the Clouds Roll By*, 1946; *Night and Day*, 1946; *Words and Music*, 1948) and biographical musicals of 'stars' with a show-biz background (*Lillian Russell*, 1940; *Incendiary Blonde*, *The Dolly Sisters*, both 1945).

Of these three traditions it is the last, the 'life-stories' of performers, that fared best in terms of continuation. They went on well into the 1950s and indeed into the 1970s as with *A Star is Born* (1954); *I'll Cry Tomorrow* (1955); *Lady Sings the Blues* (1972); *The Rose* (1979). What is interesting

237

is that it is mostly the biography of female performers that 'fascinates'. Generally speaking their story is one of an unprecedented rise to success followed by a slow decline through drugs, alcohol and self-neglect – even though they carry on singing. Implicitly fame is too hard or hot for them to handle. Ironically (since it was the opposite of the real-life situation), of the four films quoted above only *A Star is Born* is an exception – with the husband (played by James Mason) of the emerging star (played by Judy Garland) being the one to fall into alcoholic decline. It is worth matching this prurient concern with falling or failing female performers with the counter-practice of a literal White-washing of a male composer's biography: Cole Porter's in *Night and Day*. Porter, a Black and a homosexual, is portrayed in the film as a White straight male (played by Cary Grant). But then little in the other composer biographies was true either!

It was, however, Freed's conception of the musical that was greatly responsible for revitalizing the genre and marking it out as an MGM product, particularly during the 1940s and 1950s. His idea was that song and dance should move the narrative on, that there should be nothing arbitrary about the introduction of song and dance – indeed that the progression from speech to song to dance should be a natural one (see **naturalizing**). Apart from Judy Garland, Gene Kelly (who had been signed up from Broadway in 1940) was another star vehicle of this period to carry out Freed's conception of a greater **naturalism**. To this effect, Kelly was instrumental in introducing the contemporary urban musical such as *On the Town* (1949), which closely integrated song, dance and story and which was partly shot on location. Similarly, *An American in Paris* (made in 1951, but for which the music had been written in 1937 by George Gershwin shortly before his untimely death) portrayed the vitality of the musical scene in Paris in the late 1930s with the heavy influence of jazz and contemporary music. By the mid- to late 1940s contemporary music in musicals, under the influence of Glenn Miller and Duke Ellington (to name but two), also included Big Band Swing (see *The Glenn Miller Story*, 1953).

Freed's other smart move was to bring the Broadway director Vincente Minnelli to MGM. With a reputation for lavish and stylish musicals on stage, Minnelli was none the less also a firm believer in the integrated type of musical Freed advocated. His first film musical was with an all-Black cast, *Cabin in the Sky* (1943). He then went on to work with Judy Garland and together they produced some of their best work: *Meet Me in St Louis* (1944), *Till Clouds Roll By* (1946) and *The Pirate* (1948).

By the late 1940s, Astaire was persuaded out of early retirement by MGM and enjoyed felicitous dance pairings with Judy Garland and Cyd Charisse. He also joined the studio that housed his only 'real' rival, Gene Kelly. Their styles are so different, however, that rather than considering them as rivals – at least with hindsight – we might better see them as exemplary of the two dominant tendencies of the musical as it relates to the American cultural system: that is, to selling marriage (Altman, 1989, 27). On the one hand, there is the stylized inventive elegance of Fred Astaire; on the other, the brash energetic experimentation of Gene Kelly. Astaire is the witty, cool man about town who gets his woman. Kelly, with his edgy over-insistence on his virility, remains a man-child who is not too convinced about marriage. In terms of a legacy it is fair to say that between them and with Garland and Charisse they helped to revitalize the musical and became part of the heyday of the 1950s **colour** musical that also included other great musical stars such as Frank Sinatra and Bing Crosby.

The period 1930–60, despite some severe dips, marked the great era of the Hollywood musical. By the 1950s, the studio system was on the decline and there was an increasing need to target audiences more systematically. Popular Broadway hits still made it on to the screen (for example *Oklahoma*, 1955; *The King and I*, 1956; *South Pacific*, 1958, and – imported from Britain – *My Fair Lady*, 1964). But dwindling audiences meant that new strategies had to be developed. Thus, Hollywood linked up with the record industry as a means of targeting a new audience: the youth class. So a spate of teenager musicals was produced, mostly starring Elvis Presley – who if he could not act could certainly sing and dance. Presley, literally, sold sex through his song and dance routines (arguably his most famous rock musical is *Jail House Rock*, 1957). Britain briefly imitated this trend, primarily in the Cliff Richard series of musicals (such as *Expresso Bongo*, 1959; *Summer Holiday*, 1963). However, these solo star performances – at least in the United Kingdom – were soon superseded by pop group musicals in the form of the Beatles (*A Hard Day's Night*, 1964; *Help!*, 1965).

The trend in the so-called 'hip sixties' was also for a greater **realism** in the musical and non-musical stars. *West Side Story* (1961) is exemplary in this respect. Set in Manhattan, it tells the story of rival gangs (Whites versus Puerto Ricans). A modern *Romeo and Juliet* narrative, the film treats racism, juvenile delinquency and young love in a serious fashion. It is also one of the first musicals to create a more believable world and to end in tragedy. This greater realism in the musical gets carried into the 1970s with the disco-dance musicals of *Saturday Night Fever* (1977) and *Grease* (1978), both with John Travolta (the former film made him into a star – for a while).

The 1970s saw a profusion of rock musicals that ranged from documentary types (*Woodstock*, 1970) to realism (the Jamaican film *The Harder They Come*, 1972) to fantasy-cum-flower-power (*Godspell*, 1973; *Jesus Christ Superstar*, 1973; *Hair*, 1979). But the early tradition of the 1930s did not disappear – *the* exemplary star vehicle for the traditional musical was Barbra Streisand. Just a few of her films serve to show not just how prolific she was (and still is), but how her range goes from comedy to tragedy to performer biography and so incorporates the heritage of the traditional musical from 1930 to 1960: *Funny Girl* (1968); *Hello Dolly!* (1969) (performer biographies); *On a Clear Day You Can See Forever* (1970) (comedy); *The Way We Were* (1974) (tragedy); *Funny Lady* (1975), and so on. Indeed, even after its heyday, the musical – albeit on the decline – never fully abandoned its traditional values. For example, Robert Wise, who directed *West Side Story*, went on to direct *The Sound of Music* (1965)

– a sweetly sugary musical that in the final analysis sells marriage. And in France, Jacques Demy had a brief stab at the genre, combining realism with sweet sugariness, with *Les Parapluies de Cherbourg* (1964) and *Les Demoiselles de Rochefort* (1967).

As a genre, the musical is now very much on the wane and just occasionally reappears in fairly unextravagant forms such as the backstage musical, for example *Fame* (1980). Dancing or **road movie** musicals that use contemporary songs for their musical soundtrack represent another inexpensively produced form of musical. John Travolta resurfaces in *Staying Alive* (1983) to dazzle us with his disco-dancing technique. The Australian-produced *Strictly Ballroom* (1992) sets a teenage love story within a ballroom dancing contest. Finally, camp comes to the musical in explicit style with the very gay and very funny *Adventures of Priscilla, Queen of the Desert* (1994).

Structures and strategies   (In this section I refer to several useful and important studies on the genre: Dyer, 1977 and 1986; Feuer, 1982; Altman, 1989.) The musical is extremely self-referential; it spends most of its time justifying its existence – as, for example, with the putting-on-a-show musical (one of the most common generic types) – 'the show must go on!'. In this type of musical there is a double referentiality pointing to the narcissistic and exhibitionist nature of the genre. Apart from the sombre-ending musicals, the general strategy of the genre is to provide the **spectator** with a utopia through the form of entertainment. The entertainment *is* the utopia. So again self-referentiality is at work.

According to Dyer (1977, 3) there are five categories functioning within this utopian sensibility: abundance, energy, intensity, transparency and community. All are related to the ideological strategies of the genre: selling marriage, **gender** fixity, communal stability and the merits of capitalism. Abundance starts with the décor and the costumes – it insists on the United States' wealth and well-being. Energy is the dance and song routine, but also the camera-work – it is also the hallmark of (White) Americas' pioneering spirit. Intensity

241

derives from the sense of intimacy that the spectator takes pleasure in when watching the body perform – literally, the body 'putting-itself-on-show'. Transparency refers to the reflection the musical purports to give on the American way of life of which the folk community is an essential ingredient. Altman (1989, 25), for his part, talks of the musical as an 'ode to marriage' and the marrying of riches (as exemplified by the male) to beauty (in the form of the female). The musical must also be seen in the light of its contextual relationship with social moments (such as the Depression) and structures of pleasure – especially since it is not always the female form that we enjoy watching dance. For example, Gene Kelly and John Travolta provide, albeit in somewhat different ways, visual pleasures that have more in common with each other – starting with the insistence on virile sexuality – than the visual pleasure offered by Astaire.

Altman (1989, 27) makes the point that cause and effect are fairly tenuous in the musical and that it is less a case of chronology or psychological **motivation** than one of paralleling stories in a comparative mode. He is of course referring to the classic period of the American musical (1930–60) – although his reading still holds true for the reprise classic musical (the happy love musical) that persists after 1960. In that it reconciles terms that seem irreconcilable (starting with sexual difference), the musical 'fashions a myth out of the American courtship ritual' (1989, 27). The musical then is based on the principle of duality or pairings, of male/female oppositions, which it ultimately resolves. Thus the paralleling serves to set up a series of binary oppositions, starting with the one based in gender. Each of the two characters embodies the opposite of the other and it is those oppositions that must be resolved for marriage to occur (1989, 24). These oppositions are what Altman calls dual-focus structures (1989, 19). They generate a chain of oppositions: sexual, background, national origin, temperament, age, colour of hair. Thus, for example, in *Gigi* (Vincente Minnelli, 1958) characters are paired: Gigi with Gaston, and Gigi's grandmother with Gaston's uncle. Settings, locations, trips and songs are paired. Roles and activities are paired: Gigi is the girl-child about to emerge into woman-hood; Gaston is an established businessman, she is frivolous, he serious. However, as their story develops he takes to fun and she to being more serious. Their marriage then becomes a merging of adult and child qualities as well as a containment of the generational problematic and its potential incestual value. Gaston is after all a generation older than Gigi – a gap mirrored, in reverse, in the uncle/grandmother love affair (see Altman, 1989, 22–7).

Opposites eventually attract and can be melded. Even Gene Kelly, who is an interesting exception to the dual-sexuality focus, is eventually brought into the community: which means marriage, children and so on. We mostly remember Kelly dancing alone, the child-like clown and self-centred show-off who in the end has to grow up. In this way, says Altman (1989, 57), Kelly embodies an American dream – he keeps the 'good' of his childlikeness and also matures. In this respect only, he is also in the vein of the female child role rather than the serious mature male role. Opposites are, then, finally reconcilable, and this applies to all the binary oppositions that the musical generates. This includes the work/entertainment opposition which is often a strategy of the backstage musical. This type of musical opposes the 'real' with 'art'. The real world of work is drab and ordinary; that of the stage is ideal and one of beauty. In *Silk Stockings* (Rouben Mamoulian, 1957) – a remake of *Ninotchka* – Cyd Charisse is the serious (that is, dull) businesslike Soviet representative and Astaire the happy-go-lucky (that is, fun-loving) Hollywood director. Charisse comes to learn that entertainment is in fact good business. This type of opposition can generate a slightly different one if both characters represent different types of 'art'. Thus, in a musical one character can be a musician or ballet dancer, the other a music-hall entertainer or tap-dancer. The former sees her or his 'art' as high art and therefore serious work and, conversely sees the other's work as enter-tainment, not serious – therefore hardly work at all, and certainly low art. In reverse the entertainer sees the other as a snob who has not lived. By the end of the musical both

243

come to see the merit of the other's work (see *An American in Paris*, or, on a slightly different tangent of opposing theatre worlds, *The Barkleys of Broadway*, 1949).

The musical therefore functions ideologically to resolve the fear of difference. In this way, it functions as a text which disguises one of society's paradoxes. By extension, of course, this means that it makes invisible the other sets of paradoxes that are inherent in society, thereby ensuring society's stability. Thus the musical also makes safe the notion of the community as *the* place to be. Musicals that fall into this category are typically called 'folk musicals', and implicitly deal with the American folk. Small town or agricultural communities are common in this type of musical (as in *Oklahoma* or *Seven Brides for Seven Brothers*, 1954). Central to these musicals are home and the family. Family groupings, the extended family – all work towards the well-being of the community. To this effect, this 'joyous' folk musical nearly always gets threatened by a baddie or gang warfare – the 'other' outside who threatens the stability of the community. Although they are less present, even large cities are represented as a coherent community. For example, St Louis in *Meet Me in St Louis* is humanized to the level of a small-town community (Altman, 1989, 275).

This same levelling also occurred for all-Black-cast musicals (directed and composed by Whites) – of which in the heyday of the musical genre there were only a few. Apart from the first all-Black-cast musical, *Hallelujah* (Vidor/Berlin, 1929), *Cabin in the Sky* (Minnelli/Duke) and *Porgy and Bess* (Preminger/Gershwin, 1959) are the two most often quoted. These latter two films contain the Black characters within a safely boundaried community (Catfish Row and Kittiwah Island for *Porgy and Bess*) and give a White-eyed version of the Black folklore. Similarly, *Hallelujah* contains the Black characters within the family household consisting of shanty houses and the cotton fields. This film, however, is based not on the traditional oppositions evoked above for all-White musicals but on the opposition chain of religion/**sexuality**, virtue/sin (!). In terms of Black folklore, it includes a further opposition, this time in relation to 'Black' music – or rather the White's perception of it: church music and jazz, where the former is associated with 'virtue and goodness' the latter with sin and woman-temptress. Other than these full-blown White-eyed visions of Blackness, there is the isolated case of Paul Robeson playing a slave on a cotton farm in *Show Boat* (Whale/Kern, 1936), in which he sings *Old (sic) Man River*), or an ennobled African helping the White man (*Sanders of the River*, Alexander Korda, 1935; *King Solomon's Mines*, Stevenson, 1937, in both of which he sings African songs). In all cases he is contained within a White colonialist environment. As a last measure of this levelling and **normalizing**, tap-dancing which is a Black tradition, is totally recuperated into White musicals with no acknowledgement of its Black origins until the 1970s when tribute is finally payed to that heritage in *Black Joy* (1977) and *Thank God it's Friday* (1978).

Altman (1989, 32ff.) isolates four key functions of the cinematic **apparatus** in the musical construction: **settings**, **iconography**, music, dance. A key technique for settings was to use repetition for comparative purposes, to underscore the duality of the sexual oppositions. Therefore, work and home spaces have similar settings or décor; or the two spaces in which the protagonists move (and dance) – be they work or home – mirror each other. Similarly, the proliferation of other couples serves as mirrors to the main couple or pair. In terms of iconography, what dominates is the duet and the solo shot. But even in the presence of the solo shot the spectator fills it in because she or he knows that the coupling is preordained (1989, 39). Similarly with the music. The duet is there for the maximum tension and climax of the narrative. However, the solo carries most of the musical and, as with the solo shot, the spectator fills it in with the missing other (1989, 40). Finally, dance: the camera dances with the characters. It either adopts the position of a watching audience and is, therefore, static and panning left to right; or it is fluid using tracking or crane shots (as we saw with Busby Berkeley). As with the other key functions, the camera catches solo, duet or group dancing. In order to invest these shots with

245

energy – particularly when the camera is static – the tendency is to cut up the shooting with close-ups on feet, hands and faces. The exception to this rule is, as we have seen, Astaire, who insisted on full shots for his routines – whether solo, duet or ensemble.

Dyer (*The Movie 75*, 1981, 1484) speaks of a standard model for a genre as having three periods: primitive, mature, decadent. We have seen how the musical has had a chequered career, reflecting partly audience taste, partly finance (the musical is a very expensive genre to produce), partly due to social conditions (emergence of a youth class, greater choice of leisure pursuits, periods of economic recession). This entry has mostly talked about the first two periods, so a brief word is necessary on the last. By the decadent phase Dyer means that the time in the genre's development has come when its **codes and conventions** can be questioned. Until the 1960s and 1970s the musical did not question itself – as we have seen it indulged in narcissistic auto-satisfaction. Arguably, the rock musical of the 1960s started the questioning of the codes and conventions of the genre. It is interesting to note that some critics qualify *Easy Rider* (Dennis Hopper, 1969) as a rock musical – even though there is no on-screen singing and dancing, just a soundtrack of rock music – whereas most see it as a **road movie**. The point in this debate is not really what genre it is but rather that it typified, for some, a definite change in the orientation of the musical because the message of the film was politicized in its counter-cultural aspirations and because the use of contemporary songs on the soundtrack was a break with copyright law. Similarly, Blacks started putting their own culture and music up on screen in films like *Shaft* (1971) and *Superfly* (1972) – which in some ways backfired because Hollywood co-opted their work in a series of blaxploitation movies (see **Black cinema**).

A film-maker often quoted in the context of the decadent period of the musical is Bob Fosse. *Sweet Charity* (1969) and *Cabaret* (1972) are exemplary of his challenge to Hollywood. He mixes elements of art cinema with movie entertainment – the influences of Federico Fellini and Bertolt Brecht respectively are felt in these films. High and low art are therefore reconciled from the beginning. Dance style goes from the fluid to the ugly and brash. The camera-work similarly goes from the fluid to the vertiginous. And there is 'no such thing as happiness'. Nor, incidentally, is there any such thing as the good all-American folk community, or the merits of capitalism. All is either a bit seedy, decadent or just plain vulgar. No 'Nice, nice Miss American Pie' here. But perhaps the musical to end all musicals is Robert Altman's *Nashville* (1975). Nashville, the so-called heart of country and western music and all-America folk, literally disintegrates before the spectator's eyes. Altman's musical goes nowhere, comes from nowhere, it tells you nothing, it is *not* about country and western music, no one mirrors anyone, and, finally, what pairing there is is dysfunctional from beginning to end. Nothing is reconciled and the film ends in a solo performance.

myth (*for more detailed discussion see* **denotation/connotation, semiology/semiotics**) Myth has become a key concept in semiotics to refer to the way in which reality is represented. Roland Barthes is the main philosopher associated with this concept, the principles of which he set out in his book *Mythologies* (1957). Having shown how myth operates to produce meaning (see **denotation/connotation**), he proceeds to analyse certain aspects of popular culture and explain how these cultural artefacts produce meaning. Cultural artefacts have a mythic function, they are just so many ways by which we understand the culture in which we find ourselves. Myth mediates reality. Myth is a concept that primarily refers to a process of signification by which any given society 'explains' its history and culture. Myths are part of everyday life and change across time. History and culture inform myth but, equally, myth serves as a way by which history and culture are 'explained' as a natural process. Myth, then, is part of the **ideological** process of **naturalization**. The **structuralist** and anthropologist, Claude Lévi-Strauss argued that 'a dilemma or contradiction stands at the heart of every living myth. The impulse to construct the myth arises from the desire to resolve the dilemma' (quoted in Cook, 1985, 90). We can see how this concept of myth is at the heart of **classic narrative cinema**'s discursive strategy of order/disorder/order-renewed. **Dominant cinema** seeks always to resolve a dilemma. In terms of film as a cultural artefact, Barthes's assertion that film is a sign system that functions mainly on the level of myth which then loses all tangible reference to the real world equally refers to mainstream cinema and its desire for the 'reality-effect'. Mainstream cinema spends a lot of effort disguising the fact that what it is showing is pure illusionism.

narrative/narration (*see also* **classic narrative cinema**, **diegesis**, **dominant cinema**, **Oedipal trajectory**)   Narrative involves the recounting of real or fictitious events. Narrative cinema's function is storytelling not description, which is, supposedly, a part function of the **documentary**. Narrative refers to the strategies, **codes and conventions** (including **mise-en-scène** and **lighting**) employed to organize a story. Primarily, narrative cinema is one that uses these strategies as a means of reproducing the 'real' world, one which the **spectator** can either identify with or consider to be within the realms of possibility. Even **science fiction** films have a narrative with which the spectator can identify (for example forces of good fighting it out with those of evil). The **motivation** of the characters moves the story along to make a 'realist' narrative. In mainstream cinema it is traditionally the male who is the prime motivator of the narrative – that is, it is his actions that set the narrative in motion. However, female characters can also act as prime motivators of the narrative even though they mostly remain as object. For example when the woman is at the centre of the enigma around which the film revolves, as is often the case in **film noir**, she is still, usually, object not **subject** of the narrative. She is the object of investigation, since it is her 'enigma' or story that must be probed, investigated and finally resolved by the male protagonist (for a classic in this mode, see *Laura*, Otto Preminger, 1944).

Because narrative exists in so many cultural forms (novel, film, theatre, mythology, painting, etc.) it appears 'as natural as life itself' (Lapsley and Westlake, 1988, 129). And it is this naturalness, or **naturalizing** process that film theorists have sought to contest, at least since **structuralism**. Narrative structures and narrative analysis of film first became an area of theoretical investigation as part of the structuralist debates on cinema. The study of the spheres of action and narrative functions in fairy tales by Vladimir Propp (1920s) and the structure of folk narratives by Claude Lévi-Strauss (1950s) were systems applied by film theorists to film narrative (see Metz, 1972 and Heath, 1981). Structuralist narratology looked for common structures underlying the diversity of narratives – as if seeking a grammar of narrative. Theorists currently interested in this approach are now turning to the work of Gérard Genette (1980) because he makes clear and useful distinctions between three types of narration, allowing one to speak of film as a narrative function, the narration going on within the film and the narrating of the film itself. Thus, he distinguishes between narrative, **diegesis** and narrating. He uses *narrative* to refer to the undertaking to tell an event. Where film is concerned narrative would refer then to film as a narrative statement, to its function as a narrative text. His second term, *diegesis*, refers to the succession of events and their varied relations that make up the particular story. Thus, with film, diegesis refers to the story we see projected up on screen and refers, therefore, to both the storyline and the visual mise-en-scène. His third term, *narrating*, refers to the act of **enunciation**. In film this third term refers, first, to the acts of utterance within the film, the 'act of producing a form of words which involves a human subject' (Hawthorn, 1992, 57). It refers, therefore, to the characters whose utterances motivate the narrative. In the second instance, enunciation refers to the **spectator**–text relations. In other words, the narrative is being narrated to us. We are witnessing the act of narrating.

A primary focus on narrative by Anglo-Saxon film theorists, however, has been on classic narrative cinema as exemplified by

Hollywood, especially the cinema of the 1930s to the 1950s. The classic narrative, for the most part, negates the female point of view and is predominantly based on male **sexuality**; thus films tend to be Oedipally over-determined (that is, there is a dominance of Oedipal narratives). Narrative in cinema tends to follow a fairly standard set of patterns which can be defined by the triads order/disorder/order and order/enigma/resolution. These triads often, but not exclusively, trace the successful or unsuccessful completion by the male protagonist of the **Oedipal trajectory** – that is, simply put, to enter successfully into the social conventions of patriarchy, find a wife and settle down. In this way the narrative achieves closure. In order for these triads to have a cohesive structure, the film narrative is structured on the principle of another strategic triad: repetition/variation/opposition. To keep the film diegesis tight, visual or discursive elements get picked up again during the unravelling of the narrative (repetition) and/or altered somewhat (variation) and/or, finally, shown in a completely contradistinctual way (opposition). A good example of this strategy, which all films use to varying degrees, can be found in the various car sequences that punctuate *Thelma and Louise* (Ridley Scott, 1991). Compare the first car sequence, where the characters escape from the drudgery of their humdrum existence (one form of a life sentence), with the final one, which represents an exhilarating assertion of their right to an alternative resolution to their predicament than that of a life sentence in prison. (For further reading see Bordwell, Staiger and Thompson, 1985; Bordwell, 1986; Branigan, 1992; McMahon and Quin, 1986.)

naturalizing (*see also* **ideology**) A process whereby social, cultural and historical constructions are shown to be evidently natural. As such, naturalizing has an ideological function. Thus, the world is 'naturally' shown in film (and in television in much the same way) as White, bourgeois, patriarchal and heterosexual. These images of western society are accepted as natural. Naturalizing, then, functions to reinforce dominant

251

ideology. Naturalizing discourses operate in such a way that **class**, race and **gender** inequalities are represented as normal. **Images** construct woman as inferior and object of the male **gaze**. Black **sexuality** is represented as potent and, therefore, dangerous and to be contained. The working class gets fixed as naturally subordinate (intellectually and economically) to the middle classes. And so on. Very slowly resistances to this naturalizing process are emerging through the work of a handful of film-makers. An exemplary film which takes on board the naturalizing of inequalities and exposes the ideological function of such a process is Mike Leigh's *Ladybird, Ladybird!* (1994). (For further reading see Lapsley and Westlake, 1988, chapter 5; Bordwell, Staiger and Thompson, 1985; Neupert, 1995.)

naturalism (*see also* **realism**)   A term closely associated with realism. Naturalism first came about in the theatre of the late nineteenth century with the work of, among other dramatists and theatre directors, the Frenchman André Antoine. Antoine's **theory** was to get the actors to move away from the theatrical **gesturality** so prevalent at the time. To do this he created the principle of the fourth wall, which meant that the actors would not address or acknowledge the **audience**. They acted as if the audience was not there. In this regard, the proscenium arch of theatre is effectively abolished and the audience feels as if it is witnessing a slice-of-life realism; it as if viewers are literally dropping in, unseen (a fly on the fourth wall!), on the goings-on of the people on stage. To sustain this effect the décor is realistic, the subject matter contemporary and dialogue delivered naturally – 'they speak just like us'. Actors enter the personae of their characters rather than represent them. They impersonate their characters and reveal their complexity from within. This form of naturalistic acting would later become labelled **method acting** (interestingly, the French talk of actors as 'encamping' their roles).

Antoine went on to direct films and took this principle of naturalism with him, adapting it to the cinema. He insisted on location shooting, the use of a multi-camera point of view (which he believed would parallel the effect of the fourth wall) and an **editing** style that would involve the **spectator** in the narrative (through identification with the mediating camera). He was, incidentally, the first to show female nudity in **narrative** cinema (*L'Arlésienne*, 1922).

Naturalism as an effect, then, places the spectator voyeuristically. We take up the position of the mediating camera. The characters seem so natural, their dialogue or verbal interchanges so real, the **setting** and **mise-en-scène** so totally realistic that an easy identification takes place. We are there alongside the characters. Take, for example, *On the Waterfront* (Elia Kazan, 1954) and the use of the **diegetic** audience to place us as one of the protagonist's entourage (Marlon Brando as Terry Malloy). The reality of what we see before us, with which we identify, stitches us into the illusory nature of the representation so that it appears innocent, natural. In this way, naturalism has an ideological effect much like **naturalizing**. It purports to show reality but in fact has little to do with the representation of the contradictions which underlie social structures and political processes. It gives, therefore, a surface **image** of reality.

neo-realism – *see* **Italian neo-realism**

New German cinema – *see* **Germany/New German cinema**

New Wave/*Nouvelle Vague* *see* **French New Wave**

Oedipal trajectory (*see also* **classic Hollywood cinema, Imaginary/Symbolic, psychoanalysis, suture**) The term *Oedipal trajectory* is a concept used in film psychoanalytic theory to refer to a convention of classic Hollywood cinema whereby the male protagonist either successfully or unsuccessfully fulfils the trajectory through the resolution of a crisis and a movement towards social stability. In other words, after much difficulty (depending on the film **genre**), he finds a woman and 'settles down'. In psychoanalytic terms, the cinematic concept of the Oedipal trajectory is based in Sigmund Freud's conception of the Oedipal complex or crisis and Jacques Lacan's account of the mirror stage. In referring to the Oedipal myth, Freud seeks a means whereby he can explain a child's acquisition of 'normal' adult sexuality. Freud was primarily concerned with the male child's Oedipal phase. The Oedipal phase is also, in Lacanian terms, the latter stage of the mirror phase. The male child who at first is bonded to his mother (through the breast) imagines that he is a united whole with her. However, once he is held up to the mirror by his mother, he perceives his difference from her. He becomes aware of the illusory nature of his unity with his mother and yet still desires unification. The desire for the mother is now sexualized. He is, however, aware of the father whom he currently hates because he has 'lawful' access to the mother, and he, the child, does not. The male child now reads his difference from his mother as one of castration. That is, to his (un)informed eye the mother is castrated. She is not like him, she does not have a penis. To identify or to seek unity with the mother would mean that, in both instances, he would be without penis: in identifying with her he becomes like her, in uniting with her he runs the risk of punishment from the castrating father since he assumes that the father has the power to castrate. How else would the woman/mother lack a penis? So he now moves to identify with the father and sets about to complete his socio-sexual trajectory successfully by finding a female (m)other – that is, someone who is just like his mother. The Oedipal trajectory thus involves identification with the father and objectification of the mother. The male child can now move towards social stability by becoming like his father.

In terms of cinema **narrative** the male protagonist moves, through the resolution of a crisis, towards social stability. In mainstream cinema, the female is a stationary site (that is, passive object) to which the male hero travels and upon which he acts (that is, the active **subject**). If he fails to achieve this trajectory, as is often the case in **film noir**, then it is possible to talk about masculinity in crisis. He fails to find social stability by failing to marry the female other (in a film noir, for example, either he or she dies). It is interesting to note that the other genre in which the male hero does not 'settle down' is the **western**. But in this instance the failure to complete the trajectory is often read positively. Implicit in the western, with its assertion of the **myth** of the west (frontiersmanship, etc.), lies the notion that the cowboy or gunslinger or western hero cannot *yet* settle down: the west is still to be won.

From a psychoanalytical perspective, cinematic narratives that embrace the Oedipal trajectory articulate how the threat of castration (as represented by the woman who lacks) is dispelled and the masculine role of the patriarch is assumed. Two strategies are employed to contain the threat: **voyeurism** and **fetishism**. These strategies form part of the narrative. Thus, with the first strategy, the woman is objectified through the **gaze**, is voyeuristically placed as object of surveillance and therefore containable, safe. The male gaze probes and investigates her. She cannot return the gaze because she is not subject. She is the object (the mother) in the mirror that reinforces or confirms the male's subjectivity. And the male, in recognizing his difference (his subjectivity), asserts his superiority over the female (m)other. The alternative strategy is to fetishize the female, to construct her as a fetishized object, to deny her sexual difference. By a fragmentation of her body and an over-investment in parts of the body (breasts, legs, etc.), the woman becomes commodified as a whole and unified body. The body is fetishized and denied its differ- ence. The body is rendered phallic, a masculinized female image (tight slinky black dresses, high heels and painted finger- nails are good examples of this). Both strategies reinforce the notion of a naturally stable male subjectivity and reaffirm the naturalness of the patriarchal order to which the female must comply through her passivity and, of course, to which the male complies through his activity (see **naturalizing**).

The female Oedipal trajectory is only just coming into focus as an issue in film **theory**. And it is particularly in relation to women's films and **melodrama** that it is being investigated in terms, partly, of mother/daughter relations but also, subliminally, lesbian relations. Clearly the female child is never completely free from desiring her mother. Because of their sameness, there is unity in identification. As with the male child, the mother is her first love-object. But there is no perceived difference, so there is no fear of castration. What then will motivate her to turn away from her mother and desire the father? Freudians argue that she turns away through penis envy. The mother cannot provide her with a penis so she will turn to the father for him to provide her with it in the form of a child. Lacanians, at least feminist Lacanians, argue that since she must enter into the social order of things – that is, patriarchy – she will be obliged to turn from the mother even though she will never fully relinquish her desire of the mother. To fulfil her Oedipal trajectory and enter into the social order of things, the female child must function to confirm male subjectivity. To withhold such confirmation means punishment – either through marginalization or death. In classic narrative cinema, independent women eventually 'come to their senses' and marry the guy (if it's **comedy**), or are 'brought to their senses' (if it's a film noir or **thriller**). (For further reading see Kaplan, 1992; Krutnik, 1991; Modleski, 1988, 42–55; Penley, 1989.)

180-degree rule (*see also* **30-degree rule**)   Also known as the imaginary line, this is a 'rule' that ensures consistency of the **spectator**'s perspective. Essentially, when shooting a scene, cameras should stay on one side of this imaginary line, otherwise the spectator would get disorientated as the diagram

---------------------------- ◘ ◘ ◘ ---------------------------

C₁   C₂

illustrates. The three cameras are on one side of the line pointed at the object on the line. As the film unravels on screen, the spectator takes up any of those three camera positions depending on which **shot**-position has been chosen at any given time and edited into the final cut (camera 1, 2 or 3). There is perfect logic in this perspectival **gaze** for the spectator. But what if a camera went the other side of the line? The spectator's perspective would be reversed: she or he would be seeing things back to front. If the object was two characters in a conversation (a two-shot), their positions would be reversed. Character *A* would be in character *B*'s position.

The only time crossing the line is 'permitted' is for the **reverse-angle shots** which are commonly used by **Hollywood** to film dialogue.

opposition – *see* **narrative, sequencing**

oppositional cinema – *see* **counter-cinema**

paradigmatic/syntagmatic – *see* **structuralism/post-structuralism**

parallel reversal   A useful term used by Modleski (1988, 19) in her discussion of the **narrative** structure of Alfred Hitchcock's *Blackmail* (1929). She uses it to describe how the closing sequence parallels or repeats an earlier one, near the beginning of the film, but with the positions reversed. In the early sequence of this film, the female protagonist, Alice White, is visibly annoyed at having to wait for her boyfriend, a detective, Frank Webber. She is waiting for him in his place of work, Scotland Yard. He comes to greet her, at which point she ostensibly flirts with another detective. He whispers something in her ear, she laughs and then exits with Frank but without telling him the joke. At the end of the film, Alice is similarly placed between two men, one of whom is Frank – and again at Scotland Yard – but this time it is she who is the butt of the joke between the two men and thus she who is excluded.

parallel sequencing – *see* **editing**

patriarchy – *see* **Imaginary/Symbolic**, **Oedipal trajectory/psychoanalysis**

performance – *see* **gesturality, star system**

plot/story – *see* **classic Hollywood cinema, discourse, narrative**

point of view/subjectivity – *see* **subjective camera, subjectivity**

politique des auteurs – *see* **auteur, French New Wave, mise-en-scène**

postmodernism (*see also* **modernism, structuralism/post-structuralism, theory**) This term entered into critical **discourse** in the late 1960s. As a concept it was seen as exemplifying a counter-position to modernism, especially modernism in its latest manifestation as total theory: structuralism. And for this reason it is a term often associated with post-structuralism, to which it is, arguably, connected. Although the two concepts do indeed co-exist, some critics feel that postmodernism – also known as the postmodern – refers more to an age, particularly the 1980s and 1990s, than to a theoretical movement to which, of course, post-structuralism belongs. There appears to be no easy definition of postmodernism. Indeed there are many different ways in which it is perceived. These are never totally contradictory readings but, depending on the positioning of a particular thinker, writer or theorist, it can be given a different interpretation. This of course points to its pluralism as a concept and is something to be welcomed after the strictures of modernism and structuralism. It is also a reason why postmodernism gets aligned with post-structuralism, which is similarly pluralistic in its approach. Post-structuralism is more readily concerned with opening up the problematics in modernism and as such constitutes a critical theory of

259

modernism. Postmodernism is perceived more as an historical condition within which are contained social, political and
cultural agendas and resonances. These are interpreted,
depending on the positioning of the writer or theorist, either
as reflective of a mentality of 'anything goes', therefore
nothing works, or of a questioning of the modernist ideals
of progress, reason and science. In the first instance, theorists
claim that the postmodern condition signals the death of
ideology. In the second, it heralds a new scepticism about
the modernist belief in the supremacy of the western world,
the legitimacy of science to legislate the construction and
function of **gender**, and the advocacy of high art over popular
culture.

Ultimately, then, postmodernism is a vague term. However,
in its eclecticism lies its power to be non- or anti-essentialist,
it neither has nor provides a fixed meaning; in its pluralism
lies its ability to be read either positively or negatively.

*A first set of readings – mainstream postmodern culture and oppo-
sitional postmodern culture* Some critics see the postmodern
as an effect that is a reaction against the established forms
and canons of modernism. In this regard it takes issue with
modernism's positive belief in progress and a unified underlying reality. Postmodernism reacts against modernism's
optimistic belief in the benefits of science and technology to
human kind. But, as the entry on modernism makes clear,
this optimism is only part of the picture. Certain modernists
did not share this optimism but mistrusted science and technology. Viewed in this light, then, postmodernism continues
the pessimistic vein that already prevailed in modernism.
According to Fredric Jameson (1983), postmodernism, as an
effect, also represents the erosion of the distinction between
high art and popular culture. The postmodern does not really
refer to style but to a periodizing concept 'whose function
is to correlate the emergence of new formal features in culture
with the emergence of a new type of social life and a new
economic order' (Jameson, 1983, 113). In other words, it is
a conjunctural term at the interface between artefact and the
new moment of capitalism. This new moment of capitalism

is varyingly called post-industrial or post-colonial society, modernization, consumer society, media society. The artefact is what is produced by and within that moment in capitalism. What is significant is that the term *postmodern* is consistent with the way in which western contemporary society defines itself – that is, in relation to the past (post-colonial), but also in relation to social practice (modernization, consumer) and technology (media). In its consistency with western definitions, the postmodern looks back, is retrospective, is not defined as other, but as *post*modern, as coming after. In its lack of history (defined only in relation to the past), it rejects history, and because it has none of its own – only that of others – the postmodern stands eternally fixed in a series of presents. This reading places postmodernist culture as ahistorical.

According to this view, the postmodern era has little of the optimism of post-structuralism. It is more akin to a cult than to a movement. Although Anglo-Saxon theorists refer to this concept as postmodernism or postmodernity, it is instructive to note that the country whence the term emanated, France, deliberately omits the 'ism': *le postmoderne*. This very omission warns us that this is a non-collective phenomenon and that, by implication, it focuses on the cult of the individual (a position not all critics agree with; see below). Curiously, this contemporary hedonism recalls the aesthetic culture of the symbolists at the end of the nineteenth century – particularly in France. The *fin de siècle* mood of that time – a direct reaction to the political, intellectual and moral crises taking place – manifested itself in a neoromantic nihilism wherein the individual artist became a cult figure. The death of ideology at that time left the artist in the presence of a spiritual void. How to fill the abyss of nothingness? The response was aestheticism, art for art's sake, as an end in and of itself which led to a self-sufficient formalism. In other words, only form, not content, could fill the void.

It is this pessimistic vein which finds its heritage first in the tragic modernist and later in the ahistorical postmodernist cultures. Both are traumatized by a technology that has created

261

ideological structures of suppression and domination never seen before. Modern technology allowed **images** of this technology at work to be recorded (by the camera) and be brought to our attention. If there was not much footage of the First World War shown publicly, archival film shows enough of the horrors of trench warfare. More recently, images of the apocalyptic events of the Holocaust and the dropping of the atomic bomb have left modernist and postmodernist alike with seemingly unanswerable questions. How to invent, comes the cry, when invention can lead to such wholesale destruction of humanity? In answer to this daunting set of questions, modernism in its pessimistic mode presents a world as fragmented and decayed and one in which communication is a virtual impossibility. In its response to these same questions, according to theorists providing the ahistoric reading of postmodernity, postmodern culture, which can see itself only in relation to the past, bifurcates. The majority tendency is unoppositional, a unidirectional reflection towards the past, providing a conservative cultural production – that is, mainstream culture. The minority is avant-garde and oppositional.

In relation to the contemporary cultural aesthetic, then, the postmodern adopts two modes. In its mainstream mode, it manifests itself through mannerism and stylization, through pastiche – imitation of what is past. In its oppositional mode – that is, in its despair at the nothingness of the abyss – it turns to parody, an ironization of style, form and content (as in Samuel Beckett's plays and novels). Whether mainstream or oppositional, the postmodern aesthetic relies on four tightly interrelated sets of concepts: simulation, which is either parody or pastiche; prefabrication; **intertextuality** and bricolage. What separates the two tendencies is that the oppositional postmodern aesthetic experiments with these concepts and innovates through subverting their **codes**, whereas the mainstream postmodern aesthetic merely replicates them. Hence the need for two distinguishing terms for the first concept, simulation: 'parody' and 'pastiche'. Parody is the domain of oppositional art. Pastiche pertains to the symptomatic in that it imitates previous **genres** and styles, but, unlike parody, its imitation is not ironic and is therefore not subversive. In its uninventiveness, pastiche is but a shadow of its former thing (parody). Postmodern art culls from already existing images and objects and either repeats or reinvents them as the same. To make the distinction clear, we could turn to the world of fashion and say that punk is parody, chic-punk is pastiche.

The three remaining concepts, then, are either played out in a parodic or pastiche modality. As you will see, there is considerable overlap between the concepts. In postmodern cinema, images or parts of sequences which were fabricated in earlier films are reselected. In much the same way that prefabricated houses are made up of complete units of pre-existing meaning, so the visual arts see the past as a supermarket source that the artist raids for whatever she or he wants. A film could be completely constructed out of prefabricated images (and even sounds). This is particularly true for mainstream postmodern cinema. For example, a film-maker wanting to insert a song and dance routine could select Gene Kelly's dance routine of the title song in *Singin' in the Rain* (1952), for a **flashback** she or he could clip in the beginning of *Sunset Boulevard* (Billy Wilder, 1950), and so on. Robert Altman's *The Player* (1992) makes reference to this pastiche culture of prefabrication (two studio scriptwriters discuss a possible script which they describe as *Out of Africa* meets *Pretty Woman*).

In this context of prefabrication, note how clever Quentin Tarantino's films are. While they appear to be a **mise-en-abîme** of filmic quotes, the orchestration of the quotes is so brilliantly achieved that what appears pastiche is in fact parody. He selects the quotes and then brutally overturns them. Take, for example, *Reservoir Dogs* (1991). The ten-minute torture scene in the empty warehouse, which is horrendous in its horror, is also excessively comic because the torturer, the psychopathic Mr Blonde, dances to a 1970s song, *Stuck in the Middle with You* – a song that relates to a paranoid if not drugged perception of 'reality'. Meantime as he slices up his victim he asks, in tune with the song, 'was that as good for you as it was for me?' According to Tarantino, the filmic quotes are Abbott and Costello monster movies which combine the comic with the horror (*Sight and Sound*, Vol. 2, No. 8, 1992). They also, in their seemingly gratuitous violence, recall many a Scorsese scene of violence (for example *Taxi Driver*, 1976). This scene, as with other quotes in the film, also pulls from the **B-movies**. Again they are pushed to their limits. This particular torture scene derides the false bravura of cops and gangsters who 'shoot it out' – here ears are cut off, faces are slashed (before even a gun is shot!), and people torched – all to the sound of music and dancing. Not even *The Saint Valentine's Day Massacre* (1967) or *The Godfather* (Francis Ford Coppola, 1972) could match these extremes of violence-in-**excess**. It is precisely in scenes like this one that the film achieves the parodic. Through this use of violence, Tarantino exposes the **spectator**–film relationship as one of sadomasochism. We might bleed with Mr Orange as he lies in the wharehouse dying, but we also find ourselves dancing with Mr Blonde. Compounding the parodic is Tarantino's expressed intention of making us brutally aware of the manipulative hand of the director – 'he can shoot scenes like this' – and our collusion with him 'we choose to watch'. In this respect, Tarantino's work must be seen as oppositional. This makes the point that oppositional culture, postmodern or otherwise, can reach mass audiences. Tarantino is one of today's successful postmodern film-makers who can dissolve the divide between high art and low art without reducing his film to pulp, that is, to a mere series of good images.

Intertextuality, which in many respects can be seen as closely aligned with mise-en-abîme and as overlapping with prefabrication, is a term which refers to the relation between two or more texts. All texts are necessarily intertextual, that is, they refer to other texts. This relation has an effect on the way in which the present constructed text is read. All films are, to some degree, always already intertextual. Within mainstream pastiche cinema, the most obvious intertextual film is the remake. Within the parodic mode and of the more contemporary and popular film-makers, Tarantino's films are exemplary in the way that they refer to other texts. *Pulp Fiction*

(1994), for example, refers in many of its décors to the paintings of Edward Hopper – so in part the intertext is composed of painterly texts. Tarantino readily acknowledges his references to the film texts of Jean-Luc Godard. And certainly *Bande à part* (1964) with its own references to the American **musical** – which Godard reinscribes in a parodic mode – is a text to which *Pulp Fiction* refers. Tarantino talks about his film being based on three storylines that are the oldest chestnuts in the world, filmic **narratives** based on pulp fiction: a member of the gang taking out the mobster's wife whom he must not touch; the boxer who is supposed to throw the fight; gangsters on a 'mission' to kill (*Sight and Sound*, Vol. 4, No. 5, 1994, 10). Characters within film can also be intertextual of course. Again to cite Tarantino's film: Butch, the boxer, is an intertext of the character of Mike Hammer in *Kiss Me Deadly* (Robert Aldrich, 1955) and the look of the actor Aldo Ray in *Nightfall* (Jacques Tourneur, 1956).

Finally among these concepts comes bricolage. This is an assembling of different styles, textures, genres or discourses. In oppositional postmodern art this takes the form of replicating within one discourse the innovations of another. For example, the deconstruction of time and space that occurs in the *nouveau roman* is replicated in the films of Marguerite Duras, Alain Resnais and Alain Robbe-Grillet through a use of **montage** that disorientates. The most common replication in cinema of other textural mediums is the plasticity of video and painting which can be found in many of the 1980s film-makers' work – both mainstream and oppositional.

In mainstream postmodern cinema genres are mimicked and not renewed. In terms of subjects, themes and style, the spectator of today is reviewing either images of modernist cinema or mediatic images of its own age. With a few exceptions there are no social or political films (Stephen Frears, Neil Jordan and Dennis Potter are a few who come to mind in the British and Irish environment). Some of the major issues of the 1980s and 1990s go unheard. This dearth of subjects coincides with a cinematographic mannerism which manifests itself in at least three ways. First, by a prurient (necrophiliac?) fixation

265

with genres and images of a bygone cinema – nostalgia at its worst. Second, by a servile simulation of television visual discourses. And, finally, by manipulating and elevating virtual reality and computer graphics to the status of real. It is in this sense that mainstream postmodern film-makers of today display a disdain for culture with a capital C. All culture, 'high' and 'low', is assimilable or quotable within their texts so that the binary divide is erased. The dissolution of the divide would be a good thing, but the result still has to have meaning. Instead, in their formalism and mannerism they aim purely and simply for the well-made image – 120 minutes of good publicity clips. They invent nothing. John Orr (1993, 12) points out that this cinema of pastiche lends itself to a double reading or, rather, contradictory readings. This cinema will appeal to right and left, Black and White. *Forrest Gump* (1994) is an excellent example, since both the left and the right have found it consonant with their own ideologies. As Orr says (1993, 12), this cinema, while so patently empty, is also potentially dangerous – schizoid, as Orr puts it.

A second set of readings – negative versus positive readings of the postmodern (Here I am drawing on the useful and illuminating analyses to be found in Huyssen, 1990; Nicholson, 1990; Bruno, 1987; Hawthorn, 1992; Kuhn, 1990.) In terms of current writing about postmodernism, there are at least as many positions as there are areas of concern. What follows is a summary of those positions as they affect readings of postmodern cinema. There is of course some overlapping or cross-fertilization but it is worth spelling them out if only to reiterate the pluralism of postmodernism. Postmodern discourses have been elaborated with reference to architecture, human sciences and literature, the visual arts, technology, cultural theory, social, economic and political practices, feminism and gender. As has already been mentioned, these discourses generate either positive or negative readings of the postmodern.

Negative readings tend to focus on what is perceived to be the essential schizophrenia of postmodernism: a schizophrenia which can, for example, be detected in contemporary architecture's random historical citations which have been pasted or pastiched on to so many postmodern façades (Huyssen, 1990, 237). Roman colonnades are mixed with Georgian windows, and so on. Jameson believes that this schizophrenia comes about as a result of a refusal to think historically (Kuhn, 1990, 321). Baudrillard sees this post-industrial society as the society of spectacle that lives in the ecstasy of communication (Bruno, 1987, 67). This society, he believes, is dominated by electronic mass media and is char-acterized by simulation (Kuhn, 1990, 321). Baudrillard explains that this post-industrial society is one of reproduc-tion and recycling, so rather than producing the real it reproduces the hyper-real (Bruno, 1987, 67). By this he means the real is not the real, is not what can be reproduced but, rather, that which is always already reproduced which is essentially a simulation (1987, 67). The hyper-real, then, is a simulacrum of the real. Perfect simulation is the goal of post-modernism; thereby no original is invoked as a point of comparison and no distinction between the real and the copy remains (1987, 68). In this implicit loss of distinction between representation and the real, Baudrillard perceives the death of the individual.

In order to make this point clearer it is useful to compare the effects of the industrial machine on the individual (the **subject**) versus those of the post-industrial one. Whereas the industrial machine was one of production, the post-industrial one is one of reproduction (1987, 69). In the former case, the industrial machine leads to the alienation of the subject – the subject no longer commands the modes of production. In the latter, the post-industrial machine leads to the fragmenta-tion of the subject, to its dispersal in representation (1987, 69). It has no history, is stuck in the ever-present. It is in effect without memory. According to Jacques Lacan, the experience of temporality and its representation are an effect of language (1987, 70). If, therefore, the subject has no experience of temporality, has no link with the past or the future, then it is without language – that is, it lacks the means of representing the 'I'. This creates a schizophrenic condition in which the subject fails to assert its **subjectivity** and fails also to enter

267

the Symbolic Order. Therefore it is stuck in the Imaginary, perhaps even in the pre-Imaginary (see **Imaginary/Symbolic**). The question becomes 'who am I?' – even 'who made me?'. It is remarkable that the past decade or so has witnessed a spate of monster films on screen and that the question of reproduction has been central to the narrative (for example *Jurassic Park*, Steven Spielberg, 1993; *Mary Shelley's Frankenstein*, Kenneth Branagh, 1994) and identity (*Interview with the Vampire*, Neil Jordan, 1994). An analysis of these films would doubtless produce the missing link between past, present and future – that is, the figure of the mother who is so pre-eminently absent from these films as site of reproduction, the reproduction machine of post-industrialization (male technology) having reproduced her (genetic engineering).

Postmodernism, as we know, refers to a general human condition in the late capitalist (post-1950s) world that impacts on society at large, including ideology, as much as it does on art and culture. Certain theorists, amongst them so-called neo-conservatives (Huyssen, 1990, 255), see postmodernism as a dangerous thing both aesthetically and politically. In terms of aesthetics, the danger resides in the popularization of the modernist aesthetic which, through the dissolution of the divide between high art and low art, promotes hedonism and anarchy. It promotes anarchy because it removes the function of modernist art as critique – 'anything goes' – and hedonism in that it takes the subjective idealism of modernism to the point of solipsism (Hawthorn, 1992, 110). That is, the individual subject becomes the only knowable thing. Politically speaking, because it reacts against modernism's belief in knowledge and progress, postmodernism rejects meaning in the sense of believing that the world exists as something to be understood and that there is some unified underlying reality. Ideology becomes distinctly unstable in this environment.

Postmodernism is not necessarily perceived negatively, particularly by those living in it – primarily the youth generation, but also other groupings (as I will explain). Postmodernism in its positive mode celebrates the present and is far more accepting of late capitalism and technology. It also celebrates the fact that mass communication and electronics have revolutionized the world (Hawthorn, 1992, 111). Postmodernism delights in and is fascinated by technology. The Internet represents the height of communication in the present through mass technology. Virtual reality can 'let me be there' without moving. Late capitalism means a dispersal of the productive base: commodities are produced where it is most advantageous, the labour market has become internationalized and fragmented. But it has also produced multinational corporations, which means that capital itself is concentrated in the hands of the few. For example, the world is so small that Reebok or Nike can have their central office in New Jersey or Eugene, Oregon but not have a factory outlet anywhere in the United States. The factories are placed in parts of the world where labour is cheapest.

To the criticism that postmodernism has lost the edge of art as critique and that, in its art-for-art's-sake positioning, it resembles the *fin de siècle* mood of the nineteenth century, postmodern art appears – within its celebratory and playfully transgressive (of modernism) mode – to reject this function of art or proposes that popular culture is just as capable of offering a critique as high art. In this latter respect, the populist trend of postmodernism (as exemplified by pop art and its reference to comic-strip culture, and by pop music: rock, punk, acid) – in its deliberate counter-culture positioning – challenges modernism's hostility towards mass culture (Huyssen, 1990, 241). It also rejects modernist belief in the 'perpetual modernisation of art' (1990, 238) and questions the exploitation of modernism for capital greed and political need. To explain: during the 1940s and the Cold War of the 1950s, modernism, in the form of abstract expressionism (as seen in the paintings of Willem de Kooning), was a school virtually 'invented' and subsequently institutionalized as canonical high art by the United States (read: the CIA and art critics). This was done for propagandistic and political ends. The intent, successfully carried out, was to move the centre of the art world out of Europe (and the threat or taint

269

of communism) and to make New York the world capital (in both senses of that word) of art.

Postmodernism's effect of dissolving the binary divide between high and low art has, domino-style, generated others. The positive side of 'anything goes' is that dichotomies no longer function tyrannically as exclusionary. Modernism had represented a masculinization of culture, due in part to a bohemian lifestyle that excluded most women at least at first (Hawthorn, 1992, 109), but due also to the primary areas of modernism: architecture, painting, film, theatre (the modernist novel coming, arguably, later in the 1930s). Thanks to its creative relationship between high and low art, postmodernism has made space for minority cultures, has brought about a fragmentation of culture that is positive. Thus, where **gender** and race are concerned, this dissolution of binary divides and deprivileging of a meritocracy within dichotomies have led, first, to a pluralism within the question of subjectivity and, second, to a questioning of defining one group in relation to the concept of 'otherness'. In its rejection of universal norms, postmodernism refutes generalizations that exclude, and advocates a plurality of individualized agency (Nicholson, 1990, 13). In this respect, therefore, gender and race are no longer dichotomized. Postmodernism represents, then, a cultural liberation.

Small surprise that for some groupings – particularly those who had previously been excluded by the high principles of modernism – postmodernism is seen as liberating and celebratory. Voices from the margins, minority cultures, are finding spaces within contemporary culture. In the western world this has meant hearing, among others and in differing degrees of volume, the voices of Blacks, women, women of colour, gays, lesbians, ecologists, animal rights supporters, disabled people and so on. Some of these voices are finding their way on to film. Since the 1980s, for example, there has been an emergence of Black men and women film-makers and Black **stars**, gay and lesbian film-makers are coming on mainstream – marking the beginnings of a pluralism therefore in this highly competitive arena.

This pluralism has extended into film theory perhaps with greater speed than into the film-making practices themselves. And this is due in part to postmodernism's impact upon or coincidence with developments in cultural studies towards a mapping of our cultures – seeing culture as pluralistic (starting in the 1960s with Raymond Williams *et al.*). It is also due to its conjuncture with feminism. Feminist criticism exposed the masculine determinations of modernist art and culture and as such, albeit through a differing optic, echoed the post-modern position. In its critique of the normalizing function of patriarchy, feminism joins up with postmodernism's critique of the modernist belief in knowledge and its use of 'master narratives' to legitimate scientific research and the pursuit of knowledge (Kuhn, 1990, 321). In the name of knowledge, modernism has presented a very dislocated and partisan view of the world – one that excludes more than it includes, one that belongs to a particular gender, class, race and culture (Nicholson, 1990, 5). Feminism rejects modernism's belief in reason and objectivity and its concomitant belief in total theory. Feminism opposes, therefore, all generalizations because they exclude.

Because feminism raises the questions of identity, identifi-cation and, ultimately, history (or lack of it where woman's place is concerned), postmodernism seems, then, a natural ally to feminism (although not all feminists agree; see Nicholson, 1990). Counter to modernism's construction of the individual as a single subjectivity in relation to the 'other', postmodernism and feminism make possible the notion of a 'plurality of individual agents' (Nicholson, 1990, 13). For example, there is no longer a single standard norm wherein gender, identity and sexual orientation are fixed as hetero-sexual (1990, 15). Furthermore, it becomes possible to talk in terms of gender- and race-based subjectivities (Huyssen, 1990, 250). (For further detail see **feminist film theory**.)

The importance of this concept of pluralism for film theory is clear. The construction of subjectivity through the cine-matic **apparatus** can be examined. This in turn generates questions around the **gaze** and leads to its investigation: who owns it, is it exclusively male? The whole debate around sexuality on screen gets opened up. The issue of spectator–text relations now becomes yet another way by which the filmic text can be understood as an ideological operation. Thus gender issues are no longer reduced to an 'either/or', but discussed within frameworks of gender fluidity, resistance to gender fixing, whether on screen or in connection with the spectator and the text.

post-structuralism – *see* **structuralism/post-structuralism**

preferred reading (*see also* **classic narrative cinema, dominant cinema, ideology**)   In mainstream cinema, **images** and films as a whole are encoded in such a way as they are given a preferred reading. They are meant to mean what they say. The narrative triad ('order/disorder/order'), the filmic **codes and conventions** germane to a particular **genre** (for example the **lighting** and décor in **film noir**), characterization (for example heroic active male, scheming female, passive female victim), the **iconography** of the image – all these become just so many ideological operations of the cinematic **apparatus**, the internal workings of the film text which create a closed text, one where the meaning is encoded from the outset. Of course the **spectator** may not necessarily accept that preferred reading. Indeed, feminist critics have been busy in the last ten to fifteen years making readings against the grain (or oppositional readings) – particularly of the film noir and the **melodrama** (see **feminist film theory**).

presence – *see* **absence/presence**

private–eye films – *see* **gangster films**

projection – *see* **apparatus, psychoanalysis**

272

projector – *see* **apparatus**

psychoanalysis What follows is a mapping of the major debates in psychoanalysis as they have been introduced into and developed in film **theory**. For the sake of clarity and easy reference, major concepts in psychoanalysis and film are given their own full development under separate entries, which are cross-referenced in this synopsis. However, it seems useful to list immediately these major key concepts: **absence/presence; apparatus; enunciation; fantasy; feminist film theory; gaze; Imaginary/Symbolic; Oedipal trajectory; scopophilia; shot/reverse shot; spectator; subjectivity; suture; voyeurism/fetishism**.

Although psychoanalysis is not such a new phenomenon in literary theory, it is relatively new to film theory. Literary theory took up psychoanalysis in the 1930s and 1940s, but it did not fully enter into film theory until as late as the early 1970s. This might surprise, given that cinema is a contemporary of Freudian psychoanalysis (both emerging at the end of the nineteenth century). And in fact in the early, experimental **avant-garde** theorizing and film-making of the 1920s (in France) there was considerable debate around the notion of the subjective camera, and film-makers strove to give visual expression to the representation of the unconscious. The delay might also surprise since cinema is so readily associated with fantasy and dreams. Again, although film theory has been in existence since around 1910, on the whole formal, authorial and sociological considerations tended to dominate (see **auteur**). It would take the coincidence in the late 1960s of two occurrences in theoretical thinking to bring about the psychoanalysis entry. On the one hand, the late 1960s witnessed a reaction against the effects of **structuralism** and its 'total theory' strategy. This reaction was exemplified by **post-structuralism**. On the other hand, this period saw a widening of the debates in Freudian psychoanalysis thanks to the writings of Jacques Lacan. These were subsequently taken up in critical theory in general and film theory in particular.

There are predominantly two strands of psychoanalysis, particularly on the question of subjectivity, that have found their way into film theory: Freudian and Lacanian. And they have so far been applied in three main areas of investigation: the film texts themselves; the **apparatus–spectator** relation which later evolved into text–spectator relations; and **fantasy**. Of course these applications have been refined and reviewed, refuted even, by theorists working in this area of film criticism. This means that psychoanalytic theory has developed significantly in film theory since its earliest applications. Despite the conviction with which some theorists have taken up psychoanalysis, particularly feminists (for reasons that will become clear), it is noteworthy that not all film theorists are confirmed adherents to the merits of psychoanalysis – so the debate remains an active, not to say controversial, one.

Freud's theory of the subject   Sigmund Freud's psychoanalytic approach was to investigate, to probe the psychological functioning of our human psyche and the relations we form with the outside world. Freud believed that we strive to fulfil our needs and desires (including, especially, sexual ones) and suffer pain if we are unable to do so. We also feel guilt for our desires, particularly if they cannot be fulfilled, and become self-critical, even self-hating. Freud maintained that, generally speaking, we repress these feelings of frustration and self-disgust into the unconscious. The unconscious does not remain perpetually buried, and can resurface in dreams or through projection. In the former case, dreams represent a return of the repressed so they are the vehicle for that which re-emerges from the unconscious. In the latter case, we impose, project our frustrations on something or someone external to us (for example, driving a car too fast or picking an argument for no ostensible reason with a loved one).

Freud determined three parts to our psyche: the id, ego and super-ego. The id is the uncontrolled, repressed part of the psyche which the ego, as the consciousness, attempts to control. The super-ego, as the term suggests, attempts to act as a higher-order authority over the id and the ego by trying to gain a greater critical conscience in relation to the workings of the psyche and to understand them. The super-ego is also identified with the 'parental' voice within the psyche. Where the boy-child is concerned, the super-ego represents an internalizing of patriarchal authority – that is, he accepts the suppression of desire (of the mother) in order to gain access to the same rights as his father. Thus patriarchy regenerates itself.

Freud distinguished between two ego-types, the realist and the narcissistic. The regulating ego mentioned above is the realist type. It mediates between the pleasure-seeking id and reality. That is, it satisfies some of the id's desires while conforming to social expectation. The narcissistic ego is far less heard of in relation to Freud – unsurprisingly, considering that it is the direct antithesis to the realist ego which presumes improvement, even the perfectability of the ego (Grosz, 1990, 31). It is, however, this ego that Lacan developed in his own analysis, so it is relevant to explain Freud's concept. The realist ego type was, Freud conceded, too simplistic in its definition. If it was the mediator between the id and reality, this meant, essentially, that it took care of its ego instincts (satisfying some of the id's desires but conforming to social norms) but apparently ignored *its* own sexual instincts. The question becomes, if it is moderating between the id and its needs and reality how can the realist ego type take part in its own sexual instincts, be part of its subjectivity? How can it be a unified subject if it is the rational moderator standing outside, aloof, from the notion of desire?

In his account of the narcissistic ego, Freud attempts to answer these questions. This ego is linked to early infant narcissism, which means that the ego takes itself as the object of its own libidinal drives. So the ego is both the subject and the object: the subject desiring the mirrored or narcissistic object or other. In this respect, then, the ego is not the unified subject (as it appears to be in the form of the realist ego) but is divided. This concept of the divided self is one that Lacan developed in his own investigation of subjectivity.

The second important point Freud makes, and which Lacan later developed, concerns Freud's description of this narcissistic ego in terms of a libidinal reservoir. According to Freud the narcissistic ego is the boundary around the libidinal reservoir (Grosz, 1990, 30). And it is for this reason that it can invest in itself as one of its libidinal objects (1990, 30). It does of course invest in external objects other than itself. This ego changes shape depending on how much it has invested outside into the external objects (object-libido), including its own body, and how much it has retained within itself (ego-libido). Grosz (1990, 29) refers to this mutation as hydraulic or amoeba-like. But, and here is the crucial point, because the ego's primary relationships are libidinal, they are based in pleasure not in reality (1990, 29). Furthermore, the ego has an object relation with its self, in that it can invest in its body as one of its libidinal objects (1990, 30). So from what source does the self assert its subjectivity, its identity? Whereas the realist ego was a self-contained entity that acted (and, therefore, had **agency**) as a rational mediator between the id and reality, it is evident that the narcissistic ego – in that it has no direct relation to reality – is not an entity, has no agency, but is 'constituted by its relationships with others. Indeed, its self-identity is . . . always mediated by others' (1990, 29).

These two central points, in so far as they concern first Lacan and then film theory, will be picked up when we come to discuss Lacan. In terms of film theory, however, Freud's account of subjectivity was important in at least one further, significant way. This part of the account concerns his notion of the Oedipal complex. The dyadic mother/child relationship, although a precursor to entry into the social, is none the less narcissistic in its mutual identification and desiring. For growth to take place into a plurality of relations and into the order of civilization and culture the child must be removed or severed from its imaginary unity with the mother. This dyadic structure must give way to a third term. This moment is what Freud terms the Oedipal complex or crisis. The father intervenes, forming a triangular structure, forbidding the child sexual access to the mother. The male child renounces his desire for his mother for fear of castration. He notes that his father has the phallus and his mother does not. He assumes that his mother is castrated and that, therefore, his father – he who possesses the phallus – has the power to castrate him. Both mother and father carry the threat of castration for the male child: he could become 'she who is without' if he disobeys either parent's prohibition (in this respect Alfred Hitchcock's *Psycho*, 1960, at first sight appears to offer a classic scenario of the castrating mother). The male child obeys the father, enters into a pact with him in that he renounces his mother momentarily until it is time for him to find his own female and accede in his turn to 'paternal' status which is the reward for renouncing the mother. The question of the female child gets less attention in Freud (and for that matter Lacan).That issue will be dealt with below.

The Oedipal crisis for the male child, then, manifests itself by this renouncement of the mother, what Freud terms primal repression. This moment of primal repression marks the founding moment of the unconscious. In other words, those unspoken sexual drives and desire for narcissistic union with the mother are repressed. The male child must repudiate his mother and become like his father in terms of masculinity, but not like his father in terms of his love object – it cannot be the mother (although, as Freud points out, it ultimately always *is* the mother). And it is here that we have the basis for the so-called Oedipal trajectory that has been associated with **classic narrative cinema**. The protagonist must successfully complete his trajectory through first resolving a crisis, usually of a triangular nature (rivalry for a woman, for example), and then attaining social stability. By way of illustration, in the **comedy** genre the protagonist is often seen resolving a misunderstanding he has had with the woman he is attracted to and eventually settling down and marrying her.

Lacan's theory of the subject – including his concept of 'jouis-sance' Since the entries on **Imaginary/Symbolic** and on **subjectivity** go into Lacan's theories of the subject in considerable detail, what follows is a brief synopsis of the key issues and a quick indication of their impact on film theory. (For more detailed explanation see also **apparatus, feminist film theory** and **suture**.)

What of Lacan and his development and rethinking of Freud's theory of the subject? First, he shifted the frame of reference away from Freud's preoccupations with the sexual drives and looked to language as the site for the construction of the subject, of subjectivity. This shift is justifiable in a number of ways, starting with the fact that Freud himself posits the Oedipal complex at an age when the child can talk. In other words, the speaking subject comes into being at the moment of the primal repression (of the desire for the mother). At the same time as the male child enters into the Oedipal complex, Freud notes that he turns his attention to objects other than his mother in order to compensate for the fear of her loss. Freud talks about the child's *fort da* game. The child throws a reel of cotton away and, in retrieving it, emits the sound '*da*'. The cotton reel, according to Freud's reading, is a substitute for the mother, the game a way of coming to terms with the loss of the mother (that is, of being separate from her, abandoned by her). The game and the word become a way of mastering her absence. That absence and control of absence is marked in language: '*da*'. For Lacan, the game represents the child's entry into language and the reel functions as a symbol standing in for what is missing. It signifies lack. According to Lacan, the child is born into the experience of lack and spends the rest of his/(her) life trying to recapture an imagined entity which is the moment he associates with pre-lack – the imagined unity with the mother.

A second reason for Lacan turning to a linguistic model follows closely on from the above and concerns the child's shift, thanks to the mirror stage, from the Imaginary into the Symbolic. The mirror stage is a kind of 'half-way house' between the Imaginary and the Symbolic. It belongs to the Imaginary domain, but moves the child from the dyad with the mother into an identification with its own specular image. Prior to the mirror stage, the child has no sense of separateness from the mother and, therefore, imagines itself as one. It is only after the mirror phase that it knows its difference and/or separateness from the mother. By this time, however, it has entered the Symbolic Order which is based in language – that is the 'Law' of the Father. Until this mirror phase, the child is pre-lack and pre-linguistic. Entry into the Symbolic is entry into language. It is also entry into lack. Language, therefore, becomes indissolubly based in and bound up with the concept of lack. Born into the experience of lack, the child as speaking subject is lack. What does this mean?

Primal repression for Freud is, as we have seen, the founding moment of the unconscious. Lacan, referring to this repression as primary, perceives this moment as an opening up of the unconscious, by which he means that the unconscious emerges as a result of the repression of desire. Lacan explains this occurrence in the following manner: the speaking subject comes into existence only because of the repression of the desire for the mother who is now lost. The child has relinquished its illusory/Imaginary identity with the mother and entered the Symbolic. Thus every time she or he enunciates 'I am' she or he also enunciates 'I am lack'. As Toril Moi (1985, 99-100) felicitously explains this difficult idea:

> The speaking subject that says 'I am' is in fact saying 'I am he (she) who has lost something' – and the loss suffered is the loss of the imaginary identity with the mother and the world. The sentence 'I am' could therefore best be translated as 'I am that which I am not' according to Lacan. ... To speak as subject is therefore the same as to represent the existence of repressed desire: the speaking subject *is* lack, and this is how Lacan can say that the subject is that which it is not.

Entry into language signifies both the birth of desire (the child recognizes it) and the repression of desire. Entry into language means entry into the social order, but it also means experiencing lack even further because desire can never be fully satisfied. Thus starts the unfulfillable search for the eternally lost object, what Lacan calls *l'objet petit-a* ('little "*a*"', *autre* meaning 'little "o"'' other, the mother).

A final reason for Lacan's choosing the linguistic model lies in the similarity between the signifying system of language and that of the subject. Words do not have predetermined intrinsic meanings, nor does the subject. Sign and referent are not and do not mean one and the same thing. For example, the word 'tree' refers to tree but it does not *mean* tree. Similarly, when the child looks into the mirror, unity with the mirror image is illusory. Furthermore, words can only be defined in relation to one another. The unified self (as Freud has shown, and Lacan makes clearer still) does not exist and subjectivity cannot be defined in a vacuum but only in relation to others.

According to Lacan there are three determining moments concerning the child's development as it moves from the Imaginary to the Symbolic – which is the necessary progression for development into the social order. The three moments are the mirror phase, accession to language and the Oedipus complex. I have already talked to some extent about the latter two moments in the discussion of the *fort da* game and submission to the Law of the Father, so I will be brief on those two points. But first let's examine the mirror stage which the child goes through around the age of six to eighteen months. When the mother holds the child up to the mirror it assumes that the reflection it sees in the mirror is itself. In this respect, it begins to develop a sense of identity separate from the mother. This is the moment in which the child sees itself as a unified being at the centre of the world. It experiences a moment of pure *jouissance* (jubilation) in this narcissistic identification. The body is taken for the love-object. The child *sees* itself as whole, whereas in actual terms until now it has sensed itself as fragmented and uncoordinated. It sees in the mirror image the ideal image, the unified/whole. This narcissistic moment of self-idealization produces misrecognition in identification. It also produces alienation. This imaginary mastery over the body anticipates what is not yet there, actual bodily mastery. This ideal image is also the one the (m)other is holding up to be seen – she holds up the ideal image. So the child also identifies with what it assumes is the mother's perception of it. The child moves from the utterance of misrecognition, 'that's me', to that of alienation, 'I am another'. That alienation has a double edge. That is, the child senses it is not that unified co-ordinated image in the mirror ('I am another') and because the perception with which the child identifies in the mirror is that of the mother's (she holds up the ideal image), the image is conditioned by the mother's look ('I am who my mother desires me to be').

Alienation occurs, then, because the image can signify as real only because of the presence of the (m)other − what Lacan, as we have seen, terms *l'objet petit-a* − and identification is possible only in relation to another. This exposes the gap between the idealized image and the subject. This means there can never be a unified self, only a divided subject. The child is a divided self between, on the one hand, the ideal image (the ego-ideal) and the false sense of unity with the self and, on the other, the need for its subjectivity to be confirmed by another.

We can see here how Lacan has reworked two key ideas in Freud's concept of the narcissistic ego: the divided self and the mediation of self-identity by others. Lacan's account of the next moment, accession to language, is also based in Freud: the *fort da* game. According to Lacan, this game represents the child's entry into language. However, Lacan also makes the point that because the other (the mother) is already present in the mirror stage so too is the notion of the Symbolic Order − that is, language. To explain: the self only signifies because of the signifying presence of the other (in this instance the mother); the other is constituted by and in the Symbolic Order, that is to say, in language. Therefore, the Symbolic is already always present in the Imaginary Order because of the presence of the (m)other. When the child enters into the Symbolic, it enters language but it also succumbs to the Law of the Father, laws of society, laws that are determined by the Other (with a capital O). The Other is a term which is coterminous with the Symbolic Order, language and the Law of the Father. Lacan's use of the term Other allows him to

281

formulate clearly the distinction between the Imaginary and the Symbolic orders. Thus in shorthand form he can refer to the capital O as distinct from the little o which refers to the imaginary relations with the other that take place within the Imaginary (the mirror-image, the mother). The capital O represents, then, the Law of the Father and the danger of castration – in these terms de*cap*itation (being de-capitalized from O to o).

In order to obtain a social identity, the child has to suppress its desire of the mother. Again, Lacan's version of the child's Oedipal phase has much in common with Freud's; but the difference is the use of a linguistic model rather than a purely bio-sexual one. This is what Lacan defines as the Symbolic Order. At the moment that the male child recognizes his desire for his mother, the father intercedes and imposes the patriarchal law. The father is the third member to enter the reflecting mirror. It is he who represents to the child the authoritative figure in the family. So the child imagines what the authoritative figurehead would say – the father is, therefore, a symbolic father. The father proscribes incest. This taboo is imposed linguistically and is defined by Lacan as the Law of the Father. Because it is based in language, patriarchal law is a Symbolic Order. In the Oedipal phase, then, the male child imagines himself to be what the mother lacks and therefore desires – that is, the phallus. However, this is proscribed by the Law of the Father, the patriarchal 'No'. Prohibition of fulfilling the incestual drive is marked in language. And the child will comply for fear of castration by the father. The male child enters into the Symbolic and adopts a speaking position that marks him as independent from the mother. Poor mother! In the pre-Oedipal phase she it is who has the power (to feed, to nurture) and, because she has the power, she is the 'phallic' mother. The post-Oedipal mother is powerless.

The male child conforms to the patriarchal law, upholds it and thus perpetuates it for generations to come – he follows in the 'name-of-the-father' so that when he says 'I' it comes from the same authorized speaking position as the language of the father, the Other. He becomes the subject of the Symbolic. However, as we know, his desire for the mother does not disappear, it gets repressed and enters into the unconscious. This means that his identification with the mother's object of desire, the phallus, does not disappear either, not altogether. For example, Lacan notes how the fetishist articulates this relation to desire around fetishistic objects such as women's shoes and bits of clothing. These are symbols of the mother's/woman's phallus in so far as it is absent and with which the fetishist identifies. We are reminded that in **film noir** the *femme fatale* is commodified in a fetishistic way (slinky black dress, high-heeled shoes, painted fingernails), but we could also consider François Truffaut's films with their constant figuration of women's legs. The transvestite similarly articulates this desire for the phallus in that he identifies with the phallus-as-hidden under the mother's dress. In other words, he identifies with a woman who has a hidden phallus. Fetishism, as we also know, is a strategy of disavowal faced by the fear of castration: the fetishist 'completes' the female body and in so doing denies difference, denies the lack. A reading of *Psycho* in this light shows not only to what degree Norman Bates had fetishized his mother for fear of castration but also how unable (unwilling) he was to forgo his desire to become or identify with his mother's object of desire, the phallus. He plays both fetishist and transvestite.

The subject represents itself in the field of the Other (language), that is, it represents itself through that which is outside of the self. A sense of fragmentation occurs which gets compounded by the fact that the subject can never fully be represented in speech since speech cannot reflect the unconscious. The subject, in representing the self, can only do so, then, at the cost of division (conscious/unconscious; self/Other). As the (conscious) subject seeks to represent the self in the field of the Other, it does so at the expense of coming after the fact or word, by which time the (unconscious) subject is already not there but becoming something else. The conscious subject utters 'I' and becomes situated as 'I': the spoken subject becomes presence. However, the

283

unconscious subject is already beyond that 'I' and becoming something else: the spoken subject now becomes absence. As the spoken subject fades, becomes lack, so the subject will attempt to recapture itself as a unified being, the idealized image (ego-ideal) of the Imaginary. But, as we recall, this image is an external one, the subject as seen from outside, the subject as it imagines others (starting with the mother) see it. Lacan reasons that this is where the subject confronts the divided notion of the self: the image of the self is accurate but delusory. It is the same and other. The subject (mis) recognizes itself both as itself and as other. The subject is decentred, lacking and fading (for further detail see **enunciation**).

The two orders, the Imaginary and the Symbolic, are, as we have seen, always co-present (sutured as Lacan puts it). The Imaginary is the field of fantasies and images associated with the mirror phase and it never disappears because it involves the **mediation** of self-identification through another. It is, therefore, always already present in adult relationships. The Symbolic is the field of social and cultural symbolism. It is through this Order, which is based in language, that the subject can be represented or constituted. It is through this Order that the subject can articulate its desires and feelings. There is, however, a third Order of subjectivity, what Lacan calls the Real. The Real Order refers to what is outside the subject, what is 'out there', what the subject bumps up against but does not make sense of immediately – because it cannot or it will not. The Real Order is what subsists outside symbolization, what has been expelled or foreclosed by the subject. If something gets excluded from the Symbolic it appears in the Real. It is what the subject is unable to speak, so it is like a hole in the Symbolic Order. Only through reconstruction can the Real be understood. The Real Order is not repression but foreclosure – it is the disaffirmation (rejection) that something exists for the subject. The Real is often experienced as an hallucination and, unsurprisingly, is linked with death and sexuality – what is 'the beyond of desire'. Thus, for example, the trauma of weaning is not understood then as such by the child but is signified in an hallucinatory form by the child making sucking noises. Fear of castration cannot be symbolized by the child, so it gets expelled into the Real Order, hallucinated say as a cut finger. The primal scene is hallucinated as the father brutalizing, perhaps even killing, the mother. The Real then is that which is prohibited the speaking subject (the subject inscribed into the Other, the Symbolic Order). Language in its first manifestation to the child is marked by the phallic signifier – the patriarchal 'No'. To break that prohibition means castration, death, lack. To enter into it means to adopt the same speaking position, that is, to be subject of that language that prohibits. This means that death and *jouissance* – because they are 'the beyond of desire', because they violate what the Law of the Father prohibits – must remain unspoken.

The key concepts we need to bear in mind when considering the impact of psychoanalysis on film theory, then, are: the construction of subjectivity and most particularly the notion of the divided self; the three orders of subjectivity, the Imaginary, the Symbolic and the Real; and, finally, the unconscious and the repression of desire. These terms of reference will be briefly elaborated upon below, but first a word about female subjectivity. (For more detail see Benvenuto and Kennedy, 1986; Grosz, 1990; Lapsley and Weslake, 1988.)

Psychoanalysis and the female subject So far in this entry, little or nothing has been said about the female subject. Freud devotes two essays to the matter but Lacan does not examine it in much detail. Indeed, for Lacan the woman does not exist as subject, she is 'not being', 'not all', she is the other of the phallic function ('*l'objet petit-a*'). Lacanian feminists and feminist theorists do, however, investigate female subjectivity and argue that there is such a thing as a female Oedipal trajectory (see **feminist film theory** and **Oedipal trajectory**).

As far as Freud is concerned, the female child enjoys a pre-Oedipal relationship with the mother that is similar to the male child. Freud sees the Oedipal complex for the girl as dynamically different from the boy (see Freud's essay: 'Female Sexuality', Freud, 1931). According to Freud, the girl sees herself as born in lack so she rejects the mother and turns to the father to get herself a penis (in the form of a baby). That desire for the father gets transferred on to a male other (who ultimately *is* the father). Successful completion for the female is, then, motherhood (getting a penis in the substitute form of a baby). However, Freud argues that because there is no castration fear, the female child never fully gives up the Oedipal complex and that she is thus always bisexually poised.

Freud and Lacan concur (in different terms) that the libido is masculine. For Lacan this is because sexual difference is inscribed in language only in relation to the phallus. Freud talks of the riddle of femininity, asks the question 'what does woman want', speaks of her as the 'dark continent'. Lacan perhaps tells us something of what is going on in this phallocratic **discourse** when he says that women do not have the fear of castration, that they enjoy something that men cannot, in that they can have the phallus in intercourse – which a man never can (not even a homosexual). Lacan states that male desire is linked to enjoyment of the phallus but at the expense of sexual enjoyment. The phallus is the signifier of the Symbolic, but it is also the reminder that one is not a unified self. Phallic enjoyment is achieved in language, that is in mastery: control, not abandonment. Lacan speculates that women derive *jouissance* (jubilation) from sex, an unspeakable enjoyment (Benvenuto and Kennedy, 1986, 185–93). This sounds very much like an assertion of the unfathomability of female **sexuality**. Whatever the case, if it is unspeakable then it is something that cannot be symbolized. If this is so, then female sexuality, to some degree or another, has been expelled to the Real Order. We know that sexuality and death are in the realm of the Real; in the realm of the inexpressible. *Jouissance* is also in the realm of the Real, it is what is forbidden the speaking subject, because it too is 'the beyond of desire' (1986, 180). Thus female sexuality becomes perceivable as hallucinatory because unspeakable, as close to death because of her surplus of enjoyment (*jouissance*). This will prove interesting when we come to consider film theory.

286

But for now what of the female subject and what of her Oedipal complex? Lacan is much less, if at all, clear about the girl child than Freud. When she perceives her sameness with her mother, she experiences her lack as being non-phallic. She discovers that she, like her mother, is castrated – is already what the male child most fears. Her sexual drives impel her towards the truly phallic, the father. The father must once again impose the Law of the Father and forbid her sexual access. When the girl child says 'I' the question becomes, whose 'I' is it? She cannot be subject of the Symbolic in the same way as the male child can because the authorized speaking position is that of the father, and language is marked by the phallus. If she cannot be subject then she must be object of the Symbolic (that is, language); and if she is object of the Symbolic then she must also be the object rather than the subject of desire (she is fixed by language since it is not hers).

The whole notion of identity for the male child is bound up with the question of sexual difference and language. As for the female child, first, she will never fully relinquish her desire for her mother because there is no recognition of it within the Law of the Father. Second, she will never fully enter into the Symbolic Order because the Law of the Father does not, in the final analysis, apply to her. And it is here that the questions surrounding female subjectivity become of real interest for feminists, because, as such, the female child is then doubly poised both sexually and in relation to language. With regard to the first point, we recall that her subjectivity is determined by her sameness with her mother. She is then doubly desiring, first, of her own sex (the mother) and also of the male sex (her 'natural' trajectory is to desire the father and, forbidden that desire by the father, she will then seek to fulfil it by finding a male other). In terms of language she is doubly positioned. She is pre-linguistic. Because she can never be subject of patriarchal language she is always outside it. She is not subject of language (unlike the male child) but object of the Symbolic Order. However, and here is the paradox, she is also *in* the Symbolic Order. As we have seen, she must be there in the patriarchal constructs of sexual identity because her reflection as (m)other has to be in the mirror for the male to recognize his difference.

It is clear that the male child has a vested interest in obeying the father and entering the Symbolic. However, it is equally clear that the female child does not have that same interest. She is never completely free from desiring her mother. Furthermore, because of their sameness, there is unity in identification. As with the male child, the mother is her first love-object. But because there is no perceived difference, there is no fear of castration. What, then, will motivate her' to turn away from her mother and desire the father? Freudians argue that she turns away through penis envy. The mother cannot provide her with a penis so she will turn to the father for him to provide her with it in the form of a child. Lacanians, at least feminist Lacanians, argue that since she must enter into the social order of things – that is, the Symbolic – she will be obliged to turn from the mother even though she will never fully relinquish her desire of the mother. However this also means that in order to fulfil her Oedipal trajectory and enter into the social order of things, the female child must function as the other that confirms male subjectivity. To withhold such confirmation means punishment through one form or another of marginalization from the social order. To provide it is not without its problems either. Whose perception of the subject is she confirming? We must not forget that the image in the mirror is also conditioned by the mother's look. The male child identifies not just with his own image but with what he assumes is the mother's perception of him. His subjectivity is, to his mind, conditioned by the (desire of the) (m)other's.

Psychoanalysis and film theory In the 1970s film theorists (primarily French: Metz, Bellour, Baudry, all 1975), recognizing the limitations of a 'total theory' structuralist approach, turned to psychoanalysis as a way of broadening the theoretical framework. Drawing on Freud's account of the libido drives and Lacan's of the mirror stage, they sought to explain how film works at the unconscious level. By establishing an analogy of the screen with the mirror, they discovered a way of talking about spectator–screen relations. They argued that at each viewing there is an enactment for the spectator of the move from the Imaginary to the Symbolic Order, that is, an enactment of the unconscious processes involved in the acquisition of sexual difference, language and subjectivity. In other words, each viewing represents a repetition of the mirror and the Oedipal stages. Bellour makes the point that cinema functions simultaneously for the Imaginary (as mirror) and as the Symbolic (through the film discourses). And the spectator is in a constant state of flux between the two. We have already noted how, in terms of subjectivity, the two Orders are always co-present (to clarify this point further see **suture**).

According to these early theorists, in that cinema functions simultaneously for the Imaginary and the Symbolic, it follows that the cinema constructs the spectator as subject. In so far as the spectator is positioned voyeuristically by the filmic apparatus, the spectator is also identified with the look, with all that that connotes in terms of visual pleasure. The projector functions as the eye, and that eye is all-seeing. Thus visual pleasure is also bound up with the principle of lawless seeing (unwatched by those on screen, the viewer watches). Going to the cinema implies the desire to repeat pleasure in viewing. But, because viewing also involves a re-enactment of the Imaginary narcissistic identification with the image and lawless seeing, it implies that there is a desire to repeat the experience of *jouissance*. Given this identificatory process, it is not difficult to see why Metz would speak of cinemagoing and viewing as a regression to childhood.

Metz argues that it is not just the process of voyeurism that is involved in film-viewing, but also that of fetishism. Fetishism and voyeurism are the two strategies adopted to disavow difference. To contain and make safe the (m)other's lack (absence of a phallus) and to allay thereby the fear of castration, the woman is made object of the gaze (voyeurism), or has a part of her body over-invested in so that what is present (for example, legs or breasts) stands in for what is absent (fetishism). Fetishism occurs on screen within the

image, as in the case of the fetishizing of the body of the *femme fatale* in film noir. But, says Metz, fetishism operates also at a far more basic level. The image as image and the cinematic apparatus as apparatus are both fetish, because they stand in for, make present, what is absent. As such, they disavow what is lacking, they disavow difference. Similarly the spectator, in watching cinema, is disavowing lack, difference. The spectator knows that presence is absence, that what is there is not there, that what is being seen is lack (absence). Yet the spectator, says Metz, disavows it and the apparatus in its seamlessness disguises this absence, it sutures the spectator into that disavowal (see **suture**).

It is in these investigations into cinema's relation to voyeurism and fetishism and its relation to the Imaginary and Symbolic Orders that these early years of psychoanalytic film theory made their greatest inroads into the advancing of film theory. Cinema was seen to embody psychic desire. The screen became the site for the projection of our fantasies and desires, that is, for our unconscious. In this way, it was presumed that the cinema positioned the spectator as desiring subject, therefore, as subject of the apparatus – starting with the camera, with which the spectator identifies. These first theorizings were not entirely unproblematic, however. Indeed, they presented at least three problems, not least of which was the exclusively phallocratic reading of cinematic practices. These issues were picked up by feminist film theorists – starting with Laura Mulvey (1975). The identified problems were, first, that in this reading it is assumed that the spectator–screen relation is only one-way; second, that the subject is male in its positioning; and third, that film texts are organized in such a way as to give a **preferred reading**.

Feminist film theorists, while acknowledging that psycho-analysis as a discourse oppresses women, none the less insisted that it was for that very reason that it was important to investigate it seriously, not simply to understand it but to be able to expose the phallocentric construction of subjectivity – starting with Freud's notion of penis envy and Lacan's asser-tion that our subjectivity is determined in relation to language and its signifier, the phallus. To understand how women have become positioned as they have, the argument goes, is to make possible a **deconstruction** of that construction. In terms of film **theory**, the film text in this context stands as a dream, a fantasy or the analysand, and the critic or theorist takes on the role of the analyst. Thus for instance feminist critics have managed to look at 'themes (such as mother/daughter bonding or Oedipal triangles) in order to understand how *patriarchal signifying systems have represented such systems*' (Kaplan, 1990, 15, her stress). Furthermore through this deconstructionist approach they have been able to give readings against the grain, that is, readings that are not the encoded, preferred reading.

During the 1980s and 1990s, therefore, problems brought about by a phallic-centred reading of cinema have been largely debated and that reading has been contested. As a result, psychoanalytic film theory has developed considerably in the areas of spectator viewing and textual analysis. Spectator positioning is now seen as more heterogeneous or pluralistic (across **gender**, **class**, race, age, sexuality, nationality and creed). The spectator-subject is as much constituting of as constituted by the filmic text (see **ideology**). So the spectator–screen relation is at least two-way. Finally, the Oedipal trajectory of the classic narrative is no longer perceived as exclusively male – particularly within film genres that are not evidently all-male, such as **melodrama** and **film noir**. The female Oedipal trajectory is now being investigated in terms, first, of mother/daughter relations and, second, of lesbian relations (even if subliminal).

I want to conclude this entry on another related issue with regard to the female Oedipal trajectory, this time in its relation to desire. Whilst from the very beginning of the introduction of psychoanalysis into film theory considerable attention had been paid to the male Oedipal trajectory *and* desire, it was not until recently that this question, as it concerned the female, came into focus. Barthes, in his book *Le Plaisir du texte* (1973), makes the distinction between pleasure and *jouissance*. He is talking primarily about literary texts, but the distinction holds good for other texts, including the bodily text. Pleasure is what the reader derives from the closure offered by realist texts. Conversely, *jouissance* is derived from modes of narration that do not provide closure. Barthes speaks of *jouissance* occurring in reading a text when his body follows its own ideas. *Jouissance* is experienced corporeally not linguistically. He encounters his enjoying body: *corps de jouissance* is his term. In this way he experiences an erotic investment in the textual object. Barthes seems to be echoing Freud's notion of the narcissistic ego here. Both pleasure and *jouissance*, says Barthes, can be experienced within the same text. We can now see that pleasure is experienced in the Symbolic Order (social order, control, closure) and can be enunciated in language. Conversely, *jouissance* is experienced within the Imaginary (since the term refers to when it was first experienced as that moment of imaginary unity with the self as reflected in the mirror). As such it remains unspoken. Since pleasure and *jouissance* can both be experienced within a same text it follows that both the Imaginary and the Symbolic can be experienced within a single text as well. The Imaginary and the Symbolic, in reading as elsewhere, are always co-present.

But let's pick up this question of *jouissance* and female desire. We recall that *jouissance* is, of course, extra-discursive. *Jouissance* is, first, that imaginary moment in the mirror phase when the image and the self are united in fusional bliss. *Jouissance* is before language, what remains unspoken. Henceforth, upon entry into the Symbolic – now that the child can speak – *jouissance* joins the realm of the Real Order of subjectivity and becomes associated with that which cannot be spoken: death and desire. We noted above that, according to Lacan, woman is both 'not all/not being' and the site of *jouissance*. We have also noted that she is sexually and linguistically doubly positioned. On the one hand, she is desiring of the Other or father and as such is *in* but not *of* the Symbolic Order. On the other, she is both pre-Oedipal and pre-linguistic. She can, therefore, experience *jouissance* far more readily than the male for whom such unspeakable enjoyment is prohibited by the Law of the Father. Viewed from this phallocentric point of view, *jouissance* is represented as woman's 'natural' realm. This is her 'deep and dark mystery'.

But, and here is a first complication, *jouissance* stands for the fusional pleasure of the Imaginary: the moment of narcissistic identification with the ego ideal. It stands also for what the subject always already desires: the desired fusion with the lost object – *'objet petit-a'* – the (m)other. This would suggest that the female subject can experience what the male subject cannot: unification with the self *and* with the mother. She has something that male subject does not. Significantly, beyond the already existing lesbian overtones in this unification, when the woman experiences childbirth for herself she identifies with, becomes her mother as well as being mother herself. She is reunited with her mother's body at the same time as she is giving birth to her self. Lesbianism, reproduction and narcissism unite in unspeakable enjoyment: *jouissance*. Equally important, since the female subject, according to this phallocentric view, can experience *jouissance,* she is 'naturally' represented in the Real Order. This means that, in terms of her sexuality, she has been expelled or disaffirmed by the male subject – he who is constituted by language which is marked by the phallic signifier. She is outside symbolization. Her sexuality remains unspoken – in phallic terms it remains a hole in the Symbolic Order, the male subject rejects that it exists. We recall that the Real is often experienced as an hallucination and is, of course, closely aligned with sexuality and death. So the male subject, in foreclosing the female subject's sexuality into the Real Order as *jouissance*, is in fact experiencing it as an hallucination, as 'the beyond of desire', as death.

It is not difficult to see that a phallocentric world will construct the female subject in such a way that she will not derive power from this. And it is noteworthy that her experience of desire, as in *jouissance*, is mute and biologically, not linguistically, based. Significantly, 'bad' motherhood gets considerable exposure in films as much as in other media. Take for example the wicked mother of Joan Crawford in *Mommie Dearest* (Frank

293

Perry, 1981), the over-zealous mother as the eponymous *Mildred Pierce* (Michael Curtiz, 1945) who is 'punished' by one of her daughters for her over-maternalizing behaviour, or the self-sacrificing but ambitious mother in *Stella Dallas* (King Vidor, 1937) who will relinquish her bond for the sake of her daughter's upward mobility. Cyborg-reproduction movies like *Alien³* (Fincher, 1992), *The Fly* (David Cronenberg, 1986) and *Coma* (Michael Crichton, 1977) attempt either to punish the woman for having sole rights to reproduction organs or to show that they are not necessary after all. And films that have men as reproducers, as in the recent Schwarzenegger movie *Junior* (Ivan Reitman, 1994), although silly, none the less say much about male fantasies.

Women in film noir are frequently punished for their refusal to conform to patriarchal signifying systems. Rather, they are first constructed as being in control of their own sexuality and then punished for it. In other words, the film noir as a genre puts on screen the 'unspeakable', feminine *jouissance*. It represents the unrepresentable, the Real Order. It is interesting to note that the male protagonist is usually unclear and confused about what is happening in the narrative – as if he is partly blinded, or as if he is hallucinating (as in *Double Indemnity*, Billy Wilder, or *Murder My Sweet*, Edward Dmytryk, both 1944). Arguably the film that best illustrates the male subject's hallucination of female subjectivity is Otto Preminger's *Laura* (1944). The male protagonist, the detective Marc McPherson, is obsessed by a portrait of a woman he believes is dead, Laura. He is obsessed to the point that he literally hallucinates her. He also pursues women whom he momentarily misrecognizes as her – only, finally, to come face to face with her, alive.

As far as film noir is concerned, we can also see that this **mise-en-scène** of the Real Order, at least where female subjectivity is concerned, makes possible a playing out of the fear of castration. Here the strong 'phallic' woman is represented as sexually armed and dangerous. The fact that she is fetishized through her dress-code should not, however, escape our attention. It tells us that she is after all contained by the

294

male and that, although she may behave transgressively throughout the film, she none the less will be put in her place by the end (for example *The Woman in the Window*, 1944; *Gilda*, 1946; *Kiss Me Deadly*, 1955). (For a sample reading of applications of psychoanalysis to film see Doane, Mellencamp and Williams (eds), 1984; Doane, 1992; Kaplan, 1980, 1983, 1990 and 1992; Krutnick, 1991; Kuhn 1982 and 1985; Lebeau, 1994; Lurie, 1980; Modleski, 1982 and 1988; Mulvey, 1989; Rose, 1986.)

psychological thriller – *see* **thriller**

queer cinema   Queer cinema has been in existence for decades
although it lacked a label. Films of Jean Cocteau and Jean Genet
in France in the 1930s and 1950s (such as *Le Sang d'un poète*,
Jean Cocteau, 1934, and *Le Chant d'amour*, Jean Genet, 1950)
are cited as the forefathers (*sic*). It is a cinema that is identified
with **avant-garde** or **underground** movements (for example
Kenneth Anger's and Andy Warhol's 1960s films in the United
States). Queer cinema itself was introduced as a concept in 1991
at the Toronto Festival of Festivals, to refer to a spate of films
that re-examined and reviewed histories of the image of gays.
These films proposed renegotiated subjectivities, men looking
at men, gazes exchanged, and so on. They also took over genres previously considered mainstream, subverting them by
bringing the question of pleasure on to the screen and the cel-
ebration of **excess**. In certain cases these films reinscribed the
homosexual text where previously it had been elided. See, for
example, Derek Jarman's historical film *Edward II*, (1991), or
Tom Kalin's murder/crime **thriller** *Swoon* (1992) (the latter is
a 'remake or retake', setting the record straight (!) of an earlier
Alfred Hitchcock film, *Rope* (1948), and a Richard Fleischer
film, *Compulsion* (1959) – both films completely elide the
homosexual dimension to the two killers' relationship).

Always a cinema of the margins, only now in the 1990s,
in the light of the tragedy of AIDS, has queer cinema become
a more visible cinema. Indeed, the New Queer Cinema, as

this cinema is also labelled, has now become a marketable commodity if not an identifiable movement. One of the leaders of the United States queer cinema is Gus Van Sant (*My Own Private Idaho*, 1991; *Even Cowgirls Get the Blues*, 1993). *New* Queer Cinema was a term coined in a 1992 *Village Voice* article by B. Ruby Rich to describe the renaissance in gay and lesbian film-making represented by the Americans Todd Haynes, Jennie Livingstone, Gus Van Sant, Gregg Araki, Laurie Lynd, Tom Kalin and the British film-makers Derek Jarman and Isaac Julien. Queer cinema is not a single aesthetic but a collection of different aesthetics – what Rich delightfully refers to as 'Homo-Pomo'. Queer cinema is above all a male homosexual cinema and focuses on the construction of male desire. Some lesbian film-makers have made films that come under this label and it is instructive that they have made films that address not just their **sexuality** (as in *Go Fish!*, Rose Troche, 1994) but that of their male counterparts (*Paris is Burning*, Jennie Livingstone, 1991). (For further reading see Dyer, 1990; Gever, Parmar and Greyson, 1993; Bad Object-Choices, 1991; Dyer, 1977; Russo, 1981.)

realism (*see also* **documentary, naturalism, seamlessness, socio-realism, suture**)   The term *realism* comes from a literary and art movement of the nineteenth century which went against the grand tradition of classical idealism and sought to portray 'life as it really was'. The focus was on ordinary life – indeed the lives of the socially deprived and the conditions they had to bear. As far as the film camera is concerned, it is not difficult to see why it is perceived as a 'natural' tool for realism, since it reproduces 'what is there' (that is, the physical environment). Film as cinema makes **absence** presence, it puts reality up on to the screen. It purports to give a direct and 'truthful' view of the 'real world' through the presentation it provides of the characters and their environment. Realism functions in film on both the **narrative** level and the figurative (that is, pictorial/photographic). In this regard, physical realism marries into psychological realism via the narrative structures. Generally speaking, realist films address social issues. However, because the narrative closure of these films tends to provide easy solutions, this form of realism on the whole serves only to naturalize social problems and divisions and not provide any deep insight into causes.

There are, arguably, two types of realism with regard to film. First, seamless realism, whose **ideological** function is to disguise the illusion of realism. Second, aesthetically motivated realism, which attempts to use the camera in a non-manipulative fashion and considers the purpose of realism in its ability to convey a reading of reality, or several readings even. As far as the seamless type of realism is concerned, film technique – supported by narrative structures – erases the idea of illusion, creates the 'reality effect'. It hides its mythical and **naturalizing** function and does not question itself – obviously, because to do so would be to destroy the authenticity of its realism (see **myth**). Nothing in the camera-work, the use of **lighting**, **colour**, **sound** or **editing** draws attention to the illusionist nature of the reality effect. The whole purpose is to stitch the spectator into the illusion – keeping reality safe.

Conversely the realist aesthetic, first strongly advocated by French film-makers in the 1930s and subsequently by André Bazin in the 1950s, is one that recognizes from the start that realist **discourses** not only suppress certain truths, they also produce others. In other words, realism produces realisms. And, although due caution must be exercised when making a realist film, this multiplicity of realisms means that a film cannot be fixed to mean what it shows – as occurs in seamless realism. The realist aesthetic recognizes the reality-effect produced by cinematic **mediation** and strives, therefore, to use film technique in such a way that, although it does not draw attention to itself, it none the less provides the spectator with space to read the text for herself or himself. In other words, technique functions in this instance so as not to provide an encoded **preferred reading**. Rather, it seeks to offer as objectively as possible a form of realism. So this type of realism uses location shooting and natural lighting. Most of its cast is composed of non-professional actors. It employs long **shots** using **deep-focus** cinematography (to counter manipulation of the reading of the image), long takes (to prevent the controlling effects of editing practices) and the 90-degree angled shot that, because it is at eye level, stands as an objective shot.

After the Second World War, the American public wanted a more realist view of the country, which it found in the spate of **films noir**. In Italy economic necessity as much as a desire for a non-manipulative realism produced **Italian**

neo-realism, which picked up on realist traditions already in place in French and Italian cinema of the 1930s. Indeed, Jean Renoir – one of the major advocates of a politically motivated socio-realist cinema – is credited with making the first film of this kind, *Toni* (1934). In the 1960s France, for its part, pursued its interest in politically motivated realist films, albeit on a small scale, with the **cinéma-vérité** and documentary works of such film-makers as Jean Rouch. Finally, from the late 1950s into the 1960s, new wave cinemas emerged from Britain, France and Germany and provided the slice-of-life realist cinema (see **British New Wave**, **French New Wave**, **New German Cinema**). (For a full discussion of the debates around realism see Lapsley and Westlake, 1988, 157–80; Williams, 1980.)

reconstructions – *see* **historical films**

repetition/variation/opposition – *see* **narration**, **sequencing**

representation – *see* **feminist film theory**, **gender**, **sexuality**, **stereotypes**, **subjectivity**

resistances – *see* **avant-garde**, **counter-cinema**

reverse-angle shot – *see* **shot/reverse-angle shot**

road movie (*see also* **genre**) Road movies, as the term makes clear, are movies in which protagonists are on the move. Generally speaking, such a movie is **iconographically** marked through such things as a car, the tracking **shot**, wide and wild open spaces. In this respect, as a genre it has some similarities with the **western**. The road movie is about a frontiersmanship of sorts given that one of its codes is discovery – usually self-discovery. The **codes and conventions** of a road movie have meant that until fairly recently this genre has predominantly been a **gendered** one. Generically speaking, the road movie goes from *A* to *B* in a finite and chronological time. Normally the **narration** of a road movie follows an ordered sequence of events which lead inexorably to a good or bad end (compare the bad ending for the travellers in *Easy Rider*, Dennis Hopper, 1969, with the reasonable solution for the protagonist in *Paris Texas*, Wim Wenders, 1984). Genderically speaking, the traveller(s) is male and the purpose of the trajectory is to obtain self-knowledge. Recently, however, women have been portrayed as the travellers (as in *Thelma and Louise*, Ridley Scott, 1991) – and in this we can perceive a readiness to subvert or parody the genre. *The Adventures of Priscilla, Queen of the Desert* (Stephen Eliot, 1994) ironizes the macho-masculinity of the genre in a different way – this time a dancing troupe of drag-queens sets off across the Australian desert and all find fulfilment in one way or another.

rules and rule-breaking – *see* **counter-cinema, jump cut**

science fiction films (*see also* **genre**)   These are considered by
some critics to be a sub-genre of the **horror** movie (see Cook,
1985, 99); by others as a **genre** distinct from horror films
(see Kuhn and Radstone, 1990, 355); by others yet again as
a sub-genre (along with horror movies) of **fantasy** films
(Konigsberg, 1993, 303). These varied critical positions point
to the difficulties in demarcating and categorizing genres in
general and this one in particular. Interestingly, the French
use all three categories *fantastique*, *horreur* and *science fiction* to
distinguish between films which other countries might be
satisfied to lump under one label, namely horror.

Science fiction as a literary genre came about in the mid-
to late nineteenth century in response to advances in science
and technology. Two exemplary authors of the genre, Jules
Verne and H. G. Wells, from opposing positions, described
science's prowess in making possible what up until the turn
of the century had seemed impossible (for example submarines and space craft). Film, in so far as it can make visible
what is invisible, seems a natural medium for this kind
of narrative. However, science fiction films have been more
erratic in their appearances on screen than most other
genres. For example there were only a few produced during
the silent era and it could be said that as a genre it came
into its own only after 1950 (for reasons that become clear
below).

The earliest examples of science fiction movies date back to Georges Méliès with his *films fantastiques* that portrayed voyages to the moon and to the centre of the earth (1902). These, however, were benign comic narratives of humans encountering a series of adventures with strange phenomena which none the less ended 'happily' – marked by a return to safety (that is, the earth's surface). Apart from Méliès's work, which was very loosely based on Verne's writing, films in this genre have tended to be grounded more in the Wellsian fear of science outstripping our understanding and taking us over. Science fiction films produce a futuristic vision where we are no longer in control of what we have created (this curiously assumes that we currently do control science). This genre relies on the **audience**'s willingness to suspend disbelief and does so by playing on our fears of science. The few science fiction films made before 1950 tended to focus on technology as the science-demon that would destroy humanity.

After 1950 the trend was for humanity to be at risk from alien intruders that either invaded the earth or caught up with humans in outer space in a space-craft or on an alien planet (upon which the humans unquestioningly had the greater right to be, it would appear). It was not until this period that this genre or sub-genre became identified as a Hollywood genre. Apart from the *Flash Gordon* serials (1936–40), what little science fiction had been produced in western culture was of European origin – the most remarkable example being Fritz Lang's *Metropolis* (1926) with its futuristic city, and William Menzies's space fantasy *The Shape of Things to Come* (1936). However, the 1950s was the period of the Cold War at its highest. 'Reds under the bed', McCarthyism and the House Un-American Activities Committee's witch-hunt of supposed communists, the threat of the nuclear deterrent (albeit only ever used by the Americans against an enemy), the threat or fear of totalitarian regimes – all of these elements fed into the American political culture of the 1950s and found a steady reflection in contemporary film production. Aliens came in their droves from outer space on to the American screen (*Invaders from Mars*, *War of the Worlds*, *It Came from Outer Space*, all 1953 films, and *It Conquered the World*, 1956, etc., etc.).

After 1968 – the next watershed year, with Stanley Kubrick's *2001: A Space Odyssey* – the genre reintroduced technology as man's (*sic*) potential enemy but in a far more ambiguous way. In this film, man's responsibility as the maker of the technology is highlighted as Hal, the computer aboard the *2001* spaceship reminds us. Although Hal is destroyed because of his severe life-threatening malfunctioning, it is never resolved whether he is friend or foe. Later, this ambiguity surrounding Hal is mirrored in the representation of the alien, once science fiction returns in the 1970s and early 1980s (*The Man who Fell to Earth*, 1976; *Close Encounters of the Third Kind*, 1977, both Stanley Kubrick; *E.T.*, Steven Spielberg, 1982). This type of alien is generally unthreatening (once you get to know 'him') and often offers us a lesson in humility before departing (presumably back whence it came). It should be remembered that the 1970s was the Age of Aquarius, peace and flower power, sentiments that could extend to an enlightened openness at least towards individual aliens. There were rumblings of nastiness about, however, as in Ridley Scott's *Alien*, made in 1979. Technology and aliens were now to be feared equally – nay, might even be present in one and the same thing as this film and its two *Alien* sequels (to date) make clear, although in a very specific way. This *Alien* trilogy addresses the effects of feminism on patriarchy and male **sexuality**. Thus, rather than a political culture feeling under threat (as in the 1950s), it is now (White) male sexual culture that feels threatened. In *Alien*, men give birth to alien babies; by *Alien³*, the only remaining woman is implanted (artificially inseminated) with an alien egg. Reproductive technology is here, man has made it and as such threatens women's reproductive rights. Although this is not the first series of science fiction films to attract feminist critics to the genre, it sums up why this genre is of interest to them: because it shows the danger of science and technology, explores the underlying social anxieties regarding especially experiments in reproduction technology, and constructs of female sexuality as monstrous (Kuhn and Radstone, 1990, 356).

The science fiction film, then, *is* politically motivated – mostly, but not entirely, negatively. Technology *should* be questioned and attitudes to outsiders *should* come under scrutiny, but this is rare, as a quick gloss over the three main categories of films discussed above will show. The three types within this genre are: space-flight, alien invaders, futuristic societies. Lang's *Metropolis* is the prototype of this last category. But it also set the agenda for a critique of futuristic urban spaces by challenging the 1920s **modernist** belief in technological progress as a source of social change – a challenge still apparent today in Ridley Scott's *Blade Runner* (1982) and *Someone to Watch over Me* (1988). Space-flight films, on the other hand, have traditionally devoted more energy to exposing the virtuosities of film technology and as such have functioned as a vehicle for prowess (in real terms for the film industry, **metaphorically** for the space industry) until the arrival of Kubrick's 1968 film *2001,* which placed grave question marks on man's faith in and assumed superiority over technology. Finally, alien invader films, because they are probably the most prolific of the three categories and, arguably, the most conservative – in that they point at otherness as threatening to life and/or social mores – represent the most 'worrying' category of all with their innate potential for misogyny, racism and nationalistic chauvinism. (For further reading see Brosman, 1991.)

scopophilia/scopic drive/visual pleasure (*see also* **gaze**)
Literally, the desire to see. Sigmund Freud used the term scopic drive to refer to the infant's libidinal drive to pleasurable viewing. As such, it is closely attached to the mirror phase and the primal scene. In Lacanian **psychoanalysis** the mirror phase refers to the moment of recognition by the male child of his difference from his mother. And the primal scene, first identified by Freud, refers to the moment when the male child,

unseen by his parents, views them copulating. In psycho-analytic film theory (in the 1970s) scopophilia was adapted to elucidate the unconscious processes at work when the **spectator** views the screen. This spectator–screen analysis revealed that a double phenomenon occurs: first, cinema constructs the spectator as **subject** (the beholder of the gaze – that is, at the moment of the mirror phase); second, it establishes the desire to look (the drive to pleasurable viewing – that is, at the moment of the primal scene). Thus, as Metz (1975) stated, at each film viewing there occurs a re-enactment of the unconscious processes involved in the acquisition of sexual difference and, simultaneously, a **voyeuristic** positioning of the spectator (the viewer watches unseen in a darkened room or theatre).

At this juncture (early 1970s), the meaning of the mirror stage (fear of castration at the sight of sexual difference with the mother) and the implications of scopophilia for masculine erotic desire and the male **fetishizing** gaze were never brought into question. This would not occur until the mid-1970s, when the issue of **gendered** spectatorship finally got addressed, first by Laura Mulvey (1975), then by other feminist critics. They developed a theory to describe the pleasure derived from the gaze (usually male) of the character whose point of view it is within the film and, also, the pleasure derived by the spectator gazing upon the female body (whether nude or not). This gaze fixes the woman and in so doing fetishizes her, makes her the object not subject of desire. It fixes her, attributes meanings to her that are derived from another (male) perception or reading of the female bodily text. To this effect the woman has no **agency**.

Cinema functions through its **codes** to construct the way in which woman is to be looked at, starting with the normally male point of view within the film. The source of pleasure offered by that point of view to the male spectator (through identification) is clear. What, however, of the female spectator? Mulvey argues that for her to derive pleasure she must adopt the masculine point of view. Later feminist critics (Doane, 1982) nuance this masculinization of the female spectator, arguing that there are two viewing places: that of the female masochist identifying with the passive female character and that of the transvestite identifying with the active male protagonist or hero. Later still, Bergstrom (1985), Studlar (1985) and Modleski (1988) propose positioning the female spectator bisexually. In this position she can identify with the female character's predicament caught within socio-economic and sexual structures that make her 'victim'. But this identification can then lead to a regendered position that allows for a critique of such structures to take place (for further discussion see **feminist film theory**, **spectatorship** and **suture**).

seamlessness (*see also* **continuity editing**, **editing**, **spatial and temporal contiguity**, **suture**)   Used to refer to the **Hollywood** film style where – in the name of **realism** – the editing does not draw attention to itself. The spectator is presented with a **narrative** that is edited in such a way that it appears to have no breaks, no disconcerting unexplained transitions in time and space. Hence its seamlessness. Editing style that draws attention to itself (for example, through **jump cuts** and **unmatched shots**) is mostly found in oppositional, non-mainstream, **counter-cinema**.

semiology/semiotics/sign and signification (*see also* **structuralism**)   Semiology was a term coined by the Swiss linguistician Ferdinand de Saussure, in his lecture series on structural linguistics (1907–11), to refer to the study of signs within society, which he believed should be possible thanks to the application of structural linguistics to any sign system. Semiotics, coined a little earlier by the American philospher C. S. Peirce, is the term that has most currency in English speaking countries and also refers to the study of signs. However, in general, the term semiotics refers more to Saussure's theories than to Peirce's. And since Saussure's theories have had the greater impact to date in film theory we will limit this discussion to his (those interested in the adoption of Peirce's theories should see Wollen, 1972).

Saussure's structural linguistic theories, which were to remain 'unknown' until Roland Barthes brought them into the limelight in the late 1950s (in his book *Mythologies*, 1957), gave birth to a new theoretical system known as **structuralism**. In his *Cours de linguistique générale* (published posthumously in 1915) Saussure set out the base paradigm by which all language could be ordered and understood. The base paradigm, *langue/parole*, was intended as a function that could simultaneously address the profound universal structures of language (*langue*) and its manifestation in different cultures (*parole*). Saussure made the vital point that the governing conventions in relation to this sign system are very arbitrary and that there is no necessary correlation between the word (the signifier) and the object or idea being designated (the signified). This arbitrariness is manifest in the differences between languages. It is also this arbitrary relationship between signifier and signified which makes it possible for this linguistic system to function as a general science of signs – meaning that it can address other sign systems, can examine other sign systems as operating like a language. Just to clarify the meaning here: semiotics, in that it studies the social production of meaning through linguistic sign systems, stresses that language as a cultural production is societally, not individually, bound. Given that there are social or cultural productions *other than language* which produce meanings (for example sport, games), that is there are other sign systems, semiotics became a useful tool with which to analyse the process of meaning production in such sign systems as literature, cinema, television and advertising and, ultimately, other forms of popular culture (pop songs, dress-codes and so on). Barthes (1957), for example, used semiotics to examine popular cultural artefacts of the 1950s and the language of mass culture.

Saussure broke new territory in the study of language which, until his new approach, had been limited to philology, that is, to how language has evolved rather than to how

308

language works, produces meaning, which is what interested Saussure. Meaning, he argued, could not exist independently from a system which, in the case of language, meant *langue* (that which *can* be uttered) and *parole* (that which *is* uttered). Language functions as a system of signs but not in a simplistic one-to-one relation (that is, language does not acquire meaning by referring to things). According to Saussure the linguistic sign was not a name that could be attached to an object but a composite of signifier and signified (word and concept). Because it is not a case of a one-to-one correspondence, language does not therefore reflect reality. Rather, language becomes a signifying system that sets 'reality' before the ears. It constitutes, **mediates** reality and as such has an **ideological** function. It is not **transparence** that it signifies, but **myth**. And it is this latter point (actually refined by Lacan) along with one other crucial one that made semiotics – especially in its structuralist formation – a fertile theoretical field to be worked by film theorists. The other crucial point is that semiotics reopened the debate around cinema as language (a debate initiated in the 1920s but closed or shut out by the *Cahiers du cinéma* group's polemical writings privileging the **auteur** as producer of meaning). Although cinema could not, in the final analysis, be seen as analogous to the base *langue/parole* paradigm, it was none the less a sign system that produced meaning, and in that respect could, like all other social or cultural productions, be seen as a language (see discusssion of Metz's work in this context under **structuralism**).

Semiotics analyses the structural relations, within a system, that function to produce meaning. Signs can be understood only in relation to other signs within the system, and this occurs, in the first instance, in two ways. A sign derives meaning simultaneously by what it is not and by what it is in combination with. Saussure referred to paradigmatic and syntagmatic axes to explain this concept. The paradigmatic axis is vertically connected to the horizontal, syntagmatic axis. The former refers to the choices available, to the possible substitutes (thereby pointing to what the sign is not – man not woman, boy, girl; cat not hat, mat). The latter refers to

309

the combination of elements actually present and how that combination functions as a signifying chain to produce meaning (the cat sat on the mat, the boy sat on the mat). In this respect meaning is produced out of differences (by what is present in relation to what is absent).

A second way by which signs produce meaning is in relation to their referential reality. The term Saussure used for this concept was *signification*. Although Saussure had identified the concept, it was Barthes (1957) who developed it more fully in his analysis of the way signs work in culture. Within what he terms the semiological system, Barthes identifies two orders of signification, **denotation and connotation**, which in turn produce a third – ideology (actually, although Barthes identifies this last order, it is Hartley (1982, 217) who suggests calling it the third). At the first level is denotation: a simple first order of meaning, the surface literal meaning. At the second level, signs operate in two ways: as connotative agents and as myth-makers. This second order of signification occurs when the first order meets the values and **discourses** of the culture (1982, 215). Connotation, as the word implies, means all the associative and evaluative meanings attributed to the sign by the culture or the person involved in using it – and as such is always sensitive to context. Myth is the way in which we are enabled to understand the culture in which we find ourselves. At this level of signification, signs activate myths, provide cultural meaning.

By way of illustration let us take a photograph of Marilyn Monroe. At the denotative level this is a photograph of the movie star Marilyn Monroe. At a connotative level we associate this photograph with Marilyn Monroe's star qualities of glamour, **sexuality**, beauty – if this is an early photograph – but also with her depression, drug-taking and untimely death if it is one of her last photographs. At a mythic level we understand this sign as activating the myth of **Hollywood**: the dream factory that produces glamour in the form of the **stars** it constructs, but also the dream machine that can crush them – all with a view to profit and expediency.

This second order of signification reflects subjective responses but ones which can only be motivated by the fact that they are shared by the community of a particular culture, a sharing that Fiske and Hartley (1978, 46) refer to as inter-subjectivity. This intersubjectivity works in two ways and it is in this respect that we can see the third order of signification coming into operation: ideology. 'This intersubjectivity is culturally determined' (1978, 46). Thus on the one hand our individual response is affected or influenced *by* the culture in which we find ourselves and, on the other, that response signifies our appertaining *to* that culture. This dynamic is a prime way in which ideology functions. Ideology inserts itself at the interface between language and political organization and as such is the discourse that invests a culture (nation) with meaning. Louis Althusser (1984, 37) – echoing Gramsci (Althusser is quoted rather than Gramsci because of his influence on film theory during the 1960s and 1970s) – makes the point that ideology is not just a case of a controlling few imposing an interpretation of the nation upon the subjects of the state, but that in ideology the subjects also represent to themselves 'their relation to those conditions of existence which is represented to them there'. In other words, they make ideology have meaning by colluding with it and by acting according to it because of the reassuring nature of national identity or cultural membership. To return to our earlier example, the photograph of Marilyn Monroe and its ideological function, the reading we now get is as follows: the film industry as exemplified by Hollywood is a powerful, rich, organized industry, in which one can succeed only by conforming to the preordained role assigned to one. Deviancy (booze, drugs or sexuality) will not be tolerated. In other words, Hollywood is about reproducing the institution, culture or ideology of the White middle-class United States to which all should aspire, or, if they do not, they will perish. Almost a Taylorization of national identity (a compartmentalized assembly-line approach)!

Semiotics in film theory, then, by opening up filmic texts in the way illustrated above, showing how they produce

311

meaning, has served among other things to uncover, make explicit the **naturalization** process of realist, mainstream cinema. Latterly as it has become inflected with other theories (**psychoanalysis**, Marxism, feminism) it has broadened its frame of reference not just to address the filmic text as producer of meaning but to examine **spectator**-positioning and the spectator's role in meaning-production. By unravelling how meaning is produced, other questions can be raised such as the way in which the inscription of sexual difference in the images is 'taken for granted'. (For fuller analyses and greater examination of the evolution of the semiotic debate see Lapsley and Westlake, 1988; Andrew, 1984; Stam, Burgoyne and Flitterman-Lewis, 1992. In terms of applying the theory see Fiske and Hartley, 1978 (although it addresses television and not film it is a very clear text for initiates to semiotics); for analyses of representation and sexuality see De Lauretis, 1984; Kuhn, 1985.)

sequencing/sequence (*see also* **editing/montage**)   A sequence is normally composed of scenes, all relating to the same logical unit of meaning. For this reason, the length of a sequence is equivalent to the visual and/or **narrative** continuity of an episode within a film (sequences can be likened to chapters within a novel). It is useful when studying film to be able to segment out a film into sequences since this gives the student or **spectator** a sense of the formal structure of the film as well as the relations between the sequences. Since film is (notionally) constructed around the formula of repetition/opposition/variation, to be able to perceive this structurally gives a first reading to the filmic text. On average a film has twenty-three or twenty-four sequences if it is a mainstream or **Hollywood** film; European cinema tends towards a lower number (eleven to eighteen). Traditionally the opening sequence of a film is composed of establishing **shots** to orientate the spectator safely, and in this respect the beginning of each sequence functions to reorientate the spectator (alternatively, the closing shot or comment in the previous sequence sets up what is to follow). The closing of a sequence is marked by some form of transition: a **fade**, **wipe**, iris or a **cut**. (In an 'iris' the image is phased in or out in imitation of the opening and shutting of the camera lens.) These transitions serve to make the film easy to read. Conversely, **jump cuts** or **unmatched shots** are two procedures used to counter the safe orientation provided by traditional transition markers. These transitions are like punctuation marks, so they will also be found within sequences. The fade and iris are soft transitions. Wipes and cuts are hard. The former are more readily associated with earlier cinema, although contemporary films do make use of them (sometimes as a homage to the cinema heritage). These soft transition markers can serve to denote a lapse in time, states of mind and the subconscious, so they are less likely to be found within a sequence but rather between sequences. Of the hard transitions, the wipe is hardly ever seen nowadays. A cut between sequences can imply a direct link between the two, in either narrative or chronology. Cuts within a sequence serve to give a rhythm (fast or slow, depending on how frequently they are used) and also allow relations of space to become clear to the spectator (so long as the various degree rules are 'obeyed': see **30-degree rule** and **180-degree rule**). If cuts are not used conventionally within a sequence they point to the idea of fragmentation or separation. (For more detail on how sequencing functions throughout a film, see **editing**).

setting Part of the total concept of **mise-en-scène**. The setting is literally the location where the action takes place, and it can be artificially constructed (as in studio sets) or natural (what is also termed location shooting). Certain film movements are readily associated with a type of setting: the distorted settings of **German expressionist** films, the dimly lit rainwashed streets and empty cold interiors in **films noir**, the natural settings of Italy's cities and countryside in **Italian neo-realism** films.

sexuality (*see also* **stereotype**)   Cinema is one structure among others that constructs sexuality. Until the impact of **feminist theory** (1970s) this was 'normally' taken to mean White male sexuality – as opposed, in the first instance, to White female passivity – that is, women perceived or constructed as sex symbols, sex goddesses (objects to be desired, rather than desiring **subjects**). Equally, sexuality was 'normally' taken to refer to heterosexuality. Finally, sexuality (and **gender**) are coded by film **genre** – for example, the sexuality of characters in a **musical** differs from that of characters in a **western**.

Debate around sexuality in film studies came about largely as a result of feminist theorizing on structures in general which position or construct woman as other in patriarchal society (see **scopophilia**). Claire Johnston (1976, 209) makes the point that while the earliest stereotyping of woman in the cinema (as vamp or virgin) has changed very little, the image of man has been privileged with greater differentiation. Early cinema required fixed **iconography** for audiences to follow the narrative, so characters were stereotyped (villain, hero, etc. for men; fallen woman, victim, etc. for women). But once cinema **codes** became familiar it was felt that this stereo-typing of the male contravened 'the notion of character' (1976, 209). In this respect, Johnston argues, **Hollywood**'s conventions around sexuality reflect dominant (by which she means patriarchal) **ideology** that stereotypes men as active and therefore part of history and women as passive and therefore 'ahistoric and eternal' (1976, 209). Thus, within mainstream cinema especially, but not exclusively, stereo-typing is not questioned. Masculinity and femininity as constructs were 'taken for granted' and their representation was not questioned – that is until the 1970s.

Annette Kuhn (1985, 5) acknowledges pre-feminist think-ing on representation in Althusser's (1984) work on ideology and in Barthes's (1957) **semiotic** and **structuralist** readings of specific **images**. However, she also points to their 'gender-blindness', to which we should add colour-blindness. The feminist and Black movement and cultural studies debates of the 1970s and 1980s, as well as the incorporation of **psycho-**

analysis into theory in general and film studies in particular, have meant that the issue of sexuality has broadened from its somewhat narrow (White) male/female binary opposition. Discussions around **spectatorship**, which is not a single entity but composed of so many different 'types' (male, female, Black, Asian, White, lesbian, gay and so on), have elucidated the limitations of this binary construct because pleasure in viewing can be derived without reference to this binary paradigm's implicit White heterosexuality. This means that representation is not limited to a reproduction of the patriarchal order – it does that but it does more. It reproduces the dominant ideology but it also reflects those who are inside and those outside the culture or **hegemony** and also the shifting relationships depending on how close to the centre of the culture they are (for example, in mainstream Hollywood and western cinema, the White female has more power than the Black female; she also has more power than the Black male in terms of the **gaze**). Thus, the debate on sexuality in the 1990s has evolved and come to be closely identified with gender (including cross-genderization and/or sexual disguise), the representation of sex and desire including its referent (male, female, **class**, race, age, heterosexuality, male homosexuality, lesbianism, cross-dressing), the historical and social contexts, and the relationship of the spectator to that representation.

The following comments should serve by way of illustration of this shift away from the binary opposition paradigm in relation to sexuality. In **classic narrative cinema** the central positioning of the White male as the site of truth and/or the natural assumption or acceptance of the predominance of the male point of view means that any other **subjectivity** is occluded. Therefore, White masculinity can be defined as more than just 'his sex'; femininity much less so – and if it is (that is, more than just her sex), it is usually transgressive or excessive (see **excess**). Woman becomes other or object to the male's subject – she is defined in relation to his centrality, his point of view. As such she is fixed as an object of his desire, but an object whose sexuality is also perceived by him as dangerous – and therefore to be punished

315

or contained (through death (or its equivalent) or marriage, respectively). This notion of fixity also applies to others whose subjectivity is denied by the centring of the White male. For example, racial difference, especially in the person of the Black male, is linked with heightened sexuality and thereby connected to sexual danger, not just for the White female but also for the White male. He is perceived as other, as an object of fascination (with colour or potency) but also of danger. Oddly, however, he is positioned much like the White woman and as such must be contained or punished. The origins of this **fetishization** of the Black male are not, however, the same as those surrounding the White female. They are fixed, first, in colonizing history and then slave history – what Jane Gaines (1988) refers to as 'racial patriarchy' – a different order of otherness. And it is in relation to those histories that the Black male is punished or contained. Thus, to conclude on this example of difference, mainstream cinema constructs Black male sexuality against a different set of histories from that of the White male. But these histories are those emanating from White hegemony – the White version of colonial and slave histories – an ideological construct exemplified in this instance by the film industry which, in its **mise-en-scène** of male blackness, pulls on those histories to construct him. D. W. Griffith's *Birth of a Nation* (1915) is the very first film to do this, but Steven Spielberg's *The Color Purple* (1986) also plays on the **myth** of the bestiality of the lustful Black man. Equally, Sidney Poitier's films of the 1950s and 1960s, which might seem to address blackness in an 'enlightened' manner, are just as problematic. Poitier's image of urbane civility does less to counter images of Black male sexual potency and more to point to the civilizing process of American education (read: 'he (Black Sidney Poitier) can be "just like us"'). Nor has that myth disappeared. The depiction of Blacks playing by White rules and losing still persists (for example the Eddie Murphy films; *A Soldier's Story*, Norman Jewison, 1984). However, this mythification and reification of blackness is being contested in the newly emergent **Black cinema**. (For further reading see: Dyer,

1986; Grosz and Probyn, 1995; Kuhn, 1985; *Screen*, 1988; *Screen*, 1992.)

shots (*see also* **image**, **match cut**, **jump cuts**, **shot/reverse-angle shot**, **unmatched shots**)   In terms of camera *distance* with respect to the object within the shot there are basically seven types of shots: extreme close-up, close-up, medium close-up, medium shot, medium long shot, long shot, extreme long shot or distance shot. In addition the terms *one-*, *two-* and *three-shots* are used to describe shots framing one, two or three people – usually in medium close-ups or medium shots.

   Close-up/extreme close-up (CU/ECU)   The subject framed by the camera fills the screen. Connotation can be of intimacy, of having access to the mind or thought processes (including the subconscious) of the character. These shots can be used to stress the importance of a particular character at a particular moment in a film or place her or him as central to the **narrative** by singling out the character in CU at the beginning of the film. It can signify the **star** exclusively (as in many **Hollywood** productions of the 1930s and 1940s). CUs often have a symbolic value. For example a character looking at her or his reflection in a mirror or in the water can have connotations of duplicity (what we see is not true) or death (as in the dream or **myth** of Narcissus). CUs can be used on objects and on parts of the body other than the face. In this instance they can designate imminent action (a hand picking up a knife, for example) and thereby create suspense. Or they can signify that an object will have an important role to play in the development of the narrative. Often these shots have a symbolic value, usually due to their recurrence during the film. How and where they recur is revealing not only of their importance but also of the direction or meaning of the narrative.

   Medium close-up (MCU)   Close-up of one or two (sometimes three) characters, generally framing the shoulders or chest and the head. The term can also be used when the camera frames the character(s) from the waist up (or down),

317

provided the character is right to the forefront and fills the frame (otherwise this type of shot is a medium shot). An MCU of two or three characters can indicate a coming together, an intimacy, a certain solidarity. Conversely, if there is a series of two and one shots, these MCUs would suggest a complicity between two people against a third who is visually separate in another shot.

Medium shot (MS)   Generally speaking, this shot frames a character from the waist, hips or knees up (or down). The camera is sufficiently distanced from the body for the character to be seen in relation to her or his surroundings (in an apartment for example). Typically characters will occupy half to two-thirds of the frame. This shot is very commonly used in indoor sequences allowing for a visual signification of relationships between characters. Compare a two-shot MS and a series of separate one shots in MS of two people. The former suggests intimacy, the latter distance. The former shot could change in meaning to one of distance, however, if the two characters were separated by an object (a pillar, a table, even a telephone for example).

Visually this shot is more complex, more open in terms of its readability than the preceding ones. The character(s) can be observed in relation to different planes, background, middle ground and foreground, and it is the interrelatedness of these planes which also serves to produce a meaning.

Medium long shot (MLS)   Halfway between a long and a medium shot. If this shot frames a character then the whole body will be in view towards the middle ground of the shot. A quite open shot in terms of readability, showing considerably more of the surroundings in relation to the character(s).

Long shot (LS)   Subject or characters are at some distance from the camera; they are seen in full in their surrounding environment.

Extreme long shot (ELS)   The subject or characters are very much to the background of the shot. Surroundings now have as much if not more importance, especially if the shot is in high-angle.

318

A first way to consider these shots is to say that a shot lends itself to a greater or lesser readability dependent on its type or length. As the camera moves further away from the main subject (whether person or object) the visual field lends itself to an increasingly more complex reading – in terms of the relationship between the main subject and the décor there is more for the **spectator**'s eye to read or decode. This means that the closer up the shot the more the spectator's eye is directed by the camera to a specified reading. André Bazin (1967, 23ff.), in his discussion of depth of field, greatly favoured what he termed the objective **realism** of the **deep focus** shot – generally found in a MLS or LS. Shots, therefore, in and of themselves have a subjective or objective value: the closer the shot, the more subjective its value, the more the meaning is inscribed from within the shot; conversely, the longer the distance of the shot the more objective its value, the greater the participation of the spectator or reader in the inscription of meaning. To avoid confusion with terms such as *subjective camera* it is better to think and speak of shots as being more or less open (MS to ELS) or closed (MCU to ECU) to a reading.

Other factors influence the readability of a shot – primarily the angle of a shot. A high or low camera angle can denaturalize a shot or reinforce its symbolic value. Take, for example, an ELS that is shot at a high angle. This automatically suggests the presence of someone looking, thus the shot is implicitly a point of view shot. In this way some of the objective value or openness of that shot (which it would retain if angled horizontally at 90 degrees) is taken away, the shot is no longer 'naturally' objective. The shot is still open to a greater reading than a CU, however; although the angle imposes a **preferred reading** (someone is looking down from on high). In terms of illustrating what is meant by reinforcing symbolic value, the contrastive examples of a low- and high-angle CU can serve here. The former type of shot will distort the object within the frame, rendering it uglier, more menacing, more derisory; conversely, when a high-angle CU is used, the object can appear more vulnerable, desirable.

These are of course preferred readings or readings that adhere to the **codes and conventions** of traditional cinema. Film-makers do not necessarily abide by these rules, however. And it is in their 'breaking', bending or subverting of cinematic rules regarding film-making in general (shots, editing, **soundtrack**, etc.) that their films can be said to have their individual hallmarks.

shot/reverse-angle shot (*see also* **suture**) Also known as shot/counter-shot, this is most commonly used for dialogue. Two alternating shots, generally in medium close up, frame in turn the two speakers. Normally these shots are taken from the point of view of the person listening. In the clearest instances the shoulder and profile of the listener are just distinguishable in the foreground of the frame and the camera is focused on the face of the speaker. But the **spectator** can assume the presence of both interlocutors even if the listener is not **foregrounded** because of the series of reverse angles. This type of shot follows visual logic (character A is framed as she or he speaks – cut to character B framed as she or he speaks). Alternatively, but less usually, the camera can frame the listener (particularly if she or he is under threat). In these two types of reverse-angle shots the position of the spectator shifts. In the first type the spectator becomes the privileged viewer of the **image** in so far as the shot permits identification with the position of the listener; in the second she or he is far more ambiguously positioned in that she or he is either excluded from the identification process because she or he does not have the power of speech, or she or he is forced to realize the collusionary role she or he plays as voyeur of the image (see **scopophilia**).

sign, **signification** – *see* **semiology/semiotics**

social realism Although it is argued that the advent of **sound**, in 1927, brought about a greater realism in film, the realist tradition was in evidence in cinema's earliest productions, as

320

for example in France whose cinematic practices were very much inflected by literary adaptations, especially those of the socio-realist novelist Emile Zola. Social realism in film refers, as it does in literature, to a depiction of social and economic circumstances within which particular echelons of society (usually the working and middle **classes**) find themselves. The earliest examples of this tradition in sound cinema, however, date back to the 1930s and it is John Grierson and his work in **documentary** that is generally credited with the introduction of the social-realist aesthetic into **narrative** cinema. Grierson, who was primarily a producer and theorist, held that documentary should be in the service of education and propaganda for the greater social good – with an insistence on quality and good taste. Grierson surrounded himself with a group of like-minded film-makers and organized a loosely formed documentary movement that was to impact on several film movements after the Second World War. There were three basic principles to which the group adhered. First, cinema should be taking slice-of-life-reality rather than artificially constructing it. Second, everyday ordinary people should act themselves in real settings. Finally, cinema should strive to catch the spontaneous or authentic gesture and uncontrived or natural speech (see Armes, 1974).

Although there are examples during the 1930s of individual films that exemplify these principles (such as Jean Renoir's *Toni*, 1934; Carol Reed's *The Stars Look Down*, 1939), it was after the war that actual socio-realist film movements could be discerned. There are three movements in cinema's history that in some way are indebted to this social realist aesthetic – all of which produced what have been termed social-problem films. First, the **Italian neo-realism** movement of the late 1940s. Then the **Free British cinema** and the **British New Wave** of the late 1950s; and, finally, the loosely formed **cinéma-vérité** group in France during the 1960s.

sound/soundtrack Before the soundtrack was introduced to cinema audiences in 1927, film was accompanied by a musical score played by an orchestra or an organist or pianist (depending on the luxury and means of the cinema theatre). Although sound on film dates from 1927, the technology for putting it in place predates the 1920s by at least a decade if not more (depending on which film historian you read). At that time there was no sense of urgency to go to the costly lengths of implementing a sound system, since cinema was proving sufficiently profitable in its silent mode, France, Germany and the United States had been competing almost since the beginnings of the film industry to synchronize sound and **image**. The first breakthrough occurred in 1911 when the Frenchman Eugène Lauste, working for the American Edison, demonstrated the first sound-on-film movie. This particular system was greatly improved in 1918 by German technicians. Systems of sound on disc synchronized to film, Phonofilm and Vitaphone, were but the latest perfections in the mid-1920s of work started in 1900. Gaumont had been working on a series of processes of synchronized sound since 1902, only to perfect it by 1928. And so on. In the end it would be the American Western Electric and the German Tobis-Klangfilm which, between them, carved up the sound market.

The moment in sound is Alan Crosland's *The Jazz Singer* (starring Al Johnson) produced by Warner Brothers in 1927. Competition and economic exigencies represent a first reason for the launch of sound at this time. Warner Brothers was desperately seeking a way to enter into stronger competition with the then four majors (see **studio system**). The launching of this film shot Warner into the status of a major. In terms of economy of scale, US **audiences** were dropping – because of the impact of the radio and access to other leisure activities – at the very moment that the film industry had invested massively in luxury grand film theatres. Sound was intended to attract the **spectator** back. Sound also made possible a bringing together into one unit elements of vaudeville with filmed images which previously had been two disparate entertainment forms in silent cinema spectacles. In the case of **Hollywood** this produced a new **genre** – the **musical**.

However, it also put an end to other generic types, such as the gestural, slapstick **comedy** associated with Chaplin and Keaton. Conversely, it created a new type of comedy: the fast repartee comedy with snappy dialogue (as with the Marx brothers and W. C. Fields) and screwball comedy – usually based on the 'battle between the sexes' with stars like Clark Gable and Cary Grant pitted against the likes of Claudette Colbert, Katherine Hepburn and Rosalind Russell (as in *It Happened one Night*, Frank Capra, 1934; *Bringing up Baby*, *His Girl Friday*, both by Howard Hawks, 1938 and 1939).

The consequences of sound for cinema were not just generic. It affected the careers of actors. It also impacted on the **narrative**. When the spoken element came in, some actors did not survive and went out because their voice did not match up to their image (this was particularly the case for Hollywood actors); other actors with theatre experience left the boards and ascended on to the silver screen. As for narrative, prior to the soundtrack sound had not been perceived as necessary nor as a crucial element to the registering of authentic reality. Now sound cinema was touted as being closer to reality. Since there could be dialogue, it was argued, there was greater space for social and psychological reality within the narrative. In the event, all critics (whether for or against sound) had to admit that once sound was improved (which it was by the early 1930s) it did permit narrative or **diegetic** economies – for example, dialogue could move the film's narrative along more speedily than intertitles. In its earliest days, however, sound was more of a regressive step for cinema because it severely limited camera movement. The new cameras fitted with sound recording systems were heavy bulky affairs and could not be moved around. Similarly, at first, a single microphone was the only means of recording sound, so actors could not move around (for an amusing send-up of the beginnings of sound see *Singin' in the Rain*, Stanley Donen, 1952). In both instances visual **realism** was lost. If this problem was quickly resolved, thanks to technical improvements, sound, as a result of these same improvements, reduced options. Renewed camera mobility and the use of the boom microphone or indeed post-synchronization of the soundtrack gave visual and aural depth to film, but improvized shooting and experimentation decreased. The consequences of sound for the film industry were that it became more labour-intensive (requiring dialoguists and sound engineers): a costly affair that was carefully regimented. The standardization of equipment – due to the cartel on the technology (predominantly Western and Tobis) – meant a standardization in production practices.

From the 1930s until the early 1950s sound was single-track and was recorded optically. Optical sound is a system whereby light, modulated by sound waves, is recorded on to film. In the 1950s magnetic tape was used to record sound which was then transferred on to the optical track of the film, and, as with the earlier system, sound was generated by the film passing through a light sensor as it was being projected (a process still used today). This evolution was a natural response to the needs of wide-screen cinema: with such a large screen, stereophonic sound was clearly essential.

In the 1970s Dolby sound, a four-track stereo system that also reduces background noise, replaced the earlier stereophonic system. Nowadays, this four-track stereo system is made up of more than fifteen separate tracks that are used to record dialogue, sound effects and music. These tracks are then transferred on to the optical track of the film (the magnetic track could be placed on to film but the cost of re-equipping film theatres would be too high). Dolby-surround, as its name implies, is a system whereby sound can be separated out and reproduced through speakers from different parts of the theatre. Currently, in the pursuit of ever greater fidelity and purity, digital sound is being exploited in post-production. This is a system whereby sound is stored in a computer (through numbers so the sound stays clean!) and can be recreated in any combination of those numbers.

Until these two most recent developments, sound was very closely related to the image. Films today that are not equipped with Dolby or Digital sound still create the same illusion. And the *audi*ence remains in collusion with this relationship. We pretend, accept that it comes straight from the screen; if it is not in synch we notice it and do not particularly like this instance of sound drawing attention to itself and pointing to the fact that what we are seeing up on screen is an illusion. Now, however, that Dolby sound is used in much of mainstream cinema, we do not object to sound drawing attention to itself (especially the wrap-around version). Its realism is not even questioned, so the collusion continues – almost in reverse. That is, we collude with its artificiality and purity.

There is a scarcity of theoretical writings around the **ideological** effects of sound, almost as if the naturalizing effect has passed unheard (but see Altman, 1992; Chion, 1982, 1985; and *Screen*, 1984). However, over the span of sound cinema a few radical film-makers have addressed the issue. Among radical film-makers who have attempted to show the importance of the soundtrack in relation to the image, we can cite Jean-Luc Godard's work during the 1960s (for example *Le Mépris*, 1963; *Pierrot le fou*, 1965). In his **deconstruction** of the two elements into two separate entities he showed the ideological problems inherent in this invisibilization process whereby image and sound are seen as one and as representing reality. (For a very full but succinct review of the development of sound technology and film see Konigsberg, 1993, 331ff., and Bordwell, Staiger and Thompson, 1985, 298ff.)

Soviet cinema/school   This term refers to a loosely knit group of film-makers who, after the Bolshevik Revolution of October 1917, experimented with film style and technique. As a result of their work they had brought the cinema of the Soviet Union to worldwide attention by the mid-1920s. This experimentation did not occur in isolation. The effect of the Revolution was to bring in its wake experimental foment in all branches of the arts. The beginnings of this experimentation date back to the Russian **futurists** (1912) who adopted an experimental and innovatory approach to language. This was to filter through into the post-Revolutionary movement of constructivism. The pre-Revolutionary movement, influenced as it was by the abstract forms of European **modernist** art,

325

believed in technique and the evacuation of fixed meanings. After the Revolution, the constructivists, seeing in technology the huge potential for change, advocated a new order in which art, science and technology in tandem with workers, artists and intellectuals would combine and work together to produce a new vision of society. Art and labour were seen as one. This notion of art as production was eagerly embraced by the newly emergent Soviet cinema of the 1920s and admirably suited the political exigencies of post-Revolutionary Russia, which needed the propagandizing effect of cinema to spread the message that all workers were pulling together to secure the national identity of the new Soviet Republics.

Lenin and Stalin were well aware of cinema's propagandistic and educative value. This was particularly the case with silent film, which was the ideal visual medium to educate the masses, a great proportion of whom were illiterate and spoke in different dialects. The earliest example of this propagandistic move was during the 1918–21 civil war, when film shows were delivered all around the country on what were called 'agit-trains'. Incidentally, it was in this area of production practices that many of the famous Soviet film-makers (such as Lev Kuleshov and Dziga Vertov) started their careers. The purpose of the film shows was to consolidate communist power over the Soviet Republics by telling of the heroic proletarian struggle that made hardship worthwhile and the civil war worth winning for the Revolutionary cause. Trains went out into the country bringing with them **documentary** footage of the goings-on in the major cities, including the activities of the Bolshevik leader Lenin. Film-makers out in the country on location with these trains took footage of the peasants at work and the rural life in these times of great physical hardship.

A second move to secure cinema in its **ideological** function was the nationalizing of the industry in 1919 and the establishment in that year of a State Film School. At first the effects of nationalizing the industry were disastrous. Many of the previously independent producers left the country and took their equipment with them. In fact the industry did not gain any stability until 1922 when a central co-ordinating company was established: Goskino, renamed Sovkino in 1925. By 1929 the industry had become such a tightly centralized structure that it was able to dictate the future trends of Soviet cinema. Indeed, in 1928 an All-Union Party Congress on Film Questions decreed that films must eschew pure formalism and focus on content and on socialist realism. The experimental wave that had brought Soviet cinema to the aesthetic forefront of world cinema gave way to the edicts of socialist realism: that is, to a representation of life as it *will* be.

But to return to the heydays of the Soviet cinema of the silent period: until 1925 the film products remained conventional. It was only in 1925, when state control over the industry was momentarily relaxed, that form and style could be experimented with in film as was already being done in other art forms. This period of Soviet film history, 1925–30, was short-lived, for the reasons evoked above. However, it had enormous repercussions worldwide. The heritage of this period goes back aesthetically, as we have seen, to the constructivists and ideologically to the 'agit-train' films. The so-called father of Soviet cinema, however, is Lev Kuleshov, with his principle of montage editing. Kuleshov's principle started from the idea that each **shot** derives meaning from its context and that if the context of a shot is changed, by placing it in a different sequence, then the whole meaning of the shot and the sequence changes. From this Kuleshov developed the idea that collision or conflict must be inherent to all visual filmic **signs**. That is, a film shot acquires meaning in relation to the shots that come before and after it. The collision of these shots creates a third order of meaning that is created in the **audience**'s mind. Thus, for example, intercutting between shots of a poor woman and her child seated at an empty table with shots of a fat bourgeois seated at a table with plenty to eat will read in the audience's mind as the oppression of the proletariat by the bourgeoisie. If these two sets of shots were not in immediate juxtaposition the reading would be different. On its own, the shot of the poor woman denotes just that and connotes her poverty, no more.

327

Kuleshov's principle of montage had an enormous influence on contemporary film-makers, the most famous of whom are Sergei Eisenstein, Vsevolod Pudovkin and Alexander Dovzhenko. Some, those who formed the FEK group (the Factory of the Eccentric Actor), went on to develop, from Kuleshov's system of montage, the principle of alienation (more readily associated with Bertolt Brecht). By placing objects or people in unfamiliar contexts they sought to alienate the **spectator** and oblige her or him to reflect on the meaning of the **image** (see **distanciation**). However, Kuleshov also introduced a second important principle, that of naturalistic acting. Again, this was followed by many film-makers, but not, significantly, by Eisenstein. Pudovkin followed Kuleshov's principles of naturalistic characterization and montage, and produced popular narrative films (such as *Mother*, 1926). Pudovkin's character's are individuals with feelings and separate identities. The plot line is, in many ways, indistinct from **Hollywood**'s own 'good' versus 'bad', although this time it is based in Russia's own Revolutionary history. Indeed, it should be recalled that Soviet audiences very much enjoyed Hollywood film products and its **stars** (Mary Pickford, Douglas Fairbanks and Charlie Chaplin were great favourites). Dovzhenko, for his part, also continued in the Kuleshov vein and in particular focused on rural Russia by showing individual idealism and effort overcoming the landed peasantry's resistance to Stalin's collectivizing programme for farms (see *The Earth*, 1930).

Eisenstein is the film-maker most readily associated with this period in Soviet cinema, at least within the western world, possibly because he obtained international recognition at the time. His film *Strike* (1925) was awarded a prize at the Paris Exhibition that year. In fact he was much admired and more successful outside the Soviet Union than in it. He lectured all over the western world: France, Germany and the United States. Doubtless the other contributing factor, over time, is the huge legacy of theoretical writings he left and which were translated into English and other languages. Eisenstein advocated a materialist theory of cinema. He saw cinema as the modality for expressing and representing revolutionary struggle. He believed that a revolutionary country should be given a revolutionary culture (cinema in his case) in order for the masses to obtain a revolutionary consciousness (small wonder Grierson admired Eisenstein's ideological educative fervour). For him, montage meant intellectual montage to make the spectator think. In this light he is close to Kuleshov's thinking. He believed in the symbolic counterpointing of human beings with objects or other animate forms to create meaning. Thus in *Strike* the slaughter of a bull is counterpointed symbolically with that of the strikers. Eisenstein eschewed characterization and went for symbolic ciphers, what he called 'typage'. The actor was but one element in a film. Thus, the proletariat was the hero of the film, not a particular individual.

Eisenstein's most famous film, *Battleship Potemkin* (1925), was commissioned by the Central Committee. It is exemplary of his radical view of film as an assault on audiences to shock them into political awareness. The film was commissioned to commemorate the unsuccessful Russian Revolution of 1905. Eisenstein focused on one incident, the mutiny on the battleship *Potemkin* and the subsequent slaughter, on the Odessa steps by the Tsarist militia, of the masses cheering and trying to bring food to the mutineers. In 1927 Eisenstein was again commissioned to make a film, this time in commemoration of the successful 1917 Revolution. His project, entitled *October*, was to prove the beginning of his falling foul of critics and the state. The film was due to come out in 1927 with other commissioned projects for the Revolution's Jubilee (which included Pudovkin's populist-montage film, *Mother*). However, Eisenstein's film had to be massively recut because of the expulsion of Trotsky from the party (mainly manoeuvred by Stalin). When the film was finally screened, in 1928, it was criticized for its formalism (although it contained superb ironizing of Kerensky, the provisional head of the Revolutionary government of 1917). In fact, because it had to be so drastically recut, the film made little sense to audiences either as an intellectual montage film

329

or as a commemoration of the 1917 Revolution. In any event, by 1928 the state had decreed that the time for montage cinema was over. The need was for morale-lifting and positive post-Revolutionary **discourses** of socialist realism. Eisenstein made only two more intellectual montage and formalistically experimental films in the Soviet Union (*The Old and the New/The General Line*, 1928; *Bezhin Meadow*, 1937), after which he was subjected to public humiliation for his use of formalism over content and was obliged (or felt obliged) to denounce his former practices. In 1938 he was commissioned to make the patriotic film, *Alexander Nevsky*, which, while it was undoubtedly an attempt to bolster Soviet national identity against the imminent threat of fascism, lacked the earlier brilliance of his film techniques even though it was the first of his films to have popular appeal with the Soviet audiences. (For further reading see Taylor and Spring, 1993; Taylor and Christie, 1994a and 1994b.)

Soviet montage – *see* **editing**, **Soviet cinema**

space and time/spatial and temporal contiguity Within **classic narrative cinema** space and time are coherently represented in order to achieve the reality effect. **Shots** reveal spatial relationships between characters and objects and as such implicate the viewer as spectating **subject**. That is, shots are organized in a specific way so that the **spectator** can make sense of what she or he sees. The way in which space is carved up within a shot (size and volume of objects or characters) also provides meaning. Equally, given that mainstream classic cinema assumes an unfolding of the traditional narrative of 'order/disorder/order-restored' (or enigma and resolution), time is implicitly chronological and so must be seen to run contiguously with space. **Art cinema** has disrupted this notion of temporal and spatial continuity through, for example, **jump cuts**, **unmatched shots**, flashforwards, looping **images** and so on. Interestingly, **dominant**

cinema has adopted many of these techniques, even though they do not serve the same disruptive function but seem to function more like cinematic jokes which the spectator can enjoy (see, for example, Robert Altman's *The Player*, 1992).

spectator/spectator–identification/female spectator (*see also* **apparatus**, **gaze**, **ideology**, **Imaginary/Symbolic**, **scopophilia**, **suture**, **voyeurism/fetishism**)   The issue of spectatorship was first addressed 'theoretically' in the early to mid-1970s as a result of the impact of **semiotics** and **psychoanalysis** on film **theory**. The relationship between cinema and the unconscious is not a new concept however. Cinema as the mediator for unconscious desire, the suitability of the screen as the projection-site for the inner workings of the psyche, had been discussed by earlier theorists in the 1920s and 1930s – as had the similitude between the mechanisms of dreams and the unconscious to those of film. But it was not until the 1970s that full consideration was given to the effect of the cinematic experience upon the spectator.

Spectatorship theory has gone through three stages. In stage one, 1970s film theory, Baudry, Bellour and Metz wrote about cinema as an **apparatus** and an imaginary signifier to explain what happened to the spectator as he (*sic*) sat in the darkened theatre gazing on to the screen. In stage two, post-1975 feminist film theory, the 'natural' assumption, implicit in those first writings, that the masculine was the place from which the spectator looks and the 'natural' acceptance that each viewing was an unproblematic re-enactment of the **Oedipal trajectory** were strongly contested (in the first instance) by the critic and film-maker Laura Mulvey. In stage three, 1980s (mostly feminist) film theory, Mulvey's writings provoked further investigations by theorists who sought to widen the debate by bringing in theoretical approaches other than psychoanalysis. What follows is a brief synopsis of those three stages and the debates surrounding them.

Stage one   Baudry, Bellour and Metz drew on Freud's analyses of the child's libido drives and Lacan's mirror stage to explain how film works at the unconscious level. Drawing on the analogy of the screen with the mirror as a way of talking about the spectator–screen relation, these authors state that at each film viewing there is an enactment of the unconscious processes involved in the acquistion of sexual difference, language and autonomous self-hood or **subjectivity**. In other words, each viewing represents a repetition of the Oedipal trajectory. This in turn implies that the **subject** of classic narrative cinema is male (Mayne, 1993, 23). Let's unpick this.

According to Baudry (1970), the cinematic apparatus produces an ideological position through its system and mechanics of representation (camera, editing, projecting, spectator before the screen). The position is ideological because dominant **narrative** cinema practices hide the labour that goes into the manufacturing of the film and the spectator is given the impression of reality. This **seamlessness** gives the spectator a sense of a unitary vision over which he (*sic*) believes he has supremacy. The spectator believes he is the author of the meanings of the filmic text and in this respect colludes with the idealism of the cinematic 'reality-effect' – all of which gives evidence to what Baudry calls the 'spectator as the transcendental subject' (as having supremacy). In reality, argues Baudry, the opposite is true: the spectator is constructed by the meanings of the text. As such, therefore, the cinematic apparatus interpellates the subject as effect of the text. Later, Baudry (1975) moved away from this anti-humanist interpretation of the cinematic apparatus and its ideological connotations and, adopting a more Freudian approach, focused on cinema's ability to embody psychic desire. He also recognized the implicit regressiveness (back to the child) in that particular positioning of the spectator as desiring subject – a point Metz would develop more fully.

Bellour (1975) talked about cinema as functioning simultaneously for the Imaginary (that is, as the reflection, the mirror) and the Symbolic (that is, through its film discourses as language). As the spectator enters into the filmic experience he (*sic*) first identifies with the cinematic apparatus: the projector functions as the eye. Second, he has a narcissistic identification with the image and then, as he moves from the Imaginary to the Symbolic, he desires the **image**. Implicit in Bellour's definition of the spectator–screen relation, which is one-way, is the notion of voyeurism and lawless seeing.

Metz (1975), echoing Bellour, talked about spectator positioning and the voyeuristic aspect of film viewing whereby the viewer is identified with the look (see **gaze**). Drawing on the analogy of the screen with the mirror, Metz perceived spectator positioning as pre-Oedipal, that is, at the moment of imaginary unity with the self. However, through his discussion of cinema practices as the imaginary signifier, he introduced the complication of the **absence/presence** paradigm. Cinema makes present (signifies) what is absent (the Imaginary) – that is, it shows a recording of what is absent. This play on absence/presence means that we are confronted with the imaginary completeness of the absent image of the child in the mirror (Lapsley and Westlake, 1988, 82). The spectator is made aware of the illusionism of the imaginary unity with the self and as such is confronted with the sense of lack. This process, Metz argued, has similar properties with that undergone by the child at the mirror stage. The male child looks into the mirror, sees his image, has a momentary identification with the self (narcissism) then perceives his difference from his mother as 'she who lacks a penis'. He then responds in two ways. First, he desires reunification with the mother and his desire is sexually motivated. Second, he denies difference and through that disavowal of difference – because of his own fear of castration – seeks to find the penis in woman (fetishization). In cinema, this Oedipal trajectory is re-enacted within both the narrative and the spectator–text relation (again it was taken for granted by Metz that the subject of the gaze is male).

Stage two Numerous problems arise out of this first stage of theorizing the spectating subject, starting with the assumption that speculation is only a one-way system (spectator to screen), that it is exclusively male in its positioning and that film texts are organized in such a way as to give a **preferred reading**. These issues did not become clear until after the

333

impact of Laura Mulvey's ground-breaking essay ('Visual Pleasure and Narrative Cinema', 1975) which sought to address the issue of female spectatorship within the cinematic apparatus and psychoanalytic framework established by the authors discussed above. Mulvey's essay represented a turning point in film theory in that it was the first to introduce emphatically the question of sexual difference as a necessary area for investigation. Indeed, she intended it to act as a catalyst – she readily admits that the essay was intentionally polemical (1989). In her essay she examined the way in which cinema functions through its **codes and conventions** to construct the way in which woman is to be looked at, starting with the male point of view within the film and, subsequently, the spectator who identifies with the male character or protagonist. She describes this process of viewing as scopophilia – pleasure in viewing.

In her analysis Mulvey made clear the implications of the dual response, as described by Metz, of the male unconscious (desiring and fetishizing) for both narrative cinema and the spectator–text relation. For this sexualization and objectification of the female form that the male gaze confers upon it is not just one of desire but also one of fear or dread of castration. She demonstrated how, as a first unconscious response to this fear, the camera (and the spectator after it) fetishizes the female form by drawing attention to its beauty, its completeness and perfection. But, in making the female body a fetish object, the camera disavows the possibility of castration and renders it phallus-like (since it no longer represents lack) and therefore reassuring. Mulvey demarcated the voyeuristic gaze as the other male unconscious response to this fear. This gaze represents a desire to control, to punish the (perceived) source of the castration anxiety, even to annihilate woman. (Mulvey mentioned film noir in this context, but for an extreme example see *Peeping Tom*, Michael Powell, 1960.)

Mulvey then went on to ask, given that the narrative of **classic narrative cinema** is preponderantly that of the Oedipal trajectory and since that trajectory is tightly bound

up with male perceptions or fantasies about women (difference, lack, fear of castration and so on), what happens to the
female spectator? How does she derive visual pleasure? Mulvey
could only conclude that she must either identify with the
passive, fetishized position of the female character on screen
(a position of unpleasure, her lack of a penis signifying the
threat of castration) or, if she is to derive pleasure, must assume
a male positioning (a masculine third person).

Stage three Mulvey's polemic met with strong response by
feminist critics (as she intended) and over the last two decades
there has been extensive work on revising, reworking and
extending Mulvey's propositions. In an attempt to refute the
phallocentrism of Mulvey's argument, Silverman (1981) and
Studlar (1985) described the cinema as an essentially masochistic structure in which the viewer derives pleasure through
submission or passivity. Doane (1984), following on from
these writings, argued that the female spectator's positioning
was twofold. She adopted either a masochistic positioning
(identifying with the female passive role) or that of a transvestite (identifying with the male active hero). Mulvey (1989)
in her afterthoughts on her earlier essay warned against this
kind of binary thinking. And, indeed, already feminists were
considering the possibility that the spectator was not so rigidly
positioned in relation to sexual identity but that it was possible
to postulate the bisexuality of the spectator's positioning
whereby she or he would alternate between the two –
suggesting a fluidity and heterogeneity of positioning rather
than an 'either/or'. Modleski (1988, 98) made the point most
succinctly in relation to the bisexuality of the female spectator. The female spectator is doubly desiring because when
going through the mirror phase the girl child's first love object
is the mother, but, in order to achieve 'normal femininity'
she must turn away and go towards her father as object of
desire. However the first desire frequently does not go away.
So, the female spectator's bisexual positioning is central to
the mother/daughter nexus. The male spectator, much as the
male character up on screen, for the most part suppresses his
femininity (often projecting it on to the female and punishing

her for it). However, as Modleski (1988, 99) argued, he can find himself bisexually positioned if the male character fluctuates between passive and active modes.

The contiguous question of spectator-as-subject in relation to meaning-production has equally been broadened. The spectator is not a passive interpellated subject of the screen. She or he holds a position of power and makes sense of the images and sounds (in fact the effect of **sound** renders the screen/mirror analogy somewhat incomplete or unsound). Even though it is a construct of cinema to endow the spectator predominantly with more knowledge than the characters (at least with mainstream narrative cinema), it does not follow that the spectator occupies only one position in relation to those characters (as the apparatus reading would have it). Cowie's (1984) discussion of film as **fantasy** made this clear. In her re-thinking or re-vamping of Laplanche's and Pontalis's three characteristics of fantasy (the primal scene, the seduction fantasy and the fantasies of castration), all of which are a **mise-en-scène** of desire, she made the point that the spectator, as subject *for* and *of* the scenario, can occupy all those positions. As such, she or he is not monolithically placed but can in fact occupy contradictory positions. As an example take *Fatal Attraction* (Adrian Lyne, 1987) – a film in which it is possible to occupy at different times within the narrative the positions of the mistress, the husband and the wife. It should not be forgotten that Glenn Close (who plays the mistress) expressed deep shock and disappointment at the audience cheering the end of the film when she is shot to death by the wife. She had assumed (naively) that sympathy or identification with her character would occur.

Essentially these three stages of the debate around spectator-positioning and identification show how there has been a shift away from the early monolithic view of the spectator (as subject of the apparatus), to a more heterogeneous one. This is doubly the case since spectator analysis has not confined itself in recent years to 'spectator as psychic phenomenon'. The debate has become enlarged (thanks in the main to cultural studies) and the spectator-as-viewer is now equally deemed to be an important area of investigation. Thus historical and empirical models of spectator or viewer analysis have been established. In this respect spectatorship has been perceived as a matter of historically shifting groups. The popularity of cinema has shifted over time and has had different effects and been differently affected depending on the makeup of those groups. Spectatorship has also been analysed in relation to **intertextuality**: an examination of all the texts surrounding the actual film text and their impact upon the viewer as reader and receiver. Exhibition – where films are screened and the effect felt by the viewer – is another important consideration, as is **audience** pleasure in identification. Finally, studies of viewer-reception, initiated in television studies, have pointed to the ecclecticism of viewers and acknowledged the difference in readings of the film depending on **class**, age, race, creed, **sexuality**, **gender** and nationality. (For an extremely thorough, comprehensive and well-written book on spectatorship read Mayne, 1993. On spectator-identification see Ellis, 1982. For specific textual analyses see Modleski, 1988. On female spectatorship see Pribham, 1988 and Kaplan, 1983. On reception, Mayne, 1993, supplies an excellent bibliography to which I would add a recent analysis, Stacey, 1993.)

stars/star system/star as capital value/star as construct/ star as deviant/star as cultural value: **sign and fetish/star- gazing and performance** (*see also* **gesturality, studio system**) *A first definition: star as capital value* The star system is generally associated with **Hollywood**, although the French film industry was the first to see its usefulness in promoting its products (especially its **comedy** series and *film d'art* productions, starting in 1908). In earliest cinema, films were anonymous productions bearing only the name of the studio. It rapidly became evident that certain performers were greater attractions than others. Henceforth, performers were perceived as having capital value. And by 1919 the star system was established. Although Florence Lawrence, 'the Biograph girl' was the first named star in the United States (1910), the first 'real' star was Mary Pickford (known as 'little Mary' in her films of that period). She was shortly followed by Charlie Chaplin. But this capital value of stars was by no means a one-way exchange. Stars made fortunes – that is, as long as they made the studios' fortunes.

Before **sound** both male and female stars were quite archetypal, so their **iconography** was easily readable. After sound, there was a shift in **stereotypes**, and roles differentiated. But, as Claire Johnston (1976) has noted, this was predominantly the case for male stars only. Female stars remained, much as before, vamps or virgins *or* full-scale sex-goddesses whose main purpose was to give the **audience** (and presumably the male star) a 'human sense of beauty and eroticism' (Konigsberg, 1993, 348). Meanwhile male stars became more complex. No longer just heroes, they could be anti-heroes, rebels-as-heroes, socially aware heroes, and so on.

Hollywood's dominance of the western film industry since the First World War has meant not only that the studios have massively exported their star commodities on celulloid throughout the European continent and the United Kingdom, but also that they have been in a position to offer lucrative enticements to import stars: most famously, arguably, in the silent era, Greta Garbo. For some film stars 'going to Hollywood' could make them into megastars, for others it could consign them to oblivion, or – ultimately – do both (for example Vivien Leigh and Richard Burton).

Officially the star system was 'over' by the 1950s owing to the Hollywood studio system collapse, but rivalry remained strong in the 1950s between Europe and Hollywood. For example, just on the sex-goddess front, Diana Dors and Shirley Ann Field in the United Kingdom, Brigitte Bardot in France, Gina Lollobrigida and Sophia Loren in Italy were star images served up to counter the US sex-symbols Marilyn Monroe, Ava Gardner and Jayne Mansfield. Rather than 'over' it would be fairer to say that the star system went into decline after the 1950s collapse and that it became a case of stars still being manufactured but of being fewer in number. Also with the increase in the youth audience from the 1960s to its present dominant position, stars are of a different order – for example, they are 'even more like us' or hulking heroes, or, again a reverse-type: nasty, malevolent villains – but still stars.

Stars sell films, but their capital exchange value goes further than that of course. Producers will put up money for films that include the latest top star. Stars can attract financial backing for a film that otherwise might not get off the ground. Film scripts are written with specific stars in mind (see Robert Altman's *The Player*, 1992, for a satire on Hollywood practices in this respect). And while films are indeed vehicles for stars, allowing them to show a wide range of skills over different genres, stars are equally vehicles for film genres (for example Fred Astaire and Ginger Rogers, and Gene Kelly are icons of the **musical**, Lauren Bacall, Humphrey Bogart and Edward G. Robinson are closely identified with **film noir** and **gangster** films). Indeed, a need to re-establish a star's commercial viability could be the impetus to disassociate her or him from one type of **genre**. (This was attempted with Anthony Perkins but was never successfully pulled off: he will always remain Norman Bates of *Psycho*, Alfred Hitchcock, 1960.)

A second definition: star as construct (What follows in this section is largely based on Dyer, 1986, and Gledhill, 1991 – two extremely lucid and useful texts on this subject.) Stars are constructed by the film industry, but stars (although not all) also have a role in their own construction, participate in their own myth-making. Similarly, star status is authenticated by the media (press, fanzines, television and radio and so on). But stars also possess markers of their own authenticity and as such are involved in their own mythification. Think, for example of Doris Day, the representative of nice middle-America woman-hood; the sexually charged and ambiguous **sexuality** of Marlene Dietrich; the swashbuckling Errol Flynn; the ice-cold maiden Catherine Deneuve with flawless feminine beauty; the socio-psychologically inept Woody Allen.

Stars are somehow baroque in their image-construction since it is so predominantly about illusionism, about 'putting there' what in fact isn't there. They are appearance in the very diversified meaning of that word: they appear on screen, but they are not 'really' there – their image on screen stands in for them so they are *apparence*, a semblance (see **absence/ presence**). The look that has been constructed of them that is up there for all to perceive is also an appearance, a carefully manufactured appearance (of flawless beauty, of rugged handsomeness, for example). The rest, as Dyer (1986, 2) puts it, is supposedly 'concealed'. Yet we as **spectator**s accept this construct as real.

As a way of measuring this sense of reality let us pick up on Gledhill's comment that stars reach their audience primarily through their bodies (1991, 210). That is, they reach us through their appearance. But, depending on whether it is a male or a female star, this 'reaching-us-with-their-bodies' changes as they age. Not for nothing do so many female stars decry the lack of roles for older, mature, even old women. For male stars, ageing is not (or is less of) an issue where their appearance is concerned. Thus it is acceptable for a male star to age so long as he is 'healthy', his appearance remains one of good, or reasonable health – read: virile health (for example Paul Newman, Clint Eastwood). Even if he grows old unhealthily, through body abuse, some types of 'unhealthiness' still do not bring about a rejection of the star-body that is reaching us. In this respect, it would be purposeful to compare the responses to Burton and his facial deterioration through alcohol (described as 'cragged', 'tragic') with the prurient reactions to Rock Hudson, the first star to be openly known to have died of AIDS (even though it was denied for a long time). Certain types of deterioration, such as physical decline from **excess** in alcohol consumption, are less negatively judged than others, it would appear.

To return to the female star and ageing: the female star has 'trouble' ageing not just for herself (loss of looks equals loss of premier roles) but also in relation to her audience. On the whole, her fans do not like her to age. Curiously, the process of ageing matters when it is a woman star – it recalls our own, ageing is too real – not the 'real' we want to see. Just to take a few random examples of stars and ageing,

Simone Signoret, whose premature ageing was always said to be a result of heavy drinking and smoking, was severely criticized for losing her looks. She, it would appear, should have exercised the control that no one expected Burton to exercise. Cancer, from which she died at the age of sixty-four, could equally been the cause for her premature ageing as her much quoted excesses. Rita Hayworth was dismissed at forty as a drunk, yet she died of Alzheimer's disease. Ageing here is seen as deviancy. Joan Crawford complained of how hard she had to work to look, and stay looking good (Dyer, 1986, 1). Marlene Dietrich spent a fortune on face-lifts. The price of being not bodily deviant is high. Brigitte Bardot and Greta Garbo left the screen before age set in – taking the appearance away, the other price to pay to 'keep up appearances'.

The star as a construct has three component parts (Gledhill, 1991, 214): first, the real person; second, the 'reel' person/the character she or he plays; third, the star's persona, which exists independently of, but is a combination of the other two. The film industry makes the multi-faceted star-image, so does the star, and the audience selects; in this regard, the star-image has four component parts (Dyer, 1986, 3–4): first, what the industry puts out; second, what the media (critics and others) say; third, what the star says and does; fourth, what we say, what we can select, even to the point of imitating the star (for example James Dean look-alikes) – and each audience will select a different meaning (for example Bette Davis means different things to Black men and women than she does to White heterosexuals, or to lesbian, gay audiences).

Star-images, then, are more than just the image. As Dyer (1986, 3–4) makes clear, they are extensive (can extend in meaning, and over the public and private spheres); they are multimedia (photography, film, press, television, and so on); they are **intertextual** (the star's image gets picked up and used by others – a sulking Dean look-alike in a jeans advert); finally, they have histories that can and do outlive their lives (especially if they die in tragic circumstances). A star, then, is a cluster of meanings and parts. It is not difficult, therefore, to see that the star phenomenon is profoundly unstable

341

(Dyer, 1986, 6) and extremely paradoxical by nature – as the next three sections will go on to show.

A third definition: star as deviant A star's life is controlled by the studio, which means there is very little room for resistance. A few stars have been able to take charge of their meaning construction (for example Mary Pickford, Bette Davis, Barbra Streisand, Meryl Streep, Robert De Niro); and this resistance becomes part of their star-image. However, in general, the star colludes in the fabrication of her or his self as star, participates in the manufacturing of her or his self as representative of 'normality'. Why for example are there still 'lavender' marriages in Hollywood – marriages of convenience to cover up the fact that one or both partners is gay? Why has fear set into Hollywood as a result of a recent outing campaign led by militant homosexuals? Gay stars are the most vulnerable in relation to the instability of the star-image because they must conceal even more than the straight star. They must convince through their performance that their appearance is 'really real'; their performance is a double masquerade.

It is not difficult to perceive that this collusion in manufacturing a star-image confronts the star with a loss of identity or, at the very least, a fragmented rather than a divided self (see **psychoanalysis** and **suture**). In terms of identity loss, the star is positioned paradoxically: she or he is pre-Oedipal playing at being post-Oedipal (being without identity, the star is like the child prior to the mirror phase and 'unaware' of his difference or her/his separateness from the mother). As a fragmented self, the star has more than one image and thus too many mirrors reflecting back the multiple self – which one is the real image or reflection? At its most extreme manifestation, this loss of identity can propel the star to seek out reunification with the lost (m)other (note the important role Liz Taylor has had in relation to a number of male stars: Montgomery Clift, James Dean, currently Michael Jackson). And it can propel them to a reunification with the absent father. The father is either absent because he has not yet had to be present, that is, the mirror phase has not been gone through (if the star is in the pre-Oedipal phase). Or, he is not yet present because the mirror phase has been so overdetermined with reflections that he has been unable to assert himself as the representative of the Law of the Father. The star as the fragmented self has recognized nothing in these multiple reflections, including his difference or her/his separation from the mother.

Bearing this in mind, let us return to the concept of deviancy. The construction of a star is about excess, excess of meaning ascribed to her or him. This excess is mirrored in the star's lifestyle. If it were not excessive (mansions, swimming pools, parties and so on) would we believe in their star status? Occasionally we accept unexcessed star-images, but they are the exception and that exceptionality is part of the star image. Excess then has positive value for studio, star and spectator. But it soon becomes translated into deviancy once it has negative value primarily for the studio. Sexuality and consumption practices are, unsurprisingly, the areas in which stars 'transgress'. Since their sexuality is set up on screen for us to consume, it is perversely through those very sets of comportment that the star will seek to deny (through excess in sexual practice and consumption abuse) and then (inadvertently?) expose the masquerade of stardom – through disfigurement or death.

A fourth definition: star as cultural value: sign and fetish As a sign (see **semiology**) of the indigenous cultural codes, institutional **metonymy** and site of the **class** war in its national specificity, the signification of the star 'naturally' changes according to the social, economic and political environment. Stars are shifting signifiers, they function as reflectors of the time and as signs to be reflected into society. During the 1950s, when youth emerged as an important class economically and culturally, teenage boys in the United States donned T-shirts, jeans and leather jackets with either Dean or Brando as their icon; in France, teenage girls mimicked the Bardot look – as well as the walk, and so on. Stars have emblematic as well as cultural value in that they 'signify as condensers of moral, social and ideological values' (Gledhill, 1991, 215).

343

Gledhill makes the point that they can also be emblematic of those values being in question (for example Garland in *A Star is Born*, George Cukor, 1954; Dean in *Rebel Without a Cause*, Nicholas Ray, 1955).

The star as sign also functions as mediator between the real and the imaginary and, as such, has spectator expectations transferred on to it. The shifts in the representation of female sexuality, just to take one example, over the past sixty years of cinema show how this process of transference and mutation occurs. In Hollywood, for example, during the 1930s and 1940s two types of feminine eroticism prevailed: the 'independent just as good as the boys' (Claudette Colbert, Bette Davis, Rosalind Russell, Katherine Hepburn) or the weak, vulnerable type (Vivien Leigh). In the 1950s the femino-masculine independent type was replaced by the dutiful wife at home supporting her husband (by staying out of the job market), or the self-parodying brunette who eventually 'settles down' (roles played respectively by Doris Day and Jane Russell). The weak type is replaced by the dumb blonde (guess who?). By the late 1960s a new type has emerged, a 'radical–liberal feminist eroticism' which attributes to women the right to decide what they do with their sexuality (Jane Fonda). This woman-in-her-own-right sexuality has persisted into contemporary cinema, but it has not always sat easily – as if by way of a backlash against feminism. As two contrastive modes of representation, see Glenn Close in *Fatal Attraction* (Adrian Lyne, 1987) and Jodi Foster in *The Accused* (Jonathan Kaplan, 1988). These shifts in representation, over time, correspond, first, to different stages in the dominant perception of the American woman's sexuality and, second, to the social, political and economic conditions that prevailed in each of those epochs.

This is also an example of the way in which stars are endowed with national iconicity and as such have cultural value. Clearly a star's meaning can shift in the move from the national to the international level. This is particularly true of the United States' perception of European stars – especially French stars. But stars also signify on a personal level. They

344

articulate the idea of personhood which is a fiction for the reproduction of the kind of society we live in (Dyer, 1986, 8). As (national) icon and (individuated) person the star functions as both extraordinary and ordinary. In the first instance, as extraordinary, she or he is an object of our speculation and impossible object of our desire. In the latter, as ordinary, she or he is 'just like us' – we can identify the stars with us – and so the star is a possible object of our desire. This binary effect functions to fetishize the star – in neither instance is the star subject, always object (see **voyeurism/fetishism**). Ellis (1982, 91–108) points to the similarity between this binary effect and the **absence/presence** paradigm. The star on screen is absence made presence and the spectator is the hearing, seeing subject. In this respect the screen is analogous to the mirror into which the spectator peers and has a momentary identification with that image (the star-just-like-us). The spectator then perceives her or his difference and becomes aware of the lack (absence, separation from, loss of the [m]other – the star as absence, as not-like-us). Finally, the spectator recognizes herself or himself as the perceiving subject, a position which in turn creates desire. As holder of the **gaze** the spectator is positioned voyeuristically, desiring to look, with all that that connotes in terms of fetishism. But the absence/presence paradigm also points to the simultaneously impossible and possible nature of that desire, which is also a feature of fetishism (desiring that which cannot be had – what is absent, adulating a fixed object – the star or icon present up on screen).

The fetish value of a star is strongly underscored by her or his **mise-en-scène**, starting with the moment of entrance on screen – awaited with impatience – a use of suspense to give added value to the star. Morphological markers, 'that seem natural or naturally the star's' (such as a certain smile, biting a lip, side-**lighting** eyes), but which privilege us into their emotions, play into the fiction that the spectator or the camera or the eye has caught them unawares (Ellis, 1982, 106). Voyeuristically we look on: unseen-'presence' watches what was once seen-presence but which is now absence – an image standing for star. Even a film itself can obtain fetish status when, for example, a star has died young and/or in tragic circumstances. The film is all that is left of her or him as movement (a recent example being River Phoenix and *My Own Private Idaho*, Gus Van Sant, 1991).

A fifth definition: star-gazing: strategies of performance Two questions will frame this last definition of stardom: who is looking at the star? and what are we looking at? The answer to the first will make clear why strategies of performance inform the answer to the second question. Essentially there are two audiences looking at the star: the diegetic and the extra-diegetic ones (see **diegesis**). That is, those on the inside looking on, and those on the outside looking in – but in both instances also looking *at* the star, if with different effect. With different effect because the spectator's look is mediated by the diegetic audience. This does not exclude the fact that the spectator's gaze is also mediated by the point of view within the film, which is usually that of the star, but we are here discussing who is looking at the star. (The entry on **spectatorship** addresses spectator-positioning more fully.)

The effect of diegetic star-gazing on the female star is one of a fairly straightforward fetishization. However, the effect on the male star is twofold. First, if those star-gazers are male, the effect is one of homoeroticism and of a feminizing of the male body (the male body is as much fetsishized by the male gaze in this instance as is the female body). This puts an interesting reading on predominantly all-male genres (**westerns** and **crime-thriller** movies). Second, if the star-gazers are female, even though the gaze is now heterosexually charged, the feminizing of the male body still takes place. Women's agencing their gaze on to the male body means they are taking up the privileged male position as holder of the gaze (see **agency**). An analysis of Clint Eastwood's positioning in relation to diegetic audiences in his two recent films *Unforgiven* (Clint Eastwood, 1992) and *In the Line of Fire* (Wolfgang Petersen, 1993) would illustrate this double effect.

The extra-diegetic audience likes to come and see its stars. This implies that the audience has certain expectations of the star. The star is the point of synthesis between representation and identification. She or he represents or re-presents the 'host culture' of which she or he is a part and with which the spectator identifies (King, 1985, 37). She or he also stands for roles she or he has played before. The extra-diegetic star-gazer, then, has come to see what the star is capable of and, depending on the star, expects either a degree of sameness (acting to type or personification) or unsameness (always changing or impersonation). And to this effect strategies of performance are mobilized by both the industry and the star to satisfy this need on the part of the audience. Irrespective of which mode of acting is in play (personification or imper-sonation), these strategies function as markers of authenticity. Thus a star who plays roles that are consonant with her or his personality (no matter how constructed that is) will be far more typecast and produce ritualistic performances far in excess of a star who impersonates.

Hollywood tends to prefer the personifying star in the belief that audiences choose films in relation to stars and a know-ledge, more or less, of what to expect (for example Eastwood, the non-verbal gunman; Jack Nicholson and the leering grin combined with a macho bravura; the Bette Davis flouncing bitchiness; the soulful Barbra Streisand and her songs; the all-American winner and tough guy, John Wayne; Tom Cruise, less of a tough guy, but still an all-American winner; and so on). Stars who impersonate (that is, who can be true to any conceivable character) are fewer in number and their popu-larity or success depends to a great degree on how far they go in suppressing the authenticating markers of their real personality or star-image. While the construction of differ-ence (from the star-image or personality) must be convincing, if the suppression is so total the audience is likely to reject that performance. In other words, if the impersonation gets to the point where the disguise prevents the signs of the star from being read, so that the star to all intents and purposes 'dis-appears', the audience feels 'cheated' of the process of spectator recognition, an essential component of the star-image. The audience can no longer select those bits of the star (authenticating markers) which it recognizes or with

347

which it identifies. In this respect, the star Meryl Streep is the one actress who comes to mind because she sails so close to this 'dis-appearance act'. This could explain why she receives such a mixed reaction to her performances, which are far from universally liked or admired.

stereotype Originally, *stereotype* was a printing term used to refer to a printing plate taken from movable type, to increase the number of copies that could be printed. Applied figuratively, this expression has come to mean, at its simplest, a fixed and repeated characterization (the drunken doctor in **westerns**, the moll with a golden heart in **gangster** movies). Initially, stereotypes came about in cinema to help the audience understand the **narrative**. However, it would also be true to say that they are a carry-over from traditions of performance in stage **melodrama** and vaudeville – the two theatre **genres** that were most readily adopted by early cinema. They also serve an economic function in relation to the narrative. We 'know' what they stand for so there is no need to elaborate their characterization. This means that stereotypes are little, if at all, nuanced. But this does not mean that stereotyping just operates at the level of secondary characters. Main roles, **stars**, can equally be reduced to stereotype (the dumb blonde or sex goddess; the hulk with no brain; the all-good middle-American – respectively: Marilyn Monroe, Sylvester Stallone, James Stewart).

Stereotypes come and go; they also change in the light of the shifting political cultural context. Take for example the representation of communists and communism in Hollywood cinema from the 1950s to the 1990s (from threat, alien force that is to be defeated, to an inept, corrupt system that is doomed to failure). Already it can be seen that stereotypes are not simple signifiers, even though they appear to represent types, norms. Because they are social–cultural productions passing as normative, they need to be examined in relation to race, **gender**, **sexuality**, age, **class** and genre as well as history.

348

Let's take these last two pointers (genre and history) as a way of explaining why stereotypes must be widely examined. Some genres rely more heavily on stereotypes than others. Why? The traditional western for example abounds with stereotypes – all the better to serve as a backcloth to the main protagonist: the hero-who-puts-things-right against all odds; the hero as positive value versus the stereotypes as negative value. Take the disaster movie – a particular favourite genre of the 1970s and early 1980s (for example, the *Airport* series and the *Towering Inferno* types of films). The narrative this time functions a bit in reverse to the western. That is, the hero is not identified from the beginning but has to identify himself (*sic*) gradually against the stereotypes present in the disaster arena (neurotic ageing female film star; bigoted priest; drunken doctor (again); dying nun; nymphomaniac; twin orphans). What purpose, then, do stereotypes serve? They clip into **codes and conventions** associated with belonging and exclusion. We, the spectators, may not be like the hero but we are certainly 'not like the others'. Stereotypes represent a release of our prejudices at the same time as they play on them. They allow us to belong to a social grouping of which they (the stereotypes) are not part.

In terms of history, certain socio-cultural groupings (just as an example) find a stereotypical characterization or representation that is, in the main, unfavourable, at best reductive – even though this representation may shift over time. Certain racial groupings, and gay and lesbian groupings, are prime examples. An examination of the evolution of the representation of Jews in different western cinemas over the past sixty years of cinema would be highly instructive of how stereotypes have shifted if not necessarily improved. And a question worth asking is, in what way, if at all, do more recent images function less stereotypically than earlier ones? Do they represent more clearly issues surrounding Jewishness or do they still slot into the problematic area of stereotypes? Or are they guilty of historicism? Compare, for example, Woody Allen's films where his Jewishness is at the centre of the narrative, with Alan Pakula's *Sophie's Choice* (1982) where Jew as victim-survivor of the Holocaust is the driving force behind one individual's suffering.

structuralism/post-structuralism (*see also* **apparatus**, **auteur theory**, **feminist film theory**, **suture**, **theory**,) The founding-stone of structuralism was structural linguistics (later to become **semiotics**) which dates back to the beginning of the twentieth century, primarily in the form of Ferdinand de Saussure's linguistic theories. However, they remained little known until the theories were brought into the limelight, in France, by the philosopher–semiotician Roland Barthes in the 1950s – especially in his popularizing essays *Mythologies* (1957). Saussure, in his *Cours de linguistique générale*, set out a base paradigm by which all language could be ordered and understood. He distinguished between language as a system (*langue*): an underlying set of rules that is universal as a concept; and language as utterance (*parole*): the speech that can be generated by those rules. The impact of linguistic structuralism in the late 1950s and through the 1960s on other disciplines was quite widespread, affecting anthropology, philosophy and **psychoanalysis** to mention but three that are of immediate importance in the context of film theory. Exemplary of this impact was Claude Lévi-Strauss's anthro-pological structuralism of the 1960s, which looked at Indian myths. Although his thesis was to have a widespread influ-ence, because he was examining **narrative** structures, it was of particular significance in the context of film theory. Lévi-Strauss's thesis was that since all cultures are the products of the human brain there must be, somewhere, beneath the surface, features common to all. This was an approach that became extremely popular during the 1960s and was adapted not just by film theoreticians such as Christian Metz but also by the Marxist philosopher Louis Althusser into his discus-sions of **ideology** and by Jacques Lacan into psychoanalysis.

The first point to be made about this popularization of structuralism, in France, is a socio-political one and relates to structuralism's strategy of 'total theory'. This populariza-tion coincided with de Gaulle's return to presidential power in France. His calls for national unity in the face of the Algerian crisis, the era of economic triumphalism which he instituted and the consequent nationalism that prevailed were

350

in themselves symptomatic of a desire for structures to be mobilized to give France a sense of national identity in the face of decolonization and radical constitutional change. Thus, the desire for total structure, as exemplified by structuralism, can be read as an endeavour to counter the real political instability of the 1960s.

The second point to be made about structuralism as it affects film theory is that it represents a rethinking of film theory through academically recognized disciplines, those of structural linguistics and semiotics, hence also its appeal to US and British theorists, among others. This pattern would repeat itself in the 1970s with psychoanalysis, philosophy and feminism, and, again in the 1980s, with history. The significance of this new trend of essayists and philosophers turning to cinema to apply their theories cannot be underestimated. It is doubtless this work which has legitimated film studies as a discipline and brought cinema firmly into the academic arena.

Initially the introduction of structuralism into film theory was perceived as a bold move to deromanticize the film-maker as auteur by introducing a more scientifically based approach that could objectively uncover the underlying structures of film. However, it ended up in rigid formalism which removed any discussion of pleasure in the viewing. Symptomatic of this desire for total order in film theory were Christian Metz's endeavours in the mid-1960s to situate cinema within a Saussurian semiology. Metz, a semiotician, was the first to set out, in his *Essais sur la signification au cinéma* (1971 and 1972), a total-theory approach in the form of his *grande syntagmatique* – a linguistic structure that could account for all elements of a film's composition. Thus cinema is a set of syntagmatic relations – that is, of universal rules (much like Saussure's *langue*), a set of relations that could be described as a grammar of film. Syntagmatic relations then relate to the possibility of combination. Each film will be constructed out of a combination of syntagms, but within these a specific selection of shots will be used (much like Saussure's *parole*). Let us take, for example, a parallel syntagm – two events

351

running in parallel. The universal rules that govern this type of syntagm mean that **cross-cutting** between the two events must occur. However, no two parallel syntagms are the same (or rarely), because each film-maker, bearing in mind the narrative and **genre**, selects the shots that make up the syntagm. Thus a film based on a fairy story that opposes two worlds (the real and the **fantasy** worlds) vastly differentiates itself from a **western** or a **thriller** even though they are similarly composed of parallel syntagms.

It is not difficult to see in Metz's endeavour the problems inherent in such a total approach. First, although structuralist theory purported to reveal the hidden structures behind film-making, it simultaneously ignored modes of production, the impact of **stars** on choices and the socio-historical context of production. Post-structuralism would make this widening possible. Thus structuralism, while it might have deromanticized the auteur, none the less continued to focus on the film-maker and on her or his product. Analysing film this way meant that a critic could scientifically and objectively evaluate a film, determine the style of a particular auteur/film-maker and indeed determine also if a particular film was consistent with that film-maker's style – hence the term *auteur-structuralism*. The focus, therefore, was on the hidden structures and codes in the text and, in this respect, answers the question of how the text comes to be – but not how it comes to mean. The problem becomes one of the theory overtaking the text and, thus, of being very limiting. What is omitted is the notion of pleasure and **audience** reception. What occurs instead is a crushing of the aesthetic experience through the weight of the theoretical framework.

Post-structuralism It took the impact of post-structuralism, psychoanalysis, feminism and **deconstruction** to make clear finally that a single theory was inadequate and that what was required was a pluralism of theories that cross-fertilized each other. Post-structuralism, which does not find an easy definition, could be said to regroup and cross-fertilize – to some extent – the three other theoretical approaches mentioned. As its name implies, post-structuralism was born out of a profound mistrust for total theory, and started from the position that all texts are a double articulation of discourses and non-discourses (that is, the said and the non-said, *le dit et le non-dit*). Because post-structuralism looks at all relevant **discourses** (said or unsaid) revolving around and within the text, many more areas of meaning-production can be identified. Thus, semiotics introduced the theory of the textual subject – that is, subject positions within the textual process, including that of the spectator and the **auteur** – and the text as a series of **signs** producing meanings.

In terms of auteur theory the effect of post-structuralism was multiple: 'the intervention of semiotics and psychoanalysis' 'shattering' once and for all 'the unity of the auteur' (Caughie, 1981, 200). Having defined the auteur's place within the textual process, auteur theory could now be placed within a theory of textuality. Since there is no such thing as a 'pure' text, the intertextuality (effects of different texts upon another) of any film text must be a major consideration, including auteurial **intertextuality**. Thus, the auteur is a figure constructed out of her or his film; for although there exist authorial signs within a film that make it ostensibly that of a certain film-maker, none the less that authorial text is also influenced by those of others.

Psychoanalysis and feminist film theory introduced the theory of the sexual, specular, divided subject (divided by the fact of difference, loss of and separation from the mother (see **suture**). Questions of the subject come into play: who is the subject (the text, the star, the auteur, the **spectator**)? These newly introduced theories also examined the effects of the **enunciating** text (that is, the text brought about by the spectator) – this included analysing the two-way ideological effect and the pleasure derived by the spectator as she or he moves in and out of the text (see **spectator identification**). To speak of text means too that the context must also come into play in terms of meaning production: modes of production, the social, political and historical context. Finally and simultaneously, one cannot speak of a text as transparent, natural or innocent, therefore it is to be unpicked, deconstructed so that its modes of representation are fully understood.

studio system (*see also* **Hollywood**) Normally identified with Hollywood, even though the first country to boast a vertically integrated studio system was France, which in 1910, had three production companies: the two majors, Gaumont and Pathé, and, on a smaller scale, Éclair. Vertical integration means that a studio controls the modes of production, distribution and exhibition. The 'official' date for the birth of the studio system is *circa* 1920. However, its earliest prototype in the United States can be found in the pioneering work of Thomas H. Ince, who in 1912 built Inceville in Hollywood, where he both directed and produced films much on the lines adopted by the Hollywood studio system from the 1920s to the early 1950s. Ince set himself up as director, producer and manager, and as such supervised all the films being made simultaneously in different studios; it was he who had the final say on everything from the script to the **editing**. From this production practice it was not long before the full-blown Hollywood studio management style emerged. This style was designed along the following lines: a production head to supervise the whole project, a division of labour and the mass production of films (mostly formula films for sure-fire success), which meant among other things shooting films out of sequence to save on costs, and the last word on the final cut resting with the director–manager–owner.

Vertical integration was initiated in the United States in 1917 when Adolph Zukor acquired Paramount Film Corporation – then a distribution company (established in 1914) – and aligned it with his own production company, the Famous Players–Lasky Corporation. This brought him control of both production and distribution. This move had important consequences both for financing films and for exhibition practices. Distribution was the way to finance films, and now that Zukor owned production and distribution he could more or less force cinema theatres to accept blockbookings – to rent and screen films as decreed by exhibitors. There was an attempt to counter this potentially monopolistic putsch. In 1917 an exhibitors' company, First National (originally called the First National Exhibitors' Circuit), was established to fight the block-booking system. It lasted some twelve years and in its heyday – 1921 – owned around 3,500 theatres. By 1922 it had entered into production. Zukor responded by buying up theatres himself, and by 1926 owned more than a thousand. During this first cycle in the studio-system's history (1913–29), four other major production companies consolidated their positions as rivals to Paramount, and full vertical integration for the five majors occurred between 1924 and 1926, the others being Fox Film Corporation (first established in 1913 and fully integrated by 1925); Metro-Goldwyn-Mayer (1924); Warner Brothers (established 1923 and integrated by 1926); RKO (1928). Alongside these five majors there coexisted the 'little three' majors – Universal Pictures (formed 1912), United Artists (1919) and Columbia (1920). They were called 'little' because they were not vertically integrated but had access to the majors' first-run theatres. (For a brief history of these companies see below.)

During the 1920s these major companies had a virtual monopoly over the film industry. Profits were enormous, but so too were costs. To counter these increasing costs – due, first, to the effect of vertical integration (an expensive system to finance) and, second, to the advent of **sound** (1927) – studios increasingly came under the control of bankers and businessmen with the effect that not only economic consid-erations but also artistic ones became more and more a matter for management-style decisions (see Bordwell, Staiger and Thompson, 1985, 320–9). Only Warner Brothers, Columbia and Universal escaped direct interference from Wall Street, because of their prudent production practices. The director was but one of many specialists hired by the studio compa-nies who were now organized into different departments. Hollywood meant business, as can be determined by the fact that from 1930 to 1948 the eight majors between them controlled 95 per cent of all films exhibited in the United States and formed a seemingly impenetrable oligopoly (Cook, 1985, 10).

The eighteen-year period of Hollywood's unrivalled studio system (1930–48) can best be summed up as follows. Each studio had a general overseer (usually the vice-president of the company), and its own 'stable' of **stars**, scriptwriters, directors and designers (which led to a 'house look'). Hollywood produced some six hundred films a year on an assembly-line process (which led to a standardization of the product but also, more positively, to a greater sophistication of **genres**). Although each company followed similar production practices, they none the less tended to specialize in certain types of films and cultivate a distinctive look (see below). Economic exigency meant that films had to follow certain criteria to guarantee box-office success. During the Depression, in order to give value for money, double features became the rule. This meant that the majors and the minor majors, alongside smaller production companies that specialized in low-budget movies (particularly Monogram and Republic), had now to turn their hand to making **B-movies** to supplement the programme. With the exception of Warners, Columbia and United Artists, all majors went bankrupt at some point during the Depression and became subject to direct interference from Wall Street (Bordwell, Staiger and Thompson, 1985, 400).

In 1948 the majors suffered a reversal in fortune with the Supreme Court–Paramount decision. Litigation had been begun against the studios in 1938, but the Second World War put a halt to it until 1948. Exhibitors brought an anti-trust action to put an end to the film industry's monopoly over exhibition. On the grounds of unfair practices, the Supreme Court issued decrees that effectively divested the majors of their power as vertically integrated systems. The big five would have to relinquish their theatres, which represented about two-thirds of their capital investment (Cook, 1985, 10), and the little three would, with the big five, have to stop restrictive practices and coercion (block-booking) in the exhibition of their films. This decision opened the doors to independent film and, to a lesser degree, to foreign imports. In 1951, several appeals later, the majors had no choice but to comply with the law and enter into fair competition with minor production companies. This was but a first step in the demise of the studio system. Rising costs meant that the double bill and the B-movie with it disappeared. The lower costs of location shooting abroad also impacted upon studio use. Outside the system other factors contributed to this decline: first, the rise in the popularity of television and, second, the effect of the House Un-American Activities Committee on Hollywood both in terms of blacklisting certain actors, directors and scriptwriters and in terms of an unspoken or implicit **censorship** whereby certain types of films just would not get made (see **Hollywood blacklist**). Attempts to regain lost **audiences** through new departures in technology – 3-D, technicolour, **cinemascope** – had only a slight impact.

To stem losses, studios rented out space to television companies and even turned their own hands to making television programmes (in 1957 RKO was bought by Desilu – Lucille Ball's and Desi Arnaz's television production company – solely for making television programmes). Departments closed, land and real estate were sold off. The studio system became a ghost of its former self. More recently, studios have been bought up by large conglomerates for whom film production is just one of their practices. The current method of producing films is usually for an independent producer to put a package together and sell it to one or other of the studios (Konigsberg, 1993, 358-9).

There follows a brief history of the major and minor Hollywood studios, listed in chronological order in each category.

Fox Film Corporation/20th Century Fox Fox Film was established in 1913 by William Fox. Originally an exhibition company (in New York), it quickly became a production company (1915) with studios in Hollywood. Fox's ambition was to be the biggest major; that ambition was to cost his company so dear that he was forced out of it in 1931. In 1935, a small production company, 20th Century, headed by Joseph M. Schenk and Darryl F. Zanuck (formerly production head at Warner Brothers), merged with Fox and the company was renamed 20th Century Fox. Zanuck, as vice-president (a post he held for over twenty years), quickly turned the ailing fortunes of the former company around, and brought it into third position to MGM. This he achieved – at least during the late 1930s, more by the type of films he produced – popular **musicals** – than by his stable of stars, which he built up only slowly. To the two he inherited from Fox – Shirley Temple and Will Rodgers – he added Tyrone Power, Sonja Henie, Alice Fay, Carmen Miranda and Betty Grable, and eventually, in the 1940s and 1950s, Henry Fonda, Marlon Brando, Marilyn Monroe, Jane Russell and Gregory Peck. In his stable of directors he could count Elia Kazan, John Ford and Joseph Mankiewicz. After 1948, Fox turned to location shooting and extended its repertoire of films to include 'realistic' crime films, **westerns**, musicals and spectaculars. To attract audiences back into the theatres, Fox led the way in new technology – producing, for example, *The Robe* (1953), the first feature-length film to be shot in Cinemascope. Fox is now owned by Rupert Murdoch.

Paramount Pictures Corporation Originally a distribution company established in 1914 by W. W. Hodkinson. As indicated above, when Zukor became president of the company in 1916, he set about vertically integrating this major, which lay second only to MGM during the studio system's heyday. During the silent era it boasted such famous names as Mary Pickford, Douglas Fairbanks, Gloria Swanson, William S. Hart and Fatty Arbuckle among its stars and Cecil B. de Mille, Erich Von Stroheim, Mack Sennett and D. W. Griffith amongst its top directors. Griffith, Fairbanks and Pickford soon left to set up with Charlie Chaplin their own independent company, United Artists, in 1919. Nor was Paramount short of stars during the sound era, when it produced mainly **comedy** and light entertainment – with occasional **epics** (such as *The Ten Commandments*, de Mille, 1952). Mae West, Marlene Dietrich, Paulette Goddard, Hedy Lamar, Dorothy Lamour, Barbara Stanwyck, the Marx brothers, Bing Crosby and Bob Hope are some of the stars that made up the Paramount stable. During its Hollywood heyday, Paramount – because it owned so many theatres – produced forty to fifty films a year, more than any other studio. Dorothy Arzner was given her first directorial role by Paramount in 1927 – and was one of the very few women to accede to directorial status during Hollywood's years of ascendancy (1930–48).

After 1948, while continuing to make films, Paramount gradually ventured into television production, becoming heavily involved in the 1960s. In 1958 the company sold off all its rights to its 1929–49 feature films to Music Corporation America. In 1962 MCA had also acquired Universal. In 1966 Paramount was acquired by Gulf and Western. Until recently it was owned by the entertainment group Paramount Communications. But in 1994 it became the centre of a protracted buy-out battle between two rival American cable companies, Viacom and QVC Network, which Viacom finally won.

Warner Brothers A production company established in 1923 by the four Warner brothers. Warner Brothers was the studio that introduced integral sound into films in 1927 with *The Jazz Singer* (Alan Crosland). This bold move was undertaken to improve the studio's status amongst the majors. Prior to this Warners had been the poor relation to the other studios because it was not yet vertically integrated. The introduction of sound revolutionized production practices, and catapulted Warners into major status. In 1928, it consolidated this status by purchasing its own theatres, first by buying out the Stanley Company (three hundred theatres), then a part share in First National, which it completely bought out in 1930. Warners was now truly integrated. Of all the companies, Warners is the one that rode out the Depression best. This was as a result of careful economic planning and strategies. The company (initially under the aegis of Darryl F. Zanuck, Warners' production head) rationalized its production into assembly-line production methods, low-budget movies and strict adherence to shooting schedules. This had two consequences. First, it meant that the company could produce fast and in significant numbers (around sixty films a year during the Depression period and thereafter through the 1930s). Second, the economic constraints influenced the product

359

itself. Therefore **gangster** films and **backstage musicals** were the genres to prevail, because they were cheap to produce. **Social realism** and political relevance combined with a downbeat image endowed Warners' films with a populism that made their products particularly attractive to working-**class** audiences (Cook, 1985, 11–12). *Little Caesar* (1930), *The Public Enemy* (1931), *I Am a Fugitive from a Chain Gang* (1933), *The Roaring Twenties* (1939), *They Drive by Night* (1940) are but a sample list of 1930s films with social content or criticism at their core. During the war this liberalism gave way to more patriotic statements that were anti-isolationist, anti-pacifist and anti-Nazi. Less known in this category is *Sergeant York* (1941), but one film which has become legend – more, it has to be said, as a love story than a film about patriotism – is *Casablanca* (1942). Warners did not have 'stables' as such, but used contract directors, actors and crews. Raoul Walsh was a long-serving contract director (1939–51), Howard Hawks made *Sergeant York* and *To Have and Have Not* (1944); actors include Paul Muni, Humphrey Bogart, James Cagney, Edward G. Robinson, Errol Flynn, James Dean, Bette Davis, Ingrid Bergman, Joan Crawford, Barbara Stanwyck, Lauren Bacall.

After 1948, Warner Brothers lost its theatres (as did the other majors because of the Supreme Court–Paramount decision), but it went on to produce numerous successful films (*A Star is Born*, 1954; *Rebel Without a Cause*, 1955; *My Fair Lady*, 1964). The company also went into television production in a big way. In 1967 Warners was sold to Seven Arts (a distributor and dealer in old films). Warner–Seven Arts distributed *Bonnie and Clyde* (Arthur Penn, 1967). In 1969 Warner–Seven Arts became Warner Communications. Warner Brothers is currently (since 1988) merged with Time Incorporated, and is now known as Time–Warner. Since joining Time Inc., the company was in continuous debt until 1992 when it made its first profit. Time–Warner is currently the largest American entertainment group.

Metro-Goldwyn-Mayer Created by a merger (completed by 1924) of three smaller studios (Metro, Goldwyn and Mayer),

MGM was the leader among the majors during Hollywood's heyday. This was the studio of stars, spectacle and glamour that produced such glossy and glittering films as *The Wizard of Oz* and *Gone with the Wind* (both 1939 and directed by Victor Fleming). No set was too lavish, no special effects too expensive – for example the earthquake in *San Francisco* (W. S. Van Dyke, 1936). MGM's house style was influenced by two factors: first, high investment in pre-production and, second, the extremely tight rein on production held by Irving Thalberg, who saw a product through from start to finish. Investment in pre-production meant that films had multiple scriptwriters, and it was not uncommon during production for numerous editors to work on a particular film, or for a director to be replaced by another after previewing. This also meant that directors for this studio during the 1930s were less visible than in others. The same could not be said of its stars. Unlike Fox, which because of its small stable of talent had to make its films its stars, MGM had a veritable galaxy of stars – and was particularly renowned for its grooming of women into stars: Joan Crawford, Greta Garbo, Judy Garland, Greer Garson, Jean Harlow, Norma Shearer are some of its greatest female stars. Mickey Rooney and Spencer Tracey were two of the great names among the male attractions. But, undoubtedly *the* male star in this stable was Clark Gable – the labourer turned crowned king of Hollywood (1937).

After 1948, MGM's fortunes declined as with the other studios. In 1969 it was bought up by a Las Vegas businessman, Kirk Kerkorian, who sold off much of its real estate and other assets. In 1981, he purchased United Artists. MGM became MGM–UA. The company was then sold to the Turner Broadcasting System, which was subsequently sold back to Kerkorian, but not before Turner had kept the MGM film library for his own purposes (that is, for his film television channel, HBO), causing a serious cash-flow problem to MGM. The company was then taken over by Giancarlo Paretti, who had to relinquish control when the French bank Crédit Lyonnais foreclosed on loans made to him. Since 1992 MGM has been operated by the Crédit Lyonnais, but is losing

$1m a day and has very few assets left (the UA film library is all that remains).

RKO Radio Pictures Incorporated As its name suggests this studio came into existence around the time of the launching of sound (1928). The Radio Corporation of America wanted to get into film production so that it could promote its own sound system, Photophone, against the Movietone system which the other majors had invested in. RCA joined forces with a distribution company which owned the Keith and Orpheum theatres – hence RKO. It became a ready-made vertically integrated company 'overnight'. In its heyday it produced nine Fred Astaire and Ginger Rogers films (most famously *Top Hat*, 1935). It also produced big hits such as *King Kong* (Ernest B. Schoedask, 1933), *Bringing up Baby* (Howard Hawks, 1938), *Citizen Kane* (Orson Welles, 1941) and *Notorious* (Alfred Hitchcock, 1946). RKO's production system was introduced early (1931) into the company's existence by David O. Selznick. Termed unit production, it was strikingly different from the other majors' systems in its unrestrictive practices of contracting an independent director to make a certain number of films free of studio supervision or interference. RKO is not associated (as are the other majors) with a specific genre, although alongside its prestige movies it did produce B-movies, particularly the **film noir** and **horror** genres. The output of B-movies greatly increased after 1940 to counter the severe losses caused by the studio's prestige-film policy. And by 1942 production of these low-budget films had become the new adopted policy.

After 1948, this company also went into decline, though more severely than its rival majors – since it would eventually disappear. It was bought up in 1948 by Howard Hughes and was subsequently sold, in 1955, to General Tyre and Rubber Company who then, in 1957, sold the studios to the television programme producing company Desilu.

The first of the three minors, *Universal*, formed in 1912 by Carl Laemmle, did not build its studios in Hollywood but in the San Fernando Valley (Universal City, 1915). The firm-handed Irving Thalberg was one of its first chiefs of production (later he went to MGM). Its most famed silent stars were Rudolph Valentino and Lon Chaney. During the 1930s Universal specialized in horror movies (*Frankenstein* and *Dracula*, both 1931) primarily because at this early stage in sound cinema they were relatively inexpensive to make, depending as they did on sets and **lighting** rather than a mobile camera (Cook, 1985, 24). In the light of the Depression it is interesting to note their popularity. But then again audiences' escapism into horror **fantasy** was matched by their keen consumption of social realist films made during the same period by Warners. This studio was the first to make a sound movie about the First World War, *All Quiet on the Western Front* (1930), which was astonishing not just for its sound effects at such an early stage in sound technology but also for its pacifist message and lack of heroization. This film, directed by Lewis Milestone, became the prototype for many European **war movies** made during the 1930s. Universal went into receivership in 1933 for two years and Laemmle was obliged to sell off his holdings in 1936. The studio was relaunched and, though far from free of economic worries, its decline was stemmed until the mid-1940s by the popularity of its top stars Deanna Durbin, Abbott and Costello and W. C. Fields. From 1946, to help its ailing fortunes, Universal adopted a new strategy which prevailed until the late 1950s: in order to attract big names that would 'sell' its products, it offered stars a percentage of the profits made on films in which they starred. This brought them James Stewart, Charlton Heston, Orson Welles, Marlene Dietrich and Janet Leigh amongst others. Also in 1946 it acquired International Pictures, an independent production company: this helped to improve the company's distribution activities.

After 1948, to counter the effects of the anti-trust decision ending the industry's monopoly over exhibition, Universal re-established a studio identity by specializing in three main genres: thrillers, **melodramas** and westerns (Cook, 1985, 24). In 1952 the studio was taken over by Decca Records. Later, in 1962, these two companies became part of Music Corporation of America, a talent agency highly invested in television production. Under MCA management Universal went on to be successful in both domains by producing small-budget movies (ultimately destined for the television screen) and big-budget blockbuster movies (such as *Jaws*, 1975 and *E.T.*, 1982, both directed by Steven Spielberg). MCA was bought up in 1990 by the Japanese electronic company Matsushita for a staggering $6.6 billion (compare with the major Paramount valued at $10 billion) – an investment repaid perhaps by Universal's big Spielberg hit, *Jurassic Park* (1993).

United Artists Corporation   Established in 1919 by Charlie Chaplin, Douglas Fairbanks, D. W. Griffith and Mary Pickford as a protest against the oligarchy of the majors, the corporation was a distribution company for their own films made by them as independents (most famously *The Gold Rush*, 1925). By 1925 the paucity of films they had produced themselves obliged the corporation to distribute films made by other production companies. During the 1930s its most important releases were *City Lights* (Charlie Chaplin, 1931), *The Private Life of Henry VIII* (Alexander Korda, 1933) and *Modern Times* (Charlie Chaplin, 1936). But the major stumbling-block to its success, the lack (because of the majors' monopoly) of sufficient theatres in which to exhibit, was not fully removed until the anti-trust decree of 1948. After 1948, thanks to the anti-trust decision, United Artists was elevated to the status of a major. Unencumbered by huge overheads of studio ownership, the company flourished (*High Noon*, 1952; *Marty*, Delbert Mann, 1955; the James Bond series, Fred Zinnermann, during the 1960s). This state of affairs prevailed, by and large, until the late 1970s when, buoyed by three Oscars in a row, 1975–7 (*One Flew over the Cuckoo's Nest*, Milos Forman, *Rocky*, John Alvisdon, and Woody Allen's *Annie Hall*, 1975–7), the company over-extended itself. Then part of the conglomerate Transamerica (since 1967), United Artists was sold to MGM in 1981. Currently, MGM–UA produces and distributes a small number of films each year.

Columbia   Originally CBC Sales Corporation, a distribution company founded by Harry and Jack Cohn and Joseph

Brandt in 1920, in 1924 it entered into production and changed its name to Columbia. During the 1930s it produced predominantly B-movies which it sold to the 'big five'. In 1932 Brandt was bought out; Harry Cohn became president and head of production as well as principal shareholder and, much like Warners, imposed a tight rein of careful pre-production planning and short production schedules. Columbia rethought its production strategy when in 1934 its investment in a more up-market movie, *It Happened One Night* (Frank Capra), brought great returns. Henceforth it would invest in both A- and B-movies. Although Columbia is not known for a stable of directors or stars (somewhat like Fox), none the less its 1930s output has been identified with one **auteur**, Frank Capra, and its 1940s films with one star, Rita Hayworth. The truth is that Columbia could ill afford to have directors and stars of its own and so it tended to buy them in (hired from other studios). As for actors, the company's practice was to have contract players and character actors, only occasionally setting out deliberately to groom an unknown into a star as it did successfully with Rita Hayworth, who became a true star with *Gilda*, Charles Vidor, 1946.

After 1948, the deregulationary effects of the anti-trust law benefited Columbia, and it began to develop a small stable of stars (Judy Holliday, Broderick Crawford and William Holden). It could afford to follow a production strategy of expensive adaptations of Broadway hits and best-selling novels. This was a successful strategy against television's increasing popularity, but sensibly Columbia also saw the benefit of making products for television and as such was the first studio to recognize the potential of this new medium to effect its own economic growth. In 1950 it created a television subsidiary, Screen Gems; the other studios did not start to follow this trend until 1955. The most renowned of Columbia's earliest television products was the cop series *Dragnet* (1953). Another key to Columbia's success during the 1950s was its readiness to back not just independents but also foreign productions (for example Elia Kazan's *On the Waterfront*, 1954, and David Lean's *Lawrence of Arabia*, 1962). In the face of

365

dipping fortunes it sold its studios in 1972 and rented space in Warner Brothers Burbank Studios (Konigsberg, 1993, 58). In 1982 the company was bought up by Coca-Cola – an irony given its Poverty Row origins, its populist nature and pro-New-Deal positioning in the 1930s (see Cook, 1985, 14–15). (Poverty Row is an area of Hollywood around Sunset Boulevard and Gower Street where Columbia and other small studios had their base, subsequently an expression used to refer to a low-budget type of production from small companies.) Columbia is now part of the Japanese Sony Group, which bought it in 1989 for $3.4 billion.

Three smaller Hollywood studios are Essanay, Monogram and Republic.

Essanay Organized in 1907 and of short duration, effectively 'dying out' in 1917 when it was bought out by Vitagraph (a New-York-based studio with studios in California, in turn bought out by Warners in 1925). Essanay built its early reputation on its westerns (360 Bronco Billy films). It was also successful with its comedies and was clever enough to attract Charlie Chaplin away from Keystone. During his two-year stay with the company (1915–17) he made 14 films – most noteworthy of which is *The Tramp*, (1915) (Konisberg, 1993, 105).

Monogram Picture Corporation/Allied Artists Picture Corporation Monogram was established in 1930 and produced very cheap products, the most noteworthy being the *Charlie Chan* series. It formed a subsidiary, Allied Artists Productions, in 1946 to produce better-quality films. In 1953 the two merged and became Allied Artists Picture Corporation. Its best-known films are *Friendly Persuasion* (William Wyler, 1956) and *The Man who would be King* (John Huston, 1975). Later it produced mainly for television, eventually (in 1980) filing for bankruptcy.

Republic Pictures Established in 1935 and particularly reputed for its fast production practices. Specializing in B-movies, it was best known for its westerns and could boast among its actors John Wayne, Gene Autry and Roy Rogers. The decline of the studio system and particularly the B-movie in the 1950s signalled the end to the company's fortunes but not before it had produced the Oscar-winning *The Quiet Man* (John Ford, 1952) and the **gender**-bending *Johnny Guitar* (Nicholas Ray, 1954, starring Joan Crawford). The company folded in 1958. (See Bordwell, Staiger and Thompson, 1985; Konigsberg, 1993, for more detail on these companies. For an analysis of their history and their 'political' positioning see Cook, 1985.)

subject/object   In standard **classic narrative cinema**, which is fixed in phallocentric language, men are the subject, women the object. The narrative **discourses** deny woman her **subjectivity** and as such set up the binary **gender** divide whereby male is active, holder of the **gaze**, and female is passive and the object of male desire.

subject/subjectivity *(see also* **apparatus, diegesis, enunciation, ideology, psychoanalysis, spectator, suture, theory)** This concept needs to be viewed within three different, if contiguous, contexts: within the film text itself, as part of the **structuralist/post-structuralist** debate on the subject and, finally, within psychoanalytic theory.

Within the film   There are subjective points of view, **shots** as well as narrative techniques, that make it clear that one particular character's point of view is being privileged within the filmic text. For example, the uses of **flashback** and intra-diegetic narrative voice-over (so privileged in **film noir** adaptations of Raymond Chandler's novels) serve as markers to the authenticity of the protagonist's subjectivity. Similarly, point-of-view shots affect the **spectator**–text relation whereby the spectator feels positioned alongside that character's subjectivity and so identifies with that character. **Shot/reverse-angle shots** represent another series of shots that stitch us into the narrative and also into character identification (see **suture**).

As part of the structuralist/post-structuralist debate   The structuralist theory of the subject was based primarily in Marxian–

Althusserian thinking which perceived the subject as a construct of material structures. Thus we are the subjects of such structures as language, cultural **codes and conventions**, institutions – what Althusser called ideological state apparatuses (ISAs). We are, he argued, interpellated as subject (see **ideology**) by ISAs such as the church, education, police, family and the media. The effect of this totalizing and anti-humanist theory (the subject as effect or construct of institutions) on spectator theory was similarly monolithic. Film, as a pre-existing structure, is like all other ISAs in its ideological functioning, and as such interpellates the spectator, thereby constituting her or him as subject. Post-structuralists (Michel Foucault, Jacques Derrida, Jean-François Lyotard) argued against this totalizing theory and proposed a different vision of the subject as simultaneously constituted and constituting – as both effect and agent of the text (for further discussion see entry on **spectator**).

*Within psychoanalysis (see also **psychoanalysis**)* According to Jacques Lacan, human subjectivity, the unconscious and language are all interrelated. The unconscious is structured like a language and so is produced in much the same way as the subject, through language. When the child goes through the mirror phase it first perceives itself as a unified being (the ego-ideal), although in identifying with the reflection it is in fact identifying with the other (what is there in the mirror) and in so doing misrecognizes itself. Second, because the child is held up to the mirror by the mother, it then perceives its similitude with or difference from the mother, senses absence, loss, separation from the mother and desires reunification with her. The mother becomes the first love-object of the child. However, the child also perceives the mother as lack: lacking the penis. This lack becomes a source of castration anxiety for the boy child as he enters into the Symbolic Order, into language (see **Imaginary/Symbolic**). The issues around the girl child's entry into the Symbolic are more complex because she simultaneously perceives her mother as her first desired object and sees herself as the same (this point is more fully developed in **feminist film theory**).

The child's entry into the Symbolic amounts to its entry into and acquisition of language. So the subject is the speaking subject. However, in order to be part of language and human society, the child must conform to the Law of the Father (the site of language) and reproduce it. To do so, the subject has to appear to be a unified being. Thus, libidinal drives for the mother have to be repressed because according to the Law of the Father they are taboo; he forbids access through the utterance of the patriarchal 'No'. These drives also have to be repressed because to be conscious of them is to be aware that one is *not* a unified being, for the following reasons. These libidinal drives represent a desire to find again the imagined unity with the mother 'pre-lack' (before the knowledge of lack). However, the child, after entry into the Symbolic, does not leave the Imaginary behind even though it must suppress these particular drives. Part of the child's trajectory is forever trying to return to the Imaginary, but since it cannot desire the mother, these particular drives will be repressed into the unconscious (that which is not spoken but which is inscribed in language as taboo or the patriarchal 'No'). The child will seek an alternative moment of imagined unity to compensate for the lack represented by the mother and will imagine an idealized image of itself as complete. In other words it will seek to return to that first stage of the mirror phase when it felt a unified being – the ego-ideal.

Thus the subject is always divided (self/other; unified/not unified). What gets repressed into the unconscious is that which recalls the subject's lack of unity. The unconscious, in this respect, threatens our sense of unity.

It is not difficult to see how this theory of the subject is relevant to film studies. We saw above, considering the structuralist/post-structuralist debate, that the spectating subject is, in a sense, a divided subject (dialectically positioned as constituted or constituting) in relation to the filmic text. Because film projects before us ideal images in the form of **stars** and a seamless reality that disguises its illusory unity (see **apparatus** and **suture**), film functions **metonymically** for this imagined

369

unity of the ego-ideal and as such allows us to identify with that ego-ideal (see **spectator**). But film also does something else. It projects our desires on to the screen, it functions as a release for our repressed unconscious state and our **fantasies**. Why do so many of us like **thrillers**, **horror movies**, **melodramas** and so forth? So film is, simultaneously, the place where the spectator can find imaginary unity *and* the site where the unspoken can be spoken – that is, a 'safe' place from which to observe our lack of unity. Pornographic and bondage films would be the most extreme in terms of visioning the unconscious, but many a film noir replicates our most deep-rooted fantasies and repressed 'hatreds or phobias'. (For more depth on this issue see Lapsley and Westlake, 1988; Kuhn, 1982; Kaplan, 1983.)

subjective camera   The camera is used in such a way as to suggest the point of view of a particular character. High- or low-angle **shots** indicate where she or he is looking from; a panoramic or panning shot suggests she or he is surveying the scene; a tracking shot or a hand-held camera shot signifies the character in motion. Subjective shots like these also implicate the **spectator** into the **narrative** in that she or he identifies with the point of view.

surrealism   (*see also* **avant-garde**, **underground cinema**)   A movement that dates back to the 1920s and which impacted on films of that time but which still has a small influence today – particularly in **horror** films. This movement, much influenced by Freud, strove to embody in art and poetry the irrational forces of dreams and the unconscious. Surrealist films are concerned with depicting the workings of the unconscious (perceived as irrational, excessive, grotesque, libidinal) and with the liberating force of unconscious desires and **fantasy** that are normally repressed.

suture (*see also* **audience**, **enunciation**, **Imaginary/Symbolic**, **Oedipal trajectory**, **psychoanalysis**, **shot/reverse-angle shot**, **spectator**, **subject/subjectivity**) This term means, literally, to stitch up (from the medical term for stitching up a cut or wound). In film **theory** the system of suture has come to mean, in its simplest sense, to stitch the spectator into the filmic text. As a critical concept it was introduced into film studies by theorists, starting with Jean-Pierre Oudart (1977), and was based on studies in child psychoanalysis conducted by Jacques Lacan in the 1960s. It is important to note that Lacan primarily addressed the psychology of the male child and that it is feminist Lacanians – Hélène Cixous, Luce Irigaray and Julia Kristeva – who brought the female child's psycho-sexual development into a central space for consideration. In a similar way, until recently, in terms of its application to film studies, film theorists have blissfully ignored the case for female spectatorship. However, **feminist film theory** has significantly redressed this imbalance (for details see also **spectator**).

Lacan used the term *suture* to signify the relationship between the conscious and the unconscious which, in turn, he perceived as an uneasy conjunction between what he terms the Imaginary and the Symbolic orders – two orders which, after infancy, are always co-present. In its initial manifestation, the Imaginary stands for the period in infancy of a child's life when it first glances at its reflection in the mirror and sees itself as a unified being. This period, which Lacan terms the mirror phase, marks the first stage of the child's acquiring an identity separate from the mother and marks the child's first understanding of space, distance and position. This moment is pre-Oedipal. It is a moment of pure *jouissance* or jubilation (see **psychoanalysis)** and narcissism in which the child, held up to the mirror by the mother, sees or senses itself as a unified being at the centre of the world. This moment cannot last, however, and there occurs a second moment, also during this mirror phase (which lasts overall from the age of six to eighteen months), when the child recognizes its difference from or sameness with the mother and senses the absence and loss of the mother – since it identifies itself as separate from her.

At this juncture, according to Lacan, the Oedipus complex plays its part in dissolving the mirror phase and pushing the child into the Symbolic. In other words, it is by means of the Oedipal phase that the child of either sex is separated from its first love-object, the mother – she who has become (m)other. The child desires unification, anew, with the mother but this time, because there is separation, absence or lack, the desire to unite is now sexually driven. In the case of the male child this desire is potentially incestuous and it is at this juncture that the Law of the Father, the Symbolic Order is imposed. The child is forbidden access to the mother by the father and the child will comply for fear of castration by the father. He represses his desire, a repression which forms the unconscious. It is the verbal prohibition imposed by the father that constitutes the threat of castration. The Symbolic Order or Law of the Father is therefore, according to Lacan, based in language, and desire is repressed as that which cannot be spoken. In obeying this Law, the male child enters into the Symbolic and adopts a speaking position that marks him as independent from the mother. He conforms to the patriarchal law, upholds it and seeks to fulfil his Oedipal trajectory by finding a female other (other than his mother). He thus perpetuates patriarchal law for generations to come – he follows in the name of the father, so that when he says 'I' it comes from the same authorized speaking position as the language of the father. He becomes subject of the Symbolic (that is, he can speak as subject of the patriarchal language).

Lacan is much less, if at all, clear about the girl child, but, feminist Lacanians have developed his thinking. According to Lacan, when the female child perceives her sameness with her mother, she experiences her lack as being non-phallic. She discovers that, she like her mother, is castrated – is already what the male child most fears. Like the male child, she at first perceives her mother as her love-object. But since she is like the mother and there is no threat of castration, what, ask feminist Lacanians, will motivate her to relinquish her desire for her mother? They argue that, since she must enter into the social order of things (patriarchal law decrees she must) and leave the Imaginary, she will turn away from the mother and enter the Symbolic Order. However, she will never fully relinquish her desire of the mother and so will always remain doubly desiring. The female child's entry into the Symbolic is again, as for the male child, an entry into the Law of the Father. Her sexual drives impel her towards the truly phallic, the father. The father must once again impose the Law of the Father and forbid her sexual access. She must repress her desire for the father and embark on her own Oedipal trajectory and find a male other (than her father). However, the question becomes, when the girl child says 'I' whose 'I' is it? She cannot be subject of the Symbolic in the same way as the male child can because the authorized speaking position is that of the father. If she cannot be subject then she must be object of the Symbolic (that is, of language); and if she is object of the Symbolic then, at least within heterosexual relationships, she must also be the object rather than the subject of desire (she is fixed by language since it is not hers).

Upon entry into the Symbolic both male and female child will feel not whole but divided – as we recall they both felt this for the first time when they entered into the mirror phase, when the mother becomes other (which Lacan signifies with a small 'o'). This time both sexes attempt to signify themselves through language, that which is outside from their selves (the language/Law of the Father). The Symbolic now becomes the Other (which Lacan signifies with a capital 'O'). The subject represents itself in the field of the Other (language) – capital 'O' because the Law of the Father. To this first sense of fragmentation comes another, felt by the fact that the subject can never fully be represented in speech since speech cannot reflect the unconscious (the repressed, unspeakable desire for the mother or the father). The subject, in representing itself, can only do so at the cost of division (conscious/unconscious; self/Other). The difference for the two sexes is of course the degree of division or fragmentation. This is in direct correlation to the *mastery* as subject *in* and *of* that language. The male child can be part of it/in the field of the Other since he follows in the name of the father, even though he is always in danger of being castrated by the big 'O' – hence the *cap*-ital letter (as in capital punishment). The already always castrated girl is excluded by it; however, in exchange she remains always doubly desiring (for more detail on the female child see **psychoanalysis** and **spectator**).

To return to the general question of division, as the (conscious) subject seeks to represent itself in the field of the Other, it does so at the expense of coming after the fact or word by which time the (unconscious) subject is already not there but becoming something else, a situation Lacan (1977, 304) refers to as 'future anterior' (see **enunciation** and **absence/presence**). In other words, the conscious subject utters or enunciates 'I' and becomes situated as 'I' (the spoken subject becomes presence). However, the unconscious subject is already beyond that 'I' and becoming something else (the spoken subject now becomes absence). As the spoken subject fades, becomes loss or lack, so the subject will attempt to recapture itself as a unified being, the idealized image of the Imaginary. However, that idealized image is a recall of that first mirror reflection and the child's identification with its own specular image. In other words, that image is an external one, the subject as seen from outside (not from within) – therefore also the subject as it imagines others see it. Lacan reasons that this is where the subject confronts the divided notion of self: the image of the self is accurate but also delusory. It is the same and other. The subject (mis)recognizes itself both as itself and as other. Thus the attempt to produce or reproduce that image is to produce a misrecognition of the self – the self as it cannot be. And it is at this juncture that the conjunction – which Lacan terms *suture* – occurs between the Imaginary and the Symbolic to close the gap opened up by this breach in the subject's identity (between recognition and misrecognition, and between the conscious and unconscious).

In summary The Symbolic does not 'dislodge' the Imaginary but functions to regulate it, which is why the two orders are described as always being co-present. This co-presence can best be summed up in the following way. The early *jouissance* or jubilation felt at the mirror stage is soon threatened by the child's realization that she or he is not a unified being at the centre of the world but part of a larger social and Symbolic order within and against which the individual is constantly trying to define her or his identity – including reasserting herself or himself as a unified being. It follows, therefore, that the psyche is also not a simplified entity as it fluctuates between the desire for the ideal of the unified being of the Imaginary and the knowledge imposed by the Symbolic that it is composed of many conflicting forces. In psychoanalytic terms, then, suture is perceived as the striving of the ego to stitch these two orders together, to fill the gaps in the rupture implicitly caused by these two orders, to unify them rather than let them split asunder and thus (one must presume) split the psyche in two. (For further reading on Lacan see Grosz, 1990.)

To return to film theory During the 1970s and early 1980s the debate around suture and its applicability to film was a contested one but one that was introduced because of a perceived need to account fully for the viewing experience of a film during its projection and to describe the relationship between film narrative and spectator. What follows is a synopsis of the arguments. In its first, simplified form, suture was perceived to be the effect of certain filmic codes that stitched the spectator into the film text. For Oudart (1977) the system of shot/reverse-angle shot is the primary suturing device in **classic narrative film**. In this series of shots, which establishes the point of view of two characters in (say) a conversation, the spectator adopts first one, then the other position and becomes both subject and object of the look. The first shot, through an **eyeline match**, positions the spectator as the one looking, character *A*. *The spectator adopts A's position and looks at character B. The next shot, reverse shot, positions the spectator as character B.* But character *B*, as we know, was the object of character *A*'s look. So the spectator adopts the position of the object that *A* looked at. However, character *B* now looks at character *A*. The off-screen space (where *A* had been in the first shot) now comes

375

into view. Thus, according to Oudart, the spectator makes sense of off-screen space and becomes stitched into the film.

In general terms, the process of suturing goes as follows. The spectator upon first encountering a cinematic **image** feels much the same jubilation or *jouissance* as does the child in the mirror phase. This image appears to be complete or unified in the same way that the child's specular image appears to it. At first, then, the spectator feels secure in an imaginary relationship with the image. But this image is an idealized image, so in fact the spectator is caught up in a fascination with a delusion, with the unreal. Yet, as we know, the Imaginary and the Symbolic are always co-present. Thus this secure imaginary relationship with the image is soon under threat as the spectator becomes aware of the image frame (imag(in)e(d) frame) and therefore of off-screen space, of absence, of the absent space off-screen. This gap, this absence or lack of point of view felt by the spectator, is similar to the breach, noted by Lacan, in the subject's identity as same and other, as absence/presence. In this instance the spectator starts wondering whose point of view it is and who is framing the image. The image starts to show itself for what it is, an artefact, an illusion and in so doing threatens to reveal film as a system of signs and codes. What relieves this exposure of film's signifying practices and sutures the spectator back into the illusion, back into her or his earlier imaginary unity with the image, is the reverse-angle shot (the second point-of-view shot). The spectator now sees that the first shot was the point of view of the character currently in the shot. Off-screen space becomes on-screen space. Absence has become presence. The artifice of film can continue. The **narrative** is safe and the spectator comfortably reinscribed into the filmic discourse.

Daniel Dayan (1974) takes this idea of deception (what Oudart also termed the tragedy inherent in cinematic **discourse**) further and examines it within the context of **ideology**. If, he argues, the system of suture renders the film's signifying practices invisible, then the spectator's ability to read or decode the film remains limited. In this way, this

376

system allows the ideological effect of the film to slip by unnoticed and to become absorbed by the spectator. Film becomes **hegemonic** rather than a reflection of reality. And it is not difficult to point to **Hollywood**, as Kaplan (1983, 132) does, and its dream factory as exemplifying these cinematic strategies of smoothing over any notion of conflict and contradiction and presenting the spectator with an unquestioning or unruptured idea of idealness of the American way of life (see **seamlessness**).

Other theorists saw this interpretation of the system of suture as too limiting both in terms of its enunciation (how it negotiates the spectator's access to film) and in its relation to ideology. With regard to the former point, Salt (1977), Rothman (1976), Heath (1981) and Silverman (1983) all argue that to limit suture to the shot/reverse-angle shot is to lose sight of the fact that, as a shot, it is not a dominant one in cinema – even Hollywood cinema – and that this shot should be seen as just one example of suture alongside other devices consistent with **continuity editing**. Nor, they argue, should suture be limited to pure cinematic devices. Silverman, especially, demonstrates how suture is synonymous with the operations of classic narrative (that is, film discourse in its widest sense of **editing** and **lighting**, as well as compositional and formal narrative elements). According to her analysis, narrative is indispensable to the system in providing the spectator with a subject position.

In terms of ideology both Heath and Rothman (albeit in different ways) turn Dayan's argument around. Rothman argues against the system of suture by saying that the dominant point–of–view sequence is in fact a three- (and not a two-) shot sequence (viewer/view/viewer). He goes on to say that the point–of–view sequence appropriates the viewer's **gaze** in the second shot to show the spectator what the viewer sees. It is not an authorized shot – that is, the viewer does not authorize it, the point–of–view sequence merely takes over her or his gaze and then cuts back in shot three to the viewer. The question of whose point of view it is, Rothman asserts, simply does not pose itself. The spectator knows it is a point-of-view shot and so is aware of that cinematic code (as much as any others). It is not then a question of deception, nor is it an attempt to render film's signifying practices invisible, and as such its function is not an ideological one. It follows, then, that classic narrative is not necessarily hegemonic and that if there is a question of ideology to be addressed in relation to cinema then it cannot be thought of (as by Dayan) in terms of some abstract ahistorical absolute but rather in terms of history. If cinema is an ideological system, Rothman's argument goes, then it is so only in so far as throughout history it has served a variety of bourgeois ideologies.

Heath does not reject suture, although he does agree with Salt and Rothman that the system cannot be reduced to the function of the single cinematic code of the reverse-angle shot. As with Silverman, he believes that suture – because it is the conjunction between the Imaginary and the Symbolic – is necessarily present at all levels of filmic enunciation and that therefore all texts suture. This is not a sweeping generalization. For Heath the concept of suture is an invaluable one because it draws attention to the fact that the image is not the unified idealized image of the Imaginary it purports to be but, rather, an incomplete one – one therefore that requires the speaking subject (uttering or enunciating from the Symbolic Order) to complete. But, as has already been pointed out in the Lacan section, the speaking subject fades as soon as it has spoken. Any notion that the image is complete is illusory and it is in this respect that the ideological representations that images construct can be taken to task. Interpreted this way then, suture, contrary to Dayan's contention, leads the way into an understanding of ideological representation.

Arguably the most lasting outcome of the debate around suture concerns the relationship of the spectator to the screen and the pleasure experienced in cinema's reconstruction within the spectator of an illusory sense of the early-in-life imagined unity. Attendant within this identification process is the separation from the mother and the implicit sexual drives that separation brings with it. Cinema in this respect becomes a **mise-en-scène** of desire: first, it constructs the spectator as subject and, second, it establishes the desire to look with all that that connotes in terms of visual pleasure for the spectator. In its early days, this debate on visual pleasure, which ran concurrently with that on suture, was completely unproblematized in terms of **sexuality** and **scopophilia**. Since then, however, feminist film theory has entered into the debate and widened it to include analyses of masculine erotic desire and the male fetishizing gaze as well as female representation and spectatorship (see also **feminist film theory** and **voyeurism/fetishism**). (For further reading see Kuhn, 1982; Lapsley and Westlake, 1988; Mast, Cohen and Baudry, 1992.)

syntagmatic – *see* **paradigmatic**

theory   This entry limits itself to a reasonably brief history of the development of theory since the beginning of the century. Specific details of major developments are given in other entries.

Although there is no attempt to be deterministic here, there does appear to be a quite convenient way of carving up film theory into epochs of theory-pluralism and theory-monism. Indeed we can determine three epochs: 1910–30s, a period of pluralism; 1940s–60s, a period of serially monistic theories; 1970s–90s, pluralism once more.

1910–30s   Cinema was very quickly perceived to be an art form. Arguably, the genesis of film theory was in France. The earliest reference to film as art occurred with the start in 1908 of Film d'Art's productions (the first of which was *L'Assassinat du duc de Guise*, set to the music of Saint-Saens). However, one of the earliest attempts to align cinema with other arts can be found in the film-maker Louis Feuillade's advance publicity sheet for his series *Le Film esthétique* (1910). In his manifesto he begged the question: since film appeals to our sight and, therefore, has as its natural origins painting and the theatre, surely cinema can provide those same aesthetic sensations? He also perceived cinema as a popular art and as an economic art (a synergy between technology and the aesthetic) and as an artistic economy (art closely allied with capital). A year later Ricciotto Canudo published in France his manifesto 'The Birth of a Sixth Art', in which he established the two main lines of debate that would preoccupy theorists well into the 1920s and in some respects into the 1930s: the debate around cinema's **realism**, on the one hand and, on the other, around a pure non-representational cinema based on form and rhythm.

A few years later a German psychologist, Hugo Münsterberg, introduced the idea that cinema was not filmed reality but a psychological and aesthetic process that revealed our mental experiences. After the First World War, the debate widened further, mainly among French critics and film-makers, and addressed issues of high and popular art, realist versus **naturalist** film, the **spectator**–screen relationship, **editing** styles (a debate much influenced by the **Soviet cinema** of the 1920s), simultaneity, **subjectivity**, the unconscious and the **psychoanalytical** potential of film, **auteur** cinema versus script-led cinema, cinema as rhythm and as **sign**. In the 1930s, following the advent of **sound**, the ground shifted and the debate centred on the very polemical issue of whether sound was a good or bad thing for the aesthetics of cinema. Certain critics claimed that it was the death-knell for experimental cinema, others thought that it brought with it the chance of a new radicalization of cinema. In this latter case, film was linked with social praxis (that is, it acted as a **transparence** on society and its interactions with individuals) but was also revelatory of mental states.

1940s–60s   This was predominantly the period where the search was on, particularly after 1946, for a total theory. Speculatively, we could say that this desire for total theory is easily understandable in the light of the Jewish and atomic holocausts – to such irrational acts only a single unified vision can provide security and stability. The two main theories to mention here are, first, the so-called **auteur theory** (1950s) and, second, **structuralism** (1960s), although we should also point out that these two were preceded by Alexandre Astruc's (1948) concept of cinema as language (*caméra-stylo* as he defined it). Seeing film as a matter of authorial signs (whether stylistic or thematic) was too limiting, denying the other structures and production practices that go into making a film (see **auteur theory**). It was also a conservative romantic aesthetic in so far as the film-maker was isolated as the aesthetic genius. Finally, it was fraught because it introduced the idea of 'great' directors.

Similarly, structuralism and auteur-structuralism, which 'replaced' auteur theory in the 1960s, ran into difficulties, this time of total theory crushing the aesthetic. Structuralism was a theory which, it was believed, could be applied to all aspects of society and culture. However, it ended up in rigid formalism which removed any discussion of pleasure in the viewing. Although this theory purported to reveal all hidden structures behind film-making (modes of production, impact of **stars** on choices, socio-historical context of production and so on), in fact it continued to focus on the film-maker and her or his product – hence the term auteur-structuralism. The most central theorist in this debate as it concerned cinema was the semiotician Christian Metz (1971 and 1972), who devised a linguistic paradigm that could account for all elements of a film's composition – almost a grammar of film (see **semiotics**). Analysing film this way meant that a critic could scientifically and objectively evaluate a film and at the same time determine the style of a particular auteur or film-maker and indeed determine also if a particular film was consistent with that film-maker's style. The focus, therefore, was on the hidden structures and codes in the text and in this respect it answered the question of how the text comes to be – not how it comes to mean. Thus, ultimately, the limitation of this total theory was its formalism (for fuller discussion see **structuralism**).

1970s–90s Total theory made it evident that a single theory would never be sufficient to explain and analyse film. Where in this total theory, for example, could one talk about the **spectator**–text relationship? However, there was no need to throw the baby out with the bath-water, hence the term **post-structuralism**. Psychoanalysis and semiotics in their structuralist phase had started to shatter the concept of the unity of the auteur. The effects of **deconstruction** theory, introduced by Jacques Derrida around 1967, would help to do the rest. Deconstruction helped to recentre the theory debate in a pluralistic context. In essence, deconstruction stipulates that a text is not transparent, natural or innocent and therefore must be unpicked, deconstructed. The non-transparency must be investigated to show just how many texts there are – all producing meaning. There is no longer any single reading of a text, nor indeed is there any final reading.

Post-structuralism, then, did several things. It defined the auteur's place within the textual process – the auteur was now a figure constructed out of her or his films (a far less authoritative position). It established the importance of **intertextuality** – the effects of different texts upon one another. There is no such thing as a 'pure' text, all texts have intertextual relations with others. As far as film is concerned, this means relations with other films and of course with the 'invisible' texts such as the modes of production, the dynamics between actors, crew and film-maker (and so on). Post-structuralism also established the fact that film has **ideological** effects, therefore the question of the **subject** comes into play (who is the subject: the text, the auteur, the spectator?). What also comes into play is the question of the effects of the **enunciating** text (the film as performance) upon the spectator. In the final analysis post-structuralism opened up textual analysis to a pluralism of approaches which did not reduce the text to the status of object of investigation but as much subject as those reading, writing or producing it.

In Anglo-Saxon countries the other significant area of film theory, **feminist film theory**, helped to develop the debate along several new lines of investigation. The whole question of gendered **subjectivity** and **agency**, not addressed since the 1920s, was re-opened. Who held the **gaze**, within and without the screen, was a fundamental issue raised in this area. **Genre** and **gender** also generated questions: if certain films were gender specific (for example **westerns** for men, **melodrama** for women), what were the ideological operations at work and what were the spectator–text relationships depending on what sort of genre was being viewed? Further, given the ostensible gendered subjectivity of the viewer, what could be said about pleasure in viewing?

Third Cinema/Third world cinema (*see also* **cinema nôvo**) Third cinema was a term coined in 1969 by film theorists and film-makers F. Solanas and O. Getino (reprinted in 1983) to distinguish it from the first cinema (**Hollywood**) and the second (European art cinema). Third World Cinema was so called because it was comprised of countries outside the two dominant spheres of power: the eastern and the western super-power blocks which no longer exist since the demise of the Soviet Union. These two terms get used interchangeably, even though this is not necessarily always strictly correct. Third Cinema is more ostensibly political in its conceptualization since it seeks both to counter the **ideologically** unsound film-making practices of the two cinemas, especially Hollywood, and to promote the cause of socialism. Third World Cinema is more general term that refers to films made by countries other than the developed industrial countries. Generally speaking, these countries do not have a fully developed film industry either – the exceptions being Brazil, Argentina, India and Egypt. The films produced by these countries, primarily in Latin America, Africa, Asia and the Middle East, or at least the films that get distributed outside these countries, often have political resonances. These films are political both in terms of making political statements in relation to their own country and in relation to dominant film practices outside their country. This politicization of Third Cinema dates back at least to the 1960s when liberation struggles and revolutions in these countries became worldwide news and film-makers made films either advocating or challenging these changes. Since that period also, the cinema of these countries has been fairly consistent in its opposition to the colonial film practices of the western world, particularly as exemplified by **Hollywood**. American and European products had swamped the screens of these countries with their pro-capitalist messages. The need was felt to project images of the indigenous realities, and this was done in a variety of ways depending on the country's political culture and the individual film-makers' vision and working conditions.

It is something of a paradox to speak of Indian cinema as a Third World cinema. It produces more films than any other nation – around nine hundred a year – and in sixteen languages. **Stars** have a major influence and standing and often play an active role in politics. Indian cinema is still a very popular form of entertainment since television is not yet a household commodity for many. The dominant popular **genres** are **musicals**, romance and adventure films. Production is dominated by Bombay Studios. However, there are a few independent film-makers and it is here that Indian cinema enjoys the political cachet attached to Third Cinema. The work of Satyajit Ray is exemplary in this context.

Cuba and Black Africa are the two regions that had to start from nothing. In 1959 Fidel Castro set up the Cuban Institute of Cinematographic Art and Industry, and **documentaries** and feature films were soon being produced. Cuba very quickly established itself on the international scene. Black Africa has moved far more slowly and it is really only Francophone Africa that has managed to establish a reputation on the international scene. The most widely known film-maker in that context is Ousmane Sembene of Senegal.

Despite major differences between the cinemas of the countries constituting Third Cinema, they do have in common a desire to address the effects of colonialism (Black Africa) or neo-colonialism (Latin America and Asia), exclusion and oppression (all countries). This Third Cinema sets out deliberately to politicize cinema and to create new cinematic **codes and conventions**. Gabriel (1982, 16ff) discusses the major themes of this Third (politicized) Cinema. This cinema addresses issues of **class**, race, culture, religion, sex and national integrity. Class struggle between the poor and the rich is at the core. But in these films the issue of race is seen within the context of class antagonism (Gabriel, 1982, 16). The preservation of popular indigenous cultures and the representation of them

385

in opposition to the dominant colonial and imperialist values espoused by the ruling classes constitutes an 'aesthetics of liberation' (1982, 16) in the cinema. Contradictions inherent in political struggle within the context of deeply rooted structures of religion are **foregrounded**, as is the struggle for the emancipation of women. Finally, armed struggle is a theme particularly identified with Latin American cinema. Indeed, indirect and direct social and political criticism of current regimes are more commonly associated with Latin American films, particularly those of Argentina (see Octavio Getino and Fernando Solanas's *La Hora de los Hornos* (*The Hour of the Furnaces*), 1968, and Leopoldo Torre Nilsson's *Piel de Verano* (*Summer Skin*), 1961. Cuba produced a political cinema including films that charted the difficulties of implementing the revolution (as exemplified by Tomás Guttiérez Alea's *Memorias del Subdesarrollo (Memories of Underdevelopment),* 1968, and Humberto Solás's *Lucia*, 1968). (For further reading see Chanan (ed.), 1983; Gabriel, 1982; Pines and Willemen (eds), 1990.)

30–degree rule (*see also* **180–degree rule**) A rule applied in the name of continuity that stipulates that, when there is a cut to another camera position, the camera should be at least 30 degrees from the previous one. If this rule is not observed and two shots are cut together of the same person or object within the scene without the camera having moved more than thirty degrees, the effect on the spectator is of a jolt as if the camera has jumped a bit. Essentially in terms of spatial logic there is not enough difference between the two shots in terms of angle (and therefore a clearly understood renewed position on the object) for the transition between the two shots to remain unnoticed. The result is a noticeable jump, what is termed a **jump cut**. The 30-degree rule serves to create an undisturbed **seamlessness** in the film because such a shift does not draw attention to itself and is logically motivated within the **narrative**.

thriller/psychological thriller – (*see also* **fantasy, film noir, gangster movies, motivation, horror movies, science fiction, voyeurism/fetishism**) A very difficult **genre** to pin down because it covers such a wide range of types of films. Thrillers are films of suspense, so clearly film noir, gangster, science fiction or horror films are in some respects thrillers, as are detective thrillers (see **gangster films**). Some purists will differentiate terror movies as being distinct from thrillers, since a thriller is supposed to instil terror into the **audience**. I shall ignore that sub-categorizing and focus primarily on the psychological thriller, bearing in mind the overlap with the aforementioned genres.

A thriller relies on intricacy of plot to create fear and apprehension in the audience. It plays on our own fears by drawing on our infantile and therefore mostly repressed fantasies that are voyeuristic and sexual in nature. *The* master of the thriller is Alfred Hitchock, the greatest creator of anticipation and builder of suspense. Almost unquestionably he is the filmmaker who invented the modern thriller. His secret is of course in the construction of his films. Often at the centre of the **narrative** is a fairly basic theme, usually a struggle around love and/or money, so that is not what grabs and enthrals the **spectator**. Fundamentally Alfred Hitchcock works through delay. He delays the action which we know is going to occur. We know Marion Crane is going to be murdered (in *Psycho*, 1960), but we do not know when or how. We, like Norman Bates, have been watching her, unseen, as we peep through the holes alongside Norman. When will terror strike? When it finally does, we almost feel relief, certainly a release from all the tension that has been building up through the set of **gazes** that have been conferred on Marion. In this respect, the attacks on women in Alfred Hitchcock's films are clearly sexually motivated. Even if in some films (such as *The Birds*, 1963) they do not die, Alfred Hitchcock's women are assailed by knives, birds or brutally strangled (*Frenzy*, 1972).

Thriller films are, then, sadomasochistic. Indeed, the psychological thriller bases its construction in sadomasochism, madness and **voyeurism**. The killer spies on and ensnares his victim in a series of intricate and sadistic moves, waiting to strike. The killer is most often psychotic and his madness is an explanation for what motivates his actions. He **agences** murderous power through his madness. Such is not usually the luck of the woman. Madness predominantly privileges women-as-victim far more than men. Their madness is a deep-rooted phobia that often has a sexual cause. Marnie's fear of men (in *Marnie*, Alfred Hitchcock, 1964) is due to her violent reaction to seeing her mother aggressed by a sailor – Marnie kills him, but is for ever stuck with the neurosis that men equal sexual aggression. She is stuck, that is, until her all-knowing husband cures her. In *Repulsion* (Roman Polanski, 1965), as the title already indicates, the heroine's revulsion at men's sexual advances is the result of the fear and repulsion she experiences when confronted by the primal scene (the parents copulating). Men who get too close to her get murdered.

Voyeurism operates within the film (is **diegetically** inscribed) but the film also operates to position us as voyeurs. One film that brilliantly exposes this process is Michael Powell's *Peeping Tom* (1960). The film itself **foregrounds** voyeurism, positions us as voyeur-director and as the victim, and in the closing shots makes us voyeur of our 'own' victim-ness (for a discussion of this point see **foregrounding**). In this way we too play out the sadistic scenario and derive pleasure from re-experiencing our primitive and infantile desires. It is noteworthy that many thrillers focus around bad parenting – or that bad parenting is the cause of psychotic behaviour. Norman Bates in *Psycho* and Mark Lewis in *Peeping Tom* both had bad parents: an overbearing mother in the first case, a disapproving father in the second. Sibling rivalry can also cause psychological disorders of a life-threatening kind (as in *Whatever Happened to Baby Jane?*, Robert Aldrich, 1962). But so too can sibling narcissism (as in *Dead Ringers*, David Cronenberg, 1988). The two identical twins, both brilliant gynaecologists (!), live in perfect harmony with one another until a woman enters their life with an amazing gynaeco-logical problem (a triple cervix). She disrupts the twins' symbiosis and symbolically castrates them (well, she would with a triple cervix wouldn't she?). Incapable of coping with woman-as-difference and terrified of separation, one of the twins takes to drugs and becomes increasingly hysterical in relation to women. He eventually drags his brother down with him and the two finally succumb to a gruesome double-death.

One final point. Although thrillers are more about fantasy than reality, they do fulfil a very real need. Otherwise why would we go to the movies? We do have a psychological fascination with horror, we like being made afraid. For this reason many thrillers have an aura of 'the possible' about them. To achieve this, the settings are as ordinary as one's own familiar environment. Alfred Hitchcock's *Frenzy* is a good example of this everyday ordinariness in which ordinary women keep getting murdered (the setting is London, more specifically the former Covent Garden, the murderer an ordinary fellow, a fruiterer). Roman Polanski combines the fantastic with the ordinary in *Rosemary's Baby* (1966) where he juxtaposes demonic possession and witchcraft with contemporary New York.

time and space – *see* **spatial/temporal contiguity**

tracking shot/travelling shot/dollying shot   Terms used for a **shot** when the camera is being moved by means of wheels: on a dolly (a low wheeled platform on which a film camera is moved) and on tracks (hence tracking shot), in a car or even a train. The movement is normally quite fluid (except perhaps in some of the wilder car chases) and the tracking can be either fast or slow. Depending on the speed this shot has different connotations (for example like a dream or trance if excessively slow, or bewildering and frightening if excessively frenetic). A tracking shot can go backwards, forwards, from left to right or right to left, and the way in which a person is framed in that shot has a specific meaning (for

389

example, if the camera holds a person in the frame but that person is at one extreme or other of the frame, this could suggest a sense of imprisonment).

transitions – *see* **cut, dissolves, fade, jump cut, unmatched shots, wipe**

transparency/transparence (*see also* **ideology**) This concept takes both these spelling forms, and refers to the notion that cinema, does not provide a window on the world, any more than television does, that is, the idea that it offers a one-to-one relationship with reality is a **myth**. Both media can, however, offer a transparence on the world: they can give a reflection *on* the world that surrounds us. Thus a **war film** like *All Quiet on the Western Front* (Lewis Milestone, 1930) gives a reflection on the horrors of the First World War trench warfare – a reflection that is closer to the truth than the dominant tendency of war films which is to glorify victory and heroize the individual.

travelling shot – *see* **tracking shot**

underground cinema The underground cinema movement in the 1960s was very important to the growth of US cinema. It was bold, outrageous and scornful of dominant cinema practices. It was also known as the New American Cinema Group: this group, formed in 1960, signed a manifesto accusing mainstream or **dominant cinema** of being morally corrupt. Underground cinema was a name coined by Stan VanDerBeek to qualify this independent film-making movement based in New York and San Francisco. This movement grew out of the 1950s Beat Generation and its revolt against conventional artistic practices. VanDerBeek was one of the practitioners of this movement, as were, more famously, Andy Warhol, Stan Brakhage and Kenneth Anger. **Censorship** was still in practice in the US (it was abolished in the late 1960s), hence the term underground, because in subject matter the films produced by this movement were proscribable products. The movement was not a cohesive group but stood as one in its determination to defy the censorship laws, which it deemed unconstitutional. And in fact it was one of the movement's most notorious films, Jack Smith's *Flaming Creatures* (1963) – a **fantasy** film about a transvestite orgy – which was hounded by the New York police and the US Customs but which, in the end, was shown as evidence before the States Supreme Court hearing on the abolition of censorship.

The collective that made up underground cinema were not necessarily film-makers, but came from different artistic backgrounds and saw in film a new way of self-expression. The heritage of this movement is traced back to Maya Deren's influential experimental film work on the subconscious, most specifically her film *Meshes of the Afternoon* (1943). And indeed she helped to finance projects by other independent film-makers, particularly Brakhage and Anger. The first so-called underground film, *Pull My Daisy* (1959), was a Beat Generation film made by Robert Frank and the painter Alfred Leslie starring Jack Kerouac as voice-over and Allen Ginsberg as the poet. Kenneth Anger's films explicitly explored homosexual fantasies, rituals and dilemmas (see *Scorpio Rising*, 1963). Andy Warhol filmed real time by placing his camera in front of a building for up to eight hours and just letting the film roll (see *Empire*, 1965 – in front of the Empire State Building). He also parodied **Hollywood genres** (for example **westerns** in *Lonesome Cowboys*, 1968). Other film-makers were more closely associated in their work with the **cinéma-vérité** tradition. Lionel Rigosin's and Shirley Clarke's documentary approach produced such politicized films as Rigosin's film on a down and out alcoholic in New York, *On the Bowery* (1955), and the clandestinely shot film among Black South Africans, *Come Back Africa* (1959); Clarke's films focused on Black ghetto subculture in Harlem: drugs and jazz (*The Connection*, 1961); adolescent crime and survival (*The Cool World*, 1963); Black male prostitute fantasy (*Portrait of Jason*, 1967).

unmatched shots Cutting from one **shot** to another so that there is no apparent **continuity** in action. This type of **editing** is typically used in **avant-garde** and **surreal** films as a means of creating a sense of disorientation in time and space. A classic example is Luis Buñuel's *Un Chien andalou* (1929).

vampire movies – *see* **horror movies**

variation – *see* **repetition**

violence – *see* **censorship**, **voyeurism/fetishism**

visual pleasure – *see* **scopophilia**

voyeurism/fetishism (*for fuller discussion see* **gaze**, **psychoanalysis**, **scopophilia**, **spectator positioning**, **suture**)   Voyeurism is the act of viewing the activities of other people unbeknown to them. This often means that the act of looking is illicit or has illicit connotations. We pay to go to the movies, but once we are sat before the screen we are positioned as voyeurs, as spectating **subject** watching the goings-on of the people on-screen who are 'unaware' that we are watching them. It is from this positioning that we derive pleasure (known as scopophilia, pleasure in viewing). Voyeurism is not limited to the spectator, however. The camera that originally filmed the action is also a 'voyeur'. Often there is a voyeuristic positioning of a character within a film. Alfred Hitchcock is

393

notorious for this (as in *Rear Window*, 1954, and *Psycho*, 1960). A film that admirably foregrounds the complexity of voyeurism and all the subject positionings possible is Michael Powell's *Peeping Tom*, 1960 (see **foregrounding** for a discussion of this film in this light).

Fetishism refers to the notion of over-investment in parts of the body, most commonly the female body. Thus, in films women's breasts or legs are often 'picked out' by the camera and are, thereby, over-invested with meaning. Similarly, dress-codes can be part of this fetishizing process. Thus, a woman might wear a slinky, tight-fitting dress and long black evening gloves. Alternatively, she might be wearing very high heels, stilettos perhaps, and have her fingernails thickly nail-polished (in deep red if it is a film in **colour**).

In psychoanalytic terms, voyeurism and fetishism are two strategies adopted by the male to counter his fear of sexual difference (between himself and the female, sexual other) and the fear of castration which he feels as a result of that difference (the woman lacks a penis, the male assumes 'she' has been castrated). Thus, adopting the first strategy he fixes the woman with his gaze, voyeuristically investigates her body, and therefore sexuality – she is the object of his investigation and in that way he safely contains her. As the object of his look and surveillance, meaning is ascribed to her by him. Voyeurism, at its most extreme, can lead to sadomasochistic behaviour. The man watches the woman, she may or may not know that he is looking at her, she cannot, however, return the gaze (because it is he who has **agency** over it and thus over her). Ostensibly, she is his victim and he the potential sadist who can violently attack or even kill her. Most **thrillers** and **films noir** depend on this sadomasochistic dynamic for their suspense. *Psycho* is an obvious example, but *The Shining* (Stanley Kubrick, 1980) is a more recent one. And by way of a rare reversal of power relations, at least until the bitter end, Kathy Bates in *Misery* (Carl Reiner, 1990) entraps her favourite popular fiction writer who has broken his leg and is therefore 'impotent'; she keeps him under constant surveillance and, when he 'dares' to 'look back' (by refusing to do her bidding and write *the* novel she wants written!), thinks nothing of brutally attacking him with axes and all sorts of penile or castrating instruments. But all ends well, he gets away – this after all is a comic thriller.

Fetishism is no more kind to the woman. Fetishism is a strategy to disavow difference. The male seeks to find the 'hidden' phallus in the woman. This fetishization takes place by a fragmentation of the body and an over-investment in the part of the body (or a piece of clothing) that has been fragmented off. The purpose of this over-investment is, ultimately, through perceiving them as perfection themselves, to make those parts figure as the missing phallus. The female form is contained this time by a denial of difference. She is phallic, therefore safe. Marlene Dietrich was a fetished form particularly in Von Sternberg's films – she takes on a masculinized female form (see Kaplan, 1983, 49ff.). Marylin Monroe was kept sexually safe by over-investment in her breasts and legs. More recently, many of Kathleen Turner's and Theresa Russell's roles have them (phallically) dressed in tight black dresses, stiletto heels with highly varnished nails and long sweeping hair – the deep voice just adds the finishing touch.

W

war films (*see also* **genre**)   Given the devastating effects of wars, especially world wars, on the populations of the nations involved, it comes as some surprise that war movies are very much a minority genre – both in the west and the east – and that, as far as colonized and formerly colonized countries and nations are concerned, there is even less **transparence**. What transparence there is tends to glorify or put forward the heroics of a particular triumphant nation. Only rarely do these films look at the horrors of war. Within western cinema on the whole, the vanquishing nation or colonizer's rightness in its endeavours has hardly ever been questioned or indeed explained – that is until recently.

The west has known two world wars since the birth of cinema. It has also been involved in various combats with regard to decolonization (particularly France) and wars that have been partially the outcome of the Cold War waged between the two superpowers (the United States and the former Soviet Union). What follows is a synopsis, largely based upon these various periods, of the representations of war in western movies.

The Great War 1914–18 and its representation in cinema 1914–39   The Great War had been the 'war to end all wars'. The loss of life had been colossal, almost beyond belief – at least 8.5 million servicemen died on the two sides of the combat (the Allies lost 5 million, the Central Powers 3.5) and a further 21 million combatants were wounded. The loss of life on the eastern front (Germany's eastern border) was as great as that on the western front, yet it is the latter front that is the more notorious in film and in history books – perhaps because of the devastating futility of the trench warfare fought out on both sides along the Franco-German border.

In Europe during this period, the propagandist nature of films only lasted for the early part of the hostilities. But the patriotic **melodramas** did their bit to help enlistment. *England Expects* (1914), *The Fatherland Calls* (*Das Vaterland ruft*, 1914) and *French Mothers* (*Mères françaises*, 1916) are just a sample of the titles that were intended to encourage men into battle and women to support their patriotic sons, lovers and husbands in the war effort. However, audience taste soon waned for these films that demonized the enemy or glorified the sacrificial spirit of the ordinary indigenous population. Preference was felt for the escapist nature of American comedies and series. Paradoxically, in terms of patriotic fervour it would be the United States that would pick up where Europe left off. Until 1917, when the Americans went to war, the United States had adopted an isolationist position in relation to the war, an isolationism that was reflected in the film output. And what few films were made about war were pacifist in nature (for example, *War Bride*, 1916, urges women to abstain from bearing children until fighting ceases). By 1917 all had changed and films became increasingly militantly pro-war (for example *The Kaiser – The Beast of Berlin*, 1918). The change of attitude came about largely as a result of Germany's offensive against the trade embargoes placed upon it and the two other countries of the Central Powers alliance (Austria-Hungary and Italy). To counter the Allies' attempts to deprive it of trading and receiving materials, Germany in 1915 launched a submarine (U-boat) campaign against the United Kingdom and the mercantile activities of the United States (one famous sinking was of the British liner *Lusitania* in 1915). Anti-German sentiment, not expressed until this period, at the loss of American lives during this campaign was partly responsible for the United States joining forces with the Allies

(France, the Soviet Union and the United Kingdom). Now the German was exposed on film as a ruthless rapist intent on ravishing America's virgins (*The Little United States*, 1917, starring Mary Pickford as the almost hapless victim) or a terrorizing colonialist who would invade America's shores (for example *The Sinking of the Lusitania*, 1918). In terms of content, these films did little more than transpose into American culture the jingoistic tone and stereotyping of earlier British and French films (such as *The Outrage*, Cecil Hepworth, 1915; *Herr Doktor*, Louis Feuillade, 1917).

Only after the war could a more acerbic eye be turned upon the savagery of war. But even so the number of films produced was minimal. For example, in the immediate aftermath of the war, France produced only one, and it focused on the horrors of war: Abel Gance's *J'accuse* (1919). Not until the tenth anniversary of the Armistice would the French film industry produce another film on the atrocities of that war. If anything, the United States was the more prolific. Capitalizing on the success of Charlie Chaplin's *Shoulder Arms* (1918), **Hollywood** was quick to realize that there was a taste for war movies, and during the 1920s several grand-scale reconstruction films of the United States' fighting role in the war were made. *The Four Horsemen of the Apocalypse* (1921), *The Grand Parade* (1925) and *What Price Glory* (1926) are just three examples of films that reconstructed battle scenes (often using veterans as extras). William Wellman's *Wings* (1927) pays homage to the fighter pilots of the war (then in their infancy). His film won the first Oscar ever, for best film.

The film to describe most explicitly the merciless horror of trench warfare was one of the earliest **sound** films to be made, Lewis Milestone's *All Quiet on the Western Front* (1930). The effect of this film was all the stronger since it was the first to bring the sound of war to the **images**. A strongly pacifist film, it portrays both the Allies and the Germans as victims of war, a senseless war. Jean Renoir's *La Grande Illusion* (1937) also picks up on this theme, but by the late 1930s, with war again imminent, the pacifism of his film was met with **censorship**. During the early 1930s, Germany also produced anti-war films, most famously Georg Pabst *Westfront 1918* (1930). However, given that moment in history and the rise of Nazism, the tendency was for the Germans to pay tribute to their war heroes, particularly those working in the submarines (*Morgenrot/Dawn*, Gustav Uciciky, 1933).

With the advent of the Second World War, the First sunk into oblivion as a film theme until the late 1950s. Stanley Kubrick's *Paths of Glory* (1957) and Joseph Losey's *King and Country* (1964) were just two films among a handful that returned to that period and seriously questioned practices operated behind the war scene by officers in power over young conscripts. In both Kubrick's and Losey's film the issue is that of courtmartials: three Frenchmen in the former film, a British soldier in the latter. More historically accurate films like these appear periodically in attempts to put the record straight (showing for example the effects of blinding gas in *Aces High*, Jack Gold, 1976) or to put on record war efforts that had been neglected (for example the contribution of Australian and New Zealand servicemen to the war in *Gallipoli*, Peter Weir, 1981).

The Second World War   If ever proof were needed that wars do not end wars then perhaps the devastating mortality figures of the Second World War will stand as testimony. Over thirty million service people and civilians died in this six-year war that left the world divided into two ideological parts (at least): the capitalist west and the communist east (of course geography does not oblige with such a neat schism: Cuba is in the west and Japan in the east!). The boundaries of traditional warfare had been blown apart by the dropping of the atomic bomb first on Hiroshima and then on Nagasaki (two important Japanese seaports). The savagery of this war can be measured by the fact that almost as many civilians as service people perished (14.7 million civilians including the systematic annihilation of 5.7 million Jews and an unaccountable number of gypsies and homosexuals; 15.3 million service men and women).

In the United Kingdom as elsewhere the **documentary** was perceived as a vital instrument for both morale boosting

399

and propaganda (see **ideology**). Already in the First World War the documentary had been used to chronicle some parts of the war, that is once the ban on cameramen (*sic*) was lifted in 1915, thus permitting them to go to the front. These documentaries included footage of the disastrous battle of the Somme. Documentary was already a strong tradition in the United Kingdom, harking back to work done for the GPO Film Unit by the Grierson Group – a group of documentarists headed up by John Grierson (see **documentary**). This film unit was renamed the Crown Film Unit in 1940. These documentaries focused both on the home front and on hostilities overseas. *London Can Take It* (Harry Watt and Humphrey Jennings, 1940) portrayed life going on as normal in London during the day despite the night raids by German fighter planes. This film was extremely influential in the United States in obtaining funds for Britain's war effort. In the same vein of Britons 'getting on with it' were Jennings's *Heart of Britain* (1941), showing ordinary people coping in the north of England, *Listen to Britain* (1942) about the British facing up to the hardships of wartime and *Fires Were Started* (1943) about the London fire service. *Target for Tonight* (Watt, 1941) portrayed the RAF bombing raids on Germany, showing what all the home-front hardship was for: victory. (The film was a studio reconstruction, although real RAF pilots were used.) Nor was the focus uniquely on the confrontation with Germany on European soil. Films from the Service Film Units provided images of campaign victories in North Africa (*Desert Victory* and *Tunisian Victory,* both 1943) and the Far East (*Burma Victory*, 1945).

If the war can be said to have had any positive impact on the film-making industry, as far as the United Kingdom and France were concerned it did free up slots for new talent to emerge. The American presence in Europe 'went home'. (The United States had not joined the war until 1941 after the Japanese had bombed its naval base at Pearl Harbor in the Pacific.) As for the French presence, certain of the established names, including immigré Germans and Austrians fleeing Nazi Germany, escaped to Hollywood. The new talent

400

emerged from their lesser roles into that of film-maker: David Lean, Sidney Gilliat, Frank Launder and Charles Frend in the United Kingdom, Robert Bresson, Jacques Becker and Henri-Georges Clouzot in France. In the United Kingdom many of the films produced were about the RAF, the naval forces and the merchant navy. Exceptionally with the new generation of film-makers, the shift in emphasis was away from **class**, still very much in evidence in other established film-makers' work (see Anthony Asquith's *The Way to the Stars*, 1945). Their films exemplified group solidarity dissolving class lines, and they stressed the ordinariness of people fighting the war (see *In Which We Serve*, Lean, 1942; *San Demetrio, London*, Frend, 1943). The importance of women in the war was also signalled (see two 1943 films: *The Gentle Sex*, Leslie Howard, about the women in the Auxiliary Territorial Services, and *Millions Like Us*, Launder and Gilliat, about women working in a munitions factory).

For France the story was completely the reverse. As an occupied country (1940–44) France could not address the war either as resistant to the Germans or as collaborator. This is why the few films that did appear to have a 'message' commenting the time were read so conflictually as simultaneously resistant and collaborationist. A classic example is Clouzot's *Le Corbeau* (1943), a film about a small town riddled with fear as a result of a spate of poison-pen letters. Another example is Jean Grémillon's *Le Ciel est à vous* (1944), about a female aviator who, after successfully completing a transatlantic flight, returns to the bosom of her family and carries on as good mother and housewife. In post-war France very few films indeed reflected the immediate past. Those that did eulogized the work of the French Resistance (eight films in all immediately after the liberation), most famously perhaps *La Bataille du rail* (René Clément, 1946).

In Germany propaganda had been underway throughout the Nazi régime since the early 1930s (with Goebbels as Hitler's propaganda minister). The work of Leni Riefenstahl is most often mentioned in this connection (see *Triumph of the Will*, 1934) although during the war she was virtually inactive. The

401

primary message of Germany's propaganda was its Aryan superiority, its victorious war campaigns and its heroism. The most notorious 'documentary' film was Dr Franz Hippler's *The Eternal Jew* (*Der Ewige Jude*, 1940) which purported to document the evils that Jews had wreaked on Germany (including causing Germany the loss of the First World War) and showed them as degenerate, even barbaric, in their traditions and culture and as corrupters of German aesthetics. Apart from the documentary propaganda, the German film industry produced a fair number of historical films which, in particular, praised former great leaders of the nation (for example *Bismarck*, 1940). Historical films were also produced to target Germany's reviled enemy, Britain. These films attacked Britain as the evil oppressor in Ireland (*The Fox of Glenarvon*, 1940, and *My Life for Ireland*, 1941 – both made by Goebbels's brother-in-law, M. W. Kimmich). Alternatively, Britain was the imperialist creator of concentration camps run by Churchill during the Boer War (*Uncle Kruger*, 1941). This last piece of propaganda was in fact based in truth. During the Boer War the British did set up concentration camps in which some twenty thousand women and children perished.

Both Germany and Britain exploited the historical reconstruction to propagandistic ends: the Germans to show their courage, their genius and their sense of vision as a nation that was politically and culturally unified, the British to extol their indomitable spirit against all odds (what is now termed the Dunkirk spirit – oddly since Dunkirk refers to a 'valiant' retreat by the Allies in 1940 when France was occupied). Bismarck, Schiller, Bach and Diesel were just some of the geniuses Germany paraded before its cinemagoing **audiences** (in films of the same titles). Britain turned to Nelson, exhorting Britain to go to war against Napoleon (*That Hamilton Woman!*, Alexander Korda, 1941); to Disraeli and his defiance of Bismarck (*The Prime Minister*, 1941); and to Henry V and his rallying call to the English for one more effort to overcome the enemy (*Henry V*, Lawrence Olivier, 1944).

The war established a documentary tradition for the Soviet Union, United States and Japan. The Soviets often compiled documentaries exemplifying the collective spirit of a united Soviet Republic (see *A Day at War*, 1942, with a hundred contributions from the front and *Berlin*, 1945, with forty contributions capturing the taking of Berlin). The documentary was exploited far less in Japan and on the whole extolled the duty to fight, but not without giving a realistic portrayal of the dangers of war (see Yamamoto's *The War at Sea from Hawaii to Malaya*, 1942, a reconstruction of the bombing of Pearl Harbor). In the United States documentaries were used to explain why the country had engaged in the war – a necessary procedure given its isolationism and fairly neutral pacifism during the first two and a half years of hostilities. Most exemplary was Frank Capra's documentary series *Why We Fight* (1942–45). The seven documentaries that make up this series document the rise and spread of fascism, the aggression of those fascist nations on others and, finally, the threat of fascism to America. Questioning the merits of engagement does not arise. Indeed the series was commissioned by the United States War Department. The maverick style in which John Ford's equally propagandistic film *The Battle of Midway* (1942) was made and finally shown to President Roosevelt for approval also points to a committed unquestioning stance. Ford, a lieutenant–commander serving in the Pacific, brought back to the United States actual footage of the Battle of Midway, determined to make a film for the mothers of America so that they would be proud of their sons' bravery in war and be moved to support American engagement (and send more sons to fight). It was made in total secrecy, shown to the President and approved for general distribution. John Ford had become the John Wayne of war documentaries.

Before the United States joined the war it produced several films, made in Britain, in support of the British. For example, the British film *That Hamilton Woman!* was a United Artists London film. As already mentioned, this film was an historical reconstruction. Others showed British courage in the face of German bombing raids (William Wyler's *Mrs Miniver*). More usually, however, these films took the form of an

403

American serviceman participating in a British campaign (as with *A Yank in the RAF*, Henry King, 1941). These types of film also had the merit of not upsetting the isolationist camp in the United States which, despite Roosevelt's wish to assist Britain in the war effort, had a strong hold on how the nation conducted itself. Furthermore, these films were muted and were not allowed to be particularly anti-fascist for fear, according to the **studios**, of political and economic reprisals – although why this fear arose is questionable since by 1940 Hollywood could not export to most of mainland Europe because it was occupied by the Germans, who had imposed a complete ban on the import of American products, including films. This fear may point to the widely acknowledged belief at the beginning of the war that the Germans would win the war and that it would be foolish to lose future markets. A simple example will illustrate this fence-sitting attitude. In 1939 (just prior to the war) Warners released Anatole Litvak's *Confessions of a Nazi Spy*, an explicitly anti-Nazi film. Germany, which still had a diplomatic presence in the United States, expressed its indignation and Warners were warned off making any such film in the future.

If until the United States' engagement in the war Hollywood played a rather minimal and unpartisan role in relation to the war effort, such was not the case once Pearl Harbor brought the United States into the war. Roosevelt put pressure on the studios to participate in the propaganda and morale-boosting necessary to get the United States behind the fight. Stars helped either by joining up (Clark Gable, James Stewart), by entertaining troops or getting ordinary Americans to buy war bonds (Bing Crosby, Bob Hope, Rita Hayworth, Bette Davis, Marlene Dietrich). The war film took off. **Comedies**, **musicals**, and combat films, films depicting the effects of the war on European citizens – all of these came pouring out of Hollywood, under the strictest of government guidelines. In the period 1942–45 Hollywood produced some five hundred war movies out of a total output of 1,700 films. The earliest films obeyed the governmental criteria of patriotism against fascism (see two 1942 films,

Yankee Doodle Dandy, a musical, and *Remember Pearl Harbor*, a war film with a clear call to arms).

On the whole the **stereotyping** in the war films reveals a curious mixture of jingoism, ambivalence and naivety. The jingoistic attitude prevailed in the representation of the Japanese. They were the evil, sadistic torturers who would go to any lengths to win (as in *Across the Pacific* and *Wake Island*, both 1942, and the fiercely anti-Japanese *Purple Heart*, Lewis Milestone, 1943). As far as the Germans were concerned, they were either the evil Nazi (*Hitler's Children*, 1942) or the good German (*The North Star*, 1943). They could in fact be a blend of the two as in Conrad Veidt's Nazi in *Casablanca* (Michael Curtiz, 1942). Veidt, it will be recalled, was the fetish star of the **German expressionist** films (so not a little irony here since Hitler held the Jews responsible for the decadence of expressionism!). The ambivalence in these particular films can be understood in the light of the large numbers of German immigrants and second-generation Germans residing in the United States. The open hostility to the Japanese, however, resides in their otherness and purported inscrutability.

But, in terms of stereotypes, by far the oddest response was to the Soviets. In films such as *Mission to Moscow*, *North Star* and *Song of Russia* (all 1943), Soviets were cast as ordinary people just like the 'folks back home'. Ideologically there was little to separate the two 'great nations': the Soviet Union was a virtual reflection of the United States: singing, dancing and uncomplicated. Stalin was Uncle Jo, and his repression of dissidents a necessary step for national and international security in the time of war (let it not be forgotten that the United States had incarcerated thousands of Japanese-Americans in California, under the same pretext of national security). This whitewashing of a precarious ally – after all the Soviet Union had signed a non-aggression pact with Hitler which broke down only when the Germans decided to invade the Soviet Union in June 1941 – is not astonishing in the light of war. Beyond the strategic need for fighting to take place on Germany's eastern front, thus dispersing German resources and weakening the enemy, there was doubtless a more hidden agenda that explains this naive representation of the Soviets. The Soviet armed forces were needed if public support for the war was to be maintained 'back home'. Presidential popularity, therefore security of office, is and always has been notoriously tied – in times of combat – to the number of 'body bags' sent home. Eleven million Soviet combatants died in this war and seven million civilians (over half the total deaths in this war). American casualties were not light, but in relation to those figures they are certainly less awesome (292,131 combatants and 6,000 civilians).

The idea that the United States was fighting a just war and that sacrifices were necessary was not a mood that prevailed, however. By 1943, doubtless because returning servicemen were bringing the message home that the war was not being won, several films had begun to reflect a greater reality in sharp contrast to the heroization and fervent patriotism expressed in the general run of war movies. Several films reflected the setbacks and defeats suffered by American troops against the Japanese. *Bataan* (Tay Garnett, 1943) ends with the massacre of an American patrol. *Air Force* (Howard Hawks, 1943), *Thirty Seconds over Tokyo* (Mervyn Leroy, 1944) showed the gruesome reality of air combat. *The Purple Heart* depicted the torture of American prisoners of war at the hands of the Japanese.

Immediately after the war several American war movies began if not to question then certainly to expose the futility of war, its horrors and the atrocious conditions under which it is fought (as in *The Story of GI Joe*, William Wellman, and *They Were Expendable*, John Ford, both 1945). But by the late 1940s Hollywood was back to its more jingoistic practices, undoubtedly as a result of the Cold War and the activities of the House Un–American Activities Committee (HUAC). An exemplary film in this context is *The Sands of Iwo Jima* (1949), subtitled *The Marines' Greatest Hour*, and starring John Wayne. War-wearied Britain dropped the genre only to return to it with grand-scale heroization of the RAF in *The Dam Busters* (Michael Anderson, 1955). This jingoism and heroization was sharply contrasted by the sense of loss and defeat apparent in

the few films made by the losing nations, Germany and Japan
– it is revealing that they were not post-war films as such
but products of reflection, coming some ten years after the
end of hostilities. Kon Ichikawa's two films on the devasta-
tion and dehumanizing effects of war, *The Burmese Harp*
(1956) and *Fires of the Plain* (1959), reveal the full horror to
which Japanese troops were exposed. In the first film a former
army scout becomes a Buddhist monk who roams across Japan
burying the war dead; in the second, which is set towards
the end of the war, starving troops are reduced to canni-
balism. The desperate lengths to which Germany would go
in the face of the inevitable loss of the war is virulently
described in *The Bridge* (1959). Short of manpower, young
adolescents are conscripted to defend a bridge, futilely, since
they get blown up.

As with the **western**, the war movie, at least until this
period, had a fairly unchanging **iconography**. Combat is
either on a grand scale (military manoeuvres, tanks and so
on) or on a small, even individual one (as with fighter pilots).
Quite frequently there is a target to be obtained (a hill, a
bridge). There is an ensemble within the corps of servicemen
with whom we identify (see **spectator identification**) and
who display different types of courage. Comradeship is paramount. The enemy is absent except as an impersonal other
(and therefore bad). There were, of course some exceptions
to this uncritical heroic representation of war. Class conflict
destroying prisoner of war morale is central to David Lean's
The Bridge over the River Kwai (1957), and the corruption of
officers and their indifference to the fate of their men is
exposed in Stanley Kubrick's film (based in the First World
War) *Paths of Glory*. As with other genres in the 1950s,
psychology was being introduced as a mainspring to character **motivation**. Thus, a certain number of films which
attempted to go counter to the dominant trend tried to
examine the psychological effects of warfare – as in Lewis
Milestone's *Halls of Montezuma* (1950), about combat fatigue;
and Robert Aldrich's *Attack!* (1956), which looks at officers'
cowardice and the fear of fighting.

In general, vanquishing nations tend not to look too closely at the ambiguities of war. This is also true of film. Questions can be asked only if there is doubt, and victory is less conducive to doubt than defeat. And it is worth noting that, as far as the United States was concerned, only when the ignominy of defeat became undeniable and questions had to be asked – as they were over Vietnam – did an 'unglorious' look at war become more commonplace. But before that came the Cold War.

The Cold War and Vietnam   The term Cold War refers to the hostilities between the two superpowers and their allies following the Second World War. The fear of nuclear war (as exemplified by the effects of dropping atomic bombs on Hiroshima and Nagasaki) proscribed military confrontation (even though both powers reputedly stockpiled nuclear arms). So war was conducted on economic, political and ideological fronts. This was the epoch for the spy, counter-espionage, paranoia about the spread of communism or capitalism and, finally, the age of intervention into the political arena of countries too small to prevent the encroachment of the two superpowers who annexed them as satellites.

The Cold War produced anti-communist films from Hollywood (such as *The Red Menace, The Red Danube*, both 1949; *I Was a Communist for the FBI*, 1951; *Big Jim McClain* and *My Son John,* both 1952). These were virulent anti-communist **melodramas** where protagonists either wake up to the dangers of communism, and sniff it out or die for their mistake in believing that communism was a good thing. Alternatively the Red Menace could take an alien form, as in *Red Planet Mars* (1952) and *Invasion of the Body Snatchers* (1956). Paranoia was also felt at the risk of nuclear war. This mood generated a series of films either in the apocalyptic mode (*The Beginning or the End?*, 1947; *White Heat*, 1949) or in the post-holocaust one (*Five*, 1951; *The World, the Flesh and the Devil*, 1959). Unsurprisingly, the Soviets produced their own anti-American films. Mostly these focused on the imputed evildoings of the CIA (for example *Secret Mission* and *Conspiracy of the Doomed*, both 1950).

However, perhaps the film-maker most associated with Cold War movies is the American Sam Fuller. He made three films based on US intervention during the hostilities between North and South Korea: *Steel Helmet*, *Fixed Bayonets* (both 1951) and *Hell and High Water* (1954). They are all extremely violent films – since he mostly made **B-movies** he suffered less interference from the censors. But his representation of violence set a precedence for movies to come, particularly in the 1960s and 1970s films of Arthur Penn and Sam Peckinpah (for example *Bonnie and Clyde*, 1967 and *The Wild Bunch*, 1969, respectively). Fuller's influence extended beyond the depiction of violence, however. His editing style, which **deconstructed** the **seamlessness** of traditional Hollywood practices, considerably influenced Jean-Luc Godard and later certain film-makers of the **New German Cinema** (Rainer Werner Fassbinder and Wim Wenders), and later still Martin Scorsese. Fuller's modernity or prescience is (arguably) evidenced by the fact that he was the first to portray the Vietnam War as an issue for the United States, long before it became officially engaged in the war. His 1958 film *China Gate* tells the story of an American legionnaire fighting for the French in Vietnam. As opposed to the traditional role of a legionnaire as detached from any patriotic or personal motivation, his fighting the communist enemy is personalized. He sees their defeat of the Vietcong as the imperative that will allow him to take his son (the progeny of his marriage to a Eurasian woman) back to the United States.

All wars remain remarkably difficult to 'talk' about in films – unless they are the jingoistic films we associate, say, with John Wayne (*Green Berets*, John Wayne/Ray Kellogg, 1968) and Sylvester Stallone (*Rambo*, George Pan Cosmatos, 1976). The 'truth' about the war – with one or two brave exceptions (usually censored) – rarely comes out until some decent amount of time has elapsed and the nation's psyche has had time to recover. Interestingly, this was not the case with Japan. After 1952, when the occupation of Japan by the American Allies was over, Japan made several post-Holocaust films about the atomic bombing of Hiroshima and Nagasaki that had brought the country to an abrupt cessation of hostilities with the Allies. Until that date, Japan was not permitted to broach the subject from a critical or realistic point of view. Once the ban was lifted, a variety of films on the subject of the effects of the atomic Holocaust were made. The horror of the holocaust was represented in Kaneto Shindo's *Children of the Atom Bomb* (1952), Heideo Sekigawa's *Hiroshima, Hiroshima* (1953) and Akira Kurosawa's *Record of a Human Being* (1955). The effects of the atomic fall-out, such as producing monsters and mutants, is the subject of Ishiro Honda's **horror** movie *Godzilla* (1955). Conversely and more typically, in the west, issues raised by the atomic bombing – such as the kind of reasoning that makes such attacks possible – did not get raised until the mid-1960s, some twenty years after the event. In 1964 Stanley Kubrick launched a virulent satire on those in charge and capable of unleashing atomic warfare (*Dr Strangelove*, 1964) and in 1965 Peter Watkins made a politically uncompromising film that examined the effects of a nuclear attack on Britain (*The War Game*).

With regard to Vietnam, the United States was, perhaps surprisingly, not so slow to produce films that attempted to view critically the impact of that war on the American mentality, particularly that of the American GI. The war was officially over by 1976. Martin Scorcese made *Taxi Driver* in the same year. Then in 1978 and 1979 came Michael Cimino's *The Deer Hunter* and Francis Ford Coppola's *Apocalypse Now*. These films focus on the effect of the war on the individual and in that light can be seen as progressive. They do not, however, question America's legitimacy in fighting that war. In Scorsese's film the neglected and despised Vietnam veteran becomes a self-appointed vigilante of urban New York and finally wins acclaim as a hero. In the other two films the real issue of why the war was being fought is again side-stepped and, although the protagonists are clearly severely disturbed by what has happened to them in Vietnam, there is no mistaking that the cause for the action in both films is the sadism of the enemy, the unknown other. The only film of the period that came close to a committed questioning of the United

States' involvement in Vietnam was Hal Ashby's *Coming Home* (1978), starring Jane Fonda (who had been politically active against the war). In the late 1980s and early 1990s a smattering of films have attempted to address that war more realistically, with portrayals of American brutality, the horror of the actual fighting, the racism suffered by Black Americans from their own compatriots – and so on (for example *Platoon*, Oliver Stone, 1986 and *Hamburger Hill*, John Irvin, 1987).

westerns (*see also* **genre**) Also known as the Horse Opera or Oater, the western became a genre that was very early incorporated into the film industry's repertoire. The first, official, western was by the American film-maker Edwin S. Porter, *The Great Train Robbery* (1903). Although the western is considered an exclusively American genre, this is not the case. The French, for example, were making westerns and exporting them successfully to the United States at least until the First World War – most famously the *Arizona Bill* series, starring Joë Hammond (1912–14). And, of course, later on in the history of this genre the Italians turned to making the so-called spaghetti westerns (1965–75).

In a sense, the silent westerns (though of course they were accompanied by music) were simply carrying on where reality had left off. The 'civilizing' of the west was virtually completed when cinema was born, and the cowboy's life as a herder had more or less come to an end as a result of the landrush and subsequent homesteading. The effect of this great migration west was to close off the open range. The landrush to all intents and purposes made the cowboy defunct. Given the mythic value of the cowboy as far as westerns are concerned, it comes as some surprise that as herders cowboys only existed fully for a brief period: 1865–80 – at which point the beef boom foundered. Homesteading was complete, the new towns and cities were established and there was no more need for driving the cattle west to feed the people. These factors – civilization and the open range or wilderness – are two first keys to the typology of this genre. The hero

411

(*sic*) is constantly operating at the point of conjuncture of these two opposing values. He never really wants to accept civilization, as embodied by the woman (who brings with her from the east the notion of community, family and so on). Rather he is always desiring to be on the move in the Wild West. The cowboy, with his restless energy and rugged, dogged individualism, is in the western the embodiment of American frontiersmanship, or at least the **myth** of that frontiersmanship. However, the fact that the cowboy or gunman is always represented as being caught between the two values points to the **ideological** contradictions inherent in the myth of that frontiersmanship. The hero's actual ambivalence reveals the nation's own ambiguous attitude towards the west. Civilizing the west meant giving up the freedom it represented, a high price for Americans to pay for national unity. However, the duration of the genre – possibly the longest lasting one of all – points to America's fascination with the frontier – as a site of hope for something new and better.

The tradition of the cowboy as mythic hero dates back to the western dime novels published from the 1860s. These novels dramatized lives that were both real and fictional and elevated the cowboy to mythic status. In the early days of cinema, at least, these novels were the primary sources for the western movie, which is a part explanation for the highly ritualized nature of this genre. These novels also heroized outlaws (Jesse James being a favourite) and indeed lawmen. And as we shall see, the heroization of the outlaw also became a typology of this genre. In fact, real-live outlaws and cowboys – especially cowboys who had been rodeo riders – came into the film industry up until as late as the 1930s and 1940s (Gene Autry and Roy Rogers are two well-known names). Buffalo Bill starred in his own film *The Adventures of Buffalo Bill* (1913). A reformed bank robber, Al Jennings, starred in several early westerns. However his films did not glamorize the west, rather they told the truth about the sordid money-grabbing practices that were so prevalent (as in *The Lady in the Dugout*, 1918). These were not the **images** the public wanted to see, so his career soon ended.

Audience expectation, then, is a second factor explaining the ritualistic and formulaic nature of the western. This ritualization needs to be discussed before continuing with the history of this genre. The dime novels tried to explain 'how the west was won', even though of course it was not won. It was taken away from the Indians by the 'few' property speculators, and what was left over from the good gold-mining terrain and profitable land, which they kept, was sold to the beleaguered pioneers who had come so far for so little. Dime novels could not tell this story any more than films. Audiences wanted to see the west as it should have been, that is as myth. The ritualistic narratives of the western do, however, reveal the ideological contradictions of this myth. Rituals are about the fear of loss of control, of mastery (*sic*). Thus the eternal repetition, as represented by rituals and the formulaic construction of the genre as well as the audience's own ritual in going repeatedly to see these films, reflects the desire to reassert that control and mastery (we know this is not the truth, it is myth, but we keep going back to see it because we want it to be so). The narrative rituals of robbery, chase and retribution, of lawlessness and restoration of law, are **iconographically** inscribed in the western, right down to the very last detail and gesture. Attacks are repeated in different ways. The stage-coach chase is replaced by the wagon-train attack, the train robbery, the cavalry charge or the Indians swooping down on 'innocent' homesteaders. Cattle drives, gold prospecting and railroad building are epic markers saluting the glory of going west. The ritual of the gunfight (in or out of the saloon), the pushing through the saloon swing-doors and swagger up to the bar – all are images that we immediately associate with the genre. All, of course, constitute a massive cover-up of how the west was colonized in the name of capitalism. That story would be told, but only rarely, and Al Jennings was one of the first to tell it so. However, back to history.

The first western hero was one of his own making, Gilbert M. Anderson. He persuaded Thomas H. Ince to let him star in *The Great Train Robbery*. Just as importantly, it was he who took the western out west in the name of authenticity. He formed his own production company, Essanay, and made a large number of films starring himself as Bronco Billy. The Bronco Billy series lasted from 1910–18 (for example *Bronco Billy's Redemption*, 1910; *The Making of Bronco Billy*, 1913). He was quickly followed by William S. Hart, who made his debut in 1914. He too strove for authenticity and worked first for Ince, then for Paramount. Hart's films were quite pessimistic and bleak. He played the same role of the baddie who is really good deep down inside and who gets redeemed by the end of the film. His most accomplished film is *Tumbleweeds* (1925), which he produced and in which he starred. It contains extraordinarily realistic footage, including the settlers' landrush sequence composed of three hundred wagons and at least a thousand men, women and horses.

By the late 1910s the western, by now a great favourite, spawned five big western **stars**, whose careers went well into the 1920s – some lasting as long as into the 1930s (that is into **sound**). The five 'greats' were, first, Tom Mix, who wore highly stylized outfits, the first to do so, a tradition that carried on through into the fringed shirts, soft leather gloves and gaily painted leather boots worn by Roy Rogers. More macho in image and in action were Buck Jones and Tim McCoy, great stuntsmen who had, like Mix, started out their careers in rodeo and wild west shows. The last two, Hoot Gibson and Ken Maynard, were often paired in films. Between them they significantly developed the iconography of this genre: Mix's costumes have already been mentioned; the horse became a focal point, almost a second hero; cowboys started to sing.

The first western **epic** is James Cruze's *The Covered Wagon* (1923), closely followed by John Ford's *The Iron Horse* (1924). What is exceptional about Cruze's film, apart from the mammoth undertaking of attempting to put into film the enormity of the migration west, was that it was shot not in the studios but on location and was therefore a reconstruction of the migration as it had been experienced. Thus there were river crossings, Indian attacks and struggles through arduous weather conditions, all of which worked to give the film a **realism** that no other western to that date had produced. Lasting two hours, the film convincingly evoked the two-thousand-mile trajectory undertaken by the pioneers.

The other contemporaneous epic, *The Iron Horse*, tells the end-part of the pioneering American spirit, the building of the railroads west. In this respect, this film and Cruze's are the bookends of the history of that epoch, at least the mythic version of it. Clearly, in this epic context, the mythical value of these films has nationalistic overtones. Indeed, Ford, the son of an immigrant family from Ireland, makes no attempt to disguise his commitment to the concept of America as the land of opportunity and to the Lincolnian belief in the America as one nation (he dedicated his film to Abraham Lincoln). The overriding message of this film is a belief in progress (the iron horse replaces the horse). However, not at any price: unity among men, not individualism, is the only way of achieving it.

John Ford is arguably the greatest western film-maker of all time, although Howard Hawks is a strong rival. Ford started his career making westerns for Universal, the largest producers of the genre until the early 1920s (see **studio system**). In 1920, after three years with Universal, he went over to Fox. His film career spans over forty years (*The Man Who Shot Liberty Valance*, 1962, is a late example of his work in this genre alone). It is often said that, because of his own immigrant past and his desire to belong, he was obsessed with American history and with the notion of the family. Whatever the case, it is certain that the notion that unity creates stability and a sense of community is central to his films, including the western. In this respect his vision seems to go counter to the ideology inherent in the western of the wandering cowboy or gunhand who must restlessly move on. However, this first disposition of Ford's in fact enhances the tension in his film between the opposing values of *wild*erness and civilization precisely because, for the most part, his heroes do not settle down but live out and with this contradiction (as in *My Darling Clementine*, 1946; *The Searchers*, 1956). His

415

fetish star was John Wayne who, when he first worked with Ford, almost got himself thrown out of the studio for being insubordinate.

Back to the history of this genre. The advent of sound brought about a big drop in the production of the western, at least as an A-movie. The drop occurred largely because there was so little dialogue. The audience was now used to 'talkies' and the western did not adapt well at first. As an action–packed film, before sound, it had little need for much talk. Clint Eastwood's almost silent movies of the 1980s and 1990s merely carry on this tradition (although he is not that heavy on action either!). Interestingly however, during the 1930s, westerns continued to be produced as **B-movies** and were very popular. As a B-movie, a western was a low–budget product that could be quickly and cheaply produced to fill the double-bill requirement. The double bill was a practice introduced during the Depression years to attract audiences by giving two films for the price of one. The smaller studios, Monogram and Republic in particular, were largely responsible for this output although, among the majors, Warners was also a significant producer. It was the B-westerns that launched the singing cowboy – starting with John Wayne in 1933 (*Riders of Destiny*) and closely followed by Gene Autry (*Tumbling Tumbleweeds*, 1935) and Roy Rogers. As a type the B-western was iconographically simplistic and ideologically populist. The goodies and the baddies were easily identifiable. The former wore white, the latter black, and unquestionably the goodies would win. No room here for redemption – bad is bad. By the mid-1950s the B-western (and the B-movie in general) had disappeared after the Supreme Court's decision in the Paramount case of 1948 finally took effect by breaking up the major studios' cartel (see **studio system**). But it did not go out with a whimper. In 1952 and 1954 Republic won best director Oscars for, respectively, Ford's *The Quiet Man* and Nicholas Ray's *Johnny Guitar*.

Briefly in the late 1930s there was a big surge once more in production of A-feature westerns. A first cause was the

416

United States' isolationism in the face of the war in Europe. The revival of the genre reflects an inward-looking nationalism that is simultaneously nostalgic, having regard for things American but things of the past, in this instance, the nation's heroic and civilizing expansion into the west. By curious coincidence John Wayne, *the* true grit American as we now know him, finally attained star status in this brief period of production upswing when he starred in Ford's *Stagecoach* (1939). Pioneers were celebrated (as in *The Westerner*, 1940, with squeaky-clean Gary Cooper). Often the narrative depicted the individual fighting against giant corporations (railroad companies, banks, etc.). Certain outlaws were also celebrated. A particular favourite was Billy the Kid (see *Billy the Kid*, 1941 and Howard Hughes' *The Outlaw*, 1943 but not released until 1946 – see below). This heroization of outlaws, as already mentioned, was part of the mythologizing of the west started by the western dime novels of the 1860s. Because the west was largely monopolized by land-grabbing companies, to take the law into one's own hands was perceived as a legitimate practice. An outlaw in these circumstances came to represent freedom in much the same way as the cowboy. The outlaw asserted individual 'rights' over the big bosses. Similarly the lonesome lawman was a hero in his standing up to the baddies who threaten to disrupt the community.

There was, however, the burgeoning of another type of western: one that was more socially critical and which set a trend that would be more fully developed in the 1950s. William A. Wellman is credited with being the progenitor of this so-called 'modern western' which, because it deals with social issues, is also described as the psychological western. In the first of these films, *The Ox-bow Incident* (1943), Wellman polemicizes against the lynch law. The rough justice meted out in western folklore is severely criticized but not through a goodies-versus-baddies confrontation. Collusion and passivity on the part of 'decent, ordinary folk' are as much responsible for the lynching of the innocent men as those baying for their blood. In this uncompromising film Wellman takes to task

417

the ideological functioning of the traditional western: nostalgic escapism at the service of corporate capitalism. He repeated this in his 1944 film criticizing the White colonization of the west, *Buffalo Bill*.

The introduction of **colour** on a bigger scale in the mid- to late 1940s meant that violence now appeared more real. This was greeted with considerable consternation by the censors. But far more to their consternation were the implications for sex on screen. Sex did not come on to the screen in the western until the late 1940s and even so it came in with great difficulty. Howard Hughes's *The Outlaw* was made in 1943 and was a vehicle for his new star, Jane Russell. However, the league of decency (see **censorship**) created a furore over its premiere, complaining that the over-exposure of Jane Russell's breasts was indecent. The film was withdrawn and rereleased with a few cuts in 1946. Jane Russell was the first of a number of actresses to play the role of a 'smouldering', sexy, décolletée Mexican woman. Sex was launched, but it had to be had with **stereotypes**. Plenty of hot-blooded foreign womanhood but not 'nice, nice Ms American pie' – she had to be kept virginal at all costs. Until this eruption of sex the characterization of women was fairly peripheral. The western is a man's movie. A man with a horse, a man in action, a loner who leaves the woman behind rather than staying. His lust for adventure far outweighs his lust for women. As a genre, the western is the antithesis to the **melodrama** and domesticity. The western stands out in its refusal to complete the **Oedipal trajectory**. It is very rare for the hero, having once rescued the abducted but pure woman, to go on to marry her. The hero's 'job' is to make the west safe for the virgins to come out and reproduce, but not with him, that is the job for the rest of the community. He has to 'move on out'.

In the western very few exceptions exist to the misrepresentation of the frontierswomen. Women are either floozies in the saloon, who are to be driven out of town (not until after good use however) or shot, or pure as the driven snow and totally vulnerable to marauding men and, of course,

418

abducting Indians. In truth, cowgirls did exist, gun-toting just like the men, and dressed in men's clothes. Indeed a recent film, *The Ballad of Little Jo* (Maggie Greenwald, 1993), is based on a real woman whose gender was discovered only after her death. During the 1930s only a handful of films paid homage to the role of women in the west. *Annie Oakley* (1935) was a first, starring Barbara Stanwyck, followed by *Plainsman* (1936) with Jean Arthur in the role of Calamity Jane. And two films starring Mae West, *Klondike Annie* (1936) and *My Little Chickadee* (1940) complete the list. The 1950s did not see any great improvement on this tally. Again, only a handful come to mind. Wellman's quite authentic film about frontierswomen and their dangerous and stressful drive out west to find husbands (*Westward Women*, 1951), is one. So too is Ray's *Johnny Guitar,* starring Joan Crawford as the gunslinging cross-dressed Vienna who, once she has cleared the town of the threat of a lynch mob and their leader (another woman, Emma, played by Mercedes McCambridge), none the less dons her feminine clothes again. In all these films, cross-dressing occurs and represents **diegetically** an embodiment of power and independence. And, as far as the female **spectator** is concerned, despite the fact that in some of the films the woman gives up her clothes and gets her man, there is none the less an identification with that empowerment. Not that those in feminine attire necessarily lack force. Barbara Stanwyck had several strong roles to play – most brilliantly in *Forty Guns* (Sam Fuller, 1957) where she is a ranch boss with forty hired guns. Finally, Marlene Dietrich (playing true to type) was the star in *Rancho Notorious* (Fritz Lang, 1952).

By the 1950s the western's hero had become more complex, more psychologically motivated (see **motivation**). He had a past. The introduction of **psychoanalysis** into this genre is credited to Wellman (as mentioned above), but it took off in a big way in the 1950s in part owing to the influence of the **film noir**. The broody, introspective, angst-ridden film noir protagonist reappears with spurs. Something in his past has deeply scarred his persona. He still rides in and out of the wilderness as before, but now that *wild*erness is also part of his temperament and embedded in his psyche. The other exemplary film-maker of this new type of western was Anthony Mann, who worked with James Stewart as his fetish star. Before turning to the western Mann had made several films noir (such as *T-Men*, 1947, and *Raw Deal*, 1948) so the cross-over of mood is quite visible in his films. He gave an uncompromising vision of the west. His heroes are often solitary, mentally and morally divided personae (as was their film noir prototype), bent on revenge and yet wanting to find peace of mind and thereby rest from their avenging souls (see *Winchester '73*, 1950; *Bend of the River*, 1952; *The Naked Spur*, 1953 – all Stewart vehicles). Mann's westerns are intentionally violent – a tradition followed by Arthur Penn (as in *The Left-Handed Gun*, 1958) and Sam Peckinpah (*The Wild Bunch*, 1969).

The demise of the studios in the early 1950s led to location shooting, and this, coupled with the implementation of **cinemascope** and colour, gave the western increased visual realism alongside this greater psychological realism. Although on the whole the western, then as before, was seen as an escapist genre, none the less certain films, especially those made during the first half of the 1950s, can be read as commentaries on the contemporary political arena of McCarthyism as well as reflections of the political uncertainties of the Cold War. *High Noon* (Fred Zinnemann, 1952) and *Johnny Guitar* are the two that are most often cited as allegories of McCarthyism and the fear and mistrust brought about by the Cold War. The former film was scripted by Carl Foreman, a communist who was blacklisted (see **Hollywood blacklist**) and he clearly meant his loose adaptation of the novel *The Tin Star* (by John W. Cunningham) to act as an indictment of US justice and society. In the film the hero (played by Gary Cooper) is the lone marshal who has to gun down an ex-convict and his gang bent on revenge. The marshal tries to drum up support but no one will come to his assistance. A similar instance of community cowardice and a refusal to get involved is present in *Johnny Guitar* (which was shot in Spain in 1954 while Ray was in self-imposed exile, and also free of the constraints of Hollywood). In this film the community hide behind the law to rid themselves of alien people – even though, in the end, Vienna and Johnny put a stop to it.

High Noon certainly re-established the reputation of the western, and the 1950s produced many great westerns. Indeed the traditions of this epoch of films are at least partly a progenitor to Clint Eastwood's 1980s and 1990s westerns. Alan Ladd's portrayal of nervous heroism in *Shane* (George Stevens, 1953), Gregory Peck's unsuccessful attempts to outrun his past as the fastest gun in the west in *Gunfighter* (George King, 1950) and the restless, drifting hero coming into town and then leaving having resolved a problem of a community in crisis – these are all hallmarks of Eastwood's performance as exemplified in two films also directed by him, *Pale Rider* (1985) and *Unforgiven* (1992).

Until the 1950s Indians on the whole were represented as killers, abductors and pyromaniacs – hardly ever as individuals, certainly not with any attempt to understand or reflect their side of history. The 1950s marks an occasional shift from this trend with just a few films. In these rare films there is a new respect for the Indian (*Broken Arrow*, Delmer Daves, 1950) and a bitter condemnation of the exploitation of the Indian by the White man (*Devil's Doorway*, Mann, 1950). Kevin Costner's *Dances with Wolves* (1990) is but one of the last in a short line of this attempt to redress the history of the west.

By the 1960s, in an attempt to attract audiences back into the cinemas, the western went super-epic. The psychological realism was dropped in favour of bulk value for money: widescreen productions filled with as many stars as possible (like John Sturges's *The Magnificent Seven*, 1960, with seven stars and reworked three times). The community had gone, and with it the notion of service. Group solidarity was in but only among the gang. Alternatively the protagonist was motivated by revenge, but, contrary to the complex western of the 1950s, there was no visible reason or moral point of view

421

that explained this motivation (see Henry Hathaway's *Nevada Smith*, 1966). What also prevailed was an aesthetics of violence not seen heretofore. One explanation could be the abolition of film **censorship** in the United States, since this new, even excessive, violence characterizes many films of that decade (notably Arthur Penn's *Bonnie and Clyde*, 1967). Another could be that the old-established generation of film-makers (particularly Ford and Hawks) were coming to the end of their careers and a new way had to be found of telling what is intrinsically the same story. The western had become as action-packed as in its early silent days, but on the whole it lacked inventiveness, bar a few smash hits (like *Butch Cassidy and the Sundance Kid*, George Roy Hill, 1969). A third reason might be that it was a genre out of touch with the climate of the times. The United States had proved to itself that it was still a violent and corrupt country (the Watergate scandal, the assassinations of President Kennedy, his brother Robert Kennedy and Martin Luther King), so the myth of pioneering spirits, frontiersmanship and a united nation – with all that it denotes of optimism, wholesomeness and integrity – did not sit easily with reality.

The western, perhaps the longest-lasting genre, looked set to die out. But its fortunes were revived, largely thanks to its moving eastward to Europe and its shift in emphasis from reality to parody. The success of the so-called spaghetti westerns (so called in the belief that they were shot in Italy; in fact they were, for the most part, shot in Spain) came about as a result of a fortunate meeting in 1964 between the Italian film-maker Sergio Leone and a fairly unknown actor Clint Eastwood. The quiet, almost static aloofness of the 'man with no name', as Eastwood was known in his first film, *A Fistful of Dollars* (1964), in combination with Leone's ironic treatment of the western proved to be unbeatable. And if the genre has been revitalized on the American front, then its regeneration is in large part due to the parodying it underwent under Leone's direction. The genre itself was called into question – a criticism of the ideological operations at work in Hollywood's mythic construction of the west. The footage was not all action-packed, the pace was slowed down. Eastwood hardly spoke and barely moved. Eastwood claims that he deliberately cut out most of the dialogue to facilitate direction since he and Leone had no common language. This first film was such a success that Eastwood went on to make three more. Other American actors went to Europe to work with Leone (Henry Fonda, Charles Bronson and Rod Steiger). And the whole series of spaghetti westerns lasted a decade. But the western was changed for ever, away from the prevailing optimism, puritanism and nationalism it had displayed before. The genre had been **deconstructed**, it could now go back west.

The success of the spaghetti westerns is their difference. Their caricatural nature pokes fun at the iconography of the western. The baddies are not only bad, they are ugly and dirty. The films themselves are cynical in tone. Sleaziness and dishonesty are the order of the day. Only one man, Eastwood, can clean it all up and even then not for long if the first sequel to *A Fistful of Dollars* is anything to go by – *For a Few Dollars More* (1966). Following the success of these films, Eastwood returned to the United States, since when he has been directing and producing and starring in his films. He has become the icon of the contemporary western to the point that he is almost solely identified with it. (For further reading see Bold, 1987; Buscombe, 1988; Tuska, 1976; Wright, 1975.)

wipe A transition between two **shots** whereby the earlier one appears to be pushed aside by the latter, creating the effect of wiping off a scene and replacing it with another.

women's films – *see* **melodrama and women's films**

zoom   The zoom lens was developed in the 1950s, constituting another technological attraction for **audiences**, as did the introduction of **colour** and **cinemascope** in the same decade. A zoom **shot** is one that is taken with the use of a variable focal length lens (known as a zoom' lens). A zoom-forward normally ends in a close-up, a zoom-back in a general shot. Both types of shot imply a rapid movement in time and space and as such create the illusion of displacement in time and space. A zoom-in picks out and isolates a person or object, a zoom-out places that person or object in a wider context. A zoom shot can be seen, therefore, as **voyeurism** at its most desirably perfect.

BIBLIOGRAPHY

Abel, R. (1984) *French Cinema: The First Wave, 1915–1929*, Princeton, Princeton University Press

Althusser, L. (1984) *Essays on Ideology*, London, Verso

Altman, R. (1989) *The American Film Musical*, Bloomington, Indiana, Indiana University Press

Altman, R. (1992) *Sound Theory/Sound Practice*, New York and London, Routledge

Anderson, L. (1954) Only Connect!, *Sight and Sound*, Vol. 23, No. 4, April/June

Andrew, D. (1984) *Concepts in Film Theory*, New York and Oxford, Oxford University Press

Andrew, D. (1995) *Mists of Regret: French Poetic Realism*, Princeton, Princeton University Press

Armes, R. (1974) *Film and Reality: An Historical Survey*, Harmondsworth, Pelican

Astruc, A. (1948) Naissance d'une nouvelle avant-garde, *Le Film*, No. 144

Attille, M. and Blackwood, M. (1986) Black Women and Representation, in: Brunsdon, C. (ed.) *Films For Women*, London, British Film Institute Publishing

Bad Object-Choices (1991) *How Do I look?: Queer Film and Video*, Seattle, Bay Press

Bakari, I. (1993) Le Facteur X du nouveau cinéma afro-américain, *Ecrans d'Afrique*, No. 4

Barsam, R. M. (1992) *Non-Fiction Film: A Critical History*, Bloomington and Indianapolis, Indiana University Press, revised edition

Barthes, R. (1957) *Mythologies*, Paris, Editions du Seuil (also available in English translation: London, Paladin, 1989, trans. A. Lavers)

Barthes, R. (1973) *Le Plaisir du texte*, Paris, Editions du Seuil

Baudry, J.-L. (1970) Cinema; effets idéologiques produits par l'appareil de base, *Cinéthique*, Nos 7–8, translated as Ideological Effects of the Basic Cinematic Apparatus, in: Rosen P. (ed.) (1986) *Narrative, Apparatus, Ideology*, New York, Columbia University Press

Baudry, J.-L. (1975) Le Dispositif, *Communications*, No. 23, translated as The Apparatus: Metaphysical Approaches to Ideology, in: Rosen, P. (ed.) (1986), *Narrative, Apparatus, Ideology*, New York, Columbia University Press

Baudry, L. (1992) From the World in a Frame, in: Mast, G., Cohen, M. and Baudry, L. (eds) *Film Theory and Criticism*, New York and Oxford, Oxford University Press, fourth edition

Bazin, A. (1967) *What is Cinema? Vol. I* (essays selected and translated by H. Gray), Berkeley, University of California Press

Bellour, R. (1975) Le Blocage symbolique, *Communications*, No. 23

Benveniste, E. (1971) *Problems in General Linguistics*, Miami, University of Miami Press

Benvenuto, B. and Kennedy, R. (1986) *The Works of Jacques Lacan: An Introduction*, New York, St Martin's Press

Bergstrom, J. (1985) Sexuality at a Loss: The Films of F. W. Murnau, *Poetics Today*, Vol. 6, Nos 1–2

Black, G. D. (1994) *Hollywood Censored: Morality Codes, Catholics, and the Movies*, Cambridge, Cambridge University Press

Bogle, D. (1988) *Blacks in American Film and Television: An Encyclopedia*, New York and London, Garland Publishing Company

Bogle, D. (1994) *Coons, Mulattoes, Mamies and Bucks: An Interpretative History of Blacks in American Films*, Oxford, Roundhouse Publishing Company, third edition

Bold, C. (1987) *Selling the Wild West: Popular Western Fiction 1860–1960*, Bloomington and Indianapolis, Indiana University Press

Bordwell, D. (1986) *Narration in the Fictional Film*, New York and London, Routledge

Bordwell, D. and Thompson, K. (1980) *Film Art: An Introduction*, Reading, Massachusetts, Addison-Wesley Publishing Company (fourth edition (1993), New York, McGraw Hill)

Bordwell, D. and Thompson, K. (1994) *Film History: An Introduction*, New York, McGraw Hill

Bordwell, D., Staiger, J. and Thompson, K. (1985) *The Classical Hollywood Cinema: Film Style and Production to 1960*, London, Routledge and Kegan Paul

Bottomore, T. (1984) *The Frankfurt School*, London and New York, Tavistock Publications

Branigan, E. (1992) *Narrative and the Comprehension of Film*, London and New York, Routledge

Bratton, J., Cook, J. and Gledhill C. (eds) (1994) *Melodrama: Stage, Picture, Screen*, London, British Film Institute Publishing

Brooks, P. (1976) *The Melodramatic Imagination: Balzac, Henry James, Melodrama and the Mode of Excess*, New Haven, Yale University Press

Brosnan, J. (1991) *The Primal Screen: A History of Science Fiction Film*, London and Sydney, Orbit Books

Bruno, G. (1987) Ramble City: Postmodernism and *Blade Runner*, *October*, No. 41

Brunovska Karnick, K. and Jenkins, H. (eds) (1995) *Classical Hollywood Comedy*, New York and London, Routledge

Brunsdon, C. (ed.) (1986) *Films for Women*, London, British Film Institute Publishing

Burch, N. (1973) *Theory of Film Practice*, New York, Praeger

Burch, N. (1990) *Life to Those Shadows*, London, British Film Institute Publishing (trans. and ed. by B. Brewster)

Burns, E. (1983) *Introduction to Marxism*, London, Lawrence & Wishart, ninth reprint

Buscombe, E. (ed.) (1988) *The BFI Companion to the Western*, London, André Deutsch/British Film Institute Publishing (reissued (1995), London, British Film Institute Publishing)

Butler, J. (1990) *Gender Trouble*, New York and London, Routledge

Cameron, I. (ed.) (1992) *The Movie Book of Film Noir*, London, Studio Vista

Caughie, J. (ed.) (1981) *Theories of Authorship*, London, Routledge & Kegan Paul

Cawelti, J. G. (1992) *Chinatown* and Generic Transformation in Recent American Films, in: Mast, G., Cohen, M. and Baudry, L. (eds) *Film Theory and Criticism*, Oxford, Oxford University Press, fourth edition

Chanan, M. (ed.) (1983) *Twenty-Five Years of the New Latin American Cinema*, London, British Film Institute Publishing

Chion, M. (1982) *La Voix au cinéma*, Paris, Cahiers du Cinéma, Editions de L'Etoile

Chion, M. (1985) *Le Son au cinéma*, Paris, Cahiers du Cinéma, Editions de L'Etoile

Christie, I. and Taylor, R. (eds) (1993) *Eisenstein Rediscovered*, London and New York, Routledge

Comolli, J.–L. and Narboni, J. (1969/1977) Cinéma/Idéologie/ Critique, *Cahiers du cinéma* (October–November 1969); English

427

translation in: *Screen Reader: Cinema/Ideology/Politics*, London, Society for Education in Film and Television, 1977

Cook, P. (1980) Duplicity in *Mildred Pierce*, in: Kaplan, E. A. (ed.) *Women in Film Noir*, London, British Film Institute Publishing, revised edition

Cook, P. (ed.) (1985) *The Cinema Book*, London, British Film Institute Publishing

Copjec, J. (ed.) (1993) *Shades of Film Noir*, London and New York, Verso

Cowie, E. (1984) Fantasia, *m/f*, No. 9

Creed, B. (1993) *The Monstrous Feminine: Film, Feminism and Psychoanalysis*, New York and London, Routledge

Culham, S. (1988) *Animation From the Script to the Screen*, London, Columbus Books

Davies, K., Dickey, J. and Stratford, T. (eds) (1987) *Out of Focus: Writings on Women and the Media*, London, The Women's Press

Davis, A. (1981) *Women, Race and Class*, New York, Random House

Dayan, D. (1974) The Tudor Code of Classical Cinema, *Film Quarterly*, Vol. 28, No. 1

De Lauretis, T. (1984) *Alice Doesn't: Feminism, Semiotics, Cinema*, Bloomington, Indiana, Indiana University Press

De Lauretis, T. (1985) Oedipus Interruptus, *Wide-Angle*, Vol. 7, Nos 1–2

De Lauretis, T. (1989) *Technologies of Gender: Essays on Theory, Film and Fiction*, London, Macmillan (first published by Indiana University Press in 1987)

De Lauretis, T. and Heath, S. (eds) (1980) *The Cinematic Apparatus*, New York, St Martin's Press

Diawara, M. (ed.) (1993) *Black American Cinema*, New York and London, Routledge

Doane, M. A. (1982) Film and the Masquerade: Theorising the Female Spectator, *Screen*, Vol. 23, Nos 3–4

Doane, M. A. (1984) The Woman's Film: Possession and Address, in: Doane, M. A., Mellencamp, P. and Williams, L. (eds) *Re-vision: Essays in Feminist Film Criticism*, Frederick, Marylands, The American Film Institute/University Publications of America

Doane, M. A. (1987) *The Desire to Desire: The Woman's Film of the 1940s*, Bloomington, Indiana, Indiana University Press

Doane, M. A. (1992) *Femmes Fatales: Feminism, Film Studies and Psychoanalysis*, New York and London, Routledge

Doane, M. A., Mellencamp, P. and Williams, L. (eds) (1984) *Re-vision: Essays in Feminist Film Criticism*, Frederick, Marylands, The American Film Institute/University Publications of America

Donald, J. (1989) *Fantasy and the Cinema*, London, British Film Institute Publishing

Dyer, R. (1977a) Entertainment and Utopia, *Movie 24*

Dyer, R. (ed.) (1977b) *Gays and Film*, London, British Institute Publishing

Dyer, R. (1980) *Stars*, London, British Film Institute Publishing

Dyer, R. (1986) *Heavenly Bodies: Film Stars and Society*, London, Cinema British Film Institute Series, Macmillan

Dyer, R. (1990) *Now You See It: Studies in Lesbian and Gay Film*, London and New York, Routledge

Ellis, J. (1982) *Visible Fictions*, London and New York, Routledge & Kegan Paul

Elsaesser, T. (1987) Tales of Sound and Fury: Observations on the Family Melodrama, in: Gledhill, C. (ed.) *Home Is Where the Heart Is: Studies in Melodrama and the Woman's Film*, London, British Film Institute Publishing

Elsaesser, T. (1989) *New German Cinema: A History*, London, British Film Institute Publishing

Feuer, J. (1982) *The Hollywood Musical*, London, Macmillan

Fischer, L. (1989) *Shot/Countershot: Film Tradition and Woman's Cinema*, Princeton, Princeton University Press and London, British Film Institute/Macmillan Education Ltd

Fiske, J. and Hartley, J. (1978) *Reading Television*, London and New York, Methuen

Flitterman-Lewis, S. (1990) *To Desire Differently: Feminism and the French Cinema*, Urbana and Chicago, University of Illinois Press

Foucault, M. (1977) *Discipline and Punish: The Birth of the Prison*, New York, Pantheon (trans. A. Sheridan)

Foucault, M. (1978) *The History of Sexuality*, Vol. 1, New York, Pantheon (trans. R. Hurley)

Freud, S. (1931) Female Sexuality, reprinted in *The Standard Edition of the Complete Works of Sigmund Freud*, London, Hogarth Press, 1953–74, Vol. 21, pp. 64–145 (trans. James Strachey)

Gabriel, T. H. (1982) *Third Cinema in the Third World*, Ann Arbor, Michigan University Press

Gaines, J. (1988) White Privilege and Looking Relations: Race and Gender in Feminist Film Theory, *Screen*, Vol. 29, No. 4

Genette, G. (1980) *Narrative Discourse*, Oxford, Blackwell (trans. J. E. Lewin)

Gever, M., Parmar, P. and Greyson, J. (eds) (1993) *Queer Looks*, New York and London, Routledge

Gidal, P. (1989) *Materialist Film*, London and New York, Routledge

Givanni, J. and Reynaud, B. (1993) Images de femmes noires, *CinémAction*, No. 67

Gledhill, C. (1980) *Klute* 1: A Contemporary Film Noir and Feminist Criticism, in: Kaplan, E. A. (ed.) *Women in Film Noir*, London, British Film Institute Publishing, revised edition

Gledhill, C. (ed.) (1987) *Home is Where the Heart Is: Studies in Melodrama and the Woman's Film*, London, British Film Institute Publishing

Gledhill, C. (ed.) (1991) *Stardom: The Industry of Desire*, London and New York, Routledge

Godard, J.–L. (1980) *Introduction à une véritable histoire du cinéma*, Paris, Albatros

Grant, B. K. (ed.) (1986) *Film Genre Reader*, Austin, University of Texas Press

Grant, J. (1987) *Encyclopedia of Walt Disney's Animated Characters*, New York, Harper & Row

Grosz, E. (1990) *Jacques Lacan: A Feminist Introduction*, London and New York, Routledge

Grosz, E. and Probyn, E. (eds) (1995) *Sexy Bodies: The Strange Carnalities of Feminism*, London and New York, Routledge

Hardy, P. Milne, T. and Willemen, P. (eds) (1986) *The Encyclopedia of Horror Movies*, New York, Harper & Row

Harper, S. (1987) *Historical Pleasures:* Gainsborough Costume Melodrama, in: Gledhill, C. (ed.) *Home is Where the Heart Is: Studies in Melodrama and Women's Film*, London, British Film Institute Publishing

Harper, S. (1994) *Picturing the Past: The Rise and Fall of the Costume Drama*, London, British Film Institute Publishing

Haskell, M. (1974) *From Reverence to Rape: The Treatment of Women in the Movies*, Harmondsworth, Penguin Books

Hartley, J. (1982) *Understanding News*, London, Methuen

Hawthorn, J. (1992) *A Concise Glossary of Contemporary Literary Theory*, London, Edward Arnold

Hayward, S. (1992) *A*history of French Cinema: 1895–1991 – Pioneering Filmmakers (Guy, Dulac, Varda) and Their *Heritage, Paragraph*, Vol. 15, No. 1

Hayward, S. (1993) *French National Cinema*, London and New York, Routledge

Heath, S. (1978) Difference, *Screen*, Vol. 19, No. 3

Heath, S. (1981) *Questions of Cinema*, London, Macmillan

Hill, J. (1986) *Sex Class and Realism: British Cinema 1956–63*, London, British Film Institute Publishing

Hoffer, T. J. (1981) *Animation Reference Guide*, Westport, Connecticut, Greenwood Press

hooks, b. (1981) *Ain't I a Woman: Black Women and Feminism*, Boston, Long Haul Press

hooks, b. (1992) *Black Looks: Race and Representation*, London, Turn–around

Hull, G., Scott, P. B. and Smith, B. (eds) (1982) *All the Women Are White, All the Blacks Are Men, But Some of Us Are Brave*, New York, The Feminist Press

Huyssen, A. (1986) *After the Great Divide: Modernism, Mass Culture and Postmodernism*, London, Macmillan Press (Language, Discourse, Society Series)

Huyssen, A. (1990) Mapping the Postmodern, in: Nicholson, L. (ed.) *Feminism/Postmodernism*, New York and London, Routledge

Jakobson, R. (1960) Concluding Statement: Linguistics and Poetics, in: Sebeok, T. (ed.) *Style in Language*, Cambridge, Massachusetts, MIT Press

Jameson, F. (1983) Postmodernism and Consumer Society, in: Foster, H. (ed.), *Postmodern Culture*, London, Pluto Press

Jancovich, M. (1929) *Horror*, London, B. T. Batsford

Johnston, C. (1973) *Notes on Women's Cinema*, Screen Pamphlet, London, Society for Education in Film and Television

Johnston, C. (1976) Women's Cinema as Countercinema, in: Nicholls, B. (ed.) *Movies and Methods*, Berkeley, University of California Press

Jones, J. (1991) The New Ghetto Aesthetic, *Wide Angle*, Vol. 13, Nos 3 and 4

Kaplan, E. A. (ed.) (1980) *Women in Film Noir*, London, British Film Institute, revised edition

Kaplan, E. A. (1983) *Women and Film: Both Sides of the Camera*, New York and London, Methuen

Kaplan, E. A. (ed.) (1990) *Psychoanalysis and Cinema*, New York and London, Routledge

Kaplan, E. A. (1992) *Motherhood and Representation: The Mother in Popular Culture and Melodrama*, London and New York, Routledge

Kennedy, L. (1993) Is Malcolm X the Right Thing?, *Sight & Sound*, Vol. 3, No. 2

King, B. (1985) Articulating Stardom, *Screen*, Vol. 26, No. 5

Knight, J. (1992) *Women and the New German Cinema*, London and New York, Verso

Konigsberg, I. (1993) *The Complete Film Dictionary*, London, Bloomsbury

431

Krutnik, F. (1991) *In a Lonely Street: Film Noir, Genre, Masculinity*, London and New York, Routledge

Kuhn, A. (1982) *Women's Pictures: Feminism and Cinema*, London and Boston, Routledge & Kegan Paul

Kuhn, A. (1985) *The Power of the Image: Essays on Representation and Sexuality*, London and New York, Routledge & Kegan Paul

Kuhn, A. (1988) *Cinema, Censorship and Sexuality 1909–1925*, London and New York, Routledge

Kuhn, A. (ed.) (1990) *Alien Zone*, London and New York, Verso

Kuhn, A. (ed.) with Radstone, S. (1990) *The Women's Companion to International Film*, London, Virago

Lacan, J. (1977) *Ecrits: A Selection*, London, Tavistock Publications (trans. A. Sheridan)

Lapsley, R. and Westlake, M. (1988, reprinted in 1992) *Film Theory: An Introduction*, Manchester, Manchester University Press

Lebeau, V. (1994) *Lost Angels: Psychoanalysis and the Cinema*, London and New York, Routledge

Lesage, J. (1974) Feminist Film Criticism: Theory and Practice, *Women and Film*, Vol. 1, Nos 5–6

Lovell, A. and Hillier, J. (1972) *Studies in Documentary*, London, Secker & Warburg

Lurie, S. (1980) Pornography and the Dread of Women, in: Lederer, L. (ed.) *Take Back the Night*, New York, William Morrow

Macdonell, D. (1986) *Theories of Discourse: An Introduction*, Oxford, Blackwell

McMahon, B. and Quin, R. (1986) *Reel Images: Film and Television*, South Melbourne, Australia, Macmillan

Mast, G., Cohen, M. and Baudry, L. (eds) (1992) *Film Theory and Criticism*, Oxford, Oxford University Press, fourth edition

Matthews, T. D. (1994) *Censored*, London, Chatto & Windus

Mayne, J. (1984) Women at the Keyhole: Women's Cinema and Feminist Criticism, in: Doane, M. A., Mellencamp, P. and Williams, L. (eds) *Re-vision: Essays in Feminist Film Criticism*, Frederick, Marylands, The American Film Institute/University Publications of America

Mayne, J. (1993) *Cinema and Spectatorship*, London and New York, Routledge

Merquior, J. G. (1985) *Foucault*, London, Fontana Press

Mellen, J. (1974) *Women and Their Sexuality in the New Film*, New York, Dell

Metz, C. (1971) *Essais sur la signification au cinéma, Tome I*, Paris, Editions Klincksieck

Metz, C. (1972) *Essais sur la signification au cinéma, Tome II*, Paris, Editions Klincksieck. Both volumes translated by M. Taylor (1974) as *Film Language: A Semiotics of the Cinema*, New York, University of Oxford Press

Metz, C. (1975) The Imaginary Signifier, *Screen*, Vol. 16, No. 3

Modleski, T. (1982) Never To Be Thirty-Six Years Old: *Rebecca* as Female Oedipal Drama, *Wide Angle*, Vol. 5, No. 1

Modleski, T. (1988) *The Women Who Knew Too Much: Hitchcock and Feminist Theory*, New York and London, Methuen

Modleski, T. (1992) Time and Desire in the Woman's Film, in: Mast, G., Cohen, M. and Baudry, L. (eds) *Film Theory and Criticism*, Oxford, Oxford University Press, fourth edition

Moi, T. (1985) *Sexual/Textual Politics: Feminist Literary Theory*, London and New York, Routledge

Moraga, C. and Anzaldúa, G. (eds) (1981) *This Bridge Called My Back*, New York, Persephone Press

Mulvey, L. (1975) Visual Pleasure and Narrative Cinema, *Screen*, Vol. 16, No. 3, reprinted in *Visual and Other Pleasures* (Mulvey, 1989)

Mulvey, L. (1977) Notes on Sirk and Melodrama, *Movie*, No. 25, reprinted in *Visual and Other Pleasures* (Mulvey, 1989)

Mulvey, L. (1987) Notes on Sirk and Melodrama (updated), in Gledhill, C. (ed.) *Home is Where the Heart Is: Studies in Melodrama and Woman's Film*, London, British Film Institute Publishing

Mulvey, L. (1989) *Visual and Other Pleasures*, London, Macmillan

Neale, S. (1980) *Genre*, London, British Film Institute Publishing

Neale, S. (1985) *Cinema and Technology: Image, Sound and Colour*, London Macmillan/British Film Institute Publishing

Neale, S. (1990) Questions of Genre, *Screen*, Vol. 31, No. 1

Neupert, R. (1995) *The End: Narration and Closure in the Cinema*, Detroit, Wayne State University Press

Nichols, B. (1991) *Representing Reality: Issues and Concepts in Documentary*, Bloomington, Indiana University Press

Nicholson, L. (ed.) (1990) *Feminism/Postmodernism*, New York and London, Routledge

Nowell-Smith, A. (1987) Minnelli and Melodrama, in Gledhill, C. (ed.) *Home is Where the Heart Is: Studies in Melodrama and Woman's Film*, London, British Film Institute Publishing

Orr, J. (1993) *Cinema and Modernity*, Cambridge, Polity Press

O'Sullivan, T., Hartley, J., Saunders, D. and Fiske, J. (1992) *Key Concepts in Communication*, London and New York, Routledge, sixth edition

433

Oudart, J.-P. (1977) Cinema and Suture, *Screen*, Vol. 18, No. 1

Paul, W. (1994) *Laughing Screaming: Modern Hollywood Horror and Comedy*, New York, Columbia University Press

Penley, C. (1985) Feminism, Film Theory and the Bachelor Machines, *m/f*, No. 10

Penley, C. (1988) *Feminism and Film Theory*, New York, Routledge, and London, British Film Institute Publishing

Penley, C. (1989) *The Future of an Illusion: Film, Feminism and Psychoanalysis*, New York and London, Routledge

Pines, J. and Willemen, P. (eds) (1990) *Questions of Third Cinema*, London, British Film Institute Publishing

Place, J. (1980) Women in Film Noir, in: Kaplan, E. A. (ed.) *Women in Film Noir*, London, British Film Institute, revised edition

Pribham, D. (ed.) (1988) *Female Spectators*, London and New York, Verso

Reid, M. A. (1993) *Redefining Black Film*, Berkeley, Los Angeles and Oxford, University of California Press

Renov, M. (ed.) (1993) *Theorizing Documentary*, New York and London, Routledge

Rentschler, E. (1988) *West German Filmmakers on Film: Visions and Voices*, New York and London, Holmes & Meier

Rheudan, J. (1993) The Marriage of Maria Braun: History, Melodrama, Ideology, in: Friedan, S., McCormick, R. W., Petersen, V. R. and Vogelsang, L. M. (eds) *Gender and German Cinema, Feminist Interventions*, Oxford, Berg Publishers

Rose, J. (1986) *Sexuality in the Field of Vision*, London, Verso

Rosen, M. (1973) *Popcorn Venus: Women, Movies and the American Dream*, New York, Coward McCann & Geoghegan

Rothman, G. (1976) Against 'The system of the suture', in: Nicholls, B. (ed.) *Movies and Methods: An Anthology*, Berkeley, University of California Press

Russo, V. (1981) *The Celluloid Closet: Homosexuality in the Movies*, Harper & Row

Salt, B. (1977) Film Style and Technology in the 1940s, *Film Quarterly*, fall

Salt, B. (1983) *Film Style and Technology: History and Analysis*, London, Starword

Schatz, T. (1981) *Hollywood Genres*, New York, Random House

Screen (1984) Special issue on the soundtrack, Vol. 25, No. 3

Screen (1988) Special issue on race, Vol. 29, No. 4

Screen (1992) *Sexing the Subject: A Screen Reader in Sexuality*, London and New York, Routledge

Showalter, E. (ed.) (1989) *Speaking of Gender*, New York and London, Routledge

Silverman, K. (1981) Masochism and Subjectivity, *Framework*, No. 12

Silverman, K. (1983) *The Subject of Semiotics*, Oxford, Oxford University Press

Snead, J., MacCabe, C. and West, C. (eds) (1994) *White Screen, Black Images: Hollywood from the Dark Side*, New York and London, Routledge

Solanas, F. and Getino, O. (1983) Towards a Third Cinema, in: Chanen, M. (ed.) *Twenty-Five Years of the New Latin American Cinema*, London, British Film Institute Publishing

Sorlin, P. (1991) *European Cinemas, European Societies 1939–1990*, New York and London, Routledge

Stacey, J. (1993) *Star Gazing: Hollywood Cinema and Female Spectatorship*, London and New York, Routledge

Stam, R., Burgoyne, R. and Flitterman-Lewis, S. (1992) *New Vocabularies in Film Semiotics: Structuralism, Post-Structuralism and Beyond*, New York and London, Routledge

Stead, P. (1989) *Film and the Working Class*, London and New York, Routledge

Stephens, M. L. (1995) *Film Noir: A Comprehensive Illustrated Reference to Movies, Terms and Persons*, McFarland, North Carolina and London, McFarland & Co. Inc. Publishers

Studlar, G. (1985) Masochism and the Perverse Pleasures of the Cinema, in: Nichols, B. (ed.) *Movies and Methods*, Vol. 2, Berkeley, University of California Press

Tasker, Y. (1993) *Spectacular Bodies: Gender, Genre and the Action Cinema*, Comedia Series, New York and London, Routledge

Taylor, C. (1986) The L.A. Rebellion: New Spirit in American Film, *Black Film Review*, Vol. 2, No. 2

Taylor, R. and Christie, I. (eds) (1994a) *The Film Factory: Russian and Soviet Cinema in Documents 1896–1939*, London and New York, Routledge

Taylor, R. and Christie, I. (eds) (1994b) *Inside the Film Factory: New Approaches to Russian and Soviet Cinema*, London and New York, Routledge

Taylor, R. and Spring, D. (eds) (1993) *Stalinism and Soviet Cinema*, London and New York, Routledge

Tudor, A. (1989) *Monsters and Mad Scientists: A Cultural History of the Horror Movie*, Oxford, Basil Blackwell

Turim, M. (1989) *Flashbacks in Film: Memory and History*, New York and London, Routledge

Turner, G. (1988) *Film as Social Practice*, London and New York, Routledge

Tuska, J. (1976) *The Films of the West*, New York, Doubleday & Co. Inc.

Weiss, A. (1990) *Vampires and Violets: Lesbian Representation in the Cinema*, London, Pandora Press

Wilkins, M. (1989) I'm Gonna Git You Sucka: A Glance at the Blaxploitation Era, *Black Face*, No. 1

Williams, C. (ed.) (1980) *Realism in the Cinema*, London and Henley, Routledge & Kegan Paul

Williams, L. (1984) When the Woman Looks, in: Doane, M. A., Mellencamp, P. and Williams, L. (eds) *Re-vision: Essays in Feminist Film Criticism*, Frederick, Marylands, The American Film Institute/ University Publications of America

Winston, B. (1995) *Claiming the Real: The Documentary Film Revisited*, London, British Film Institute Publishing

Wollen, P. (1972) *Signs and Meaning in the Cinema*, London, Secker & Warburg

Wollen, P. (1982) *Semiotic Counter-Strategies: Readings and Writings*, London, Verso

Wood, R. (1992) Ideology, Genre, Auteur, in: Mast, G., Cohen, M. and Baudry, L. (eds) *Film Theory and Criticism*, Oxford, Oxford University Press

Wright, W. (1975) *Six Guns and Society: A Structural Study of the Western*, Berkeley, Los Angeles and London, University of California Press

INDEX OF FILMS

NAME INDEX

449

SUBJECT INDEX

456

461

pluralism 380; postmodernism and 270–2
poetic realism, French 117, 141–3, 300
politique des auteurs 13–14
postmodernism 221, 259–72
post-structuralism 19–20, 98, 223, 259, 352–3, 368, 382–3
power theory 110–13
prefabrication, parody and 263–4
preferred reading 80, 118, 272, 319, 333–4
presence (absence/presence) 1–4, 333, 345–6
private-eye films 148–9
psychoanalysis 273–95; absence/presence and 2–3; auteurism and 19–20; avant-garde and 21, 273; female subject and 285–8; feminism and 104–5, 108–9, 285, 290–5; film theory and 288–95; flashbacks and 122, 125–30; Freudian 274–7; gaze/look and 150–1; gender and 154–5, 285–8; and horror movies 177–8; melodrama and 206–7, 210, 212; modernism and 226; scopophilia and 305–7; sexuality and 275–7, 283, 286–8; spectator and 331–7; stars and 342–3; structuralism and 16; subjectivity and 274–95, 368–70, *see also* Imaginary/Symbolic; Oedipal trajectory
psychological horror movies 176–7

queer cinema 296–7
quota agreements 89–90
QVC Network 359

race *see* black people
Radio Corporation of America (RCA) 362
Rank Organisation 134
realism 226–7, 298–300; art cinema and 9; in Black (African American) cinema 29; in British New Wave 31; cinemascope and 38; in classic Hollywood cinema 47–9; colour and 52–3; comedy and 55; deep focus and 65, 79; in dominant/mainstream cinema 75; ego-type 275; French poetic realism 117, 141–3, 300; Italian neo-realism 37, 191–4, 299–300; melodrama and 208; in musicals 240; narrative and 143, 298; seamlessness and 48, 84, 298–9, 307; socialist 327, 330; sound and 323–4
realistic motivation 233
Reason, Age of 221–3
reception theory 12
reproduction, human 94
Republic Pictures 30, 356, 366–7, 417
reverse-angle shots 49, 257, 320, 375
RKO Radio Pictures Inc 30, 235; history of 355, 357, 362
road movies 49, 300–1

science fiction 50, 91, 93, 165, 302–5
scopophilia 305–7, 334; colour and 52–5; feminism and 103–4, 306; foregrounding and 130
Screen (journal) 18

underground cinema 9, 59, 391–2
United Artists Corporation 33;
history of 355, 358, 361, 364
United States of America: art
cinema in 9, 10; auteurism
in 15; avant-garde in 22, 228–9;
Black cinema in 24–30; buddy
films in 33–4; censorship in 9,
35, 36–7; Cold War and 408,
409; colour movies in 50, 51–2;
documentaries in 74; film noir
genre in 116–17, 166; film
trade agreements and 89–90;
Great War and 397–8; Second
World War and 403–6;
underground cinema 9, 59,
391–2; Vietnam War and 46,
231–3, 410–11, *see also*
Hollywood
Universal Pictures 415; history
of 355, 362–4
unmatched shots 392

vampire movies 174–5, 177
Viacom 359
Vic Films 32
Vietnam War 46, 231–3, 410–11
visual pleasure *see* scopophilia
Vitagraph 366
Vitaphone 322

vorticists 143
voyeurism 189, 255–6, 289–90,
306, 345–6, 388–9, 393–5

war films 46, 161, 396; Cold War
408–9; Great War (1914–18)
396–9, 400; Second World
War (1939–45) 399–408, 410;
Vietnam 46, 231–3, 410–11
Warner Brothers 29, 134;
gangster movies and 146–7;
history of 355, 359–60;
musicals and 236; sound
and 322
Western Electric 322
westerns 5, 68, 163–4, 165;
feminism and 105; gender in 1,
418–19; history of 411–23;
iconography of 179–80, 413;
stereotypes in 349
wipe 81, 423
Women and Film (journal) 101–2
women's films: female
melodramas 208–15; feminism
and 105, 106–7; ideology in
184; Imaginary/Symbolic
and 189
Woodfall Films 32, 135

zoom shots 424